LEGAL RESPONSES TO TRAFFICKING IN WOMEN FOR SEXUAL EXPLOITATION IN THE EUROPEAN UNION

The phenomenon of trafficking in women for sexual exploitation, which in the last decade has changed from a marginal 'non-issue' to a legitimate concern in many parts of the world, has become familiar through newspaper coverage. Now, finally, legislators and law enforcement agencies have begun to act. In Europe many EU Member States have (or are developing) at least some sort of anti-trafficking policies (with some of them in the forefront of global anti-trafficking efforts). Moreover, the EU itself has become markedly more active with regard to curbing trafficking in human beings, as part of its migration control and police and judicial co-operation functions.

However, even co-ordinated efforts such as those being worked on by the EU tend to produce only short-term 'cures' to a problem that is in truth global and structural in nature and which cannot be eradicated—or necessarily even significantly reduced—through policing and migration control measures alone. Too often there is little debate on broader measures which might be targeted to address the 'root causes' of trafficking, such as poverty, under-development, general lack of economic and migration opportunities and, above all, gender inequality.

Against this background, this book deals with present efforts to control trafficking in women for sexual exploitation. In doing so it examines claims that what is needed effectively to prevent and tackle trafficking is a 'comprehensive' approach, and at the very least one that is far more wide-ranging and coherent than what exists today. It also analyses the assertion that destination countries, and more specifically Member States of the EU, could and indeed should, take more action against trafficking through regional co-operation, particularly in the framework of the EU, rather than as individual Member States.

The book will be of interest to a wide range of scholars in EU law, human rights, comparative law, sociology, feminist theory and politics, as well as policy-makers, practitioners and NGO activists in various European countries.

Volume 14 in the series Modern Studies in European Law

Modern Studies in European Law

1 Soft Law in European Community Law *Linda Senden*
2 The Impact of European Rights on National Legal Cultures *Miriam Aziz*
3 Partnership Rights, Free Movement and EU Law *Helen Toner*
4 National Remedies Before the Court of Justice: Issues of Harmonisation and Differentiation *Michael Dougan*
5 The National Courts Mandate in the European Constitution *Monica Claes*
6 EU Environmental Law: Challenges, Changes and Decision-Making *Maria Lee*
7 European Union Law and Defence Integration *Martin Trybus*
8 Principles of European Constitutional Law *Armin von Bogdandy & Jürgen Bast*
9 EU International Relations Law *Panos Koutrakos*
10 Effective Judicial Protection and the Environmental Impact Assessment Directive in Ireland *Áine Ryall*
11 The European Court of Justice and the EU Constitutional Order: Essays in Judicial Protection *Takis Tridimas*
12 The European Union, International Law and the Promotion and Protection of Democracy *Richard Burchill*
13 EU Food Law: Protecting Consumers and Health in a Common Market *Caoimhín MacMaoláin*

Legal Responses to Trafficking in Women for Sexual Exploitation in the European Union

Heli Askola

·HART·
PUBLISHING
OXFORD – PORTLAND OREGON
2007

Published in North America (US and Canada) by
Hart Publishing
c/o International Specialized Book Services
920 NE 58th Avenue, Suite 300
Portland, OR 97213-3786
USA
Tel: +1 503 287 3093 or toll-free: (1) 800 944 6190
Fax: +1 503 280 8832
E-mail: orders@isbs.com
Website: www.isbs.com

Hart Publishing, 16C Worcester Place, OX1 2JW
Telephone: +44 (0)1865 517530 Fax: +44 (0)1865 510710
E-mail: mail@hartpub.co.uk
Website: http://www.hartpub.co.uk

British Library Cataloguing in Publication Data
Data Available
ISBN-13: 978-1-84113-650-9 (hardback)
ISBN-10: 1-84113-650-6 (hardback)

Typeset by Hope Services Ltd, Abingdon
Printed and bound in Great Britain by
TJ International Ltd, Padstow, Cornwall

In memory of my grandfather

Acknowledgements

This book is based on a PhD thesis which was submitted to the European University Institute (EUI), Florence, in 2005. I have some particular debts I wish to acknowledge here, although it is impossible to name everyone who has helped me over the years. They are simply so many and they have contributed in such various ways that I cannot do all of them justice here.

I am pleased to acknowledge here my debt to my supervisor, Professor Neil Walker, without whose unflagging support and helpful comments the thesis certainly would not have been completed—let alone on time. I also wish to thank the members of my examining jury, Bruno de Witte, Kees Groenendijk and Thérèse Murphy, for their helpful comments and encouragement. Furthermore, I am immensely grateful to Dr Urfan Khaliq, whose comments and suggestions were invaluable. I also owe a debt of gratitude to my 'Swedish correspondent', Tuulia Svanehav, whose support has always been unwavering. In addition, I would like to recognise the financial support of the Academy of Finland and the European University Institute.

Finally, let me simply thank all others—family members, friends and colleagues in Finland, Italy and the UK in particular—who have supported and advised me in so many ways since I first started this project (rather by coincidence) in 2001.

Contents

Acknowledgements vii
Abbreviations xi
Table of Cases xiii
Table of Legislation xv

1. *Introduction* 1

1.1. THE BACKGROUND, AIM AND STRUCTURE OF THE BOOK 1
1.2. DIVERGENCE, CONVERGENCE AND COUNTRY STUDIES 9
1.3. SOME COMMENTS ON TERMINOLOGY AND THE NATURE OF THE PROBLEM 15

2. *Feminism, Prostitution and Trafficking: A Complex Approach* 22

2.1. THE BACKGROUND: SEXUAL SLAVERY AND SEX WORK REVISITED 21
2.2. TALKING ABOUT TRAFFICKING: DEBATES AND DEFINITIONS 28
2.3. TOWARDS A MORE COMPREHENSIVE UNDERSTANDING? 36

3. *EC Free Movement Law, Freedom and Prostitution* 43

3.1. NOTIONS OF FREEDOM AND THE LEGAL REGULATION OF PROSTITUTION 44
3.2. FREEDOM IN EUROPEAN LAW 52
3.2.1. The Common (Sex) Market? Freedom and Prostitution in EC Law 52
3.2.2. Some Girls are Freer than Others: EC Law and its Outsiders 59
3.3. CONCLUSIONS 64

4. *Trafficking as Irregular Migration* 67

4.1. THE EUROPEAN MIGRATION POLICY CONTEXT 69
4.1.1. Crowded Houses, People's Homes or Fortress(es in) Europe 69
4.1.2. (Im)Migration Policy Dilemmas and the European Union 73
4.2. FEMALE MIGRANTS, MIGRATION POLICIES AND EXPLOITATION 80
4.2.1. From Structural Causes to Exploitative Situations 80
4.2.2. Helping Trafficking Victims through Short-Term Residence Permits? 88
4.3. CONCLUSIONS 96

5. *Criminal Justice Co-operation Against Trafficking* 99

5.1. TRAFFICKING OFFENCES IN THE MEMBER STATES 100
5.1.1. On the Goals and Contents of the Criminal Provisions 100
5.1.2. Applying the Laws: Female Caricatures and Invisible Men 108
5.2. TRAFFICKING AND THE THIRD PILLAR 120
5.2.1. Harmonising or Not—Repressive Emphasis with Vague Results 120
5.2.2. Anti-trafficking Co-operation: Security, Justice or Freedom? 127
5.3. CONCLUSIONS 131

6. *Trafficking and Human Rights* 133

6.1. FEMALE MIGRANTS AND INTERNATIONAL HUMAN RIGHTS 134
6.1.1. Actual Victims of Trafficking: Included if Invisible? 134
6.1.2. Potential Victims of Trafficking: Marginalisation of the Marginalised? 141
6.2. EXCLUSION OF MIGRANT WOMEN FROM DEBATES ON WOMEN'S RIGHTS 145
6.3. THE EUROPEAN UNION'S HUMAN RIGHTS DIMENSION 153
6.4. CONCLUSIONS 159

7. *Towards a More Comprehensive Approach to Trafficking?* 161

7.1. ANTI-TRAFFICKING IN THE SHORT TO MEDIUM TERM 163
7.2. PREVENTING TRAFFICKING IN WOMEN IN THE LONG RUN 172
7.2.1. Development, Migration and Gender Empowerment 172
7.2.2. Sexual Ideologies and the Market for Sexual Services 181
7.3. FINAL REMARKS 187

Bibliography 189
Index 215

Abbreviations

ACP	African, Caribbean and Pacific (states)
AFSJ	Area of Freedom, Security and Justice
CAT	Convention Against Torture and Other Cruel, Inhuman or Degrading Treatment or Punishment (UN)
CATW	Coalition Against Trafficking in Women
CE	Council of Europe
CEDAW	Convention on the Elimination of All Forms of Discrimination Against Women
CEECs	Central and Eastern European Countries
CRC	Convention on the Rights of the Child
EAW	European Arrest Warrant
EC	European Community
ECHR	European Convention on Human Rights
ECJ	European Court of Justice (EU)
ECOSOC	Economic and Social Council (UN)
ECR	European Court Reports
ECtHR	European Court of Human Rights
EHRR	European Human Rights Reports
EP	European Parliament
EPP	European Public Prosecutor
ETS	European Treaty Series
EU	European Union
GA	General Assembly of the United Nations
GAATW	Global Alliance Against Trafficking in Women
GU	Gazzetta Ufficiale (Italy)
HIV	Human Immunodeficiency Virus
ICCPR	International Covenant on Civil and Political Rights
ICESCR	International Covenant on Economic, Social and Cultural Rights
ICMW	International Convention on the Protection of the Rights of All Migrant Workers and Members of Their Families (International Convention on Migrant Workers)
IGO	inter-governmental organisation
ILO	International Labour Organisation
IOM	International Organization for Migration
JHA	Justice and Home Affairs
LNTS	League of Nations Treaty Series
NGO	non-governmental organisation
ODIHR	Office for Democratic Institutions and Human Rights (OSCE)

OECD	Organisation for Economic Co-operation and Development
OJ	Official Journal of the European Union (Communities)
OSCE	Organisation for Security and Co-operation in Europe
QMV	qualified majority voting
SEA	Single European Act
SFS	Svensk Författningssamling
SOU	Statens Offentliga Utredningar (Sweden)
TAMPEP	Transnational AIDS/STD Prevention among Migrant Prostitutes in Europe
TEC	Treaty Establishing the European Community
TEU	Treaty on European Union
ToA	Treaty of Amsterdam
UN	United Nations
UNFPA	United Nations Fund for Population Activities
UNHCHR	United Nations High Commissioner for Human Rights
UNICEF	United Nations Children's Fund
UNODC	United Nations Office on Drugs and Crime
UNPD	United Nations Population Division
UNTS	United Nations Treaty Series

Table of Cases

European Court of Justice

Case 34/79 *Regina v Henn and Darby* [1979] ECR 3795..54
Joined Cases 115/81 & 116/81 *Adoui v Belgian State and City of Liège, Cornuaille v Belgian State* [1982] ECR 1665 ....53-54, 86
Case 238/83 *Caisse d'Allocation Familiales v Meade* [1984] ECR 2631 60
Case 121/85 *Conegate Ltd v HM Customs & Excise* [1986] ECR 1007 54
Case C–355/93 *Eroglu v Land Baden-Württemburg* [1994] ECR I–5113 60
Case C–85/96 *Martínez Sala v Freistaat Bayern* [1998] ECR I–02691....................57
Case C–249/96 *Grant v South-West Trains* [1998] ECR I–621..............................58
Case C–230/97 *Awoyemi (Criminal proceedings against)* [1998] ECR I–6781......60
Case C–122/99 & C–125/99 *D and Sweden v Council* [2001] ECR I–4319 58
Case C–184/99 *Grzelczyk v Centre public d'aide sociale d'Ottignies-Louvain-la-Neuve* [2001] ECR I–6193..53
Case C–268/99 *Jany and Others v Staatssecretaris van Justitie* [2001] ECR I–8615 ....54-55, 57, 59, 86, 109
Case C–540/03 *European Parliament v Council* (27 June 2006) 61

European Court of Human Rights

A v the United Kingdom (1999) 27 EHRR 61...137
Ahmed v Austria (1996) 24 EHRR 278..95
Airey v Ireland (1979-80) 2 EHRR 305 137
Assenov and Others v Bulgaria (1999) 28 EHRR 652..137

Chahal v the United Kingdom (1996) 23 EHRR 413 95
Cruz Varas v Sweden (1992) 14 EHRR 1..95

HLR v France (1997) 26 EHRR 29 95

Marckx v Belgium (1979-80) 2 EHRR 330 137

Osman v the United Kingdom (2000) 29 EHRR 245 138

Soering v the United Kingdom (1989) 11 EHRR 439 95

Vilvarajah v the United Kingdom (1991) 14 EHRR 248 95

X and Y v the Netherlands (1986) 8 EHRR 235..137

Z and Others v the United Kingdom (2002) 34 EHRR 97 137

Table of Legislation

TREATIES

International

International Agreement for the Suppression of the Slave Traffic (1904), 1 LNTS 83 123
International Convention for the Suppression of White Slave Traffic (1910), 3 LNTS 278 123
Convention for the Suppression of Traffic in Women and Children (1921), 9 LNTS 415 123
Slavery, Servitude, Forced Labour and Similar Institutions and Practices Convention (1926), 60 LNTS 253 136
Convention Concerning Forced or Compulsory Labour (1930), ILO Convention No 29, 39 UNTS 55 136
International Convention for the Suppression of the Traffic in Women of Full Age (1933), 150 LNTS 431 123
Convention for the Suppression of the Traffic in Persons and of the Exploitation of the Prostitution of Others (1949), 96 UNTS 271 123
The Convention on Migration for Employment (1949), ILO Convention No 97, 120 UNTS 70 143
Convention Relating to the Status of Refugees (1951), 189 UNTS 150 76
Supplementary Convention on the Abolition of Slavery, the Slave Trade, and Institutions and Practices Similar to Slavery (1956), 266 UNTS 40 136
Abolition of Forced Labour Convention (1957), ILO Convention No 105, 320 UNTS 291 136
International Convention on the Elimination of All Forms of Racial Discrimination (1966), 660 UNTS 195 146
International Covenant on Civil and Political Rights (1966), 999 UNTS 171 ..... 135–6, 138, 140
International Covenant on Economic, Social and Cultural Rights (1966), 993 UNTS 3 142
Vienna Convention on the Law of Treaties (1969), 1155 UNTS 331 164
Convention on Migrations in Abusive Conditions and the Promotion of Equality of Opportunity and Treatment of Migrant Workers (1975), ILO Convention No 143, 1120 UNTS 323 143
Convention on the Elimination of All Forms of Discrimination against Women (1979), 1249 UNTS 13 ..... 137-8, 143, 145-6, 159, 177

International Convention on the Protection of the Rights of All Migrant Workers and Members of Their Families (1990), A/RES/45/158 ......85, 136, 143–4, 169
Convention Concerning the Prohibition and Immediate Action for the Elimination of the Worst Forms of Child Labour (1999), ILO Convention No 182, 38 ILM 1207 136
United Nations Convention against Transnational Organized Crime (2000), A/55/383 123
Protocol to Prevent, Suppress and Punish Trafficking in Persons, Especially Women and Children, supplementing United Nations Convention against Transnational Organized Crime, A/55/383, Annex II 100–1, 103, 107, 123–6, 132, 139, 164, 169
Protocol against the Smuggling of Migrants by Land, Sea and Air, supplementing United Nations Convention against Transnational Organized Crime A/55/383, Annex III 123

Council of Europe

European Convention for the Protection of Human Rights and Fundamental Freedoms (1950), 218 UNTS 221, CETS No 5 ......95, 135–7, 153, 158
Council of Europe Convention against Trafficking (2005), CETS No 197 ......95, 157–8, 165

EU

Agreement between the Governments of the States of the Benelux Economic Union, the Federal Republic of Germany and the French Republic on the gradual abolition of checks at their common borders (Schengen Agreement) 60, 70, 73, 75
Single European Act [1987] OJ L 169/1 60
Convention implementing the Schengen Agreement of 14 June 1985 between the Governments of the States of the Benelux Economic Union, the Federal Republic of Germany and the French Republic on the gradual abolition of checks at their common borders (Schengen Convention) 60
Convention on Mutual Assistance in Criminal Matters between the Member States of the European Union [2000] OJ C 197/1 128
Convention on the establishment of a European Police Office (Europol Convention) [1995] OJ C 316/2 128
Partnership Agreement between the members of the African, Caribbean and Pacific Group of States (ACP) of the one part, and the European Community and its Member States, of the other part (Cotonou Agreement) [2000] OJ L 317/3 175

Treaty Establishing the European Community (consolidated version) 43, 53–4, 59, 61, 74, 92, 175
Treaty on European Union (consolidated version) 6, 43, 121, 172
Treaty Establishing a Constitution for Europe [2004] OJ C 310/1 ....10, 59, 79, 121, 131, 153, 155–6, 158

Secondary EU legislation

Decisions

Council Decision 2002/187/JHA of 28 February 2002 setting up Eurojust with a view to reinforcing the fight against serious crime [2002] OJ L 63/1 128
Commission Decision 2003/209/EC of 25 March 2003 setting up a consultative group, to be known as the 'Experts Group on Trafficking in Human Beings' [2003] OJ L 79/25 163
European Parliament and Council Decision 803/2004/EC of 21 April 2004 adopting a programme of Community action (2004 to 2008) to prevent and combat violence against children, young people and women and to protect victims and groups at risk (the Daphne II programme) [2004] OJ L 143/1 170

Declarations

The Hague Ministerial Declaration on European Guideline for Effective Measures to Prevent and Combat Trafficking in Women for the Purpose of Sexual Exploitation (Ministerial Conference under the Dutch Presidency of the EU, The Hague, 24-26 April 1997) 20, 172
Brussels Declaration on Preventing and Combating Trafficking in Human Beings (European Conference on Preventing and Combating Trafficking in Human Beings – Global Challenge for the 21st Century, organised under the Danish Presidency of the EU, Brussels, 18-20 September 2002) 7, 170, 172

Directives

Directive 2000/43/EC of 29 June 2000 implementing the principle of equal treatment between persons irrespective of racial or ethnic origin [2000] OJ L 180/22 ....62–3, 77
Directive 2000/78/EC of 27 November 2000 establishing a general framework for equal treatment in employment and occupation [2000] OJ L 303/1 62
Directive 2002/90/EC of 28 November 2002 defining the facilitation of unauthorised entry, transit and residence [2002] OJ L 328/17 77
Directive 2003/86/EC of 22 September 2003 on the right to family reunification [2003] OJ L 251/12 61–2

Directive 2003/109/EC of 25 November 2003 concerning the status of third-country nationals who are long-term residents [2004] OJ L 16/44 ....62, 169
Directive 2004/38/EC of 29 April 2004 on the right of citizens of the Union and their family members to move and reside freely within the territory of the Member States amending Regulation (EEC) No 1612/68 and repealing Directives 64/221/EEC, 68/360/EEC, 72/194/EEC, 73/148/EEC, 75/34/EEC, 75/35/EEC, 90/364/EEC, 90/365/EEC and 93/96/EEC [2004] OJ L 229/35 52
Directive 2004/81/EC of 29 April 2004 on the residence permit issued to third-country nationals who are victims of trafficking in human beings or who have been the subject of an action to facilitate illegal immigration, who cooperate with the competent authorities [2004] OJ L 261/19 ....92–4, 126, 132, 157, 164–5, 168
Directive 2004/83/EC of 29 April 2004 on minimum standards for the qualification and status of third-country nationals and stateless persons as refugees or as persons who otherwise need international protection and the content of the protection granted [2004] OJ L 304/12..........74, 94
Directive 2004/113/EC of 13 December 2004 implementing the principle of equal treatment between men and women in the access to and supply of goods and services [2004] OJ L 373/37 ....59, 186
Directive 2005/85/EC of 1 December 2005 on minimum standards on procedures in Member States for granting and withdrawing refugee status [2005] OJ L 326/13..........74

Framework Decisions

Framework Decision 2001/220/JHA of 15 March 2001 on the standing of victims in criminal proceedings [2001] OJ L 82/1 125
Framework Decision 2002/465/JHA of 13 June 2002 on joint investigation teams [2002] OJ L 162/1..........128
Framework Decision 2002/584/JHA of 13 June 2002 on the European arrest warrant and the surrender procedures between Member States [2002] OJ L 190/1 128
Framework Decision 2002/629/JHA of 19 July 2002 on combating trafficking in human beings [2002] OJ L 203/1..........5–6, 88, 99, 121, 124–7, 154, 169, 171
Framework Decision 2002/946/JHA of 28 November 2002 on the strengthening of the penal framework to prevent the facilitation of unauthorised entry, transit and residence [2002] OJ L/328/1..........77, 126

Joint Action

Council Joint Action 2002/629/JHA of 24 February 1997 concerning action to combat trafficking in human beings and sexual exploitation of children [1997] OJ L 63/1 ....99, 122

Regulations

Regulation 2836/98/EC of 22 December 1998 on integrating of gender issues in development cooperation [1998] OJ L 354/5 176
Regulation 539/2001/EC of 15 March 2001 listing the third countries whose nationals must be in possession of visas when crossing the external borders and those whose nationals are exempt from that requirement [2001] OJ L 81/1 .... 75, 83
Regulation 343/2003/EC of 18 February 2003 establishing the criteria and mechanisms for determining the Member State responsible for examining an asylum application lodged in one of the Member States by a third-country national [2003] OJ L 50/1....................74
Regulation 806/2004/EC of 21 April 2004 on promoting gender equality in development cooperation [2004] OJ L 143/40....................176

Resolutions

European Parliament Resolution on the exploitation of prostitution and the traffic in human beings [1989] OJ C/120/352....................54
European Parliament Resolution on trafficking in human beings [1996] OJ C 32/88....................134
European Parliament Resolution on the Communication from the Commission to the Council and the European Parliament on trafficking in women for the purpose of sexual exploitation [1998] OJ C/14/39....................94

Miscellaneous

Action Plan of 3 December on how best to implement the Provisions of the Treaty of Amsterdam on an area of freedom, security and justice [1999] OJ C 19/1....................121
The Prevention and Control of Organised Crime: A European Union Strategy for the Beginning of the New Millennium [2000] OJ C 124/1....................121
Charter of Fundamental Rights of the European Union [2000] OJ C 364/1....................10, 59, 131, 153–7
Comprehensive Plan of 28 February 2002 to combat illegal immigration and trafficking in human beings [2002] OJ C 142/23....................121
The Hague Programme: Strengthening freedom, security and justice in the European Union [2005] OJ C 53/1....................62, 157
EU Plan on Best Practices, Standards and Procedures for Combating and Preventing Trafficking in Human Beings [2005] OJ C 311/1....................163–5, 167–70, 173

1

Introduction

THE IDEA BEHIND this book is simple and can also be easily summarised to frame this introductory chapter. The book seeks to examine the actual and potential overlap of two commonly expressed claims about the phenomenon which is now generally referred to as 'trafficking in women for sexual exploitation': first, that what is needed effectively to prevent and tackle such trafficking is a comprehensive approach, or at the very least one that is far more wide-ranging and coherent than that which exists anywhere today; secondly, that destination countries, and more specifically Member States of the European Union (EU), should take more action against trafficking through regional co-operation, particularly in the framework of the Union, as it is perceived to be more capable of tackling trafficking as a transnational matter than individual Member States. As these issues have not been extensively explored together before, this book seeks above all to create a framework of analysis in which the interconnections between the push for a more 'comprehensive' approach and the role of the European Union can be broadly conceived. This introductory chapter has three functions: it presents the background against which the research questions and the structure of the book are explained; it introduces a theme of convergence and divergence which underlines the choice of country studies selected; and finally it explains some matters about terminology and method.

1.1 THE BACKGROUND, AIM AND STRUCTURE OF THE BOOK

As a book on the European (especially EU) responses to the phenomenon of trafficking in women for sexual exploitation, this would scarcely have been meaningful a decade ago. But since the early 1990s trafficking in human beings, especially in women and children, has been transforming from a relatively marginal 'non-issue' to a legitimate concern, and one which increasingly attracts lawyers as well. In fact, in the last few years 'fighting' trafficking in human beings has become 'fashionable' to such an extent that in 2002 a European conference on trafficking in humans[1] at the European Parliament gathered together over 1,000 participants from all over Europe to listen to statements by several high-level speakers on how 'trafficking has now become the priority it should be'[2] and how 'trafficking in

[1] The EU/IOM STOP European Conference on Preventing and Combating Trafficking in Human Beings—A Global Challenge for the 21st Century, held in Brussels, 18–20 Sept 2002.

[2] Statement by Justice and Home Affairs Commissioner Antonio Vitorino, 18 Sept 2002.

human beings is universally considered a serious crime'.[3] Although the rhetoric does not necessarily match the reality—and this is part of the problem—it is nonetheless true that most, if not all, EU Member States now have—or are developing—at least some sort of anti-trafficking policies. Moreover, the European Union has become decidedly more active with regard to trafficking in human beings owing to both the evident EU interest in the (im)migration side of the issue and its close fit with police and judicial co-operation under the current Third Pillar—both of which connect with the EU's aim of building an Area of Freedom, Security and Justice (AFSJ).

Despite the increased attention the issue has received, quite often anti-trafficking policies seem to stem from narrow analyses of the phenomenon, its underlying causes, its characteristics and its consequences. This is perhaps not surprising, for what makes trafficking in women for sexual exploitation so problematic is that in addressing it one easily enters into a myriad of heated and endless debates about, among others, 'illegal' migration, prostitution, human rights, the nature of work and exploitation, globalisation, the socio-economic inequalities both within and between countries, market liberalisation, consumerism and the commodification of the human body, as well as the alleged growth and transnationalisation of organised criminal activity. Trafficking in general is a vast, complicated and elusive topic, and it is hard to resist the compulsion to take a restricted approach in order to tackle at least one side of the issue effectively and to offer some explanations and strategies for action. Thus, some consider trafficking in women for sexual exploitation mainly as a sub-category of irregular/illegal migration;[4] some see it primarily as an integral part of the question of (forced) prostitution or the sex trade;[5] others consider it in the framework of the global marketisation of sexual representation;[6] a few approach it from the point of view of economic analysis,[7] while many find trafficking to be mainly a problem of transnational organised crime;[8] and a growing number of commentators consider

[3] Statement by Director Emanuele Marotta, Ministry of Interior, Italy, 20 Sept 2002.

[4] B Ghosh, *Huddled Masses and Uncertain Shores* (The Hague, Martinus Nijhoff, 1998). This is also the principal perspective of one of the main actors in the international scene, the International Organization for Migration (IOM), an intergovernmental organisation committed to promoting 'humane and orderly migration' (from the IOM mission statement, available at www.iom.int/en/who/main_mission.shtml (accessed 25 May 2006).

[5] N Demleitner, 'Forced Prostitution: Naming an International Offense' (1994) 18 *Fordham International Law Journal* 163; D Leidholdt, 'Sexual Trafficking of Women in Europe' in A Elman (ed), *Sexual Politics and the European Union* (Providence, NJ, Berghahn Books, 1996).

[6] I Taylor and R Jamieson, 'Sex Trafficking and the Mainstream of Market Culture' (1999) 32 *Crime, Law and Social Change* 257.

[7] P Williams, 'Trafficking in Women and Children: A Market Perspective' (1997) 3(4) *Transnational Organized Crime* 145; A Schloenhardt, 'Organized Crime and the Business of Migrant Trafficking' (1999) 32 *Crime, Law & Social Change* 203; A Jahn and T Straubhaar, 'A Survey of the Economics of Illegal Migration' (1998) 3(3) *South European Society and Politics* 16.

[8] S Shannon, 'Prostitution and the Mafia: The Involvement of Organized Crime in the Global Sex Trade' (1997) 3 *Transnational Organized Crime* 119; G Bruinsma and G Meershoek, 'Organized Crime and Trafficking in Women from Eastern Europe in the Netherlands', *ibid*, 105; P Mameli, 'Stopping the Illegal Trafficking of Human Beings. How Transnational Police Work Can Stem the Flow of Forced Prostitution' (2002) 38 *Crime, Law & Social Change* 67.

it first and foremost a (women's) human rights issue.[9] Yet it is clear that some of these analyses, extremely valuable as they are in offering insights into the problems in certain areas, easily produce a lopsided understanding of the larger web of issues at stake. To focus, for example, on only the migration aspect of trafficking, although justifiable (as trafficking is fundamentally connected to broader migration issues), necessarily leaves some relevant aspects out of the analysis. Put simply, though trafficking in women for sexual exploitation is about migration, it is not *only* about migration. A 'migration analysis', if it leads to a 'migration response', is therefore less than sufficient.

Among the European Union Member States (in particular in the 'old' EU–15) the prevailing approaches to trafficking in women for sexual exploitation (and trafficking in human beings in general) have in particular focused on more decisive responses from the criminal justice system (such as introducing harsher penalties) and migration authorities (involving measures aiming at stricter border control and improved quality of travel documents). The above is perhaps too broad a characterisation; the statement is accurate regarding those Member States (eg the Netherlands, Belgium and Italy) which as destination countries have been clearly alert to trafficking since the early 1990s and which have legislated on it—mostly, but not exclusively, adopting criminal provisions, as some of the measures go beyond the purely 'criminal' towards the social protection of trafficking victims.[10] There are also Member States where, for various reasons, the problem has only recently been gaining attention and acknowledgement, and then largely as a result of broader international and European concern over it (eg the Nordic Member States). Finally, there are countries where the topic has at least initially raised altogether different concerns (the 10 new Member States have been largely countries of origin and transit rather than destination). Although there is, for this as well as for other reasons, divergence between Member States, much of current anti-trafficking activity is undeniably directed towards the control of borders and the prosecution of traffickers. Yet some working in the field of practical anti-trafficking action are beginning to concede that, beyond law enforcement and migration checks, there is a need to protect and assist the victims of trafficking (not least because securing their testimony is often crucial for successful prosecution) and, moreover, the need to try and prevent trafficking from occurring in the first place.

[9] For a selection see S Toepfer and B Wells, 'The Worldwide Market for Sex: a Review of International and Regional Legal Prohibitions Regarding Trafficking in Women' (1994) 2 *Michigan Journal of Gender & Law* 83; S Farrior, 'The International Law on Trafficking in Women and Children for Prostitution: Making it Live Up to its Potential' (1997) 10 *Harvard Human Rights Journal* 213; L Chiang, 'Trafficking in Women' in K Askin and D Koenig (eds), *Women and International Human Rights Law. Vol. I* (Ardsley, NY, Transnational, 1999).

[10] For an overview of the laws of the Member States at the time of the first Commission Communication see T Kootstra, *Background Study on Basic Principles for a Code of Conduct Within the Member States of the European Union to Prevent and Combat Trafficking in Women* (Utrecht, Dutch Foundation against Trafficking in Women, 1996).

Typically, but not always, trafficking is a cross-border phenomenon. In Europe, trafficking in women for sexual exploitation (stereo)typically involves recruiting and transporting women from the poorer countries of the world into the old (and increasingly new) Member States of the European Union. It is often mentioned how the more 'traditional' countries of origin in Asia and Africa were increasingly overtaken by Central and in particular Eastern Europe[11] and the Balkans[12] in the 1990s; in the new millennium, the Balkans and the former Soviet Republics[13] remain significant source areas. Anxiety over these flows was the self-interested reason behind the initial European Union concern with the different responses to trafficking by its Member States, although more principled reasons for taking European-level action (including harmonisation) have also been put forward.[14] Moreover, there have now been initiatives by the EU (or some of its institutions at least) for the development of a response to trafficking that would not only result in a more convergent approach across the EU Member States, but also a more 'comprehensive' one. This resonates with the language which has become increasingly common in the international (especially human rights) arena and which understands a 'comprehensive approach' as a combination of the 'three Ps' of combating trafficking in human beings: prevention, prosecution and protection. An apt early characterisation of this language (which is now increasingly prevalent in regional fora) is provided by the United Nations Economic and Social Council: '[e]ffective action to combat international trafficking in women and children requires *a comprehensive approach* in the countries of origin, transit and destination that includes *preventive measures* to educate potential victims and their families, as well as to frustrate traffickers, *enforcement measures* against traffickers and all those who assist them and *protective measures* to aid victims of trafficking, including protection for those victims who would assist in the prosecution of the traffickers'.[15] In other words, protection, prosecution and prevention should be considered interconnected parts necessary for a comprehensive approach, and there should be a balance between the three prongs.

[11] IOM, *Trafficking and Prostitution: the Growing Exploitation of Migrant Women from Central and Eastern Europe* (Migration Information Programme, 1995).

[12] IOM, *Victims of Trafficking in the Balkans* (Geneva, IOM, 2001). See also D Haynes, 'Used, Abused, Arrested and Deported: Extending Immigration Benefits to Protect the Victims of Trafficking and to Secure the Prosecution of Traffickers' (2004) 26 *Human Rights Quarterly* 221.

[13] P Twomey, 'Europe's Other Market: Trafficking in People' (2000) 2 *European Journal of Migration and Law* 1; D Hughes, 'The "Natasha" Trade: The Transnational Shadow Market of Trafficking in Women' (2000) 53 *Journal of International Affairs* 625.

[14] For one example of the latter (the 'responsibility' of the EU as an area of destination) see A Diamantopoulou, *Fighting Modern Slavery: The EU's Role in Supporting Victims of Trafficking* (Conference Paper from the EU/IOM STOP European Conference on Preventing and Combating Trafficking in Human Beings, Brussels, 18–20 Sept 2002).

[15] Resolution 1998/20 (Action to combat international trafficking in women and children), 28 July 1998, preamble (emphasis added). In a similar vein see the consistent stream of resolutions by the Commission on the Status of Women over the past decade, advocating a 'comprehensive approach' (see, eg, Trafficking in women and girls, A/RES/59/166, 10 Feb 2005); alternatively, see the Action Plan to Combat Trafficking in Human Beings by the Organisation for Security and Co-operation in Europe (24 July 2003).

The aim of creating a more comprehensive approach stems from the gradual realisation in some quarters that to tackle trafficking merely from the point of view of (organised) crime/external migration control will not prove sufficient to stop or necessarily even significantly reduce it. But the creation of a more 'comprehensive' approach to trafficking in women for sexual exploitation, however justified and needed, is complicated precisely because the phenomenon raises several (often controversial) legal and policy concerns relevant to several different policy areas. It is hardly surprising that no country has a comprehensive strategy against trafficking, considering the complexity of the issues at stake and the variety of ways in which the problem can be framed. For instance, and in many ways most centrally, trafficking involves sometimes extreme but sometimes less obvious violations against the victims' most basic human rights. It is equally true that in destination countries it is viewed as a serious form of (transnational) crime, threatening not only the health and safety of those trafficked but the security of the destination society, while sending countries see it as abuse against their nationals who are migrating for better opportunities and to send remittances to their families in their countries of origin. More broadly, trafficking is associated with globalisation forces that affect migration patterns, and the situation of female migrants in particular, while in Europe trafficking can be seen in the light of the dual migration regime in which the free movement of 'EU citizens' goes hand in hand with restricted entry for some groups of 'third country nationals'. Last but not least, trafficking for sexual exploitation points to the issue of prostitution, which—against an increasingly globalised background—raises highly contested issues of public morality and public order as well as gender equality and social justice.

Drawing up a comprehensive approach in one national system is one thing; formulating an approach that would be comprehensive across the EU (or Europe) is quite another. Yet this seems to be exactly what is implicated by the increasing EU interest in trafficking. The first Commission Communication on trafficking in 1996 already recognised that it 'cannot be tackled effectively without a multi-disciplinary and coordinated approach which involves all concerned players—NGOs and social authorities, judicial, law enforcement and migration authorities—and which involves both national and international cooperation.'[16] More recently, the Council Framework Decision of 19 July 2002, which replaced the previous (1997) Joint Action[17] and which requires EU Member States to 'harmonise' their laws on trafficking in human beings (under Justice and Home Affairs co-operation), states that it is 'necessary that the serious criminal offence of trafficking in human beings be addressed not only through individual action by

[16] See Commission Communication of 20 Nov 1996 on Trafficking in Women for the Purpose of Sexual Exploitation, COM(96)567 final, at 6; see also the second Commission Communication of 9 Dec 1998 Proposing Further Action in the Fight Against Trafficking in Women, COM(98)726 final.

[17] Joint Action Concerning Action to Combat Trafficking in Human Beings and Sexual Exploitation of Children, 97/154/JHA [1997] OJ L 63/2.

each Member State but by a comprehensive approach.'[18] A summary of what seems to be meant by this approach is provided by the information sheets, which discuss the development of a 'comprehensive European strategy', prepared by the European Commission for International Women's Day, 8 March, in 2001. After repeating the EU engagement in this area the document goes on to state that the desired approach:

> involves national and international co-operation. It is necessary to address the phenomenon throughout the trafficking chain (recruiters, transporters, exploiters, other intermediaries and clients). A variety of measures, including explicit legal protection to all individuals, and preventive measures, as well as measures to ensure adequate protection of, support for, and assistance to the victims, are required. Since women are in a position of vulnerability to become victims, there is also a clear need to tackle this problem from the angle of promoting gender equality.[19]

The EU involvement in anti-trafficking also signifies that, as at the EU level generally, the planned method is to use law as the 'natural' vehicle to reach a desired goal, in this case the suppression of trafficking. The vision of a 'comprehensive European strategy', however, raises thorny issues, not least because the Union itself lacks or has limited competence in several areas that would be relevant to this kind of approach.[20] While some of the concerns raised have a clear connection to the EU (for instance, free movement issues and some aspects of external migration), others are still considered very much the domestic concern of each EU Member State (most obviously, the prostitution dimension fundamentally connects trafficking for sexual exploitation to the diverse criminal justice policies of the Member States). Indeed, arguably the above-mentioned Framework Decision approaches the limits of how far the EU can currently go in criminal law approximation.[21] Trafficking is, of course, not a unique phenomenon in this respect. However, because of the complexity and evolving nature of trafficking and the way in which it contests the established boundaries of policy areas, these questions are particularly relevant with regard to EU action against trafficking. Against this

[18] Council Framework Decision of 19 July 2002 on Combating Trafficking in Human Beings, 2002/629/JHA, [2002] OJ L 203/1, preamble. On this see also COM(2000)854 final/2 [2001] OJ C 62E/324 and European Parliament Report, A5-0183/2001, 30 May 2001.

[19] Trafficking in Women. The Misery Behind the Fantasy: From Poverty to Sex Slavery. A Comprehensive European Strategy. available at http://europa.eu.int/comm/justice_home/news/8mars_en.htm (accessed 3 Apr 2006), subsequently used as the basis of background document 'Trafficking in Human Beings: the European Response' (Justice and Home Affairs Directorate General, 2002).

[20] After amendments to the Treaty of Amsterdam, preventing and combating trafficking in persons now *is* an EU objective under the implementation of the Area of Freedom, Security and Justice, but EU powers in this area (including the approximation of rules on criminal matters) are limited. See Arts 29 and 31 TEU.

[21] F Medved and P Cullen, 'Counteracting Human Trafficking: An Analysis of European Union Policy' in M Anderson and J Apap (eds), *Police and Justice Co-operation and the New European Borders* (The Hague, Kluwer Law International, 2002), at 204, point out that 'you can only "approximate" what is already there'—and, as was stated above, many Member States had left trafficking completely or mostly unaddressed in criminal laws.

background, striving for a comprehensive approach seems either an almost utopian project or a process involving ominously sweeping generalisations, considering the gaps in existing research into the complexities of trafficking and scant knowledge of 'what works'.[22] This does not preclude the possibility of a 'common European strategy' against trafficking, but it does bring into focus the need to investigate the obstacles that have to be overcome.

Instead of dismissing the idea of 'comprehensive European approach' out of hand, this book examines it more closely, for it is plain that it has a sensible basis, in that a sounder European policy is required. Despite the difficulties envisaged, this is an area because developments around the topic have recently been and will in all likelihood continue to be rapid, not least because of the easily perceived connection to anxieties over security and policing. This obvious, but relatively recently made link will probably ensure that trafficking remains on the European agenda. Even if the space to create a more comprehensive response may be getting smaller, some recognition of the need for it remains.[23] Yet the overwhelming attention given to trafficking in recent years also raises serious concerns, for although the calls both for a comprehensive approach and for 'more Europe' have become more frequent, there has been little discussion of exact content of the approach and the part the EU should and could play. More specifically, if the 'comprehensive European approach' is merely a façade for the continuation and deepening of the current tendencies in developing a common policy, in particular regarding the over-emphasis on repressive measures, such developments can turn out to be more harmful than beneficial.[24] Even if all Member States move towards a common approach (for instance focus mainly on crime/migration control with minimal humanitarian or long-term preventive measures), this does not amount to a 'comprehensive' approach unless it entails correcting the current skewed emphasis of anti-trafficking action. Otherwise, the net effect of a European approach is likely to be limited or even detrimental.

The idea of a comprehensive approach, if taken seriously, implies a fuller understanding of the heterogeneity of trafficking in women for sexual exploitation and its causes. It suggests some sort of equilibrium—for example, that the interests of

[22] See, eg, E Kelly, *Journeys of Jeopardy: A Review of Research on Trafficking in Women and Children in Europe* (IOM Migration Research Series, No 11, 2002).

[23] Note the impetus given by the so-called Brussels Declaration which emerged from the 'European Conference on Preventing and Combating Trafficking in Human Beings: A Global Challenge for the 21 Century' (organised on 18–21 Sept 2003 under the Danish EU Presidency), which was subsequently included in the programme of the Greek Presidency in the first half of 2003. See Council Conclusions of 8 May 2003 [2003] OJ C 137/1.

[24] See, eg, the Presidency Conclusions of the Tampere European Council (15–16 Oct 1999), which connect trafficking to the fight against transnational crime and to smuggling. This tendency is admitted by the Commission 'so far the European Union has been more active in taking initiatives on the development of penal legislation and law enforcement and judicial co-operation than on the prevention of trafficking and the protection of victims': Trafficking in Women. The Misery Behind the Fantasy: From Poverty to Sex Slavery. A Comprehensive European Strategy, above n 19. See also, eg, K van Impe, 'People for Sale: The Need for a Multidisciplinary Approach Towards Human Trafficking' (2000) 38 *International Migration* 113.

states and the European polity (sovereignty, control) are carefully balanced against the human rights of individuals, be they EU citizens or not—which is surely in demand but which is not clearly visible in current European approaches. In legal and policy terms, comprehensiveness thus seems to entail a much more radical reconsideration of the implications that trafficking has in the policy areas that, separately and together, affect the understanding of and responses to the phenomenon in the European Union setting. In terms of the European Union as a special legal construction, the investigation needs to tackle the actual and desirable role of the Union beyond its current focal point as regards the Area of Freedom, Security and Justice. A truly comprehensive approach seems to mean crossing the boundaries of established policy areas; probing issues such as the relationship between increasing free movement of EU nationals and increasing limits on the movement of others through an increasingly Europeanised external migration policy; taking on board the role of transnational organised crime; studying the most appropriate law enforcement response both in Member States and at the Union level; and taking into account the situation of victims, both current and potential. Moreover, as will be argued in the following chapter, since trafficking in women for sexual exploitation is a phenomenon that in complex ways raises the gendered power differentials between men and women, it is helpful to examine the issues raised through a critical feminist lens.

This book is in some ways a pilot investigation of uncharted territory. The stunning proliferation of anti-trafficking research and activity in the last few years has involved optimistic calls on the EU to take a more active position in anti-trafficking efforts without addressing the particulars of the role of the EU in potentially contributing to but also in hampering anti-trafficking efforts.[25] This work therefore aims to examine more closely the overlapping legal discourses and legal frameworks around trafficking in the EU setting in order to tease out their consequences for a more wide-ranging approach to trafficking in women for sexual exploitation. It is not a manual on how to devise a comprehensive approach to trafficking, or even to the more specific problem of trafficking in women for sexual exploitation; this book instead focuses on the legal aspects of anti-trafficking action in the EU framework that seeks to overcome Member States' divergences. To go beyond that requires more knowledge than currently exists. Instead, the central objective behind the book is to examine the following questions: how is trafficking in women for sexual exploitation conceptualised in the Member States and in the EU setting? What is the role of the European Union in the relevant policy spheres regarding anti-trafficking, and its relationship with the Member States' policy convergence/divergence? What implications do the intersections of these areas and continuing European integration have for the possibilities of formulat-

[25] L Hauber, 'The Trafficking of Women for Prostitution: A Growing Problem Within the European Union' (1998) 22 *Boston College International and Comparative Law Review* 183; E Uçarer, 'Trafficking in Women: Alternate Migration or Modern Slave Trade?' in M Meyer and E Prügl (eds), *Gender Politics in Global Governance* (Lanham, Mld, Rowman & Littlefield, 1999); V von Struensee, 'Sex Trafficking: A Plea for Action' (2000) 6 *European Law Journal* 379.

ing a more comprehensive approach to trafficking in the European Union? The last question is particularly pertinent, as in many ways the phenomenon of trafficking challenges some of the premises often taken for granted regarding the internal organisation of European law, the relationship between the Union and its Member States and between European integration and global developments.

The structure of this book broadly follows 'policy spheres' that are relevant to the EU's engagement with trafficking. This is done in order to allow a broader discussion than the axiomatic categorisation of trafficking in the AFSJ frame typically permits and to facilitate the identification of the interconnections and overlap between different spheres and discourses. After Chapter 2, which introduces the main theme of feminist insights into 'comprehensiveness' that runs through the book, Chapters 3 to 6 tackle the clusters of problems raised with regard to trafficking in the areas of free movement, external migration, criminal justice and human rights. Chapter 3 connects trafficking in women for sexual exploitation and the measures to be taken against it to the exclusive logics that underpin the 'fundamental freedom' of free movement of persons within European Union, as this aspect vitally, if in many ways invisibly, informs the EU's engagement with anti-trafficking action. The reverse of this freedom, control over external migration, is tackled in Chapter 4, which examines trafficking as a form of irregular migration into the EU Member States, perceived as requiring and justifying stricter migration control measures. Closely bound with the external migration dimension is the matter of (organised) crime and its involvement with trafficking—seen as necessitating a stricter law enforcement and European co-operation response—which is dealt with in Chapter 5. Chapter 6 examines the problems raised in previous chapters against the truism that trafficking is above all a phenomenon that raises severe human rights concerns, not only because of the violations involved in trafficking itself but because of the possible violations in the implementation of anti-trafficking measures and because of the 'root causes' of trafficking. It also examines the EU's human rights dimension. Chapter 7 brings all these strands together and further discusses whether or not it is possible to move towards a more wide-ranging approach to trafficking in the European Union.

1.2 DIVERGENCE, CONVERGENCE AND COUNTRY STUDIES

It is possible to formulate the above concerns on the feasibility and desirability of a 'common European comprehensive anti-trafficking policy' somewhat differently and to connect them to a wider discussion on the prospects of European legal integration. This theme relates to whether or not European (Union) legal systems can be seen as converging as a result of European integration which has largely been pursued through the use of law as a steering mechanism.[26] Although these

[26] For the purposes of this work the expression 'convergence/divergence debate' will be used as shorthand for the standpoints that relate to whether (and if so, how) European legal systems are 'approaching' one another.

debates on convergence and divergence in European integration have their roots in European private law (where conscious legal harmonisation has been most prevalent), the discussion is currently becoming increasingly relevant to fields outside private law. Indeed, trafficking in women for sexual exploitation today touches upon these debates in several ways. To take just one example: as Harlow points out, both the drafting of the EU Charter of Fundamental Rights[27] and the promotion of greater Justice and Home Affairs co-operation are 'steps in the direction of legal unity'.[28] This in turn makes the debates on convergence relevant and topical *vis-à-vis* trafficking, which is specifically mentioned in the Charter as 'prohibited' (Article 5(3)) and which, as one of the crimes the Union is to prevent and combat, explicitly falls within the developing police and judicial co-operation.[29] While this is not the place to engage in a full debate on the intricacies of the convergence/divergence debate, it is perhaps useful to outline its main characteristics, and in particular those aspects relevant to this work.

Put simply, the proponents of 'the convergence view' consider that European legal systems are in many respects developing along common lines and achieving greater uniformity ('approaching one another') due to globalising forces, similar economic and social situations, etc. In Europe this sentiment is in particular connected to the process of 'Europeanisation' through the harmonisation of national laws in the EC (and EU) framework, which is alleged to create greater convergence of national legal systems. Moreover, the convergence of national systems is seen as not only possible but welcome. In the area of private law this idea was expressed by Markesinis, who claimed that there is (although admittedly 'gradual' and 'patchy') convergence between common law and civil law systems.[30] One commentator extends this idea to consider it even 'obvious' that European legal systems are converging, not only in private law, but also in the fields of criminal and administrative law.[31] This view, in emphasising convergence through harmonisation, is quite often (although not always) connected to the notion of law as something that can be 'engineered' and the assumption that, at least to some degree, law develops (and can be developed) not due to societal pressures, but

[27] Charter of Fundamental Rights of the European Union [2000] OJ C 364/1.

[28] C Harlow, 'Voices of Difference in a Plural Community' in P Beaumont, C Lyons and N Walker (eds), *Convergence and Divergence in European Public Law* (Oxford, Hart, 2002), at 199.

[29] The Charter was of course included in the Draft Constitutional Treaty (Treaty establishing a Constitution for Europe [2004] OJ C 310/1). Considering the uncertain future of the Constitution, this book takes note of some of the changes proposed by it, but generally assumes it may never enter into force.

[30] B Markesinis, 'Learning from Europe and Learning in Europe' in B Markesinis (ed), *The Gradual Convergence* (Oxford, Clarendon Press, 1994), 30. See also B Markesinis, *Foreign Law and Comparative Methodology: A Subject and a Thesis* (Oxford, Hart, 1997).

[31] G de Groot, 'European Education in the 21st Century' in B de Witte and C Forder (eds), *The Common Law of Europe and the Future of Legal Education* (Deventer, Kluwer, 1992), 7–11. About convergence in public law, see Beaumont, Lyons and Walker (eds), above n 28. Certainly in the areas of migration policy and criminal law convergence debates have been increasing especially since the adoption of the Amsterdam Treaty.

indeed irrespective of them.[32] This means, among other things, that it is possible to develop law by 'borrowing' (what are often referred to as 'legal transplants') from other legal systems.[33]

The opposite view is perhaps most famously represented by Pierre Legrand's well-rehearsed argument that European legal systems 'have not been converging, are not converging and will not be converging'.[34] Legrand's view is based on a division between law as formal rules and concepts and law as habits and customs, that is as a legal culture (in particular what he calls its '*mentalité*'): although the former may (seem to) be becoming more 'harmonised' as the pro-convergence authors maintain, this does not mean the *mentalités* are (in fact, in Legrand's view this is even impossible when it comes to civil law *v* common law, due to their different way of reasoning).[35] In this view law is fundamentally connected to culture: law is not just rules but a reflection of its cultural environment. In a similar vein, Teubner has challenged convergence and the idea of easy transplantability of law; yet his notion of 'legal irritants' (which 'unleash an evolutionary dynamic in which the external rule's meaning will be reconstructed and the internal context will undergo fundamental change'[36]) is not as unconditional. Legrand and others clearly have a point, in that rules should be understood as part of a wider context, and since there does not currently exist a (legal) culture that could properly be characterised as, for example, European, convergence will unavoidably be accompanied by divergences.[37] Yet at the same time it must be borne in mind that 'legal culture' is a far from straightforward concept.[38] Questions about its significance *vis-à-vis* the possibility of (some degree of) legal adaptation (and the ways of measuring the 'success' of such processes) are still very much debated.[39]

Moreover, there is an interesting and unresolved tension in Legrand's argument between his recognition of the nature of legal culture (as *not* uniform and hiding power relations) and his celebration of the centrality of 'legal cultures' that should

[32] See, eg, W Ewald, 'Comparative Jurisprudence (II): The Logic of Legal Transplants' (1995) 43 *American Journal of Comparative Law* 489, who draws from the works of Alan Watson.

[33] As will be discussed in ch 2, legal feminism has a troubled relationship with law, but many do subscribe to this belief that law can be engineered.

[34] See P Legrand, 'European Legal Systems Are Not Converging' (1996) 45 *International and Comparative Law Quarterly* 52, at 61–2.

[35] For a wider sample of his views, see P Legrand, 'Against a European Civil Code' (1997) 60 *Modern Law Review* 44; P Legrand, *Fragments on Law-as-Culture* (Deventer, WEJ Tjeenk Willink, 1999); P Legrand, 'Public Law, Europeanisation and Convergence' in Beaumont, Lyons and Walker (eds), above n 28.

[36] G Teubner, 'Legal Irritants: Good Faith in British Law or How Unifying Law Ends Up in New Divergences' (1998) 61 *Modern Law Review* 11, at 12.

[37] But see L Friedman, 'Is There a Modern Legal Culture?' (1994) 7 *Ratio Juris* 117.

[38] R Cotterell, 'The Concept of Legal Culture' in D Nelken (ed), *Comparing Legal Cultures* (Aldershot, Dartmouth, 1997); compare L Friedman, 'The Concept of Legal Culture: A Reply' in *ibid* and Legrand (1999), above n 35, at 27–34.

[39] See, eg, D Nelken and J Feest (eds), *Adapting Legal Cultures* (Oxford, Hart, 2001); P Legrand and R Munday (eds), *Comparative Legal Studies: Traditions and Transitions* (Cambridge, Cambridge University Press, 2003).

be mentioned.[40] Interestingly, in passing Legrand does point out that there is a parallel here with 'cultural' essentialism (which should be resisted) and essentialism in feminism, but he does not connect this observation (as would seem natural) to the challenges posed by critical movements such as feminism to his idea of 'legal culture'.[41] Much of legal feminism sees law (in the wider meaning of legal culture) as a site of constant struggle over competing interests (or even a site of oppression of marginalised groups) to a much broader extent than Legrand seems willing to concede. Feminist challenges to law, divergence and essentialism as well as law reform will be discussed further in the next chapter, but it should be mentioned now that the convergence/divergence debate can be seen as more layered (there is perhaps convergence in divergence and vice versa). For instance, the experience of women's exclusion from actively participating in legal culture seems to sit uneasily with Legrand's idea of 'community to which we belong'. Moreover, legal feminism often questions the centrality of cultural differences and points out that, despite variations, the pervasiveness of female subordination runs, albeit in varying ways, *across* cultures. For example, one need not take an essentialising feminist view (although it remains a relevant concern) to argue that the understanding of 'the French legal culture' of rape (or domestic violence or incest) may raise similar criticisms to that of 'the English legal culture'.

Mirroring these ideas and the notion of 'contingent' (as opposed to certain and unconditional) convergence[42] against the increasing debates around trafficking in women for sexual exploitation, it can be said that there is a clearly visible tendency in the European Union towards harmonising, or trying to harmonise, the laws of the Member States with regard to trafficking in the (admittedly limited) Justice and Home Affairs framework for which the EU currently has competence. That is a conscious project of producing converging laws. It remains to be seen to what extent such convergence (for instance, transplanting the offence of trafficking into the criminal laws of all EU Member States) can/will go beyond the level of rules to the level of actual transformation and, beyond that, implementation. As Harlow notes, '[e]mpirical evidence shows that national . . . attitudes and culture profoundly affect implementation of Community directives and policies; where these do not harmonise well with national . . . structures, they may be transported and lip-service may be paid to them, but they will remain largely a dead letter'.[43] Yet at the same time the rudimentary European Union interest in the area is in fact derived from the spontaneous efforts of (certain) Member States to develop policies to 'combat' trafficking, which stem from developments *within* these societies. However, there are diverging views on the meaning of the concept of trafficking as well as on appropriate action against it between Member States (most famously, as

[40] See Legrand (2002), above n 35, at 236–40. See also N Walker, 'Culture, Democracy and the Convergence of Public Law: Some Scepticisms about Scepticism' in Beaumont, Lyons and Walker (eds), above n 28, who notes Legrand's consciousness of the vulnerability of his cultural claim *vis-à-vis* internal strife within that same culture, at 264–5.

[41] Legrand, above n 34, at 77–8.

[42] See Walker, above n 40, at 258.

[43] Harlow, above n 28, at 210.

will be discussed below, between Sweden and the Netherlands), as well as within them. Yet this does not necessarily prevent the emergence and development of convergence in certain areas, contingent (or even unexpected) as it may be.

The theme of divergence and convergence features in all the policy areas mentioned above as relevant for a 'comprehensive European strategy' against trafficking in women for sexual exploitation. Responding to the situation of (often irregular) migration of women involved and victimised in prostitution (often but not always by organised criminals) raises several very different yet inter-connected issues. This project explores these dimensions of 'European' anti-trafficking responses, and in so doing takes heed of Nottage's attempt at the 'middle way': it will be engaged in 'taking rules seriously while not neglecting the context, and trying to uncover patterns of convergence and divergence'.[44] Part of what makes trafficking in women for sexual exploitation particularly fascinating in this respect is that it is one of those issues where (sometimes relatively) abstract discussions on convergence and divergence become extremely concrete. The harmonisation of rules on free movement, the emerging and tentative criminal law co-operation with regard to organised crime, the diverging national policies on prostitution (and attitudes behind them), victim protection, human rights and public order all coalesce in anti-trafficking responses. While some aspects of anti-trafficking strategies tie in closely with distinctive national experiences and practices, others are at the various stages of being 'Europeanised', and many are seen as requiring more or less active co-ordination and co-operation between different levels. Thus, just as the intersections of different frameworks need to be examined, so do the possibilities and difficulties involved in the bringing into line of divergent national conceptions.

The focus of the country studies of this work is in particular on the anti-trafficking measures of three EU Member States, which were chosen with the underlying rationale that in examining the convergence/divergence aspects of approaches to 'prevention, prosecution and protection' one is led to scrutinise the underpinning attitudes to sexuality and its role in commercial sex in general and prostitution in particular. Before going any further it is useful to sketch the prevailing approaches to commercial sex (which will be discussed in more detail below). Although it is impossible to categorise all approaches as falling within certain ideal 'models', they are traditionally divided into prohibitionism, regulationism and abolitionism. Prohibitionism condemns prostitution and other commercial sexual activities as immoral and criminalises involvement in them (in particular for prostitutes and pimps but possibly also for customers).[45] The

[44] L Nottage, *Convergence, Divergence, and the Middle Way in Unifying or Harmonising Private Law* (EUI Working Paper Law No 2001/01, Florence, EUI, 2001), at 34.

[45] This approach is rather (in)famously followed in the United States. See, eg, E Miller, K Romenesko and L Wondolkowski, 'The United States' in N Davis (ed), *Prostitution: An International Handbook on Trends, Problems, and Policies* (Westport, Conn, Greenwood Press, 1993); R Weitzer, 'The Politics of Prostitution in America' in R Weitzer (ed), *Sex for Sale: Prostitution, Pornography and the Sex Industry* (New York, Routledge, 2000); on the exception of Nevada, see M Bingham, 'Nevada Sex Trade: A Gamble for the Workers' (1998) 10 *Yale Journal of Law and Feminism* 69.

so-called regulatory approach also (often) condemns commercial sex as a social or moral evil, but tolerates it as 'unavoidable'; the state regulates prostitution through licensing prostitutes or through brothels. As opposed to the above approaches, the abolitionist model does not officially condemn women involved in sex industries on moral grounds (they are often seen as victims) but the exercise by others of control over them. Thus abolitionist countries seek to abolish both state control of prostitution and control by pimps. When abolitionism is accompanied by client criminalisation, those who use their 'services' for sexual gratification are also considered criminally liable.[46] It must, however, be added that these characterisations are somewhat deceptive, in that they do not always reveal the nexus of ideology and treatment. On the one hand, prohibitionism and abolitionism (and client criminalisation) have the same ultimate aim: the elimination of prostitution; yet, apart from legal provisions that criminalise certain actors or acts, they have little to say about what should be done about prostitution as a current phenomenon. Regulationism, on the other hand, does focus on prostitution as a phenomenon in full swing: it is premised on the perceived need to do something about prostitution *now*. In terms of ideology, however, classic (and even the newer form of) regulationism has none; it simply grapples with prostitution through state control in an effort to prevent nuisance, crime and the spread of disease.

The underlying commonality between prohibitionism, abolitionism and regulationism is that they all wish away the problem by either not really wanting to deal with the phenomenon now or not having any ideology apart from somehow dealing with prostitution at present. While the Member States of the European Union have, at least at first glance, notoriously incompatible policies in this regard, they also have some things in common. In traditional terms, some can be characterised as more or less regulationist (Austria), while the majority are officially abolitionist (Italy, France); some states, most notably the Netherlands, have recast legalised prostitution as work (arguably not in regulationist terms but to accept sex work as work), while Sweden, while also subscribing to abolitionism, has also criminalised buying sexual services as well. In many EU Member States the issue of prostitution is currently significant, not least because of the increasing topicality of the trafficking debate. As this project evaluates also the effect of prostitution policies, the emphasis must be on states having not only different policies on prostitution but also active and evolving policies against trafficking as destination countries. In addition, considerations of regional balance and population feature as relevant factors. This book will thus particularly concentrate on anti-trafficking measures in three jurisdictions which currently have differing approaches: Sweden, the

[46] For brief summaries of the 'traditional' approaches to prostitution and their problems see, eg, L Brussa, *Survey on Prostitution, Migration and Traffic in Women: History and Current Situation* (Strasbourg, Council of Europe, 1991), at 6–10; N van der Vleuten, *Survey on 'Traffic in Women'. Policies and Policy-Research in an International Context* (Leiden, Research and Documentation Centre Women and Autonomy, 1991), at 17–22. See also J Drexler, 'Governments' Role in Turning Tricks: The World's Oldest Profession in the Netherlands and the United States' (1996) 15 *Dickinson Journal of International Law* 201.

Netherlands and Italy (which, like most EU countries, allows prostitution but does not consider it 'legitimate' work). Sweden and the Netherlands in particular have been often juxtaposed as representing the two feminist 'solutions' to prostitution. However, this choice allows the exploration of not only differences but also commonalities: for instance, what these three countries have in common is that they are all part of 'Fortress Europe', in that as members of the European Union they have increasingly restricted legal (external) migration (also but not only for prostitution), though they (paradoxically) also need the cheap workforce provided by (female) migrants.[47]

1.3 SOME COMMENTS ON TERMINOLOGY AND THE NATURE OF THE PROBLEM

Rather than concerning trafficking in human beings more generally, this work is limited to the specific concern of 'trafficking *in women for sexual exploitation*' with particular reference to prostitution. There are particular reasons for this. First, as will be seen, this type of trafficking is possibly the major form, and certainly the major connotation, of 'trafficking'.[48] This is neither to deny that other trafficking occurs nor to claim that it is not important or serious. However, it is 'trafficking in women for sexual exploitation' which has prompted the most substantial response from society in general as well as from legal systems.[49] At the same time the fact that 'trafficking in women for sexual exploitation' is actually only a part of the larger trafficking phenomenon means that 'trafficking in women for sexual exploitation' actually offers a window of opportunity to examine both the particularities and the generalities of the phenomenon.[50] Secondly, trafficking in women *for sexual exploitation* is a particularly gender-specific phenomenon, which (in a manner slightly different from, for instance, trafficking in maids for domestic work) invokes difficult issues of sexuality, freedom, choice, gender equality, and so on.[51] As such it is also a more equivocal, and thus more interesting, subject than, for

[47] All three are also 'old' Member States (at least when juxtaposed to the 10 'new' Member States of Central and Eastern Europe). There is no case study on the new Member States because this book focuses on states that have been and are primarily countries of *destination*, as it is *their* policy choices and priorities that have been driving the the EU approach, and the new Member States have been required to adapt to the priorities of EU as a destination area.

[48] Another important form of trafficking is, of course, trafficking in children. Even though trafficking in children also raises separate concerns (which will not be addressed here) it should be noted that much of it consists of trafficking in girls (under 18) for sexual exploitation. This phenomenon, like trafficking in children for sexual exploitation in general, in many ways overlaps with trafficking in women for sexual exploitation. This is particularly evident when the girls trafficked are under age but over the age of consent (ie 16–17-year-olds).

[49] Indeed, there has been something of an over-emphasis on this aspect, but this emphasis merits investigation and is thus retained in this work.

[50] Eg, how and why the response to trafficking in women for sexual exploitation is different from or similar to the response to trafficking in women or men for work in sweatshops, or to trafficking in men for construction work. While this book concerns almost exclusively 'trafficking in women for sexual exploitation', it has a number of things in common with other forms of trafficking (especially with trafficking in girls for sexual exploitation).

[51] About these issues see below ch 2.

example, trafficking in young children (which, practically all can agree, is always 'wrong'). Thirdly, as 'trafficking in women for sexual exploitation' has indeed in recent years emerged as a 'hot' topic, especially among human rights activists and research organisations, this attention not only means that arguments in this field are perhaps more developed and sophisticated but also that the problem typical of trafficking studies, the dearth of available information, is less acute.

It should be emphasised that the lack of reliable data on trafficking practices remains a cause for concern: it is very difficult to obtain accurate figures on the numbers of trafficking victims, partly because the existence/extent of trafficking has not yet been fully recognised in many countries.[52] One often hears the statement that women and children constitute 'the vast majority' of those trafficked in. This is, of course, a claim that is extremely hard to prove or disprove, considering that there are no even remotely accurate figures on the number of people (women, men or children) who are trafficked regionally, let alone globally. The few estimates which have been suggested in the past have now been quoted so often that they are 'official truths' despite the lack of firm empirical backing (such as the now classic IOM figure of 500,000 women trafficked into Western Europe per year[53] or a United Nations estimate of 4 million people[54] or the US estimates that 45–50,000 women and children are trafficked into the United States per year[55]). At best they are educated guesses, for beyond the obstacle formed by the highly clandestine nature of all forms of trafficking, in human beings, the end result of studies on trafficking crucially depends on what one sets out to examine and how one defines trafficking as opposed to other 'irregular' migration movements—and, as will be discussed in the following chapter, this is a contested issue in itself.

[52] Knowledge is still limited, for instance, with regard to the mechanics of trafficking networks or how the demand side of prostitution interacts with trafficking (do customers prefer foreign women as the 'exotic' alternative or are they just taking what is on offer, etc). On these issues, see Kelly, above n 22.

[53] IOM Trafficking in Women Conference (New Jersey, 6 July 1998), quoted, eg, in Stiftelsen Kvinnoforum, *Trafficking in Women for the Purpose of Sexual Exploitation: Mapping the Situation and Existing Organisations Working in Belarus, Russia, the Baltic and Nordic States* (Stockholm, Stiftelsen Kvinnoforum, 1998); C Galiana, *Trafficking in Women* (European Parliament Working Paper, Brussels, 2000); R Coomaraswamy, *Trafficking in Women, Women's Migration and Violence against Women* (Report of the Special Rapporteur on Violence Against Women, its Causes and Consequences, UN Doc E/CN.4/2000/68); von Struensee, above n 25; K Corrigan, 'Putting the Brakes on the Global Trafficking of Women for the Sex Trade: An Analysis of Existing Regulatory Schemes to Stop the Flow of Traffic' (2001) 25 *Fordham International Law Journal* 151.

[54] Quoted, eg, in G Caldwell, S Galster and N Steinzor, *Crime & Servitude: An Exposé of the Traffic in Women for Prostitution from the Newly Independent States* (Report of the Global Survival Network, Washington, DC, Global Survival Network, 1997), B Young, 'Trafficking of Humans Across United States Borders: How United States Laws Can be Used to Punish Traffickers and Protect Victims' (1998) 13 *Georgetown Immigration Law Journal* 73; Coomaraswamy, above n 53; Corrigan, above n 53. Compare United Nations Fund for Population Activities, *State of the World's Population* (UNFPA, 2000) which estimates the number of *women* bought and sold at 4 million per year.

[55] CIA Briefing, Global Trafficking in Women and Children: Assessing the Magnitude (1999), quoted in A O'Neill Richard, *International Trafficking in Women to the United States: A Contemporary Manifestation of Slavery and Organized Crime* (Washington, DC, DCI Exceptional Intelligence Analyst Program, Center for the Study of Intelligence, 2000); subsequently in S Tiefenbrun, 'Sex Sells but Drugs Don't Talk: Trafficking of Women Sex Workers' (2001) 23 *Thomas Jefferson Law Review* 199; S Feve and C Finzel, 'Trafficking of People' (2001) 38 *Harvard Journal on Legislation* 279.

Some terminological clarifications are necessary at this stage as 'trafficking in women for sexual exploitation' not only invokes powerful imagery but also involves a conceptual minefield (an obstacle frequently lamented upon especially with regard to trying to define the issue in legal terms).[56] Although the issue will frequently recur in this book, a working definition should be established. In this book 'trafficking in women for sexual exploitation' is generally understood (in line with what could be called a slowly establishing minimum consensus) to mean the illicit commercial exchange of (not goods, as in 'drug trafficking', but) people, and specifically women, for a sexually exploitative purpose, usually involving movement across borders. 'Trafficking in women for sexual exploitation' is a part of the phenomenon of 'human trafficking' or 'trafficking in human beings' (as not only women but men and, in particular, children can be and are trafficked), although the initial concern over the 'traffic in persons' specifically related to women and girls, who are still considered the primary victims[57] of 'trafficking in humans'. On a related note, 'trafficking in women' is particularly connected to 'sexual exploitation' as opposed to 'non-sexual' exploitation. Based on existing information, it is widely agreed that while humans are trafficked for non-sexual exploitation, such as the exploitation of labour in the textile industry, domestic work or construction work, sexual exploitation appears to be what trafficking in women is typically about.[58] 'Sexual exploitation' in this context typically refers to the 'exploitation' of prostitution but can extend to other forms of sexual exploitation.[59] All forms of trafficking are seen as involving an element of force, coercion, deception or misrepresentation of some sort; they are therefore seen as differing from what is often called 'human smuggling' or 'smuggling in human beings', which in turn is usually understood as (mere) facilitation of unauthorised entry into a country (even though, as will be seen, this distinction is not unproblematic). Both human trafficking and especially human smuggling are often understood to be part of irregular or 'illegal' migration.[60] Trafficking does not, however, necessarily imply either, as it may involve regular entry to the country of destination.

[56] The expression 'trafficking in women for sexual exploitation' is loaded with various and sometimes conflicting meanings, a fact which leads to terminological confusion. The English term 'trafficking' is sometimes used outside the English language as well, as in many languages the corresponding term would refer to 'smuggling', while what could be called trafficking is translated as 'trade in women' ('*kvinnohandel*', '*naiskauppa*', '*vrouwenhandel*', etc.).

[57] As regards the term 'victim', it is problematic in the sense that the label of 'victim' can be seen as one-dimensional and disempowering, especially (but not only) by those who in a libertarian vein emphasise women's agency as decision-makers and who see focusing on victimhood as counterproductive. In this work 'victim' is used not in this sense but particularly where victimhood is a relevant aspect of the legal treatment of trafficking, as it often is (eg, when identification as a victim is required for a residence permit, etc.). For a discussion of this argument see J Goodey, 'Sex Trafficking in Women from Central and East European Countries: Promoting a "Victim-Centred" and "Woman-Centred" Approach to Criminal Justice Intervention' (2004) 76 *Feminist Review* 26, at 34.

[58] But see M Wijers and L Lap-Chew, *Trafficking in Women, Forced Labour and Slavery-like Practices in Marriage, Domestic Labour and Prostitution* (Utrecht, STV, 1997).

[59] On the controversy over whether prostitution is always 'exploitative' see below ch 2.

[60] The 'illegality' of non-nationals is a thorny issue, as 'illegality' can be caused by irregular entry, irregular residence or irregular employment (or activity). 'Illegal' also tends to be a strongly stigmatising

The above characterisations remain necessarily somewhat abstract, which is why many of those writing about trafficking like to start their work with a 'story of a trafficking victim'[61] in order to give the reader a framework in which to place the phenomenon. These nutshell descriptions, which tend to highlight the egregiousness of the 'flesh trade', are a way of not only outlining the topic but also highlighting the seriousness of the abuse involved. However, by invoking powerful images of sexual slavery, debt bondage, kidnapping and so on, which certainly place the issue squarely within the ambit of 'trafficking', they avoid some of the difficult issues, which evoke the grey areas of choice and coercion. Sometimes they also tend to go hand in hand with military terminology, such as 'combating trafficking', which is hardly the most fruitful way of approaching an issue as complex as trafficking, and can be a cover for promoting or justifying simplistic (military or policing type) analyses and responses.[62] The use of military terminology also implies that this 'war' is something that can be 'won' through fighting enough. In other contexts 'trafficking in women for sexual exploitation' is still understood fluidly, in that its use can range from the 'relatively independent prostitute' receiving help to obtain (illegal) access to another country to set up her 'business' there to a teenager kidnapped from her home village and delivered to a brothel in the same country, kept under lock and key. At times, the term is used by some academics, media commentators, organisations and state authorities to describe phenomena in the spheres of irregular migration or prostitution in ways which obscure rather than clarify what exactly is meant.[63]

While over-generalisations are dangerous, it is possible to outline the typical circumstances of trafficking processes for purposes of clarification. Apart from outright kidnapping, which is relatively rare, often brokers or 'boyfriends' recruit marginalised and often unemployed young women eager to migrate in search of a better life with promises of paid work or marriage abroad. The women are then transported[64] to their destinations and delivered to their 'employers', around which point it is revealed that deception has taken place regarding either the nature of the work (in prostitution) or its conditions and arrangements.[65] Often

expression, which is why many tend to use 'irregular' instead. 'Irregular' is used in this book to refer to migrants defined as such by immigration laws and regulations in receiving countries.

[61] Eg, 'Yelena left her life of poverty in her hometown of Dniprodzerzhynsk, Ukraine . . . she was trafficked across Europe, forced into sexual slavery, and held captive in various brothels and hotel rooms': Corrigan, above n 53, 151.

[62] On 'illegal' migration and the use of security rhetoric, see M Beare, 'Illegal Migration: Personal Tragedies, Social Problems, or National Security Threats' (1997) 3(4) *Transnational Organized Crime* 11.

[63] This is the case especially when terms implying voluntary choice (like sex work) are used together with terms implying lack of choice (slavery-like conditions, etc). See, eg, '80 Rescued Sex Workers Kidnapped', *The Guardian*, 10 Dec 2004, where under age trafficking victims are characterised as sex workers.

[64] Some women enter the destination country legally either because they come from countries whose nationals are not required to have a visa for a short period stay in a Member State or they are in possession of a short stay visa or even of a longer term work permit, for example as an 'entertainer'.

[65] The latter often relates to the highly distorted view of the reality of prostitution offered by recruiters (sometimes called the 'Pretty Woman syndrome', after the 1990 film which painted a fairytale picture of a happy emancipated sex worker with whom a handsome millionaire falls in love):

the victims' passports and money are taken away to prevent them from leaving; blackmail through the extortionate debts incurred to the organisers of the migration is common. The important aspect is that upon reaching their destinations, if not before, the victims become trapped in coercive and abusive situations from which escape is both difficult and dangerous. Traffickers use a wide range of manipulative and coercive tactics—horror stories of 'breaking in' with physical (beatings, rape) and mental (intimidation, threats and isolation) abuse abound both in newspapers[66] and IGO and NGO reports.[67] The methods of control during the exploitative phase actually range from physical restraint and violence to threats of violence, of informing the victims' families that they are working abroad in prostitution or of reporting their situation as 'illegal immigrants' to the authorities. As migrants in more or less irregular circumstances and as victims of sexual violence the women are particularly vulnerable to continued exploitation by, amongst others, brothel-keepers. At worst, trafficking-related exploitation ends with death at the hands of brothel owners, pimps or customers and, at best, with escape, discovery through a police raid or eventual meeting of the 'debt'. Long-term consequences for survivors involve multiple psychological, physical and health problems (the latter often related to sexually transmitted diseases (STDs)).[68]

Part of the *problematique* of trafficking has been and is still that, if and when those trafficked into sexual exploitation are in fact discovered (for example during a police operation etc), they are typically likely to be arrested, detained and ultimately expelled because they tend to be in violation of the destination countries' laws either because of irregular residency or irregular activities (as in most EU Member States involvement in prostitution is often not permitted for non(EC)-nationals, and especially not for those of them who are in the country irregularly).[69] Because victims are engaged in prohibited activities, there has been a tendency summarily to expel victims before they have a chance to file a complaint, to assess whether it is safe to return to their home countries or (in some cases) to apply for asylum.[70] In brief, trafficking victims are often treated more like criminals than like victims of a serious crime, and this is why many human rights

T Kootstra (ed), *One year La Strada: Results of the First Central and Eastern Program on Prevention of Traffic in Women* (Utrecht, Dutch Foundation against Trafficking in Women (STV), 1996).

[66] M Specter, 'Traffickers' New Cargo: Naive Slavic Women', *New York Times*, 11 Jan 1998.

[67] Coomaraswamy, above n 53; Galiana, above n 53; Caldwell, Galster and Steinzor, above n 54.

[68] The adverse physical and mental health effects of trafficking are becoming increasingly well documented. On trafficking in women see, eg, London School of Hygiene & Tropical Medicine *et al*, *The Health Risks and Consequences of Trafficking in Women and Adolescents. Findings from a European Study* (LSHTM et al, 2003). More generally, see B Gushulak and D MacPherson, 'Health Issues Associated with the Smuggling and Trafficking of Migrants' (2000) 2 *Journal of Immigrant Health* 67.

[69] Organisation for Security and Co-operation in Europe, *Trafficking in Human Beings: Implications for the OSCE* (ODIHR Background Paper 1999/3, Warsaw, OSCE, 1999).

[70] On how Member States are seeking to tackle this dimension through developing protection schemes for victims see below ch 4. On asylum and non-refoulement see ch 6. For an overview of some existing frameworks, see J Apap and F Medved *Protection Schemes for Victims of Trafficking in Selected EU Member Countries, Candidate and Third Countries* (Geneva, IOM, 2003).

activists speak of re-victimisation at the hands of the authorities. Initial consent issues, which should in principle be irrelevant for women who have been trafficked (as even if the victims did know they would work in prostitution in the destination country, once they arrive they are then deprived of their basic human rights) contribute to the perception that the women trafficked are actually 'migrant prostitutes', abuse of whom is taken less seriously.[71] Summary expulsion as illegal immigrants means that, as little consideration is given to the situations to which the victims are sent, their future fate in the country of origin can involve stigmatisation resulting in re-entry into prostitution (this time as a 'voluntarily' 'migrant prostitute') or re-trafficking, as the victims' vulnerability towards traffickers remains after expulsion.

As is clear from the above portrayal of trafficking, it is a complex phenomenon which interacts with law in various ways, which is precisely why this book engages in a discussion of measures against trafficking in women for sexual exploitation from a broad socio-legal perspective, aiming at a synthesis of ideas around the role of the EU. Trafficking raises a series of legal issues, in particular in the EU setting, but it is not enough to define the problem in terms of legal rules, for nowhere is it more obvious than with regard to trafficking that the letter of the law can be far removed from what actually takes place. Moreover, as trafficking is a phenomenon that has only recently become the focus of serious legal attention, the laws in books and official statistics reveal relatively little. This also has to do with the fact that trafficking is typically an underground criminal phenomenon the continuation of which relies on it remaining outside state intervention; moreover, it also connects to its invisibility as violence against women and migrants in irregular positions, both of which have tended to be marginalised in systems of justice. It is thus crucial to recognise the broader setting of economic, cultural and social factors (ranging from the moral attitudes of actors to structural issues of modern Western societies) which inform the understandings of trafficking as a legal (or non-legal) issue. Much of the analysis in this work will be based on, among others, a wide range of official and unofficial reports from states' authorities, international organisations, research bodies and NGOs.[72]

[71] This distinction between 'innocent' and 'guilty' victims is not only extremely difficult to make (as women may be conscious that involvement in prostitution was to be expected, etc), but it is also a problematic reflection of sexual double standards, which will be further discussed in ch 2.

[72] As regards the country studies, a source of information worthy of mention is provided by the so-called national rapporteurs on trafficking in human beings. In accordance with the recommendations of the 1997 Hague Declaration (The Hague Ministerial Declaration on European Guidelines for Effective Measures to Prevent and Combat Trafficking in Women for the Purpose of Sexual Exploitation, adopted at the Ministerial Conference under the Dutch Presidency of the European Union, The Hague, 24–26 Apr 1997), some European countries have now appointed national rapporteurs on trafficking to report to the government on trafficking 'the scale, nature and mechanisms of trafficking in women and the effectiveness of policies and measures concerning this [*sic*] phenomena'. Most importantly for this project, both Sweden and the Netherlands have appointed such rapporteurs. In Sweden this is the task of Rikskriminalpolisen (State Criminal Police), which publishes annual reports on trafficking; in the Netherlands, the national rapporteur is an independent expert whose office also publishes an annual report of the developments in the Netherlands.

2

Feminism, Prostitution and Trafficking: A Complex Approach

> To encourage a mindless expansion of sexual options, without critiquing the sexist structure in which sexuality is enacted and reducing the dangers women face, only exposes women to more danger. . . . An exclusive focus on danger, however, is just as perilous. It makes women's actual experience with pleasure invisible, overstates the danger until it monopolises the entire frame, positions women solely as victims, and doesn't empower our movement with women's curiosity, desire, adventure and success.[1]

THIS CHAPTER SEEKS to demonstrate why, in order to ask (and to try and answer) some of the most relevant questions about anti-trafficking responses with regard to formulating a more comprehensive approach, it is necessary to draw from feminist investigations into sexuality, prostitution and violence against women as well as from feminist theories of law and society. The topic of 'trafficking in women for sexual exploitation', of course, already in the choice of those words implies a focus on the gender-specific[2] nature of the phenomenon of trafficking in human beings. However, although it is commonly believed that the majority of those victimised in what is generally called trafficking in persons or trade in humans are, indeed, likely to be women or girls trafficked particular for exploitation in prostitution, this in no way forces the conclusion that investigating the phenomenon requires asking questions about the significance of gender (in)equality.[3] This chapter therefore makes the case for why any attempt at a fuller understanding of and response to trafficking cannot afford to ignore the fact that the phenomenon is fundamentally a manifestation of a complex range of gender(ed) inequalities. Moreover (and in a related vein) it argues that an investigation into feminist legal perspectives is necessary to explain the multiple roles of law as it potentially empowers and facilitates, yet simultaneously constricts and

[1] C Vance, 'More Danger, More Pleasure: A Decade after the Barnard Sexuality Conference' in C Vance (ed), *Pleasure and Danger. Exploring Female Sexuality* (London, Pandora Press, 1992), at pp xvi–xvii.

[2] 'Gender' is, it should be noted, often used instead of 'sex' to separate what is seen as the social and 'constructed' from the biological and 'natural', enabling challenges to the apparent 'naturalness' of differential treatment based on gender rather than sex. Compare however T Murphy, 'Feminism on Flesh' (1997) VIII *Law and Critique* 37 on under-theorised feminist understandings of 'sex' (as opposed to gender).

[3] See, eg, B Ghosh, *Huddled Masses and Uncertain Shores* (The Hague, Martinus Nijhoff, 1998).

even hampers, the construction of more comprehensive strategies towards trafficking in women for sexual exploitation.

In order to examine the wide range of equality concerns raised by prostitution and trafficking for sexual exploitation, this chapter draws from the complex web of feminist scholarship, which—despite its heterogeneity—has as its unifying forces the struggle for the recognition of women's experience and self-determination and the criticism of existing social, political and economic relations.[4] To start with, it is necessary to explore the background against which trafficking should be examined; to do this the voluminous feminist research on prostitution is discussed with particular reference to the role of law. This scholarship provides a strong basis for subsequent analysis, not least because of the emphasis by feminist research on elaborating how the law intersects with the (female) body[5] and (female) sexuality.[6] This analysis is then taken forward in the following section where the changes which have taken place in European sex industries are discussed, together with how feminist (and other) analyses of sexual exploitation conceptualise the phenomenon of trafficking in this changed setting. The last section provides the stepping-stone to the analysis of the following chapters. After some preliminary discussion on the inter-relationship between feminism and law, it argues that any analysis of trafficking in women and the law that aims to provide a more comprehensive approach must come to grips with a very complex policy setting, in which questions about how the law incorporates and perpetuates common beliefs about 'female nature' or appropriate female behaviour have to go hand in hand with examining broad trends, global developments and strategic opportunities and risks.

2.1 THE BACKGROUND: SEXUAL SLAVERY AND SEX WORK REVISITED

The most central feature of any feminist analysis of prostitution is a challenge to the prevalent notions about prostitution (as an immoral but necessary evil that has to be controlled and confined or as something to be formally prohibited but otherwise ignored), 'prostitutes'[7] (as a deviant group of 'fallen' women engaged in immorality or as simplistic puppet-like victims) and customers (as driven by

[4] About the earlier division into the main branches of liberal feminism, socialist feminism and radical feminism and several other categories (eg, black feminism and post-modern feminism) see V Bryson, *Feminist Debates* (London, Macmillan, 1999), at 8–44.

[5] See, eg, Z Eisenstein, *The Female Body and the Law* (Berkeley, Cal, University of California Press, 1988); J Bridgeman and S Millns (eds), *Law and Body Politics* (Aldershot, Darthmouth, 1995); J Bridgeman and S Millns, *Feminist Perspectives on Law. Law's Engagement with the Female Body* (London, Sweet & Maxwell, 1998).

[6] S Edwards, *Female Sexuality and the Law* (Oxford, Martin Robertson, 1981); C Smart, *Law, Crime and Sexuality: Essays in Feminism* (London, Sage Publications, 1995).

[7] The use of the term 'prostitute' remains contested for several reasons, not least because of the pejorative connotation of 'to prostitute' as 'to corrupt, to defile'; to some it conveys a (false) idea that being a prostitute implies an identity rather than something done to (or done by) the woman in prostitution, while others reject it because it implies an 'indiscriminate' sale of sex. Offered alternatives such as sexual slave, prostituted woman, sex worker and whore, while used by some, are even more loaded. Generally, women in prostitution will be used in this book.

biological sex urges unique to men).[8] Beyond that crucially important common element, it is the feminist controversy over the inherent—or not—oppressiveness of prostitution which has become most famous, and these debates, at times mischaracterised, also impinge on the now prevalent understandings of trafficking in women for sexual exploitation. Therefore it is necessary to discuss the issue before examining the feminist engagement with trafficking in women for sexual exploitation. Feminist attention to prostitution can be placed in the so-called 'phases' of feminism in a way that illustrates how prostitution first became a feminist issue, then a bitter bone of contention, but also a topic of indispensable insights; these phases also serve to clarify the role of the feminist engagement with law at different stages.[9]

The nineteenth century attack against the discriminatory regulation of prostitution in England (and later in other European countries), which took place during the 'first phase' of feminism, is a classic example of early feminist activism. First phase feminism was of course most concerned with women's exclusion from the public sphere and the struggle to achieve formal equality between men and women.[10] As regards sexuality, it criticised the sexual double standard, which took men's sexual promiscuity for granted but punished (both morally and legally) females who engaged in similar behaviour or who otherwise transgressed what was considered the proper feminine role. The feminist campaigners saw 'the prostitute' as a scapegoat who was both sexually exploited by private actors (men) and harassed by the public authorities (the police). The criticism was targeted at this regime of discrimination but rarely moved beyond it. The blatant discrimination and bias of laws such as the English Contagious Diseases Acts, which created a system regulating prostitution (segregating women in prostitution as a special class, subjected to mandatory health checks in an attempt to protect prostitute-using men from venereal disease), were famously criticised during this period.[11] While campaigning for the abolition of the Acts (and to raise the age of sexual consent), the feminist campaigners were also among the first to focus early attention on the (alleged) 'traffic' in (English) girls for prostitution abroad. Soon referred to as the 'white slave trade', the issue became a general moral purity crusade (even a moral panic[12]) against the sexual exploitation of 'innocent girls', the reverberations of which still echo in today's anti-trafficking debates.

[8] See H Benjamin and R Masters, *Prostitution and Morality* (New York, The Julian Press, 1964); V Bullough, *History of Prostitution* (New York, University Books, 1964); J Decker, *Prostitution: Regulation and Control* (Littleton, Colo, Fred B Rothman & Co, 1979).

[9] About the phases of feminist legal scholarship see, eg, N Naffine, *Law and the Sexes: Explorations in Feminist Jurisprudence* (Sydney, Allen & Unwin, 1990), at 1–19; Smart, above n 6, at 187–192.

[10] On early feminism generally see, eg, J Mitchell, 'Women and Equality' in A Phillips (ed), *Feminism and Equality* (Oxford, Basil Blackwell, 1987).

[11] About the Contagious Diseases Acts (1864, 1866, 1869) and the attack against them for restricting the rights of women in prostitution see J Walkowitz, *Prostitution and Victorian Society* (Cambridge, Cambridge University Press, 1981); see also Bridgeman and Millns, above n 5, at 711–19.

[12] 'Moral panic' is a term first coined in the 1970s to describe an exaggerated social reaction to behaviour that is seen to pose a threat to society.

Prostitution became the target of more integral analyses during the second feminist phase, when the emerging radical feminist analysis of society and male dominance identified sexuality as a central site of women's subordination. It was asserted that in a male-dominated society gender hierarchy is sexualised and eroticised in ways that make domination of women by men seem sexy.[13] Prostitution, besides being harmful to women involved directly in it, was argued to damage all women. It was maintained that prostitution is paradigmatic to the female condition, since it allows men to (continue to) objectify and subordinate women as their sexual servants. Prostitution became reformulated as an exploitative institution where women are turned into sexual commodities to be consumed; this institution is imposed by (patriarchal) society on women constrained by poverty, sexual discrimination and few viable economic alternatives—hence consent to prostitution came to be seen as problematic even in the presence of apparent 'choice'.[14] The invaluable insight here is an awareness of prostitution as connected with gender inequality and the structures of society rather than the individual deviancy of the 'prostitute' (perceived as deviating from the role of the 'good wife and mother'). This makes it possible to reconstruct the problem not as a private issue related to innate female traits that make some women 'fall' or to 'natural' male needs, but as a complex structural problem caused and upheld by lack of equal social and economic opportunities and sexual hierarchies that underpin the predominantly male demand for commercialised sex.[15]

Unlike early feminist scholarship, which generally believed that the law should and could be impartial and thus called for reform within the system, the second phase of feminism also mounted a more radical attack against the view of law as neutral, objective and rational. It was asserted that the seemingly universal values of law turn out to be 'masculine' and the reason the law has those characteristics is that the law is 'male' and incorporates (only) male experience. The most famous second phase argument comes from MacKinnon, who (instead of arguing that women are either the same as or different from men and should be treated accordingly) brings forth the claim that women are *dominated* by men, and that this situation is incorporated in the legal system which treats women as men see them, perpetuating their marginalisation.[16] As regards prostitution, it was argued that

[13] This kind of analysis focuses on aggressive sexual domination by men (and the adjacent female submission) and highlights the centrality of prostitution, along with pornography, rape and incest. In MacKinnon's famous words, '[s]exuality is to feminism what work is to Marxism: that which is most one's own, yet most taken away': C MacKinnon, *Towards a Feminist Theory of the State* (Cambridge, Mass, Harvard University Press, 1989), at 3.

[14] See, eg, K Millett, *The Prostitution Papers* (St Albans, Paladin Books, 1975); K Barry, *Female Sexual Slavery* (New York, New York University Press, 1979); C Pateman, *The Sexual Contract* (Oxford, Polity Press, 1988), at ch 7. See also A Dworkin, 'Prostitution and Male Supremacy' (1993) 1 *Michigan Journal of Gender and Law* 1; S Jeffreys, *The Idea of Prostitution* (Melbourne, Spinifex Press, 1997).

[15] J O'Connell Davidson, *Prostitution, Power and Freedom* (Cambridge, Polity Press, 1998).

[16] See C MacKinnon, *Feminism Unmodified* (Cambridge, Mass, Harvard University Press, 1987); MacKinnon, above n 13. See also the influential argument by C Gilligan, *In a Different Voice* (Cambridge, Mass, Harvard University Press, 1982); for other examples see T Dahl, *Women's Law: An Introduction to Feminist Jurisprudence* (Oslo, Norwegian University Press, 1987); R West, 'Jurisprudence and Gender' (1988) 55 *University of Chicago Law Review* 1.

the sexual exploitation of women is upheld by laws designed with the male (sexual) interest in mind. In other words, they stem from a sexual double standard, stigmatising 'the prostitute' while condoning the continuation of exploitation in practice.[17] Thus an attack was directed against the legal system for targeting the women in prostitution, rather than the men who visit them or their pimps and procurers, and more generally for doing nothing to change the background conditions of inequality, abuse and discrimination against women, which push some of the most vulnerable women into exploitation.[18] However, this kind of analysis was also easily overstated and essentialised, leading to a monolithic and undifferentiated understanding of oppression of women by 'men and their laws', which conceals the complexity of and variations in subordination, overemphasises the role of the sexual and is insufficiently alert to the diverse motivations of the actors in prostitution.[19]

The problems with the extremes of an 'exploitation' analysis (under which prostitution *is* sex discrimination[20]) soon came to attract strong criticism. This phase is in particular connected to the third phase of feminism, the emergence of prostitutes' rights movements and post-modernist resistance to the essentialism employed by some in making the 'exploitation' argument. The exploitation understanding was criticised for reducing all women in prostitution to nothing but passive victims of patriarchal society and denying their agency in making informed choices about engaging in it. It was argued that prostitution is not always inherently exploitative; it can also be well-paid (especially as far as 'women's work', typically systematically undervalued, is concerned) and hard work, which should be a matter of individual choice.[21] Some argued that prostitution, when freely chosen, is an act of sexual self-determination, which can even be liberating, not least economically.[22] In terms of law, this shift is connected with increasing feminist awareness of law's heterogeneity and multiplicity which questions the notion of monolithic oppression by the law. Smart describes this development by arguing that it sees the law as 'gendered'.[23] In other words, the analysis moves away from fixed categorisations of 'man' or 'woman' to the processes whereby the law itself fixes specific forms of gender division. The law is then 'relocated as one of the

[17] Barry, above n 14; see also K Barry, *The Prostitution of Sexuality* (New York, New York University Press, 1995).

[18] Millett, above n 14.

[19] E McLeod, *Women Working: Prostitution Now* (London, Croom Helm, 1982).

[20] 'Women in prostitution are denied every imaginable civil right in every imaginable and unimaginable way, such that it makes sense to understand prostitution as consisting in the denial of women's humanity, no matter how humanity is defined': C MacKinnon 'Prostitution and Civil Rights' (1993) 1 *Michigan Journal of Gender & Law* 13, at 13.

[21] Hence the use of terms such as 'sex work', 'sex worker', 'client', etc. See, eg, K Kempadoo and J Doezema (eds), *Global Sex Workers. Rights, Resistance, and Redefinition* (New York, Routledge, 1998); K Lerum, 'Twelve-Step Feminism Makes Sex Workers Sick: How the State and the Recovery Movement Turn Radical Women into "Useless Citizens"' (1998) 2 *Sexuality & Culture* 7.

[22] See G Pheterson (ed), *A Vindication of the Rights of Whores* (Seattle, Wash, The Seal Press, 1989); F Delacoste and P Alexander (eds), *Sex Work: Writings by Women in the Sex Industry* (San Francisco, Cal, Cleis Press, 1998).

[23] Smart, above n 6, 190–2.

range of practices through which gender is *acquired*, a process of which gender and gender differences are an *effect*'.[24] Prostitution laws are a frequently cited example in this regard, illustrating as they do the reproduction of gender difference by even gender-neutral statutes.[25]

The third phase criticism of essentialism also problematises the focus on incorporating 'women's experience' into law.[26] Difficult issues are raised regarding what constitutes the real problem of prostitution, who may voice concerns about it and what to demand in terms of legal intervention. The 'sex work' logic highlights the ways in which sexual activity is used as a basis for dividing women in general into 'good' and 'bad'.[27] From the perspective of the emerging sex worker lobby the main problem with prostitution was formulated as that of forced and/or child prostitution and of morality-based stigmatisation and discrimination against those women who choose sex work, who are condemned, in a sexist manner, for promiscuity.[28] Indeed, much of the oppression of sex work comes from discriminatory legal regimes and treatment by the authorities, which make the work unsafe, in turn rendering women in prostitution stigmatised and vulnerable to exploitation by pimps and to customer harassment and violence.[29] Thus, it was argued that most problems relating to prostitution could be solved by empowering women in general and those in prostitution in particular (through, for example, trade unions and labour laws) to resist the exploitation of their work; this has the underlying rationale that it would in fact be possible to transform the sale of sex *per se* from oppressive and dominating into a non-oppressive and equal commercial sexual transaction.[30] While this view seems to embrace the diverse voices of all women, including those working in the world of commercial sex,

[24] J Conaghan, 'Reassessing the Feminist Theoretical Project in Law' (2000) 27 *Journal of Law and Society* 351, at 363 (emphasis in original). See also Smart, above n 6; Naffine, above n 9.

[25] See, eg, M Frug, *Postmodern Legal Feminism* (New York, Routledge, 1992), ch 8, where it is argued that the American legal approach to sex work simultaneously 'sexualizes, terrorizes and maternalizes' the female body.

[26] The main criticism levelled against the focus on the 'experience of women' is that it (at least implicitly) assumes that most, if not all, women can be assumed to have a common, unified understanding of material issues. The accusation of essentialism in particular involves the charge that feminism has taken the situation of a highly selected group (namely white, Western, middle-class, heterosexual women) and claimed that this represents the (essential) experiences of (all) 'women'. This 'essential woman' was arguably often created by silencing dissenting voices of, eg, black, lesbian and working-class women. See, eg, b hooks, *Ain't I a Woman? Black Women and Feminism* (Boston, Mass South End Press, 1981), M Kline, 'Race, Racism, and Feminist Legal Theory' (1989) 12 *Harvard Women's Law Journal* 115 and A Harris, 'Race and Essentialism in Feminist Theory' (1990) 42 *Stanford Law Review* 581.

[27] G Phetersen, *The Prostitution Prism* (Amsterdam, Amsterdam University Press, 1996); N Roberts, *Whores in History: Prostitution in Western Society* (London, Harper Collins, 1992).

[28] See, eg, A Lucas, 'Women and Prostitution' in K Askin and D Koenig (eds), *Women and International Human Rights Law. Vol. I* (Ardsley, NY, Transnational, 1999), at 688, who condemns both forced prostitution (lack of consent) and child prostitution (no capacity to consent), but maintains that 'despite the constraints all women face, there is a *phenomenological* difference between being physically forced into prostitution and being "coerced by circumstance"' (emphasis in original).

[29] This is of course most forcefully felt where prostitution is illegal: P Alexander, 'Prostitution: *Still* a Difficult Issue for Feminists' in Delacoste and Alexander (eds), above n 22.

[30] See the discussion in L Shrage, 'Should Feminists Oppose Prostitution?' (1989) 99 *Ethics* 347.

precisely in view of the diversity of 'prostitution' and the relatively short duration of 'prostitution careers', it remains doubtful whether women in prostitution have unified interests any more than other women.[31] Moreover, at times prostitutes' independence and the freedom of their choices have been exaggerated.[32] In order to argue that sex work can be a 'choice', or at any rate a decision, to some, one does not need wholeheartedly to embrace all present aspects or manifestations of prostitution, and ignore questions about the broader context in which such choices are made.

Since the extreme ends of the 'exploitation' and 'work' views (one claiming that prostitution enforces women's subordinate position and the other considering prostitution as a sphere in which women make liberating choices about their lives and sexuality) seem irreconcilable, the debates on coercion and choice are often dichotomised into two symmetric polarities. Even though the polarisation has led to an oft-lamented lack of 'room for variation, overlap and considerations of social context' between prostitution as either 'liberating' or 'exploitative',[33] there is much common ground between them. Practically all feminist analyses consider the well-being and security of all women in prostitution to be a central concern and agree that much is wrong with the poor and dangerous conditions in which much prostitution takes place; they also frequently criticise the lack of economic and social options available to many women.[34] Most importantly, feminist analyses of why prostitution is currently problematic from the point of view of gender equality are much more nuanced. Many feminist analyses can be read as interpreting female sexuality caught in a dilemma between exploitation and suppression, or liberation and control. Female sexuality is often abused and exploited, for instance in prostitution; at the same time, it is repressed by norms and practices that label sexually active women as immoral. Tellingly enough, despite their diverging underpinnings, both a work and an exploitation understanding find support in the widely divergent stories about the lives of women in prostitution.[35] In these stories choice and coercion are interwoven. Some women were forced to enter or to stay in prostitution by boyfriends and/or pimps; others were driven by a combination of circumstances such as childhood sexual abuse, drug addiction or

[31] About this and other problems of prostitutes' organisations see, eg, L Mathieu, 'The Emergence and Uncertain Outcomes of Prostitutes' Social Movements' (2003) 10 *European Journal of Women's Studies* 29.

[32] See, eg, H Montgomery, 'Children, Prostitution, and Identity' in Kempadoo and Doezema (eds), above n 21 (which focuses on the 'motivations and perceptions' of 'child prostitutes').

[33] See, eg, Lerum, above n 21, at 23.

[34] It is further agreed that the prevalent legal approaches to prostitution often leave a lot to be desired (see below section 2.3). The agreement on certain issues is explicitly noted and discussed, eg, in M Simmons, 'Theorizing Prostitution: The Question of Agency' (1999) 2 *Sexuality & Culture* 125.

[35] For interesting accounts of prostitutes' experiences see, eg, C Jaget (ed), *Prostitutes: Our Life* (Bristol, Falling Wall Press, 1980); McLeod, above n 19; C Høigard and L Finstadt, *Backstreets: Prostitution, Money, and Love* (University Park, Penn, Pennsylvania State University Press, 1992) and Delacoste and Alexander, above n 22. For a revealing analysis of how women who work as prostitutes themselves solve the contradiction between prostitution as, on one hand, a threat to their survival (being a 'victim' of prostitution) and, on the other hand, the means of survival (being a survivor because of prostitution), see J Phoenix, *Making Sense of Prostitution* (London, Macmillan, 1999).

systematic racism and homelessness that lead to lack of other opportunities; and some women choose prostitution rationally and consciously as the best available economic option. Some women in prostitution are exploited and abused by customers and pimps; others work independently and find that, in general, violent customers are few and far between. These circumstances can change and overlap.

2.2 TALKING ABOUT TRAFFICKING: DEBATES AND DEFINITIONS

Regardless of how much or how little women in prostitution are exploited, what they in general *do* have in common is the fact that for them prostitution is primarily an economic institution.[36] Although the supply of women in prostitution obviously cannot be directly equated with poverty alone (not all poor women turn to prostitution after all), the sale of sexual services is nonetheless vitally connected to complex economic and structural gender inequalities.[37] This issue is highlighted with regard to recent global developments. As the third phase criticism rightly demonstrated, globally, regionally or even nationally, prostitution has never been a particularly homogenous phenomenon. However, the present day is still characterised by a manifest (further) diversification and transnationalisation of the commercial market for sex, much of which is due to globalisation[38] forces such as international migration, the tumultuous changes caused by the end of the Cold War and the growing gap between the rich and the poor (countries as well as people). The growing expansion of the sex industries in many countries goes hand in hand with a consistent tendency towards the 'foreignerisation' of women in prostitution in Western (and increasingly Eastern) European countries. The increasing involvement of women in prostitution outside their own countries—due to both choice and coercion—reflects the broader structural improvements in the position of the relatively privileged women in the West who, due to socio-economic improvement, no longer enter prostitution.[39] At the same time the global 'supply' of potential prostitutes is expanding due to various 'root causes', many of which relate to entrenched gendered discrimination and inequality, as well as violence against women, along with the particular impact of globalisation

[36] See Millett, above n 14; Lucas, above n 28.

[37] See, eg, C Wichterich, *The Globalized Woman* (London, Zed Books, 2000). The expansion of prostitution as many women's best economic choice is most visible in South East Asia, but other regions of the world (Latin America, South Eastern Europe) are by no means exempt.

[38] Globalisation is a complex concept, but essentially involves increased (and increasing) interconnectedness and interdependence in global economic, political and social processes: see, eg, J Mittelman, *The Globalization Syndrome* (Princeton, NJ, Princeton University Press, 2000), at 5–7. It can be viewed as a multi-faceted, continuing process rather than an outcome in itself; with the market as its driving force, it embraces further trade liberalisation and privatisation, but also the rapid development of communications technology and international financial transactions, the dismantling of border controls and increased travel opportunities (for some if not for all).

[39] A similar argument can be made in relation to trafficking in women for non-sexual exploitation (domestic work) as well as less explicitly exploitative migration practices, as many of the so-called '3D jobs' (dirty, demanding and dangerous) are increasingly performed by certain groups of immigrants.

forces (for instance economic liberalisation and restructuring) on those (mainly women) already most impoverished and marginalised.[40]

In addition to the supply side, the demand side of the equation has begun to face more scrutiny. For long the focus on female agency (or lack thereof) in prostitution has deflected attention from the element of *male* agency.[41] Now it is increasingly pointed out that the sex sector has become a big and transnational business, which thrives on the (overwhelmingly) male demand for a range of sexual services.[42] The expansion of prostitution in Western Europe partly stems from the sexual 'liberation' of the 1960s and the freedom to embrace sex; yet this sexual freedom has come to seem peculiarly one-sided: it entails that for the major part one sex is 'free' to provide for the other (or, as in the case of trafficking in women for sexual exploitation, forced to do so), rather than free to explore what sexual freedom may mean for them. Feminist analyses challenge this imbalance, as well as interrogate the 'naturalisation' of the demand for sexual servicing as constant or immutable. In light of the present-day centrality of sex(uality) in modern Western cultures, this has led to sustained calls to examine the role of prostitute users and the extent to which the demand for prostitutes is constructed through gender-specific and, in the globalised setting, often increasingly racialised ideologies of sexual mastery and appropriation of the (foreign) female body, also manifested by much of pornography and exercised through men's economic buying power (most obviously in sex tourism).[43]

Increasingly analyses draw attention to how the expansion of sex industries in many countries is not due to 'natural male urges' but, as in any market, to sex business entrepreneurs (criminal or not) who actively create and expand the demand for an ever-widening range of 'sexualised' services ranging from pornography, peep-shows and striptease acts to various prostitution services.[44] Indeed, existing sex industries, like any businesses, take advantage of technological advances, seek to expand further and look for links with legitimate enterprises,

[40] See, eg, B Ehrenreich and A Hochschild (eds), *Global Woman. Nannies, Maids, and Sex Workers in the New Economy* (New York, Metropolitan Books, 2002).

[41] Highlighted by S Kappeler, 'The International Slave Trade in Women, or, Procurers, Pimps and Punters' (1990) I *Law and Critique* 219. The emphasis on the supply side is a feature of both non-feminist and feminist research, even though for the latter to imply that the problem with prostitution lies with the supply rather than with those who demand or arrange sexualised services is most often unintentional.

[42] Y Sanghera, 'In the Belly of the Beast: Sex Trade, Prostitution and Globalization' in GAATW and Foundation for Women, *Moving the Whore Stigma* (Report on the Asia and Pacific Regional Consultation on Prostitution, Bangkok, 17–18 Feb 1997).

[43] See, eg, McLeod, above n 19, at 90: '[u]nless clients do speak out, the way in which the reasons for the continuation of prostitution lie partly in men's experience of everyday life as opposed to solely in women's deviance remain shrouded'. See also B Carpenter, 'The Prostitute and the Client: Challenging the Dualisms' (1998) 21 *Women's Studies International Forum* 387, at 398, who calls for 'knowledge of why men choose *not* to buy sex' (emphasis in original). See further below section 7.2.2.

[44] About the changing nature of sex markets and the customer experience see, eg, S Cameron, 'Space, Risk and Opportunity: The Evolution of Paid Sex Markets' (2004) 41 *Urban Studies* 1643. See also A Ryder, 'The Changing Nature of Adult Entertainment Districts: between a Rock and a Hard Place or Going from Strength to Strength?' (2004) 41 *Urban Studies* 1659.

such as the transport sector, hotels and media. Prostitution, which exists in a grey area between the legal and illegal, has, in particular in the global setting, the capacity to create huge profits, which attracts and also sustains the interest of criminal enterprises. To the extent that women can be seen as the raw material of this profit-making machine,[45] those involved in organising and benefiting from it are not necessarily, if at all, interested in making sure that the women involved make informed or free choices, let alone like the job. They are aided by the fact that the globalising world paradoxically provides both new freedom of movement through international travel for tourism and business and new restrictions on travel of the 'Fortress Europe' type. With increased restrictions placed on legal migration to developed countries, prospective migrants, including asylum-seekers, are channelled to informal and even illegal ways of migrating and seek to use migration networks and more or less reliable, exploitative and criminally-minded middlemen, who agree to provide unauthorised entry in exchange for compensation (usually known as human smuggling).[46]

At the same time globalisation, which has created the transnational linkages necessary for organising the movement of large numbers of people, has also changed the context in which organised crime operates. Transnational organised crime embodies some of the features of neoliberal globalisation.[47] Especially where state control over the legal and illegal markets has been crumbling in the last decade, such as in parts of the former Soviet Union or, for example, in post-conflict areas, the new criminal groups that have sprung up are increasingly beyond state control.[48] It has also been argued that the new transnational networks which seek to exploit the opportunities provided by various globalisation processes work both above and below the level of states: above by making maximal use of the permeability of borders and the tendency towards deregulation and by organising themselves along zonal/regional lines; and below by recruiting the marginalised individuals of societies suffering from the negative effects of globalisation.[49] But it should be kept in mind that there are also traffickers and middlemen who are not organised criminals as such, and arguably the panic over

[45] This aspect is best illustrated by those developing countries more or less consciously using prostitution as a development strategy (ie, expanding into sex tourism to capitalise on the local sex industry in order to 'catch up with the rest'). This strategy has been inadvertently promoted by the IMF and the World Bank, viewing tourism as a solution to the problems of poor countries (providing loans for the expansion of the entertainment industry in those countries): Sanghera, above n 42; see also J Pettman, 'Body Politics: International Sex Tourism' (1997) 18 *Third World Quarterly* 93.

[46] On these processes in more detail, see further below section 4.2.1.

[47] Mittelman, above n 38, at 203 (this ch with with Johnston).

[48] This situation is exacerbated where the police forces (eg, in the the former Soviet Union) tend to be underfunded and ill-equipped to deal with the emerging criminal networks and new kinds of problems caused by them. As the chief of criminal investigations in the Ukrainian Ministry of Interior put it: '[g]angsters make more money [from prostitution] in a week than we have in our law-enforcement budget for the whole year': M Specter, 'Traffickers' New Cargo: Naive Slavic Women', *New York Times*, 11 Jan 1998.

[49] Mittelman (this ch with Johnston), above n 38, at 208–11. The authors note the similarities between the actions of criminal networks and transnational corporations: both engage in, eg, profit maximisation, risk reduction, product innovation and bribery: *ibid*, 212.

the growth of organised crime has also served unduly to homogenise views of typical traffickers and the background against which most trafficking takes place.[50] Operations involving trafficking take highly diverse forms.[51] What those who could be classified as traffickers in general do have in common is that they make use of the global and regional processes which channel migrants into the informal and irregular migration routes and their capacity to navigate in the new environment by subverting migration controls.

In such situations migrants can be delivered into situations where exploitative practices, such as debt-bonded sexual exploitation, are possible and where the line between abuse and non-abuse, assisted migration and exploitation, becomes a fluid rather than a fixed one. Above all, the issue highlights how in the current setting *nationality* is constructed as a crucial factor, and, as will be seen below, this is particularly relevant with regard to the European Union. Women are often more at risk of exploitation because they are, by reason of complex socio-economic factors, in less advantageous positions to negotiate the conditions under which they cross international borders.[52] This brings to the fore the various 'root causes' of trafficking (and indeed irregular migration in general), many of which relate to gendered practices, such as discrimination and violence against women and girls, ethnic background as well as dysfunctional family situations,[53] together with economic and social reasons such as unemployment and the oft-mentioned 'feminisation of poverty'.[54] While this is not to say that all migrant women are exploited, it is against this kind of complex background of gendered disadvantage and relative powerlessness that exploitation of migrant women, when it does occur, takes place. These patterns explain why it is increasingly women from non-EU countries, who through various circumstances, choose or are coerced into prostitution in the European Union.

[50] See, eg, A Aronowitz, 'Smuggling and Trafficking in Human Beings: The Phenomenon, the Markets that Drive It and the Organisations that Promote It' (2001) 9 *European Journal on Criminal Policy and Research* 163.

[51] Although operations that 'specialise' in trafficking can be classified in several ways (see, eg, Ghosh (1998), above n 3), it is extremely difficult to give generalised descriptions that fit all aspects of trafficking operations. See also the discussion about the criminal networks, eg, in L Kelly, ' "You Can Find Anything You Want": A Critical Reflection on Research on Trafficking in Persons within and into Europe' (2005) 43 *International Migration* 235. For insights into trafficking operations, see A Schloenhardt, 'Organized Crime and the Business of Migrant Trafficking' (1999) 32 *Crime, Law & Social Change* 203; V Ruggiero, 'Trafficking in Human Beings: Slaves in Contemporary Europe' (1997) 25 *International Journal of the Sociology of Law* 231, at 234–41.

[52] See below ch 4.

[53] For a discussion on these see, eg, S Lăzăroiu and M Alexandru, *Who is the Next Victim? Vulnerability of Young Romanian Women to Trafficking in Human Beings* (Bucharest, IOM, 2003).

[54] Without going in detail into the voluminous research on women's economic and social status, it can be stated that women own a minimal percentage of the world's resources, earn disproportionately less than men for the same work, have more limited educational and societal opportunities and often face multiple discrimination based on not only gender but class, race and ethnicity: see, eg, United Nations Population Fund, *State of the World's Population 2002* (New York, UNFPA, 2002); UN Division for Social Policy and Development of the Department of Economic and Social Affairs, *The Report on the World Social Situation 2001* (New York, UN Division for Social Policy and Development of the Department of Economic and Social Affairs, 2001).

For feminist as well as other analyses the problem has been how to define the exploitation of migrant women in legal terms in a way that separates 'trafficking' as a distinct concern and at the same time connects it in relevant aspects to other phenomena such as 'irregular migration' or 'human smuggling'. The debate over the legal definition of trafficking—which extends beyond the feminist circle—has practical significance which makes it far from a question of purely academic relevance because of broad trends in the immigration policy in European destination countries. Current destination countries are prima facie negatively disposed towards those present or working 'illegally' in their jurisdictions. Until quite recently, those 'trafficked' have not been seen as a distinct group and in practice the differences in the treatment of trafficking victims and of those smuggled or otherwise engaged in irregular migration have not been great: in most countries, *all* have been simply immediately expelled. Even with the often inadequate systems of assistance and protection currently available to those identified as trafficked, treating them as a distinct group in need of protection brings into sharp relief the difference in treatment vis-à-vis other irregular migrants who continue to be expelled with little consideration for their actual situations. In part owing to feminist campaigning, there is an increasing tendency to draw an ever stricter distinction between human trafficking and human smuggling (as well as other forms of irregular migration), and this is increasingly accepted by states as well, at least in principle, if not always in practice.[55]

What was originally problematic about this distinction, and still remains so to a large degree, is that it was (and still is) justified through the claim that the majority of trafficking victims are women and girls, more vulnerable to exploitation than male migrants. To say this is not to deny that large numbers of women are trafficked, above all for sexual exploitation, but rather to argue that much research has been predetermined by the conceptual understanding of trafficking, which connects it with 'women' through 'prostitution' in the vein of the nineteenth century campaign with the aim of saving the innocent victims of 'white slavery'. Even though the situation is now gradually changing to some extent at least, most studies on trafficking, for instance many of those conducted by the IOM, have tended to set their focus on trafficking in women rather than trafficking in humans.[56] Although it is currently acknowledged that women, men and children can be trafficked, the primary connotation of 'trafficking in persons' stems from the special kind of exploitation, that is, sexual, to which women are subject that frames

[55] This is illustrated, eg, by the fact that in the context of the UN Convention against Transnational Organised Crime, two separate protocols were drafted for trafficking and smuggling. See below ch 5.

[56] See, eg, IOM, *Trafficking in Women to Austria for Sexual Exploitation* (Geneva, Migration Information Programme, 1996); IOM, *Trafficking in Women to Italy for Sexual Exploitation* (Geneva, Migration Information Programme, 1996); IOM, *Trafficking in Women from the Dominican Republic for Sexual Exploitation* (Geneva, Migration Information Programme, 1996). Even the IOM quarterly bulletin (called, gender-neutrally, *Trafficking in Migrants*) has manifested astonishing conceptual confusion as to whether trafficking only (or mostly) applies to women, whether everything else is smuggling, and what exactly the difference between the two is anyway: see IOM, 'There Are Ways to Curb the Worldwide Traffic in Migrants' [2000] *Trafficking in Migrants*, No 21.

the debate now, just as it did 100 years ago.[57] The link between 'trafficking' and 'women' is thus not so much, or at least solely, the consequence of their greater numbers among trafficking victims but also its *cause*. Trafficking is a gendered construction: it is mostly women who are trafficked because they are considered to be easily duped about or coerced into sex work, while the smuggled are mostly men, who are assumed to be showing an active capacity to migrate.[58] The point is not that women or girls are not more vulnerable to exploitation; for many reasons, as argued above, this is likely to be the case. What is problematic is to take this as a starting point for a conceptual distinction according to which the 'innocent' women, and it seems they alone, must be 'saved'.

In contrast, the feminist debates bring greater nuance to the issue. Much of the debate has gone along the lines drawn as regards prostitution, as in the well-known juxtaposition of two feminist NGO coalitions strongly involved in anti-trafficking efforts but with different views on prostitution. The Coalition Against Trafficking in Women (henceforth CATW) defines sexual exploitation broadly: 'all prostitution exploits women, regardless of women's consent. Prostitution includes casual, brothel, escort agency or military prostitution, sex tourism, mail order bride selling and trafficking in women'.[59] CATW sees women's bodies as vulnerable, exploitable and open to attack in classic radical feminist style,[60] and considers all women engaged in prostitution as exploited, and as such innocent. Thus all women recruited or transported for prostitution are 'trafficked', and hence 'victims of trafficking' regardless of whether or not they accepted their involvement in prostitution or the conditions under which it is exercised. Migration for prostitution is therefore subsumed into trafficking (as, under this approach, women in prostitution cannot be, for instance, 'smuggled'). The CATW understanding involves a recognition that, due to the structural factors underpinning prostitution and the global migration setting which results in increasing difficulty to migrate independently, many, if not all, foreign women found working in prostitution in Western countries have been to some degree exploited in the process of assisted migration, and are thus 'victims of trafficking'. It provides powerful and appealing images of women in need of protection, and also separates them as a category in need of protection and assistance. However, it is also clearly over-inclusive in terms of conceptual usefulness, and (as it ends up accusing them of false consciousness) fits particularly uneasily with the reality of those women who decide to migrate for prostitution and use the assistance of acquaintances or networks to do so.[61]

[57] When the study concerns trafficking in women, the focus has almost exclusively been on sex trafficking (especially for prostitution). See, eg, IOM, *Austria*; IOM, *Italy* and, IOM, *Dominican Republic*, all above n 56.

[58] Ghosh, above n 3.

[59] Available at www.catwinternational.org/about/ (accessed 5 Apr 2006).

[60] See in particular Barry, above n 14, also Jeffreys, above n 14.

[61] For criticism of CATW's attachment to the stereotypical notion of victim see J Doezema, 'Ouch! Western Feminists' "Wounded Attachment" to the "Third World Prostitute"' (2001) 67 *Feminist Review* 16. See also B Sullivan, 'Trafficking in Women. Feminism and New International Law' (2003) 5 *International Feminist Journal of Politics* 67.

Unlike CATW, the Global Alliance Against Traffic in Women (henceforth GAATW) subscribes to the view that prostitution itself is not necessarily exploitative or harmful to women but work, which should be recognised. GAATW draws a distinction between those who choose, from whatever limited alternatives, to engage in prostitution and those who are deceived or literally coerced into it. GAATW, which can easily be interpreted as promoting a diversity-tolerant, anti-essentialist feminist view, opposes the exploitation of prostitutes as workers, as well as forced prostitution and trafficking in women for prostitution when the prostitution/conditions in which it is practised is forced. GAATW claims to 'work to empower women rather than treat them as victims'; it thus promotes better living and working conditions for women in prostitution and action against forced prostitution and trafficking.[62] According to GAATW, it is important to distinguish between women who willingly accompany a recruiter, middleman or smuggler, fully aware of their future involvement in prostitution and consenting to it, and women who are deceived and/or coerced in some way; *both* should be humanely treated but only the latter are 'trafficked'. This acknowledges part of the reality of adult migrant prostitution, that women do make choices about prostitution and migrating for it, whether they 'can' or not according to popular 'trafficking myths' that highlight the requirement that victims be 'pure' and 'innocent'.[63] The problem with the GAATW understanding is that it is at times unduly individualist in downplaying the context in which such choice is made and does not articulate how to make its critical distinction, that is, to separate the 'forced' from the 'free' and (eg, should objective or subjective criteria be used to determine what constitutes relevant coercion?).[64]

Taken as polar opposites, the views of CATW and GAATW can only seem to be alternatives: sympathy with women exercising individual autonomy leads to supporting a 'work' position (GAATW), and identifying more with the idea that gendered social structures importantly shape women's lives leads one to think the lens of 'exploitation' makes more sense (CATW). Yet despite the valid disagreement between the positions, this exclusiveness is to a degree illusory. Many migrant women, especially those in irregular situations, are exploited and victimised, and this is in part due to the constraints faced by migrant women as a group, which expose them to abusive practices. Yet despite the abuse involved in the context of trafficking, many women do show active agency by seeking to migrate, by seeking to change their conditions, by resisting victimisation, and so forth. Emphasising individual choices and agency (regarding migration and prostitution) does not automatically mean one has to ignore the setting in which decisions are made. Nor should all the agency of all female migrant be obscured or all women have to be portrayed as passive and 'innocent' in order for it to be accepted that those

[62] Available at www.gaatw.org (accessed 14 Oct 2004).

[63] J Doezema, 'Loose Women or Lost Women? The Re-emergence of the Myth of White Slavery in Contemporary Discourses of Trafficking in Women' (2000) 18 *Gender Issues* 23.

[64] For a discussion of the GAATW definition see J Chuang, 'Redirecting the Debate over Trafficking in Women: Definitions, Paradigms, and Contexts' (1998) 11 *Harvard Human Rights Journal* 65.

victimised through exploitative practices, as well as migrants in general, deserve respect as human beings notwithstanding their choices (for example, to enter prostitution). Perhaps most importantly, feminist work on prostitution and trafficking illustrates the way in which trafficking is conceptualised as the result of a wider web of factors, and emphasises the need for broader analyses of the relevance and mechanisms of the globalisation of existing sex industries, the factors that make many women vulnerable to exploitation, the growing demand for sexualised services, and the involvement of organised crime and also more mundane middlemen.

This reading of trafficking as a constructed rather than 'natural' phenomenon also underlines what trafficking and smuggling, and indeed irregular migration in general, have in common despite the categorical distinctions that are increasingly made between them. The demarcations are to a non-negligible degree artificial because, despite the distinguishing features of trafficking (deception or coercion leading to exploitation), trafficking in humans in many ways stems from and touches upon the same complex immigration issues as other forms of irregular migration, and often has a number of elements in common with it (such as avoiding border controls or obtaining false identification, not to mention human rights concerns, many of which are common to all forms of irregular migration). Emphasising the distinction between trafficking and smuggling misses the fact that they are not mutually exclusive but part of the same continuum where there is plenty of overlap, not least because unrealistic policies which attempt to channel migrants into paths that do not match the existing reality create more space for both.[65] Most typically, a person can enter an agreement to be smuggled, but becomes instead 'trafficked' when, upon arrival, debt bondage, threats or violence are used to coerce him or her into forced labour, for example, in sweatshop work or in prostitution. In such cases, when the trafficked think they are being smuggled until the deception is revealed in the country of destination, it is impossible to distinguish trafficking from smuggling until the actual exploitation occurs. In many cases the (often considerable) debt incurred with smugglers for their 'services' makes migrants highly vulnerable to assisted irregular migration that quickly assumes the contours and traits of trafficking. Another common scenario occurs when someone initially trafficked into prostitution is later smuggled or irregularly migrates to work in another county; has she then stopped being a 'trafficking victim' and become an 'illegal migrant' instead?

The problem with the official demarcation between trafficking and smuggling, which has now gained mainstream currency, can be highlighted in relation to the polarised views offered by feminist understandings. On the one hand, the CATW position (which does see women as more vulnerable to exploitation because of structural factors) arguably fits a gendered trafficking/smuggling pattern, but with the important distinction that it rejects what the distinction supposes: that a migrant woman trafficked for prostitution has to fit the model of a 'deserving

[65] See below section 4.2.1.

victim', innocent of 'illegal' intent to migrate or engage in prostitution, to merit protection. Under the mainstream view many women that CATW would recognise as victims are tarnished by involvement in irregular migration and sex work. On the other hand, the GAATW view of migrant women as agents seeks to subvert the 'passive female victim'/'active male agent' dichotomy of trafficking/smuggling. Yet considering the double transgression of migrant women into the public sphere (as 'bad' women in prostitution and as 'bad' women who leave home), highlighting the agency of migrant women in prostitution entails the risk of losing the capacity ever to 'be' a victim under the mainstream view. The usual consequence of seeing foreign women in prostitution as 'decision-making agents' seems to be to treat adult migrant women involved in prostitution as irregular immigrants with all the consequences that go with it, while victimisation by pimps or abusive customers and structural causes are rarely identified.[66] This simplification has little space for the experiences of real-life trafficking victims, who in many cases both choose and do not, perceive themselves in charge but are at the same time dependant on middlemen, and engage in irregular migration and accept their own exploitation, but are victimised as well.[67]

2.3 TOWARDS A MORE COMPREHENSIVE UNDERSTANDING?

It should be clear by now (but is worth repeating) that, like other critical movements, feminist writings on law typically see law as political and an exercise of power.[68] Feminist scholarship has been particularly engaged with interrogating the seemingly neutral, rational, objective, coherent and autonomous framework of law to reveal how the structures and methods of this system are actually gendered, and, moreover, gendered in a hierarchical way.[69] The feminist attention to law goes hand in hand with the logic of feminist scholarship on law, which often sees law as both 'the wrong and the remedy'.[70] On the one hand, laws and the legal system in general are often accused of injustice, of at once ignoring gender as a fundamental element of the social discourse of law but also of entrenching it as a

[66] J Doezema, 'Forced to Choose: Beyond the Voluntary v. Forced Prostitution Dichotomy' in Kempadoo and Doezema (eds), above n 21. Needless to say that the trafficking/smuggling divide also works to the detriment of irregularly migrating men who (as rational agents consciously break the law) 'cannot' be trafficked under this kind of understanding.

[67] On this twofold experience, see for instance the personal stories of trafficked women in C Corso and A Trifirò, . . . *e siamo partite! Migrazione, tratta e prostituzione straniera in Italia* (Florence, Giunti, 2003).

[68] See P Smith (ed), *Feminist Jurisprudence* (New York, Oxford University Press, 1993), especially part VI.

[69] See N Lacey, *Unspeakable Subjects: Feminist Essays in Legal and Social Theory* (Oxford, Hart, 1998), at 2–14. As there is no single feminist theory of law, many speak of feminist legal theories (plural), or use the singular as an overarching term for various feminist approaches to law. In feminist legal scholarship 'law' is generally understood broadly.

[70] Formulation by Conaghan, above n 24, at 376. The most famous example of this, to some extent paradoxical, approach is the case of the MacKinnon/Dworkin anti-pornography ordinances in the US: see, eg, Lacey, above n 69, at ch 3.

basis of discrimination and oppression.[71] In short, law is seen as complicit in upholding male privilege. One the other hand, law is also seen as the remedy, not least because many of the struggles for gender equality have been waged in terms of equality before the law, starting with the first phase demands for formal equality. In its different phases, feminist scholarship has claimed that for the law to fulfil its promise of justice it has to include the concerns and experiences of women. Indeed, while law is often resistant to upsetting the status quo, it is believed that change can be achieved through resistance and reform.[72] Indeed, the second phase (counter-)knowledge of 'women's experience' has arguably provided invaluable (if limited) tools for demanding law reform, especially when the claim has been couched in terms of liberal rights (such as the right to reproductive control). Most feminists thus assume that at least some legal engineering, through transplants or otherwise, is possible.

The proliferation and fragmentation of feminist perspectives have created problems regarding legal reform agendas. As feminist jurisprudence is typically grounded in the concrete lives of actual people, what is fundamental to it is that women are (and can be) seen as a group, and one which is often silenced by the legal mainstream. The recognition of diversity among women and subsequent attempts to avoid essentialism on one hand and the promotion of law reform in 'women's interest' on the other are in a tension. It is difficult to create a 'transformative critique' that demands political and legal reform to advance 'women as a group' if, assuming that the avoidance of essentialism is taken seriously, only partial knowledge of *some* women and *some* situations can be produced. Most obviously, there are several factors that separate 'the prostitute' as a unique category, most notably the stigma involved in commercial sex and the specific legal regimes around prostitution in many countries that separate women involved in prostitution from 'normal' women, the 'whore' from the 'Madonna', even if both the vilification of the prostitute and the normalisation of 'non-prostitute' women highlight that both have in common the discipline mechanism of labelling women belonging to one or the other. Certainly, the nationality of migrant women is likely to emerge as a strong dividing factor in the European setting. Yet although awareness of and methods to avoid the dangers of essentialism are crucial to the feminist legal project,[73] this does not render the claim of women's disadvantage less valid: it is simply 'multiple, intersecting and complex'.[74] In other words, one has to be careful neither to overemphasise nor *underestimate* the commonalities among women. For instance, there are both meaningful similarities and

[71] Or exclusion, as in Réaume's characterisation of feminist jurisprudence as 'an analysis of the exclusion of some women's needs, interests, aspirations, or attributes from the design or application of the law': D Réaume, 'What's Distinctive about Feminist Analysis of Law?: A Conceptual Analysis of Women's Exclusion from Law' (1996) 2 *Legal Theory* 265.

[72] See for instance A Bottomley and J Conaghan (eds), *Feminist Theory and Legal Strategy* (Oxford, Blackwell, 1993).

[73] Ie one should learn to recognise the essentialism in categories that should *not* be used in the name of feminism.

[74] Conaghan, above n 24, 369–74.

differences between women in prostitution and women in general. Women in general suffer from gendered disadvantages, such as being allocated the responsibility but not the remuneration for child-care, as lacking financial independence, and as having a disadvantaged position in a segmented the labour market and inadequate exit options from violent relationships.

While many believe that through its promise of justice law can anticipate and promote progressive societal developments (as is indeed assumed as regards the idea of producing anti-trafficking action through convergence), substantial scepticism has also been expressed on the extent to which the law can really accommodate *any* kind of feminist critique and warnings about resorting to law in general, or rights more specifically, to further feminist aims have been issued.[75] It has been argued that law is a particularly powerful discourse and resistant to much feminist intervention because it makes a claim to truth, and thus produces knowledge which 'occupies a high place in the hierarchy of knowledges', enabling it to silence feminist challenges.[76] Yet regarding prostitution and trafficking, feminist scholarship is unavoidably engaged with law, and it has been and remains difficult not to call for more law or (better) regulation to change the status quo of many traditional legal approaches to prostitution, which leave a lot to be desired from any feminist perspective. Most of the criticism targets the fact that they focus in an extremely one-sided manner on women in prostitution, while pimps and customers tend to remain invisible in terms both of the law and of its enforcement. The enforcement of the prohibitionist model straightforwardly targets the women in prostitution rather than the client or the pimp.[77] Many of the current regulatory models seem a blast from the past, in that, while allowing prostitution and to some degree eroding the legal stigma of prostitution as a special problem of female deviance, they too have been used to enforce discriminatory control over prostitutes as a group.[78] The currently prevalent model of abolitionism, which leaves selling sex itself legal, in many countries makes it almost impossible to engage legally in most forms of prostitution because surrounding activities such as advertising, soliciting, pimping, as well as owning, operating or working in a brothel are illegal. Paradoxically, even though abolitionism claims to eliminate the exploitation of women in prostitution, often the legal arrangement is used in practice to segregate the prostitute from existing systems of support—when everything around prostitution remains criminal, prostitutes' boyfriends can be charged with

[75] See, in particular, C Smart, *Feminism and the Power of Law* (London, Routledge, 1989). On one hand, eg, the discourse of rights provides powerful rhetoric which lends itself to strategic use; on the other hand, it can easily backfire on feminists as it is easily abused by those with more power. On rights see further below ch 6. See also E Kingdom, *What's Wrong with Rights? Problems for Feminist Politics of Law* (Edinburgh, Edinburgh University Press, 1991); E Kingdom, 'Body Politics and Rights' in J Bridgeman and S Millns (eds), *Law and Body Politics* (Aldershot, Darthmouth, 1995) and F Beveridge and S Mullally, 'International Human Rights and Body Politics' in *ibid.*

[76] Smart, above n 6, in particular ch 5.

[77] Lucas, above n 28; Barry, above n 17.

[78] Lucas, above n 28; Barry, above n 17.

being pimps, and renting a room to known prostitutes can be charged as brothel-keeping.[79]

While most feminists agree that law reform around prostitution is needed in many countries with repressive laws or practices of enforcement (and believe that such reform can be engineered[80]), the entrenchment of the legal regulation around prostitution, often going back several centuries, makes this difficult. This is particularly so as regards incorporating into law a complex feminist analysis with its inherent tension in understanding that the organisation of prostitution is (now) often sexist and exploitative, and thus illegitimate, and still recognising the need to support and legitimate individual women in prostitution. Aiming to challenge the often long-standing positions on prostitution laws, feminist arguments have been 'mainstreamed' into pre-existing regulatory frameworks. Thus the most common 'feminist solutions' (improvements supported by feminist insights) have become segmented into two different positions along the lines of simplified 'exploitation' and 'work' views which could be broadly termed radical and liberal. This work will look at these two in more detail, so they are only briefly summarised here. The radical, drawing from the notion of prostitution as a form of exploitation, considers the laws around prostitution from the point of view of protecting women made vulnerable by socio-economic injustices and male violence. It often advocates the decriminalisation of prostitution, but not of those who are seen as taking advantage of it, such as pimps. Some consider that it is not only the activities of the pimp and the procurer which should be criminalised, but also those of the customers of prostitution. The liberal view considers the laws around prostitution from the perspective of eliminating discrimination against women in prostitution and thus reducing the demarcation between 'good' and 'bad' women. This can involve decriminalising all involvement in prostitution also for third parties, as long as no violence is present, or recognising prostitution as legitimate work through legalisation (legal regulation in the form of licensing, regular employment and insurance benefits or even legal brothels).

Most importantly, however, law reforms should be evaluated in terms of their real impact on *all* women involved in prostitution, and in particular those who are part of the globalised flows. As Campani states, '[t]he topic of legal intervention seems, in fact, poorly proposed today if the terms of the debate focus on prostitution solely in terms of the client–prostitute relationships, maybe even the pimp, without keeping in mind the global structure of the sex industry'.[81] This connects with the other important factor that any feminist agenda recognises: *beyond* law reform *specifically* on prostitution (be it administrative or criminal), much more must be done to reduce inequalities of sex, race and class more generally if the

[79] This, as Duncan argues, makes sure that space for prostitution exists, while maintaining the prostitute as the 'legal leper' who 'contaminates' all who come in contact with her: S Duncan, '"Disrupting the Surface of Order and Innocence": Towards a Theory of Sexuality and the Law' (1994) II *Feminist Legal Studies* 3, at 22–3.

[80] See above section 1.2.

[81] G Campani, 'Trafficking for Sexual Exploitation and the Sex Business in the New Context of International Migration: the Case of Italy' (1998) 3 *South European Society and Politics* 231, at 255.

critique of prostitution as an equality issue is to have a serious impact on phenomena like trafficking. As was seen above, both the 'liberal' and 'radical' consider female sexuality as trapped between exploitation and suppression (the radical strategy turns into demands for more safety; the liberal to demands for sexual self-expression). Classic abolitionism has showed that it is not enough to criminalise exploitation if the underpinning economic, social and cultural circumstances that drive women into prostitution and men into buying sex are not addressed as well. Similarly, it is possible to recommend the official recognition of sex work as work and yet acknowledge that this change alone is not enough to transform prostitution from oppressive to non-oppressive or to eradicate the stigmatisation of some women due to sexual activity. Changing the existing reality of prostitutes as social outcasts and customers as 'natural' sex-buyers requires long-standing commitment (which is education-based) to contesting the cultural meanings of prostitution.[82] Indeed, there is a real risk that prostitution law reform alone be seen as a complete solution to the 'prostitution problem', especially when these solutions have been backed up by feminist arguments.[83] However, it is necessary to keep asking whether or not, in responding, the law takes on board a simplified or even misunderstood version of the feminist critique, which entrenches existing attitudes rather than challenges them and, moreover, eclipses all other elements of broader reform that feminist insights try to draw attention to.

It is worthwhile to elaborate on the last two points, for they have broad implications as regards the aim of devising a comprehensive approach to trafficking. First, feminist research warns against transforming analyses into practically achievable reform that conforms neatly to pre-given categories of (non-)choosing subjects and fails to acknowledge the range of coercion and choice involved. While the law has become more receptive to feminist analyses—as the case of prostitution, but also increasingly trafficking, shows—any work on this topic needs to bear in mind that broader analyses easily become banalised in legal discourse and can also drown under the logic that 'legal problems' must have (often) narrowly defined and purely 'legal solutions'. This is a real risk, considering that while it is in no small measure due to feminist influence that trafficking in women for sexual exploitation has become as topical as it now is, the current debates in the European Union and its Member States are not directed by them. This highlights Smart's concern about the need for feminist scholarship to be perhaps more cautious about according centrality to and resorting to law as a strategy.[84] Trafficking in

[82] See, eg, Carpenter, above n 43, whose analysis of the public/private division in prostitution (ie, the actors enter prostitution as embodied—women, prostitutes—and as disembodied—men, the clients) suggests that as genders are differently constituted in prostitution, it cannot be easily 'equalised' (made gender-neutral in practice). For a similar reasoning on how the cultural constructions of gender roles obstruct making prostitution equal see C Overall, 'What's Wrong With Prostitution? Evaluating Sex Work' (1992) 17 *Signs* 705. See also N Naffine, 'The Legal Structure of Self-ownership: Or the Self-possessed Man and the Woman Possessed' (1998) 25 *Journal of Law and Society* 193.

[83] As the recent law reforms in Sweden and the Netherlands (discussed in more detail in the following chapters) show, feminist critique can influence law reform to some extent at least.

[84] Smart, above n 6, 184.

women is an issue of enormous social, political, economic and cultural complexity which paradoxically contests the ultimate usefulness of the concept of 'trafficking' that gives no clear indication of how to separate the trafficked from others and which seems a clumsy tool for recognising the relative unfreedom of 'free' and the possibilities of agency in the 'unfree'. Considering this, any legal intervention, let alone those aiming at comprehensiveness, should be based on a careful and nuanced analysis and has to be alert to the instances where legal strategies might be too narrowly constructed adequately to capture this complexity.

Secondly, as was discussed above, from any feminist perspective a comprehensive approach to trafficking needs to address the broad range of factors that create, sustain and encourage it. The issue of trafficking is multi-faceted and not easily adapted for sweeping quick-fix solutions. Global developments have meant that the line between exploitative and non-exploitative practices of assisted migration is becoming increasingly difficult to draw in the middle ground, where women exercise agency in seeking to migrate but do so in a space where their options can be severely constrained by their relative lack of power. Indeed, the striking thing about the empirical reality of the migrant movements into the sex trade in the current migration environment is the existence of a large grey area, entailing the involvement, voluntarily or less so, of countless women whose stories can be very different. A comprehensive understanding of trafficking involves recognising that trafficking for sexual exploitation exists as a continuum, most of it being mundane everyday use of power and control.[85] Considering the global differences in wealth and the gender gap in income, the manifest growth of sex industries around the world is a worrying phenomenon, which is likely sexually to exploit a large number of disadvantaged women whose choices are far from free. This means that in order to tackle trafficking it is necessary to address the broad range of factors which act as constraints for women on the one hand and which sustain their sexual exploitation on the other. The strategies stemming from such an understanding seek not only to find ways of suppressing trafficking through criminal law but also of minimising and preventing the exposure of women for sexual exploitation, bridging existing gender inequalities that feed exploitation and tackling the sexist ideologies that underpin prostitution.

The nuances required to develop these kinds of multi-faceted responses pose considerable challenges to law reform in general, and even more so as regards the European Union, which seeks to harmonise the responses of the now 27 Member States, but such responses are also absolutely fundamental for any even remotely comprehensive approach to trafficking in women for sexual exploitation. The following chapters thus concentrate on the spheres identified in Chapter 1, those of EC free movement, external migration, criminal justice and human rights, in the light of the premise that, in order to be transformative and move towards comprehensiveness, a rather complex view of gender relations, current trends and the role of law has to be taken into consideration.

[85] L Kelly, 'The Wrong Debate: Reflections on why Force is not the Key Issue with Respect to Trafficking in Women for Sexual Exploitation' (2003) 73 *Feminist Review* 139.

3

EC Free Movement Law, Freedom and Prostitution

THE EU SEEMS in some ways to be an 'ideal' forum for devising common efforts against trafficking in Europe. Freedom, after all, is a central and cross-cutting feature of European integration, whereas victims of trafficking are in some ways the personification of the 'un-free', often characterised as victims of a form of 'modern-day slavery'.[1] As is frequently noted, the European Community is founded on the four 'fundamental' freedoms, the free movement of goods, capital, services and workers—not to mention the liberal origins of the 'European idea' itself. Therefore, freeing trafficking victims seems to resonate well with the aim of maintaining and developing the Union as an Area of Freedom, Security and Justice (Article 2 TEU), but it can also be linked to Community aims such as establishing prosperity through, among other things, the free movement of people and bringing Member States closer to each other (Article 14 TEC). Yet investigations into trafficking are rarely extended to address the workings of the Internal Market of the European Community—the examination usually focuses on criminal and judicial co-operation in the field of Justice and Home Affairs (with the possible exception of mentioning that the Daphne programme on violence against women, which also covers trafficking, is funded through the EC budget[2]).

The decision to omit the EC free movement law dimension is logical to the extent that most often trafficking concerns non-EU women who arrive from *outside* the European Union into an EU Member State. There are, however, various factors that make trafficking in women for sexual exploitation in the Internal Market different from international/wholly internal trafficking scenarios. Trafficking in EU citizens within the EU does occur, and did so even before the eastward enlargement in 2004; perhaps more importantly, further trafficking takes place after the first phase of recruitment and transfer into one of the Member States, and is arguably facilitated by the Schengen area (without internal border

[1] On how 'modern' slavery differs from 'old' slavery see K Bales, 'Expendable People: Slavery in the Age of Globalization' (2000) 52 *Journal of International Affairs* 461.

[2] The Daphne Programme (launched in 2000 after the original Daphne initiative and based on the competence of Art 152 TEC) was designed to assist NGOs and other bodies active in this field. The projects financed have involved setting up multidisciplinary networks, the exchange of information and public awareness-raising.

controls). Most importantly, however, it is crucial to start with the EC right of free movement in order to understand the ways in which the European Community framework of the Internal Market, as the core of the European integration project, might orientate EU anti-trafficking approaches more broadly. In other words, a discussion on the Internal Market, and the rights and actors it embraces or ignores, is necessary for situating the EU's anti-trafficking approaches in the wider setting of European integration. The Internal Market is where domestic prostitution policies meet EC rules and also where, importantly in the trafficking context, crucial gaps emerge in the treatment of non-EU citizens.

This chapter advances a two-fold argument on the present state of European integration regarding the free movement of persons in the Internal Market as supported by EC law. First, this freedom is tilted more towards the negative, obstacle-removing sense of economic freedom, which coincides well with the market-oriented framing and use of EU competence but comes with an adjacent marginalisation of so-called positive and more social notions of liberty. Secondly, this freedom of movement is exclusionary in that it goes hand in hand with the tendency towards setting up (gendered) nationality hierarchies between EU citizens and others through the 'European migration regime'. This regime is divided into two; the first regime, the supranational governing intra-EU migration, is complemented by the second, relating to the so-called external migration, 'immigration proper'. Both have implications for the formulation of an EU approach to trafficking in women for sexual exploitation. To put into context the examination of freedom in EC free movement law later in this chapter, the first section examines how trafficking can be conceptualised as a form of 'un-freedom', discussing the regulatory frameworks set up around prostitution in the Netherlands, Sweden and Italy. The following section then contrasts this reading of trafficking as un-freedom with EC law, and argues that freedom in the EC context is freedom of a particular kind. It also introduces the exclusion of non-EU actors as the reverse of the free movement of EU citizens, whilst the actual mechanics of exclusion are examined in more detail in the following chapter.

3.1 NOTIONS OF FREEDOM AND THE LEGAL REGULATION OF PROSTITUTION

Freedom, or liberty, is often understood as the right or the ability of individuals to 'do what they want', to make choices and, if they wish, to act upon them. As can be expected, a definition as broad as this is open to various interpretations about desires, abilities and obstacles. The perhaps most common conceptualisation(s) of liberty relevant in this respect was elaborated by Isaiah Berlin, who discussed the dual notion of liberty as either negative or positive.[3] Under this type of analysis, negative liberty entails the absence of obstacles or barriers to choice (in a sense 'freedom from'), while so-called positive notions of liberty stress the social setting

[3] See I Berlin, 'Two Concepts of Liberty' in I Berlin, *Four Essays on Liberty* (London, Oxford University Press, 1969).

in which decision-making occurs or the importance of active self-direction (more akin to 'freedom to'). Negative liberty, embraced by political liberalism, pertains mostly to external constraints to the choices faced by the actor (for instance physical barriers, overt coercion, but also legal obstacles); although law is considered necessary in so far as it restrains actors from infringing each other's liberty, it is considered that individuals should have a certain minimum area immune from legal intervention.[4] More positive notions of liberty are more concerned with constraints on liberty in a larger sense, concentrating on the conditions that impede the exercise of (negative) liberties, such as poverty, a lack of awareness or education (these are sometimes also embraced in conceptions of negative freedom) or on internal factors that influence the possibility to act, for example, fears, addictions, or compulsions which may smother the actor's 'truer' desires.[5]

Libertarians especially agree with Berlin about the danger of espousing positive notions of liberty, in particular that if one may not always know one's own true will (the notion of a 'divided self'), then others (for instance those deemed more rational or better-informed) may be entitled to intervene to protect the agent's 'true interests'. This second-guessing is considered by many to be a slippery slope towards authoritarianism. But it has also been maintained that the dichotomy is false,[6] or that at any rate it is possible to bridge the two to a certain extent.[7] It has also been argued that the tendency to underestimate the degree to which the actors are socially constructed, how they are allowed not only to act but to *be*, makes even these discussions of the negative and positive sides of liberty suffer from insufficient emphasis on the experiences of actors, which reveal the artificiality of the dichotomy between external and internal barriers to freedom.[8] In other words, while both the negative and positive notion of freedom provide valuable insights into liberty in its two most common senses, the negative liberty focus on external barriers is too individualistic; at the same time positive liberty, which exposes how the subject's preferences are informed by the setting in which choice is made, can turn out to be counter-productive if embraced at the cost of excessively limiting negative freedom. Hirschmann thus advocates understanding external barriers to freedom broadly and more collectively; this facilitates comprehending the ways in which internal barriers to freedom are constructed.

It is useful to look at prostitution and trafficking for sexual exploitation from this perspective. For instance, in a strictly understood negative sense of liberty, women in prostitution are 'free' in the absence of overt coercion, and 'un-free' if

[4] See, eg, JS Mill, *On Liberty and Other Essays* (Oxford, Oxford University Press, 1998), 5–128; D Miller, 'Constraints on Freedom' (1983) 94 *Ethics* 66; H Steiner, *An Essay on Rights* (Oxford, Blackwell, 1994).

[5] C Taylor, 'What's Wrong with Negative Liberty?' in A Ryan (ed), *The Idea of Freedom* (Oxford, Oxford University Press, 1979); J Christman, 'Liberalism and Individual Positive Freedom' (1991) 101 *Ethics* 343; A Sen, *Development as Freedom* (Oxford, Oxford University Press, 1999).

[6] See, eg, G MacCallum, 'Negative and Positive Freedom' (1967) 76 *Philosophical Review* 312.

[7] For instance, many exponents of negative freedom, such as John Stuart Mill and Mary Wollstonecraft, acknowledged the importance of positive conditions, education in particular, to achieving liberty.

[8] N Hirschmann, *The Subject of Liberty* (Princeton, NJ, Princeton University Press, 2003), ch 1.

they are coerced. More moderately, women in prostitution are free in the negative sense so long as prostitution (selling) is not criminalised and no-one (pimps, customers) uses violence against them. Yet the actors in prostitution can be considered less genuinely free if the decisions they make about engaging in prostitution are dictated by poverty or a lack of education (this applies not only to prostitutes but also to customers); and the women in prostitution are certainly 'un-free' from a positive liberty point of view if they are in prostitution due to drug addiction or internalised beliefs about women's role as sex providers. These views of course echo the extreme ends of the feminist prostitution debate. At one end, the 'work' view derives much of its language from the 'sexual liberation' movement; thus it embraces the negative freedom to choose to do what one wishes, including choosing prostitution as a form of paid work, or even as a form of sexual expression.[9] At the other end, the 'exploitation' view speaks of a lack of real choice and promotes (positive) freedom to live in a society without sexual violence, objectification and exploitation.[10] However, if one takes seriously the wider view espoused in Chapter 2 and Hirschmann above, one should ask questions about what social, economic and legal conditions drive women into prostitution and make it difficult to leave it for another job should they wish to do that, what circumstances make prostitution a dangerous and consuming job, and how that impacts on the internal mental landscape of the women (and men) involved in prostitution.

Regarding trafficking, in a very narrow negative sense the distinction between freely chosen migrant prostitution and trafficking is the fact that trafficking victims have been deprived of their freedom through, for example, abduction or captivity. While this is not an irrelevant occurrence, however, not all trafficking victims are locked up and physically restrained. In fact, in the strictest negative sense many of them are 'free' to leave the exploitative situation in which they find themselves; it may be that they risk (often great) harm by escaping the control of their exploiters, but they are not always physically prevented from leaving. Instead what binds them to their exploiters is a web of circumstances, revealed if the notion of barrier is pushed a little further. Trafficking victims are figuratively, if not literally, bound to their traffickers through debt-bondage, which may be illegal but is no less real for that; they are compelled through blackmail and extortion; they may also be constrained simply because they may have no viable options but to stay. Their choice is essentially either to endure it or, risky as it is, to seek help through, for example, the police, which—as their exploiters often point out to them—entails hazards such as detention and expulsion, stigmatisation and ostracism, a threat of retaliation against them and their family members, and the same (if not worse) situation of economic and social hardship that they sought to

[9] See P Alexander, 'Prostitution: *Still* a Difficult Issue for Feminists', in F Delacoste and P Alexander (eds), *Sex Work: Writings by Women in the Sex Industry* (San Francisco, Cal, Cleis Press, 1998), at 184.

[10] 'It is a fundamental human right to be free of sexual exploitation in all its forms. Women and girls have the right to sexual integrity and autonomy': CATW 'An introduction to CATW', available at www.catwinternational.org/about/index.php (accessed 5 Apr 2006).

escape through migration. Here the ways in which external and internal barriers inform each other can be seen clearly, for the wider external barriers have as their flipside the victims' internal assessment about the situation: many trafficking victims also perceive their situation (correctly) as their having 'no other choice'.

Legal regulation plays several parts in these scenarios. Let us first outline the legal situation in the three Member States chosen as case studies. The Netherlands is, of course, famous for its supposed 'tolerance' of things like soft drugs, homosexuality and commercial sex. In line with abolitionism, prostitution itself has been legal since 1810, with all forms of exploitation of prostitution (pimping, brothel-keeping) forbidden by the Law of 1910.[11] For a long time prostitution was 'tolerated' also for non-nationals as long as public order was not violated and as long as it could be restricted to certain locations.[12] After the sexual revolution and economic boom of the 1970s, the sex business, initially small-scale, became visible, and in the 1980s it became clearer that the industry was becoming complex, and difficult to influence through a 'hands off' policy.[13] At the same time, the emerging sex worker lobby started to challenge the idea of prostitutes as victims, and attention started to turn to many migrant sex workers' exploitation. This led to the adoption of the forced/free distinction: it was argued that the right to self-determination must involve the 'freedom' to choose to engage in prostitution. And, since prostitution is work, this work has to be cleansed from 'non-work' elements such as violence, abusive conditions and trafficking.[14] In 1993 there was a proposal for the legalisation of prostitution and the criminalisation of trafficking: the former was rejected, the latter passed.[15] In 1999 the renewed proposal for the former was accepted by the parliament, and in 2000 the ban on brothels (Article 250*bis*, in force since 1911) was lifted and the 'exploitation' of (profiting from) voluntary prostitution (pimping, etc) was de-criminalised.[16] Brothels

[11] The French had introduced the model of 'regimentation' (prostitutes were required to register with the police and to be medically examined for syphilis) during their occupation of the Netherlands (1810–13) with the usual biological justification—men need sex but good women should be asexual; prostitutes are needed to fill the gap but must be controlled. Even after the French left, local communities were required to regulate prostitution. In the second half of the 19th century calls for abolition by puritans, feminists, socialists who challenged it as ineffective, obtrusive and legitimising fornication became more frequent: see J Boutellier, 'Prostitution, Criminal Law and Morality in the Netherlands' (1991) 15 *Crime, Law and Social Change* 201.

[12] Note that toleration does not necessarily mean neutrality: 'the open and liberal character of public discourse contrasts with widespread ambivalent or even negative private opinions and behaviour': I Vanwesenbeeck and R de Graaf, 'Sex Work and HIV in the Netherlands: Policy, Research and Prevention' in T Sandfort (ed), *The Dutch Response to HIV. Pragmatism and Consensus* (London, UCL Press, 1998), at 88.

[13] C Brants, 'The Fine Art of Regulated Tolerance: Prostitution in Amsterdam' (1998) 25 *Journal of Law and Society* 621.

[14] Attention also turned to ways of promoting sexual health in prostitution. See, eg, T van der Helms, *The Amsterdam Intermediary Project: Ten Years Health and Social Care in Prostitution* (Amsterdam, Intermediary Project, 1999).

[15] For a critical commentary of the criminalisation process see R Haveman, *Voorwaarden voor strafbaarstelling van vrouwenhandel* (Deventer, Gouda Quint, 1998).

[16] Prostitution policies remain local. Cities are free to choose, for instance, where brothels can be situated and where street-walking is allowed, but complete prohibition of prostitution not allowed.

operate on a system of licences with requirements for safety, hygiene and self-determination of sex workers. What remain criminal are forced prostitution, (forced) exploitation of prostitution and trafficking for prostitution. Non-(EU) nationals, however, cannot work legally in prostitution unless they have a residence permit without restrictions on working—one cannot obtain employment permit for sex work, and self-employment is equally excluded.[17]

In the same abolitionist wave as the Netherlands, Sweden reformed its prostitution laws in 1918 by abolishing the previous regulatory system.[18] For most of the twentieth century Sweden had a low level of prostitution, with prohibitions against the typical forms of the exploitation of prostitutes, such as habitual profiting, procuring and (implicitly) brothel-keeping, as well as 'nuisance' practices, such as aggressive soliciting. By the 1970s this situation led to the comment that 'although there is some degree of prostitution in Sweden, even that is on the decline'.[19] This comment was premature, however, and a criminalisation response was discussed from the 1980s onwards.[20] In 1995 the Commission set up to examine what should be done about the increase in prostitution, especially in the big cities and as a consequence of a growing number of non-nationals, recommended that both the sale and purchase of sexual services should be criminalised.[21] The suggestion received criticism from enforcement authorities due to its 'impracticability' and feminist organisations and politicians who claimed, in line with a simplified 'exploitation' view, that the women in prostitution were victims, and that if anyone should be punished, it were to be the customer only. The latter claim was expressed in terms of 'prostitution is a form of male violence against women', which should be eradicated to create a truly equal society. The argument proved effective, as violence against women was starting to be accepted as a barrier in the achievement of equality between men and women.[22] The Bill to revise the approach to prostitution was included as part of a larger government package to

[17] See Implementation Decree of the Migrant Workers Act as amended by Besluit van 20 Oct 2000 tot Wijziging van het Koninklijke besluit ter Uitvoering van de Wet Arbeid Vreemdelingen [2000] Staatsblad 464) which explicitly rules out work permits for sex work; no permits are granted for prostitution exercised as a self-employed person, as this is not 'in the interests of the country', as in the Aliens Act (Wet van 23 Nov 2000 tot algehele herziening van de Vreemdelingenwet [2000] Staatsblad 495) and Art 3.32 of the Implementation Decree (Besluit van 23 Nov 2000 tot uitvoering van de Vreemdelingenwet 2000 [2000] Staatsblad 497). For background on this apparent contradiction, see J Outshoorn, "Debating Prostitution in Parliament. A Feminist Analysis' (2001) 8 *European Journal of Women's Studies* 472. There has been some discussion on granting foreign women work permits to engage in prostitution in the Netherlands, but his has not gained widespread acceptance.

[18] The regulatory system (1847–1918) had involved mandatory health checks of prostitutes twice a week. See C Holst and P Lindström, *Förbud mot köp av sexuella tjänster* (Stockholm, BRÅ-rapport 2000:4), 131.

[19] See J Decker, *Prostitution: Regulation and Control* (Littleton, Colo, Fred B Rothman & Co, 1979) (1979), above ch 2 n 8.

[20] See, eg, Socialdepartmentet, *Report About Prostitution in Sweden; Prostitutionen i Sverige. Bakgrund och åtgärder* (SOU 1981:71).

[21] Socialdepartmentet, *Report by the Committee on Prostitution; Könshandeln. Betänkande av 1993 års Prostitutionsutredning* (SOU 1995:15).

[22] On this see Socialdepartmentet, *Report by the Committee on Violence against Women; Kvinnofrid. Huvudbetänkande av Kvinnovåldskommissionen* (SOU 1995:60).

address violence against women. The law was passed in parliament and client criminalisation took effect in 1999, leaving selling legal.[23] However, suspicion of wanting to support oneself through prostitution is grounds for denying entry into Sweden under the Aliens Law; and engaging in prostitution is also a ground for expulsion for non-nationals. The legal regulation around the issue was amended later in 2001 when Sweden also criminalised trafficking in women for sexual exploitation. This amendment entered into force in July 2002.

Italy, like the majority of EU Member States, follows the model where prostitution is allowed (both for sellers and buyers) but is not really considered work or violence against women, but mainly immoral and a public nuisance. Currently criminalised are the facilitation of prostitution, the exploitation of prostitution, organising prostitution in closed surroundings (clubs, apartments) and brothel-keeping.[24] Soliciting used to be illegal, but currently it is merely a more or less tolerated misdemeanour, although aggressive soliciting can be considered a crime. Theoretically non-EU nationals can work in prostitution but need to have a valid *permesso di soggiorno* ('permit to stay'; and no work permits for prostitution are given). Trafficking in women is covered by a wide range of sections in the criminal law, ranging from slavery to trade in women and facilitating illegal immigration. Despite the official abolitionist policy, official estimates of women involved in prostitution put the figure somewhere between 25,000 and 70,000; most of these are migrants (most of whom have no permit to stay). Due to the ban on using flats for prostitution purposes, prostitution in Italy often takes the form of street-walking. The country has one of the most wide-scale trafficking (and smuggling) problems in Europe, in sex trafficking most notably from Nigeria and Albania.[25] The response has been to introduce stricter rules on human trafficking under which several cases of trafficking have been prosecuted, and to develop a system of victim protection, with a renewable residence permit (initially for six months) provided to victims if they participate in an assistance and integration programme.[26] In 2003, a Bill was introduced which, in order to clean the streets of the nuisance caused by prostitutes and cruising customers, provides for a fine for customers and stricter sanctions for prostitutes; if passed, it would allow indoor prostitution while 'encouraging' women

[23] Act on the Prohibition on the Purchase of Sexual Services (Lagen om förbud mot köp av sexuella tjänster), SFS 1998:408.

[24] The previous system of officially regulated prostitution (which started with the Cavour regulation of 1860) was abolished by the famous Merlin Law of 1958 (Legge di 20 Feb 1958 no 75, [1958] GU 55), which amended the Penal Code (Codice Penale).

[25] See IOM, *Trafficking in Women to Italy for Sexual Exploitation* (Geneva, Migration Information Programme, 1996). See also, eg, G Campani, 'Trafficking for Sexual Exploitation and the Sex Business in the New Context of International Migration: the Case of Italy' (1998) 3 *South European Society and Politics* 231.

[26] Under the current legal regime trafficking falls under the so-called Merlin provisions on exploitation of prostitution (also a provision on 'enticing' migrant prostitution) (see Arts 535–537) and the provisions on slavery (Arts 600–604) in the Penal Code; the latter, which were previously rarely used for adults, have been amended and, eg, Art 602–*bis* now includes '*sfruttamento sessuale*' which connects (also adult) sex trafficking to slavery (Legge di 11 Aug 2003 no 228, 'Misure contro la tratta di persone' [2003] GU 195). The protection of victims is included in the Immigration Law and Legislative Decree of 1998, (Art 16, Legge di 6 Mar 1998 no 40, [1998] GU 59; Art 18, decreto legislativo di 25 July 1998 no 286, [1998] GU 191).

in prostitution to undergo medical examinations through sanctions against prostitutes who cause 'STD injury' to clients.[27]

Looking at these three EU Member States against the negative/positive freedom axis discussed above provides interesting insights into the restricting and liberating power of law. In terms of negative freedom, in all three countries prostitution as such is, strictly speaking, legal, and the excesses of the regulationist systems that forced women in prostitution to undergo health checks aimed at (but ineffective in) protecting customers from venereal disease have been abolished. All three countries have a plethora of provisions to curb violence against and exploitation of women in prostitution, which provide a legal safety net for the negative freedom from exploitation. The provisions on soliciting as a nuisance arguably form restrictions on how prostitution is exercised, in an effort to balance the 'nuisance' caused by prostitution to local communities against the situation of women in prostitution who are more vulnerable to abuse in remote places. All three countries, even the Netherlands, have barriers against migrant women engaging in prostitution legally (through not granting permits, criminalisation of trafficking and smuggling, and so on). The denial of permits is justified through labelling non-nationals as less free (in the positive sense) to make emancipated choices about prostitution. Nationals are allowed to make such choices even in Sweden, which officially considers prostitution a form of violence against women and thus, from this point of view, women 'choosing' it are clearly harming themselves.

The criminalisation of clients in Sweden and the planned sanctions against customers in Italy clearly form external barriers. In both of these cases, especially in the Swedish model which condemns buying sex, one does see elements of second-guessing at work: since it is considered that prostitution is a harmful manifestation of a distorted view of gender relations, customers should be 'saved from themselves' (besides from harming others, namely women and society in general) through criminalisation that guarantees positive freedom. Women in prostitution are arguably exempt from sanction because, as victims, they would bear the brunt of criminalisation and should instead be assisted to leave prostitution; yet at the same time non-nationals are expelled on grounds of prostitution to the same 'unfree' circumstances they left behind with no sense of obligation towards them.

While, strictly speaking, prostitution is legal in all three countries, all of them also seek to repress the growth of the sex industry, considering it undesirable and perhaps something that a 'rational self', truly free, would not want to support. This is true even of the Netherlands, where a number of cities have restricted the allowed number of legal brothels to the number or area that exist now, and which have recently shut down their street-walking zones.[28] It might be argued that this

[27] See disegno di legge no 3826 of 26 Mar 2003.

[28] Amsterdam closed down its street-walking zone in 2003 due to chronic organised crime problems and the illegal exploitation of and trafficking in women. The city of Rotterdam, since closing down the street-walking zone, has been engaged in placing drug-using prostitutes in residential colleges, against their will if necessary, to get them off the streets. Most of the municipalities have given licences only to already established brothels, effectively blocking the way for establishing new ones.

is second-guessing at work again, toeing dangerously close to overt restrictions on the freedom of women in prostitution even in the Netherlands—where (part of) the rationale behind the legalisation of prostitution was to transform prostitution from a stigmatised occupation to an acceptable one and to give the women involved legal standing—for legalisation also facilitates better control by the authorities over the women in prostitution. In Italy the proposal to make it a criminal offence for prostitutes to infect their clients with a venereal disease is the most obvious manifestation of restricting the liberty of women in prostitution for a suspect purpose, and one which in effect proposes to re-introduce discriminatory regulationist controls through the back door. In all three countries, although in varying degrees, this legal ambiguity is evident not only in the law but most of all in its enforcement, which in practice targets the freedom of women in prostitution even when officially directed both at customers and prostitutes, and which is notorious for lack of enforcement when it comes to pimp/customer violence against women in prostitution. This serves to keep women in prostitution as a separate and stigmatised category of women, making it difficult for them to have reports of exploitation or violence taken seriously or to leave prostitution for another form of work should they want to.

What is noteworthy about these policies in all three countries, unsatisfactory as they may be from diverse viewpoints, is that they reflect an attempt to negotiate the tensions within 'freedom' and find some kind of acceptable (or not) balance. The exploitation of prostitution, however diversely defined, has been and is the subject of criminalisation; yet it is sporadically enforced, leaving women in prostitution 'un-free'. At the same time, increasing positive freedom through increased controls over women in prostitution is at least as problematic, in that it can considerably restrict their negative freedom sphere, and, indeed, produce dubious results. The Dutch policy, as a result of feminist liberal concerns and an active sex worker lobby, evidences the liberal state's reluctant steps towards recognising prostitution as work. In terms of liberty, it embodies arguments about (negative) free choice but also, officially at least, aims at 'transforming' attitudes to the legitimacy of freely chosen prostitution as a form of 'normal' work, thus improving the socio-economic standing of women in prostitution.[29] The Swedish policy, which aims to get women out of prostitution, by contrast emphasises the highly constrained (un-free) 'choices' that are made about engaging in prostitution in general, whereas the client criminalisation policy is an example of justifying restricting the freedom of men for the 'greater good' (education about gender equality).[30] In the (mainstream) Italian model of prostitution it is a free, if highly immoral, choice which is to a degree 'naturalised' as a necessary evil, yet with attempts to control the spread of the phenomenon; the second-guessing of the Swedish model

[29] J Outshoorn, 'Voluntary and Forced Prostitution: the "Realistic Approach" of the Netherlands' in J Outshoorn (ed), *The Politics of Prostitution. Women's Movements, Democratic States and the Globalisation of Sex Commerce* (Cambridge, Cambridge University Press, 2004).

[30] See, eg, Report by the Committee on Violence against Women, above n 22.

is faintly echoed in (often religiously inspired) condemnation of customers who abuse disadvantaged women.

As regards trafficking, all three countries evidence a factual market trend towards the foreignerisation of women in prostitution, together with a legal demarcation in the treatment of foreign and national women in prostitution, which in part comes from the general incompatibility of increasingly strict external migration rules (for instance visa or other permit requirements) with migration, including but not only for prostitution, which is not considered legitimate for non-EU nationals even in the Netherlands. Women in prostitution thus face a 'Catch-22 scenario': this demarcation, which limits the options available to would-be migrants, is one of the factors that open a space for abusive practices such as trafficking (see also below Chapter 4); at the same time the relative lack of freedom of migrants compared to (EU) nationals is used as an argument to justify upholding a demarcation between EU nationals and others in order to 'protect' the latter from exploitation. In short, it is a crude proxy for 'unfreedom'. As it is, EU Member States have tried to tackle prostitution as a domestic matter; the external side has been dealt with solely through some attention being paid to the problem of trafficking in women, approached through more effective criminal policy against it (see below Chapter 5), but without really integrating this approach with policy choices on prostitution and the underlying migration considerations. Yet at this moment it cannot be stated that the issue has been definitively solved in any Member State. Practically all of them are in the process of evaluating relevant legislation, not least because of general globalisation, international migration and criminal policy trends, but also because of the considerations of the Internal Market, which is examined next.

3.2 FREEDOM IN EUROPEAN LAW

3.2.1 The Common (Sex) Market? Freedom and Prostitution in EC Law

Domestic policy choices around prostitution have come under pressure not only because of increasing international migration but due to the 'completion' of the Common Market, that differentiates nationals of EU Member States as a separate 'privileged class' under EC law while excluding others. Without exploring all the issues around 'European citizenship', it can be said without any doubt that recent years have brought with them increasing free movement rights to nationals of Member States.[31] Traditionally the free movement of persons has been, of course,

[31] On this area of law see, eg, F Weiss and F Wooldridge, *Free Movement of Persons within the European Community* (The Hague, Kluwer Law International, 2002). See the recent directive that codifies and clarifies much of EC law in this area: Directive 2004/38/EC of 29 Apr 2004 on the right of citizens of the Union and their family members to move and reside freely within the territory of the Member States amending Regulation (EEC) No 1612/68 and repealing Directives 64/221/EEC, 68/360/EEC, 72/194/EEC, 73/148/EEC, 75/34/EEC, 75/35/EEC, 90/364/EEC, 90/365/EEC and 93/96/EEC [2004] OJ L 158/77, corrigendum [2004] OJ L 229/35. On the Directive and other recent developments see S Carrera, 'What Does Free Movement Mean in Theory and Practice in an Enlarged EU?' (2005) 11 *European Law Journal* 699.

that of (only) workers and other economically active individuals as units of production (and thus more illusory than for instance the free movement of goods). The free movement of persons is, however, ideologically becoming an ever more important aspect in a Union seeking legitimacy in the eyes of its 'citizens', even if this has proved to be a troubled path (as Ward succinctly puts it, it is still essentially about persons 'in work or seeking work, or those with plenty of money'[32]).[33] It is of course well known that the European Community has from its inception lacked a grand social vision, its primary motivation being economic.[34] Nor is it any secret that while the Community has in many respects been considered as a forerunner in the backing of gender equality (especially as regards the workplace) in its Member States, its institutions, most notably the European Court of Justice, at the same time stand accused of following a reserved or traditional (some might even say reactionary) view of gender relations.[35] Both of these aspects, the market-oriented framing and use of EU competence (aiming to remove external obstacles from the way of integration) and the gendered logic that underpins definitions such as 'workers' and 'citizens', contribute to making the freedom of movement in the EC context freedom that, following the Berlin paradigm introduced above, can be argued (implicitly and sometimes explicitly) to focus on negative integration to advance (economic) freedom, while positive integration (necessary for social freedom) remains a subservient aim. This in turn has implications for the way in which phenomena such as trafficking are conceptualised.

The issue can be illustrated by discussing the treatment of the sex sector in the EC free market. The most relevant cases regarding the negative freedom concept adopted by EC law are those on the free movement of 'sex workers' offering 'sexual services'. *Adoui and Cornuaille*[36] concerned two French women denied residence permits in Belgium on the grounds that they were (suspected of being) prostitutes, hence making the case fall under the public policy exception to free movement of workers (now Article 39 TEC) and freedom of establishment (now Article 46 TEC). The ECJ concluded that if the Member State in question allows prostitution for its own nationals (as Belgium arguably did—it did not adopt repressive measures against prostitution as such; it banned soliciting, incitement to debauchery, exploitation of prostitution, keeping a disorderly house and living

[32] I Ward, *A Critical Introduction to European Law* (2nd edn, London, LexisNexis UK, 2004), at 190.

[33] Even if recent years have seen an expansion of EC Rights towards economically inactive persons such as students (whose rights of residence in other Member States have been subject to their having sufficient resources to support themselves and medical insurance). See, eg, Case C–184/99 *Grzelczyk v Centre public d'aide sociale d'Ottignies-Louvain-la-Neuve* [2001] ECR I–6193.

[34] See C Barnard, 'EC "Social" Policy' in P Craig and G de Búrca (eds), *The Evolution of EU Law* (Oxford, Oxford University Press, 1999); M Poiares Maduro, 'Striking the Elusive Balance Between Economic Freedom and Social Rights in the EU' in P Alston (ed), *The EU and Human Rights* (Oxford, Oxford University Press, 1999).

[35] See, eg, T Hervey and D O'Keeffe (eds), *Sex Equality Law in the European Union* (Chichester, John Wiley & Sons 1996).

[36] Joined Cases 115 and 116/81 *Adoui v Belgian State and City of Liège, Cornuaille v Belgian State* [1982] ECR 1665. On the cases see also L Flynn, 'The Body Politic(s) of EC Law' in Hervey and O'Keeffe, above n 35.

on immoral earnings), then it cannot claim that the activity is sufficiently serious to deny free movement for prostitution for nationals of other Member States. This was reaffirmed 20 years later in the similar case of *Jany and Others*[37] which extended this tolerance of prostitution, based on the Association Agreements, to nationals of the (then) Candidate Countries of Central and Eastern Europe, provided the self-employment in question was 'genuine'.[38] In this case, concerning six women of Polish and Czech nationality denied permits to stay in the Netherlands on the ground that prostitution is not a socially acceptable form of work, the ECJ merely repeated the argument that since the Netherlands does not prohibit prostitution (determined by the ECJ to be an 'economic activity'[39]) for the Dutch, it cannot invoke the public policy exception to prevent the free movement of (at that time) Candidate Country nationals. The logic of these two cases is consistent with that applied in the area of free movement of goods. In two cases concerning pornography (in the broad sense), *Henn and Darby*[40] and *Conegate*,[41] the relevant UK laws on importing obscene materials were contested as violating Article 30 (now Article 28) TEC. The ECJ accepted the UK argument on the public morality exception (ex Article 36, now Article 30 TEC) in *Henn and Darby*, but rejected it in *Conegate*; the difference was that in the former case there was, despite regional variations, 'no lawful trade' in the materials in question in the UK, while in the second case (regarding inflatable rubber dolls) legislation did not as such ban the manufacturing/marketing of similar items in the UK, although there was a ban on mailing them, and restrictions on public display and sale to minors.

The general conclusion is that the public policy exceptions give Member States leeway in denying free movement on such grounds, but only so long as such limitation is not discriminatory against EC nationals. Interestingly, qualitatively in these cases life-size sex dolls were deemed no different from, for example, coffee and 'sex work' was just about as controversial an activity as driving a bus. If allowed under national rules (in other words, if there is an absence of 'repressive measures or other genuine and effective measures', according to *Adoui and Cornuaille*), they should freely circulate in the Internal Market. This, of course, is logical if the perspective is a market-oriented one, aiming at negative integration and removing external obstacles to free movement (in the negative sense), and admittedly has the healthy side-effect of highlighting the two-faced arguments

[37] Case C–268/99 *Jany and Others v Staatssecretaris van Justitie* [2001] ECR I–8615.

[38] The Association Agreements, also called Europe Agreements, cover the right to establishment, ie to take up economic activities as self-employed persons (see Title IV of each agreement).

[39] The ECJ rather tortuously defined prostitution as 'an activity by which the provider satisfies a request by the beneficiary in return for consideration without producing or transferring material goods' (*Jany*, above n 37, paras 48–9), and hence judged it to be an economic activity. See the discussion in paras 32–50 of the judgment. For a clear contrast see European Parliament Resolution of 14 Apr 1989 on the exploitation of prostitution and the traffic in human beings [1989] OJ C/120/352, which curtly states 'the practice of prostitution involves the violation of certain fundamental rights and freedoms . . .'.

[40] Case 34/79 *Regina v Henn and Darby* [1979] ECR 3795.

[41] Case 121/85 *Conegate Ltd v HM Customs & Excise* [1986] ECR 1007.

about prostitution as immoral by governments which permit, regulate and tax it without scruple. Moreover, it can be said that the ECJ was facing a choice between two limited options and merely chose to recognise the social reality; to deny the limited benefits of EC law for a group of disadvantaged women would hardly help the situation of individual women in prostitution. This is indeed true, and the value of such recognition of women's negative liberty to make decisions, whatever their quality, should not be underestimated. However, it could also be said that precisely because one is talking about a group of disadvantaged women someone should ask why it is thought women are free simply because they wish to be 'free' to migrate to sell sex. The ECJ in *Jany and Others* did emphasise the condition of prostitutes' independence (from pimps and so on), nodding towards the alleged Dutch justification for excluding non-EU nationals (which perceived them as less 'free', positively speaking). What it failed to consider is why the overwhelming majority of those who 'satisfy the request' for sexual services are women, and normally underprivileged women at that, and why most of the 'beneficiaries' of this gendered scenario are EU citizen men with money.

In short, the ECJ did not and, importantly, could not ask why and how women in prostitution might be un-free for reasons other than those that might literally coerce them into prostitution (in other words, due to factors that limit genuine choice such as poverty, discrimination, gendered socialisation or past abuse, all relatively common among women in prostitution) and whether enforcing negative freedom in such circumstances does harm or good, not just to individuals but more collectively as well. In the setting of the Central and Eastern European Countries (CEECs) it is important to link the increasing migration of women from the CEECs for prostitution to its timeframe: the 1990s (the relevant period in this case and a time of increased trafficking from the CEECs) were a decade of enormous change especially in the CEECs, where the impact of the dissolution of the Soviet Union and the end of Communist Party rule was felt most dramatically and where the ensuing political, social and economic changes, such as democratisation, liberalisation and privatisation, coincided with the intensification of the globalisation processes.[42] Although few systematic analyses have been made, there is a fair amount of evidence to suggest that women suffered disproportionately from the immediate changes brought about by the new post-communist governments. Communist rule had not rooted out discrimination against women,[43] but it had provided women with employment, relative security and well-being, which were largely swept away by the steep economic decline in the 1990s, especially

[42] About the transition see, eg, J Rupnik, 'Eastern Europe: The International Context' in M Plattner and A Smolar (eds), *Globalization, Power, and Democracy* (Baltimore, Mld, Johns Hopkins University Press, 2000) and M Goldman, *Revolution and Change in Central and Eastern Europe* (Armonk, NY, ME Sharpe, 1997).

[43] See eg, B Łobodzińska, 'The Family and Working Women during and after Socialist Industrialization and Ideology' in B Łobodzińska (ed), *Family, Women and Employment in Central-Eastern Europe* (Westport, Conn, Greenwood Press, 1995).

where 'shock therapy' was opted for.[44] The reinstatement of traditional (and often religious) sexual and social mores resurrected the ideal model for women as faithful housewives, while at the same time there was a growing trend towards early sexual initiation, commercialisation of 'free sex' as a sign of embracing the newly found market-orientation, sexual harassment of women at the workplace and domestic violence at home. In some important ways, sexual freedom became interpreted as newly liberated ex-communist men's freedom rather than women's (and the women paradoxically became increasingly disillusioned with democracy as well).[45]

As it was, the ECJ had no choice but to appear oblivious to the decades of controversy over the nature of pornography and prostitution as expressions of barriers to freedom in a more positive sense, and as tilted towards emphasising negative freedom rather than the social and cultural setting in which such freedom is exercised. The tenuous logic of embracing only negative freedom in prostitution is revealed if one takes the train of thought to its logical conclusion, and considers a truly free sex market; where unemployed women (and presumably men too) would be expected to take up work in prostitution, where prostitution contracts would be made enforceable against both parties and so on.[46] In contrast, even the governments that allow and even tax prostitution-related income recognise that prostitution is not work just like any other and negotiate the boundary between freedom to sell sex and the need to ensure that those who do so are 'free' to do it in a more positive sense (thus, for instance, higher age limits to ensure the individual has sufficient maturity to make such a choice). The provisions on prostitution also aim to diminish the scope of the phenomenon, ensuring that the 'satisfier' in this transaction is not exploited, which is an acknowledgment that her bargaining position is weaker. Simultaneously many of them seek to convey that (female) sexuality in contemporary societies is an article of trade, but not simply or only that—often it is with the underlying idea that it should not be commer-

[44] See D Iatridis, 'The Social Justice and Equality Contexts of Privatization' in D Iatridis (ed), *Social Justice and the Welfare State in Central and Eastern Europe* (Westport, Conn, Praeger, 2000); Goldman, above n 42, ch 2. For country studies see *ibid*; V Jalušič, 'Women in Post-Socialist Slovenia: Socially Adapted, Politically Marginalized' in S Ramet (ed), *Gender Politics in the Western Balkans* (University Park, Penn, Pennsylvania State University, 1999); J Heinen, 'The Impact of Privatization on the Female Workforce in Poland' in D Iatridis (ed), above; A Zajicek and T Calasanti, 'The Impact of Socioeconomic Restructuring on Polish Women' in B Łobodzińska (ed), above n 43. Note also that in South-Eastern Europe the situation of women has been further exacerbated by the destabilising conflicts in the Balkans.

[45] S Benton, 'Gender, Sexuality and Citizenship' in G Andrews (ed), *Citizenship* (London, Lawrence & Wishart, 1991), at 151, puts it neatly: '[w]hen we read of Bulgarians and Hungarians in their first year of liberation eagerly buying the new wonders of pornography, we in the West were silent. Who are we to deny our brothers the freedom so long enjoyed on our side of the former Iron Curtain?'.

[46] Note, however, that this is exactly what is advocated by some, based on its compatibility with the 'ECJ line'. See S Laskowski, 'The New German Prostitution Act—An Important Step to a More Rational View of Prostitution as an Ordinary Profession in Accordance with European Community Law' (2002) 18 *International Journal of Comparative Labour Law and Industrial Relations* 479, on the German reform where prostitution contracts were made enforceable—but only against clients *and* in practice only regarding German or other EU nationals.

cialised. This is in tension with the logic of the Internal Market that seeks to embrace rather than to restrict the growth of markets.

Indeed, it is the recognition of women's dual status as both 'choosers' and 'losers' in prostitution that is one of the very reasons why EU Member States have not taken massively 'repressive measures' to ban selling sex completely. It is not simply a matter of respecting their negative freedom to work in prostitution, it is also recognised that they, due to societal conditions, are the ones likely to suffer most from that prohibition. The ECJ in *Jany and Others* noted that there is little consensus within European countries, let alone among them, on prostitution, and then deduced that since most of them do not decidedly and firmly ban selling sex, it must be acceptable.[47] The problem with this laissez-faire approach (which in principle allows the issue to fall within Member States' margin of appreciation) is that while the ECJ is claiming not to take a stand on an issue on which Member States disagree,[48] it *does* take a stand that affects the (often admittedly inadequate) balance of domestic policies.

The cases illustrate the broader issues of gender equality and European law, and more specifically the fact that even the flagship of European social dimension, the EC gender equality policy, contains (often hidden) assumptions about gender that link with the tensions between negative and positive, economic and social freedom in European policy objectives. This is most obvious with regard to the notions of 'work' and 'worker', the definitions of which in EC law categorise people into economically active and inactive, independent or dependant, market citizens and non-citizens in ways that construct a gendered European citizenship.[49] The ECJ's definition of work is in true liberal style economically determined, as was seen in *Jany and Others.* The ideal individual in EC law is a worker who is exercising free movement rights—as these are connected to economic activity, those deemed economically inactive have fewer rights that are often derivative, like the rights of workers' family members that are linked with the status of the worker. In this scheme, sex work is remunerated, thus 'proper' work, unlike another typically female activity, unpaid care work, which is not.[50] Indeed, in a paradoxical way the caricature-like prostitutes envisaged by EC law fit the traditional idea of the economic citizen (wage-earner) exactly, as they are conceived of as self-interested economic actors, free and keen to move across borders in search of lucrative work opportunities. Thus sex work merits the benefits of EC free movement law, while unpaid care work in the home does not.

[47] *Jany and Others*, above n 37, para 57 ff.

[48] 'It is not for the Court to substitute its own assessment for that of the legislatures of the Member States where an allegedly immoral activity is practised legally': *Jany and Others*, above n 37, at para 56. Compare the Netherlands Government, which argued that although prostitution 'lends itself to an appearance of independence since the criminal prohibition of procuring means that any employment relationships must be organised illegally, prostitutes are normally in a subordinate position in relation to a pimp'.

[49] L Ackers, *Shifting Spaces. Women, Citizenship and Migration Within the European Union* (Bristol, The Policy Press, 1998).

[50] Case C–85/96 *Martínez Sala v Freistaat Bayern* [1998] ECR I–02691.

While 'proper' workers' mobility rights are guaranteed in the effort to remove obstacles from the way of economic freedom, other actors that do not fit into this model are relegated to the status of dependants, with a gendered logic and gendered effects.[51] Those typically classifiable as labour migrants are most often men or women who follow male worker patterns, whilst, generally speaking, and also in the three countries examined in this book, migrants moving for the purposes of family reunion are more likely to be women.[52] The concerns over women's role as carers and as dependant family members link with issues about women's role in the labour market, often as 'atypical' part-time workers. This brings to play concerns over the fact that gender equality has often been understood in a formalist and marginal way in EC law, resulting in the subordination of gender equality to financial considerations (for instance concerning the permissibility of indirect discrimination).[53] At the same time, when the formalist approach is abandoned, it is replaced with an equally disturbing tendency that tacitly sustains a traditional view of gender roles both inside and outside the labour market.[54] This trend is evident in the acceptance, even endorsement, of conservative models of the family (in other words, the heterosexual married family)[55] and corresponding hesitancy as regards non-conventional families, especially same-sex couples.[56]

Such instances of institutional blindness to the gendered foundations and the gendered impact of EC law's own structures merely underline the basic concern: the supremacy of economic freedom over social rights with its attendant gender politics. In short, negative integration, the removal of obstacles from the way of economic freedom, has not been followed by positive integration in the field of

[51] K Scheiwe, 'EC Law's Unequal Treatment of the Family: The Case Law of the European Court of Justice on Rules Prohibiting Discrimination on Grounds of Sex and Nationality' (1994) 1 *Social and Legal Studies* 243.

[52] For Swedish statistics see www.migrationsverket.se/pdffiler/statistik/tabe4.pdf; for Dutch statistics see www.cbs.nl/en-gb/menu/themas/mens-maatschappij/bevolking/publicaties/artikelen/archief/2004/2004-1403-wm.htm; for Italian statistics see www.istat.it/dati/catalogo/20020120_00 and www.istat.it/dati/catalogo/20040621_01/volume1.pdf (last accessed 13 Apr 2006).

[53] About this area see, eg, E Ellis, *EU Anti-Discrimination Law* (Oxford, Oxford University Press, 2005).

[54] For instance, the tendency to support the 'reconciliation' of paid work and family life at present still seems more focused on making sure women both carry the care burden *and* engage in paid work than on freeing them from traditional gendered expectations as regards child care and dependency (or creating space for more equitable arrangements): C McGlynn, 'Ideologies of Motherhood in European Community Sex Equality Law' (2000) 6 *European Law Journal* 29; C McGlynn, 'Reclaiming a Feminist Vision: the Reconciliation of Paid Work and Family Life in European Union Law and Policy' (2001) 7 *Columbia Journal of International Law* 241. See also E Caracciolo di Torella and A Masselot, 'Pregnancy, Maternity and the Organisation of Family Life: An Attempt to Classify the Case Law of the Court of Justice' (2001) 26 *European Law Review* 239.

[55] C McGlynn, 'Families and the European Union Charter of Fundamental Rights: Progressive Change or Entrenching the Status Quo?' (2001) 26 *European Law Review* 582.

[56] See Case C–249/96 *Grant v South-West Trains* [1998] ECR I–621 and, about the case, M Bell, 'Shifting Conceptions of Sexual Discrimination at the Court of Justice: from *P v S* to *Grant v SWT*' (1999) 5 *European Law Journal* 61; Cases C–122/99 and C–125/99 *D and Sweden v Council* [2001] ECR I–4319 and, on the cases, E Caracciolo di Torella and E Reid, 'The Changing Shape of the "European Family" and Fundamental Rights' (2002) 27 *European Law Review* 80.

social rights.[57] The social dimension is caught in the middle: sufficiently important to justify some EU legislation, but not enough to be equal with EU economic regulation that constricts national leeway on social matters. There is no overall EC competence in social areas and there are, despite increased emphasis on economic and social cohesion (for instance Structural Funds), no general policies on wealth distribution available at EU level. Moreover, despite the competence under Article 13 TEC to take action to combat discrimination based on sex, making progress towards expanding the scope of gender equality and non-discrimination beyond the incomplete set of labour rights remains controversial and tortuous due to its potentially far-reaching financial implications. One example is the 2004 Directive on equal treatment regarding goods and services, which goes beyond the realm of the labour market, but does not tackle areas such as education or advertising.[58] EC law in its current form has few ways to balance decisions such as *Jany* that reinforce and legitimise the further commodification of female sexuality as a 'sign' of the negative freedom of women; it has few tools to counter this with positive freedom (and it has made little use of the ones it has). Against this background the inclusion of social and equality rights in the Charter of Fundamental Rights (see below Chapter 6) was important symbolically. However, considering the lack of progressive measures to strengthen the place of, for instance, gender equality in the Constitution process at a time when the move towards a more political union is being debated, it is not sufficient in itself.[59]

3.2.2 Some Girls are Freer Than Others: EC Law and its Outsiders

In the prostitution cases the ECJ put the full force of EC free movement law behind those elements which make 'sex goods' just goods and 'sex work' just work, without having the tools to rebalance this with elements that would recognise the positive freedom relevant to a more equalised policy that addresses the constraints facing migrating women and the various gendered conditions that channel them into prostitution. This is of particular relevance to trafficking because of the demarcation between EU citizens and non-EU nationals. Even though it could be argued that the above views (expressly) relate only to EU citizens and do not necessarily have to affect the response to (arguably) external migration issues such

[57] M Poiares Maduro, 'Europe's Social Self: "The Sickness Unto Death"' in J Shaw (ed), *Social Law and Policy in an Evolving European Union* (Oxford, Hart, 2000); F Scharpf, 'The European Social Model: Coping with the Challenges of Diversity' (2002) 40 *Journal of Common Market Studies* 645. On how the contested nature of social rights results in fragmented policy see E Szyszczak, 'Protecting Social Rights in the European Union' in A Eide, C Krause and A Rosas (eds), *Economic, Social and Cultural Rights* (Dordrecht, Martinus Nijhoff, 2001).

[58] The Directive was originally announced in 2000 and was finally adopted in 2004. See Council Directive 2004/113/EC of 13 Dec 2004 implementing the principle of equal treatment between men and women in the access to and supply of goods and services [2004] OJ L 373/37.

[59] On the Charter and Constitution and the uncertainty of their future after the French and Dutch referenda see below section 6.3.

as trafficking for prostitution, the interdependent logic of intra- and extra EU migration means that in reality the former informs the latter. Indeed, whatever the other caveats of the free movement law of the market are regarding its personal scope, the most important one regarding trafficking relates to the exclusive logic(s) of EU citizenship regarding third country nationals and the general securitisation of external migration into the EU. In short, the process of building a political community of/for EU citizens through market mechanisms has been accompanied by the re-assertion of boundaries (this time external EU boundaries) and the exclusion of non-EU citizens. Non-EU nationals legally present in a Member State, including long-term residents, have been largely excluded from EU citizenship rights such as free movement, let alone more positive rights.[60] Moreover, this boundary-drawing is accompanied by external (im)migration policies, increasingly Europeanised, which seek to diminish the numbers of certain kinds of non-EU nationals. This is most notable in the case of economic migrants from the poorer countries of the world, seen as 'masquerading' as asylum-seekers, seeking and gaining entry to the Union (this in turn goes hand in hand with the perceived need to monitor the activities of migrants within the Union).

It has been argued that the broad problem behind the reluctance to extend rights to third country nationals is crucially linked to 'securitisation' of the Internal Market that singles them out (and consequently excludes them) as a potential threat.[61] This threat can take the shape of migrants challenging the bounded nature of the welfare state or a more concrete form of crime. The Single European Act (1986), which embraced the idea of an area without internal frontiers and the removal of internal border controls and replacing them with external border checks, is often recalled as the accelerator in the securitisation of migration due to the perceived need to counter the apparent security deficit caused by a lack of border controls—that is the freedom of irregular immigrants, terrorists and criminals of all kinds to travel in the European Union.[62] The most prominent example of the securitisation logic and the exclusionary tendencies accompanying freedom arguments is of course the Schengen Agreement (1985) and its Implementation Convention of 1990 (which from the beginning was accused of a lack of trans-

[60] See, eg, Case 283/83 *Caisse d'Allocation Familiales v Meade* [1984] ECR 2631; Case C–355/93 *Eroglu v Land Baden-Württemburg* [1994] ECR I–5113; Case C–230/97 *Awoyemi (Criminal proceedings against)* [1998] ECR I–6781. See also A Geddes, *Immigration and European Integration. Towards Fortress Europe?* (Manchester, Manchester University Press, 2000); T Kostakopoulou, *Citizenship, Identity and Immigration in the European Union: Between Past and Future* (Manchester, Manchester University Press, 2001).

[61] J Huysmans, 'Migrants as a Security Problem: Dangers of "Securitizing" Societal Issues' in R Miles and D Thränhardt (eds), *Migration and European Integration. The Dynamics of Inclusion and Exclusion* (London, Pinter, 1995); J Huysmans, 'The European Union and the Securitization of Migration' (2000) 38 *Journal of Common Marker Studies* 751; J Monar, *Justice and Home Affairs in a Wider Europe: The Dynamics of Inclusion and Exclusion* (ESRC 'One Europe or Several?' Programme Working Paper 7/2000, 2000, Brighton, ESRC). See also below ch 4.

[62] P Turnbull, 'The Fusion of Immigration and Crime in the European Union: Problems of Cooperation and the Fight Against the Trafficking in Women' (1997) 3(4) *Transnational Organized Crime* 189.

parency and judicial and democratic control), the structures and decisions of which were incorporated in the Treaty structure itself by the Treaty of Amsterdam. The ToA also introduced into the EC Treaty Title IV on Visas, Asylum, Immigration and other policies related to free movement of persons (about the remaining Third Pillar see Chapter 5), under which several proposals have been made and agreed on that restrict and monitor access to the EU.[63] Even though purportedly about freedom of movement, Schengen and its progeny echo the fear of the consequences of such freedom, and consequently focus on security and control.[64]

External migrants are, of course, a heterogenous group. In this respect, the situation of third country nationals legally and permanently living and working in Member States is illustrative of the complex structures of EU Law, as it has often been argued that these in particular should have more rights in EU law, regardless of any desire in some quarters to minimise external migration. The Tampere Conclusions famously stated that the legal status of third country nationals in the EU should be brought closer to that of EU nationals.[65] Thus far, however, the new Union powers on legal migration have produced less concrete results than what was hoped for in that respect. The discussions on the Directive on migration for employment or self-employment have not led anywhere.[66] The Directive on the right to family reunification[67] took three years to negotiate after the initial Commission proposal,[68] and the final result was characterised by Peers as follows: 'while the level of standards agreed in the directive might conceivably have been lower still, the compromise reached is at such a low standard that one can only conclude that the Tampere objectives of "fair treatment" for third-country nationals and "equal treatment" for long-term residents "as far as possible" have clearly not been met'.[69] It is worth recalling that family reunion is typically a gendered

[63] Note for instance developments such as the building of the common asylum system and the Schengen Information Systems. See also below ch 4.

[64] See, eg, Ward, above n 32. For earlier criticism, see D Curtin and H Meijers, 'The Principle of Open Government in Schengen and the European Union: Democratic Retrogression' (1995) 32 *Common Market Law Review* 391; M Spencer, *States of Injustice. A Guide to Human Rights and Civil Liberties in the European Union* (London, Pluto Press, 1995).

[65] 'A person, who has resided legally in a Member State for a period of time to be determined and who holds a long-term residence permit, should be granted in that Member State a set of uniform rights which are as near as possible to those enjoyed by EU citizens; eg the right to reside, receive education, and work as an employee or self-employed person, as well as the principle of non-discrimination vis-à-vis the citizens of the State of residence.' Tampere European Council Conclusions (15–16 Oct 1999, available at http://www.europarl.europa.eu/summits/tam_en.htm), 21.

[66] See original proposal COM(2001)386, [2001] OJ C 332 E/248. In 2005, the Commission released a Green Paper on Economic Migration (COM(2004) 811 final) and a Policy Plan on Legal Migration (COM(2005) 669 final) to relaunch the discussions.

[67] Council Directive 2003/86/EC of 22 Sept 2003 on the right to family reunification [2003] OJ L 251/12.

[68] COM(1999)638, [2000] OJ C 116 E/66, amended COM(2000)624, [2001] OJ C 62 E/99, and COM(2002)225, [2002] OJ C 203 E/136.

[69] S Peers, 'Key Legislative Developments on Migration in the European Union' (2003) 5 *European Journal of Migration and the Law* 387, at 406. On the Directive see also J Apap and S Carrera, *Towards a Proactive Immigration Policy for the EU?* (CEPS Working Document No 198, Brussels, CEPS, 2003). The European Parliament brought an action to annul some of the provisions of the Directive for breaching the human rights principles which form part of EC law but the action was dismissed by the ECJ in 2006. See Case C–540/03 *European Parliament v Council*, judgment of 27 June 2006.

topic, in that for various reasons many women, even those who may qualify as 'independent' immigrants, initially come as sponsored relatives, usually sponsored by husbands, and thus placed in a dependent position.[70] Likewise, the new Directive on the status of long-term residents[71] was adopted after a considerable reduction of standards even if it still retained the central right to move between Member States provided certain conditions were met.[72] Nonetheless, Member States will have 'considerable opportunities to set such stringent limits that few if any third-country nationals will be able to move in practice'.[73]

While, despite their limitations, the two recent Directives reflect the first steps forward, in that they address the possibility that (some) third country nationals might actually 'belong' in the European polity, it is hard not to notice that this belonging is full of conditions and seems to carry with it the assumption that third country nationals have to be tested and screened before being 'free' to enter.[74] Even when they are incorporated into the structures of European law it seems that their human rights still weigh less than those of EU citizens, meriting a lower level of protection. This cannot help but to reinforce the idea that unequal treatment of Union citizens and third country nationals is somehow justified. The law relating to third country nationals also remains internally incoherent, as for instance the two Directives adopted in 2000 insist on equal treatment irrespective of racial or ethnic origin or religion, emphasising a much more positive freedom.[75] For instance, the so-called Race Directive is arguably in many ways a huge step towards a more inclusive and affirmative vision of belonging in the European Union and has remarkable breadth, covering employment, education, social security, health care, access to goods and services and housing.[76] Yet it cannot counter the effect of other instruments which seem to say drawing distinctions based on nationality is quite legitimate; and, indeed, even the Race Directive incorporates this paradox into the framework owing to the major exception it makes to the ban on discrimination. Article 3(2) makes it clear that it does not cover discrimination based on nationality and is without prejudice to the conditions relating to the entry and

[70] Compare, however, Art 15 of the Family Reunification Directive, above n 67, which remedies this to some degree.

[71] Council Directive 2003/109/EC of 25 Nov 2003 concerning the status of third-country nationals who are long-term residents [2004] OJ L 16/44.

[72] For the proposal see COM(2001)127 final, [2001] OJ C 240 E/79.

[73] Peers, above n 69, at 408.

[74] Note that the new Hague Programme (adopted by the European Council on 5 Nov 2004 [2005] OJ C 53/1) replaces the Tampere principles (fair treatment of legally resident third-country nationals 'aiming at granting them rights and obligations comparable to those of EU citizens' and equal treatment of long-term residents with nationals 'as near as possible') with 'equal opportunities to participate fully in society' and furthering their 'integration'.

[75] Council Directive 2000/43/EC of 29 June 2000 implementing the principle of equal treatment between persons irrespective of racial or ethnic origin, [2000] OJ L 180/22; Council Directive 2000/78/EC of 27 Nov 2000 establishing a general framework for equal treatment in employment and occupation [2000] OJ L 303/16.

[76] M Bell, *Anti-Discrimination Law and the European Union* (Oxford, Oxford University Press, 2002), ch 3.

residence of third country nationals. The exception undermines the protective value of the Race Directive for third country nationals but is merely a symptom of the much larger problem.

The picture of migrants in the EU is of course much more varied than the above paragraphs alone suggest, not least due to numerous international agreements that often involve provisions on free movement to nationals of relevant countries.[77] The current regime involves complex layers of freedom; outside the core group of economically active EU nationals there exist various spheres for groups of 'outsiders', some more 'free' to move than others.[78] For example, the provisions of the Association Agreements relating to the right to self-employment have already been mentioned, and these are also an interesting example of the shifting and elusive boundary between inclusion and exclusion, freedom and constraint. They limited movement and residence rights for the purpose of self-employment, forcing nationals of the CEECs into self-employment even where employment might be preferred, for instance due to the relative lack of social protection in self-employment. Thus, even though in principle there might be little need for nationals of the CEECs to be irregularly employed in any Member State, there might be incentives to circumvent the legal channels for migration and to resort to irregular migration/work.[79] The situation of nationals of the CEECs of course also links with the perceived problem of a security deficit in the 2004 enlargement process.[80] As the assumption was that the 10 new Member States would be less than ready to take on, inter alia, the Title IV obligations regarding the safety of external borders, and as old Member States also feared that rather too many new EU citizens might be keen to migrate, there have been no automatic free movement rights accorded to the nationals of new Member States to move as workers (except for workers from the smallest new Member States, Cyprus and Malta). The transition period is not a novelty of course; however, that most old Member States decided to make use of the ability to delay free movement for work is telling.[81]

It is hard not to conclude that it has been quite difficult to achieve convergence on openness towards non-EU nationals, and that the EU thus remains far from

[77] About these see Weiss and Wooldridge, above n 31, at 201–39.

[78] Most notably EEA nationals enjoy the same right to move to any of the Member States and remain there for economic purposes as do nationals of the Member States. In contrast, based on the Turkey Agreement Turkish workers have a protected position in the labour market once they have been admitted under national rules, but these rights apply only in the Member State where they reside, so there are no free movement rights in the Union.

[79] E Guild, *The Legal Framework of EU Migration* (The Political Economy of Migration in an Integrating Europe Background Paper 2/2002, Coimbra, PEMINT, 2002).

[80] J Monar, *EU Justice and Home Affairs in the Eastward Enlargement: The Challenge of Diversity and EU Instruments and Strategies* (ZEI Discussion Paper C 91, 2001, Bonn, ZEI, 2001).

[81] For the first two years after accession, the 'old' Member States admitted employees from the new Member States under national rules, rather than under Community rules on free movement. In early 2006 the situation was re-evaluated—Finland, Greece, Portugal and Spain have joined the UK, Ireland and Sweden in removing restrictions, but the majority of old Member States still keep restrictions for workers from new Member States in place for the next few years. It is only after 7 years that Member States are no longer allowed to require work permits.

creating a proactive and balanced policy in this field.[82] Despite the recent Directives, the fact remains that the structure of European migration law entails powerful mechanisms of hierarchical exclusion. Moreover, as noted above, because of the gendered allocation of wealth, education and opportunities, women often become disproportionately disadvantaged in these processes. While the disadvantage of third country nationals may in part owe something to the speed at which restrictive (rather than inclusive) instruments have been adopted in the post-Amsterdam immigration agenda,[83] this does not change the fact that the balance remains heavily tilted towards exclusion and marginalisation rather than inclusion, let alone on an equal standing. Underprivileged non-EU migrant women meet a lukewarm response at best, and a truly cool reception is likely to be reserved for those who are often in irregular and socially and economically even more dependent situations. The latter are also the practical antithesis of the free and purposive independent economic agents embraced by European law and the perception of them as an alien threat is thus not surprising.[84] Yet the reason behind this perception and its continuing existence is heavily constructed by the workings of European law itself.

3.3 CONCLUSIONS

In certain ways, European free movement law has great emancipating potential which is, however, undermined by the kind of understanding of economic freedom it presupposes and crucially limited by the interpretation of its personal scope. The foreignerisation of prostitution and trafficking in the Internal Market mean that any 'European' approach to trafficking in women for sexual exploitation has to take into account not only the possibilities offered by increasing EU integration but the necessary limits European law may place on anti-trafficking efforts. First of all, free movement law directs the way in which the problem is seen in the first place; since it can only reduce prostitution to a service, it is hardly surprising if in the EU trafficking is easily set into a framework where it is seen (only) as mistreatment of irregular foreign workers and violations of negative freedom. This limited conception stems from a crude understanding of the individual and collective freedom involved in prostitution. Secondly, the notion of mobile (EU) sex workers exercising free movement entails a growing paradox because of the consistent tendency towards replacing EU women in prostitution with mainly non-EU nationals, as relatively privileged women are voting with their feet and leaving prostitution as a sign that it does not correspond to their idea of ideal market citizenship. The pool of prostitutes is being replaced by often non-European women who have far less freedom to choose how to migrate in the first place, what

[82] Apap and Carrera (2003), above n 69.

[83] G Brinkmann, 'The Immigration and Asylum Agenda' (2004) 10 *European Law Journal* 182.

[84] For an interesting angle on this see J Berman, '(Un)Popular Strangers and Crises (Un)Bounded: Discourses of Sex-Trafficking, the European Political Community and the Panicked State of the Modern State' (2003) 9 *European Journal of International Relations* 37.

work to take and on what conditions. As they lack privileges in Member States but also under European migration law, their constrained choices open the way for manipulation and exploitation.

This is particularly significant regarding trafficking in women for sexual exploitation, for there is an obvious correlation between the lack of migration rights for non-EU workers (let alone non-workers) and trafficking in so far as trafficking victims tend to be from countries that have few, if any, rights regarding migration for employment in the EU (this applies to Asia and Africa, as well as to South-Eastern Europe). The exclusionary logic of European citizenship means that at present prima facie any EU solution to exploitation is likely to be not about lowering the barriers of access to allow migrants to come as workers or about improving their status, but rather about preventing them from coming 'for their own good', but also owing to fears over social consequences and economic costs. It should be remembered that none of the above is of course a unique problem of European law, as the same issues surface in Member States as well. Nor is it the EU that is alone—or even primarily—implicated in excluding non-EU nationals from working in the Member States: indeed, the originally relatively advanced Commission proposals on asylum and migration tend to be extremely watered down in the Council. The problem is also highlighted in EC law due to the tension between building new forms of European regional citizenship and belonging on the one hand and, on the other, arguably undermining, or at the very least not supporting, universalistic human rights norms on the other.[85] This is likely to be a particularly acute issue regarding trafficking, where the spheres of exclusion based on nationality meet the gendered structures of EC law that tend to favour conventional, if not antiquated, gender scenarios.

[85] This conflict is noted, eg, by A Favell and A Geddes, *European Integration, Immigration and the Nation State: Institutionalising Transnational Political Action?* (EUI Working Papers, RSC No 1999/32, Florence, EUI, 1999).

4

Trafficking as Irregular Migration

THE ERA OF globalisation and free movement is also that of policing the border. The profound paradox in contemporary European policies on (im)migration that emerged in the previous chapter has been pointed out often, but rarely as succinctly as in the excerpt below:

> The attitude towards migration of the EU countries in this period has become highly ambivalent. On the one hand we see a firm belief that the flow of people, information, capital and goods is an asset for the further development of economies and societies. On the other hand immigration from the Third World and the former communist countries is seen as a threat to European welfare states. Migration regulations reflect this division into 'good' and 'bad' migration flows, between welcome and unwelcome migrants.[1]

In the previous chapter the focus was on the implications of free movement law within the Union to framing the approach to action against trafficking. This chapter discusses the reverse side of free movement, namely trafficking in women for sexual exploitation from the perspective of migration control policies, as a form of irregular external migration into the area of the EU Member States. As was stated above, while most EU Member States are increasingly dismantling the legal barriers that restrain free movement between them, and generally perceive this as a worthy goal, they are also engaged in a project of trying to limit access to the Union by many groups of non-EU nationals (policies popularly, if slightly inaccurately, referred to as 'Fortress Europe'[2]). The complex interactions between the parts of the dual European migration regime have profound consequences for anti-trafficking action.

A(n external) migration perspective in many ways provides the obvious angle for examining trafficking—after all, it is only recently that trafficking has been emerging as a phenomenon, which is, or should be, considered separate from the 'mainstream' of irregular migration. Yet the issue is in many ways a challenging and under-examined one, precisely due to the kind of treatment which trafficking has received as a migration issue, as the worst form of 'bad' migration. Nowadays

[1] H van Amersfoort, 'International Migration and Civil Rights: The Dilemmas of Migration Control in an Age of Globalisation' in E Guild (ed), *The Legal Framework and Social Consequences of Free Movement of Persons in the European Union* (The Hague, Kluwer Law International, 1999), at 82.

[2] Some use 'Sieve Europe' or 'Net Europe' as the intention (or effect) is not so much to block the entry of all, but to sift those seeking entry and let in desirable categories (tourists, businessmen), while keeping out the 'undesirables'.

many analyses of migration law and policy, especially in the European context, focus on the effects of the fortress tendencies. When they touch upon the issue of trafficking in women they tend to treat it as a (mere) subcategory of illegal, or at any rate irregular, migration, and implicitly or, sometimes, explicitly argue that trafficking in women for sexual exploitation is perhaps more victimising to the female migrant than other forms of irregular migration, but not essentially different. At the same time, there exists another strand of argument, claiming that—unlike men—women as a category are *uniquely* victimised in the migration process, precisely because of their female characteristics, and often due to the intersection of gender with, among others, ethnic group and class. Both these types of analyses can be linked with the previously predominant (and still prevalent) view of 'the migrant' (illegal or not) as an opportunistic male in search of economic opportunities. The former view of trafficking is a typical example of 'adding women' without any particular analytical changes caused by that addition apart from a nod in the direction of additional victimisation. The latter, in trying to carve out a different role for women, which would recognise that the male pattern does not provide an appropriate explanation, easily ends up reduced to the simplistic argument that women as a group are somehow inherently susceptible to being duped and coerced into prostitution, which in turn reinforces, rather than dismantles, the gendered stereotypes that underpin policy.

This chapter argues that it is necessary to avoid overly simplistic frameworks and to understand trafficking as a more complex phenomenon of international migration. To this end it is necessary that the legal regulation around migration that has trafficking-related implications is contrasted with the contribution of analyses of the actual position of women in international migration processes, their involvement in illegal or irregular migration and in the sex sector. In short, the study needs to connect the targets of trafficking, namely migrating women, and the objective of trafficking, namely sexual exploitation, with the relevant aspects of European, especially EU, migration policy-setting. For that it is necessary to take a closer look at what is meant by the so-called Fortress Europe, what consequences its (alleged) existence has on the incidence of trafficking in humans (in particular women), and what that means for anti-trafficking initiatives. This chapter first examines (im)migration control policies in the Member States and then developments at the level of the European Union, identifying factors that are relevant from the point of view of trafficking and tracking patterns of convergence and divergence in the current policies. It then places migrating women in this setting and discusses how the situation of migrant women involved in prostitution is constituted and influenced by the Member States' policies and how this affects the way in which trafficking and its victims are treated, with particular attention to the shortcomings and contradictions of existing policies vis-à-vis identified trafficking victims.

4.1 THE EUROPEAN MIGRATION POLICY CONTEXT

4.1.1 Crowded Houses, People's Homes or Fortress(es in) Europe

In recent years, (im)migration to the European Union has become a hot issue, in which immigration control has come to play a central role. The control side of immigration policy[3] in general involves (government) attempts to control immigration flows and to find a balance between the benefits brought by immigrants (usually as workers) and the social and economic problems they (are seen to) create.[4] This balance varies according to factors such as the rate of unemployment and the (perceived) need for immigrant labour. Even though there are differences among countries, European-wide trends can be discerned in the situation after the Second World War. Therefore, it is possible to categorise migration trends in the following way: the 1940s—early 1950s as a period of mass refugee flows; the 1950s–1973[5] as a period of recruitment of foreign workers; 1974–mid-1980s as the period of 'closing the doors' to immigrants; and the period from the mid-1980s onwards as a period involving flows of asylum-seekers and various forms of irregular immigration.[6] Writing in 2002, Joppke stated unequivocally that 'in contemporary Europe immigration policies are exclusively about stemming', by which he means that measures intended to contain existing migration flows have replaced attempts to welcome or even tolerate them.[7] In short, (im)migration has become 'a problem' to be controlled. This is also what the discourse on 'Fortress Europe' is about; the fortress is commonly understood to refer to measures related to the increasingly strict and heavily policed (im)migration regime, which Western European states are (seen as) building, increasingly together, and especially in the framework of the EU. This regime affects not only (economic) migrants and their family members, but also asylum-seekers and people fleeing from persecution.[8]

[3] The 'other' side of immigration policies, integration (citizenship issues, etc), is not discussed in this ch; although, as was seen in ch 3, it is not irrelevant, as the (perceived degree of) integration of the migrant population has consequences for migration control, and vice versa.

[4] P Stalker, 'Migration Trends and Migration Policy in Europe' (2002) 40(5) *International Migration* 151, at 163. See also S Collinson, *Europe and International Migration* (London, Pinter, 1994), especially ch 4; R Appleyard, 'International Migration Policies: 1950–2000' (2001) 39(6) *International Migration* 7.

[5] The recession brought about by the oil crisis in 1973 is often considered the turning point after which developed states stopped recruiting migrant labour, and focused on limiting the migrant population instead. On this and other reasons see S Castles and M Miller, *The Age of Migration* (2nd edn, Houndmills, Macmillan, 1998), ch 4.

[6] Stalker, above n 4, at 152–3. Compare this with G Freeman, 'Modes of Immigration Politics in Liberal Democratic States' (1995) 29 *International Migration Review* 881.

[7] C Joppke, 'European Immigration Policy at the Crossroads' in P Heywood, E Jones and M Rhodes (eds), *Developments in West European Politics 2* (Houndmills, Palgrave, 2002), at 260.

[8] After the 'closing of the doors' seeking asylum became increasingly one of the few legal ways of reaching EU Member States, leading to increasing numbers of asylum-seekers—and the subsequent labelling of most of them as 'bogus'. However, increasing asylum-seeker flows were also influenced by the increased possibilities of travel after the end of the Cold War and the conflicts on European soil.

These broad trends, and 'Fortress Europe' more specifically, are often interpreted as proof of convergence, and indeed the 'European migration regime' is being built by unifying the standards and procedures of EU Member States. Yet the jerky European policy in this field in fact builds on divergent stories of past experience and practice. Some of these divergences provide a useful background for placing trafficking in a migration policy setting before moving on to discuss what the trend towards 'Europeanisation' actually entails. The discussion will again focus on the three above-selected countries, between which there are obvious differences despite the fact that all are now part of 'Schengenland'. Sweden is a relatively new (1995) northern Member State of the EU, sparsely populated, with a large geographical area; the Netherlands (an original EEC and Schengen Member) is a geographically small and densely populated country; while Italy is a large and relatively densely populated southern Member State. Sweden and the Netherlands have a long tradition of immigration (in the Netherlands in particular linked with its colonial past) as both countries recruited foreign labour in the 1960s and have also received large proportions of asylum-seekers in the last two decades. In stark contrast, Italy is famous for being traditionally a country of emigration, and has only recently become a country of mass immigration and asylum. In each country immigration policy is affected by very different geographical factors. Sweden has a particular regional interest in Scandinavia (the Nordic passport union and labour market) and in the Baltic Sea area; the Netherlands is particularly affected by its former colonies and its large eastern neighbour Germany; and Italy's location as a Mediterranean country ties its policy choices not only to the countries south of the Mediterranean but to the Balkans as well.

The so-called 'immigration stop' of the 1970s was particularly strong in the countries north of the Alps, which started to tighten up their immigration and later asylum regimes. The Netherlands stopped recruiting foreign labour after the first oil crisis. This did not, however, lead to migrants (perceived until then as 'guestworkers') returning home; nor did it stop the flows of migrants, but rather re-directed them to family reunion, asylum-seeking and irregular channels. It was only in 1983 that it was officially recognised that the migrant population was not formed of temporary residents, but that the Netherlands had become an immigration country.[9] The trend since has been to combine efforts to integrate the immigrant population through a 'multi-ethnic approach' with increasingly strict and sophisticated control over new (im)migration and increased exclusion of irregular migrants (especially through the Linking Act 1998[10]). A completely new

[9] This is quite significant, considering the obsessive Dutch view of the Netherlands as (too) densely populated (in the past emigration of Dutch nationals was encouraged by the government for this reason). See H van Amersfoort, 'Migration Control and Minority Policy: The Case of the Netherlands' in G Brochmann and T Hammar (eds), *Mechanisms of Immigration Control: A Comparative Analysis of European Regulation Policies* (Oxford, Berg, 1999).

[10] On this Act, which excludes irregular residents from social benefits, see P Minderhoud, 'Coping With Irregular Migration: The Dutch Experience' in B Bogusz *et al* (eds), *Irregular Migration and Human Rights: Theoretical, European and International Perspectives* (Leiden, Martinus Nijhoff, 2004).

Aliens Act was adopted in 2000, covering both migrants and refugees,[11] and to fill a perceived gap in expulsion, a return policy was outlined in a 2003 document.[12] The Netherlands has actively promoted international and European-level co-operation to achieve its aim.[13] The relationship with 'Europe' has been to some extent ambiguous.[14] Racism and xenophobia emerged as increasingly politically pertinent factors in the late 1980s, have retained their relevance in the last few years and have arguably intensified in the wake of the Fortuyn killing and the murder by an Islamist activist of filmmaker Theo van Gogh in November 2004. At the same time the multicultural minority approach has given way to an assimilationist integration policy.[15] Yet the country is also dependant on migration, as it has a very open economy that relies on trade and traffic. While ethnic minorities have been particularly hard hit by unemployment, undocumented or 'illegal' migrants working in the Netherlands are inevitably flexible, and as such 'serve as lubricant for cyclical and seasonal adjustments in the highly regulated Dutch labour market, as young, highly motivated workers for jobs deemed unattractive by formal workers'.[16]

As in the Netherlands, in Sweden large-scale recruitment of (im)migrant labour (especially from Finland) prevailed in the 1960s, but, unlike the Netherlands, Sweden explicitly promoted an immigration policy based on permanence without relying on a 'guestworker' notion. Immigration restrictions on labour migration were introduced in the early 1970s after a sudden flow of workers from Yugoslavia; the recruitment of labour was stopped altogether after the recession of 1972.[17] Policy changes towards stricter control have become more visible since the mid-1980s. This occurred for various reasons: from 1983 on the numbers of

[11] Wet van 23 november 2000 tot algehele herziening van de Vreemdelingenwet (Vreemdelingenwet 2000), (2000) 495 Staatsblad 1.

[12] Measures for a more effective implementation of Dutch policy on return (Directorate-General for International Affairs and Immigration, 21 Nov 2003).

[13] A Geddes, *The Politics of Migration and Immigration in Europe* (London, Sage, 2003), ch 5. The Netherlands has, eg, been active in negotiating readmission agreements, both nationally and as a Benelux country, and supports an EU policy on readmission agreements.

[14] For instance, in some ways a more important singular influence was Germany's tighter asylum laws, which caused tightening also in the Netherlands: see M Vink, *Negative and Positive Integration in European Immigration Policies* (European Integration Online Papers 6(13), 2002, available at http://eiop.or.at/eiop/texte/2002-013a.htm). But see also M Vink, *Limits of European Citizenship: European Integration and Domestic Immigration Policies* (Constitutionalism Web-Papers No 4/2003, Belfast, QUB, 2003) about the impact of 'Europe' in strengthening EU citizens' position.

[15] H Entzinger, 'The Rise and Fall of Multiculturalism: The Case of the Netherlands' in C Joppke and E Morawska (eds), *Towards Assimilation and Citizenship: Immigration in Liberal Nation-States* (London, Palgrave, 2003). See also Geddes, above n 13, at 113–18.

[16] A Zorlu and J Hartog, *Migration and Immigrants: The Case of the Netherlands* (Tinbergen Institute Discussion Paper TI 2001-042/3, Amsterdam, Tinbergen Institute, 2001), at 11; see also P Muus, *Migration, Immigrants and Policy in the Netherlands: Recent Trends and Developments* (Amsterdam, European Research Centre on Migration and Ethnic Relations, SOPEMI, 1996). On illegal immigrants and criminality see G Engbersen and J van der Leun, 'The Social Construction of Illegality and Criminality' (2001) 9 *European Journal on Criminal Policy and Research* 51.

[17] See T Hammar, 'Closing the Doors to the Swedish Welfare State' in Brochmann and Hammar (eds), above n 9.

asylum-seekers started to rise rapidly,[18] Nordic immigration decreased while otherwise immigration grew, unemployment rose and refugee resettlement caused local problems, and immigration generally became more politicised.[19] Stricter policy, including the tightening of control over conditions of entry and readmission agreements, has coincided with Sweden's entry into the EU; while there is no absolute clarity as to the significance of this connection, Sweden is nonetheless one of the firm supporters of Schengen and asylum co-operation. Unlike that in the Netherlands, the Swedish political climate (apart from a period at the beginning of the 1990s) has not (yet) sustained the growth of a large anti-immigrant lobby.[20] Nor has the country had a very large population of irregular residents or workers. This is largely because Sweden, like its Nordic neighbours, is a highly regulated country with strong social control and strong labour unions.[21] Space for irregular residence or work is thus limited, although there are signs that this may be changing, due to shifts in political geography or the recent growth of the informal labour market, offering less-controlled spaces for the growth of unregulated work.

In contrast to Sweden and the Netherlands, Italy—as a tourism country with strong and recent tendencies towards emigration and internal migration rather than *im*migration (especially as far as the South of Italy is concerned)—retained quite a lax immigration and visa policy (infamous amongst its neighbours because Italy is also a transit country) until the surprise and panic of the early 1990s, caused in particular by the Albanian refugee crisis. Since then, immigration policy has become increasingly restrictive. Even if policy development to some degree continues to suffer from the political instability of the country,[22] the trend towards restriction is clear and, according to one commentator, amounts to a 'complete turnaround', achieved in a decade.[23] Yet migration to Italy persists, causing intense political fluctuations.[24] The fact that Italy has a vast and diverse hidden labour sector that is willing and able to absorb great numbers of (im)migrant workers (in agriculture, construction, services) has entailed the development of a

[18] During the period 1983–93 Sweden was, in proportion to the country's population, one of the major host countries as regards asylum-seekers.

[19] Hammar, above n 17, at 176–8; H Ring, 'Refugees in Sweden: Inclusion and Exclusion in the Welfare State' in R Miles and D Thränhardt (eds), *Migration and European Integration. The Dynamics of Inclusion and Exclusion* (London, Pinter, 1995).

[20] However, the 2002 'honour killing' of Fadime Sahindal (by her father, owing to her relationship with a Swedish man) has certainly made the issue more salient. Note also that Swedish immigrant policy shifted from multiculturalism to adaptation, and a decade before the Netherlands. See Geddes, above n 13, ch 5.

[21] Hammar, above n 17, Geddes, above n 13.

[22] D Papademetriou and K Hamilton, *Converging Paths to Restriction: French, Italian and British Responses to Immigration* (Washington, DC, International Migration Policy Program, Carnegie Endowment for International Peace, 1996).

[23] G Sciortino, 'Planning in the Dark: the Evolution of Italian Immigration Control' in G Brochmann and T Hammar (eds), above n 9.

[24] In both 2004 and 2005, political instability has kept its salience—as has the 'moral panic' over illegal immigration which erupts every time a ship approaches the tiny Mediterranean island of Lampedusa. Yet Italy still has a very small immigrant population (per capita) compared to most EU Member States (not to mention Sweden or the Netherlands).

large population of undocumented workers.[25] That the demand for these workers exists in the Italian economy but is not explicitly formulated (together with growing anti-immigrant sentiment, especially in the north of the country) has ensured that 'immigration has been chaotic and managed in an emergency and approximate way', although it is deemed useful.[26] The pressure of Europeanisation has a clearly visible influence in Italy's (and other southern Member States') policies: excluded from early Schengen co-operation (the only original EEC country to be so excluded),[27] Italy has, albeit in fits, striven to fulfil the criteria set by northern Member States. The most notable achievement concerns the adoption of the 1998 single text dealing with entry, residence and expulsion.[28] The second Berlusconi government (2001–6) sought to tighten the controls even more through, for example, the 'Bossi-Fini' amendment that provides tough penalties for smuggling but still does not tackle the overdue issue of weak and divergent internal control,[29] and through readmission negotiations with sending countries, most recently with Libya, which is a major hub of human smuggling. What the new left-wing coalition will do about these provisions remains to be seen.

4.1.2 (Im)Migration Policy Dilemmas and the European Union

The general trend towards deepening concern over migration flows leads to the heart of the 'Fortress Europe' debate on the transnationalisation and harmonisation of European policy in the core areas of immigration and asylum co-operation. Even though the near-literal sense in which the term is sometimes used is inaccurate (in light of the dubious existence of a 'criminal conspiracy' to produce converging stemming policies), the restrictive trend of convergence nonetheless exists. The Schengen co-operation, involving the area where internal borders have been abolished and with common rules on visas, asylum and checks at external borders, and the Dublin Convention on the co-ordination of asylum applications[30] (now

[25] The greatest contrast to this lack (or at any rate, weakness) of internal control mechanisms is of course the above-mentioned example of Sweden with its high degree of internal control.

[26] M Ambrosini, 'The Role of Immigrants in the Italian Labour Market' (2001) 39(3) *International Migration* 61, at 62. One example of the ad hoc approach to immigration is given by the several regularisation campaigns that have taken place since 1989. On these see B Nascimbene, 'The Regularisation of Clandestine Immigrants in Italy' (2000) 2 *European Journal of Migration and Law* 337.

[27] Sciortino, above n 23, at 246–7.

[28] See decreto legislativo (decree) di 25 July 1998, no 286, [1998] GU 191 ('Testo unico delle leggi sull' immigrazione', 'Turco-Napolitano' law), which consolidated in a unified text all the provisions in force, in particular Legge di 6 Mar 1998 no 40, [1998] GU 59, on the conditions of immigration and the legal status of aliens (Art 16 of which stipulated the protection and residence permits to be given to victims of (sex) trafficking who seek to escape exploitation).

[29] Legge di 30 July 2002 no 189, [2002] GU 199, amending legge 286/1998 ('Bossi-Fini' Act).

[30] Dublin Convention Determining the State Responsible for Examining Applications for Asylum Lodged in One of the Member States of the European Communities, signed in Dublin on 15 June 1990 [1997] OJ C 254/1.

replaced by a Council Regulation[31]) are just two often-cited examples of harmonisation aspirations—and also of policies criticised for raising serious human rights concerns: Schengen, regarding for instance the Schengen Information System and the status of third country nationals; Dublin, for infringing the principle of non-refoulement. Both have also been examples of persisting divergence; three Member States have reservations on the Schengen system (Ireland and the UK have 'opted out' and retain their border controls, Denmark is a member but with an opt-out on communitarised measures) and the Dublin system did not harmonise the substance of asylum legislation, and hence was criticised for making the system unworkable in practice. Asylum, however, also provides an example of the speed at which things can change when push comes to shove, in this case because of the Amsterdam five-year timetable and the (then) imminent eastward enlargement.[32]

With regard to migration, as was seen in the previous chapter, the development and consequences of Member States' policies, mainly emphasising the stemming rather than acceptance (let alone soliciting) of migrants from outside the EU, should also be seen in the light of the creation of a European Internal Market and the area without internal frontiers. The other half of the 'European migration regime' relating to immigration proper, which is becoming increasingly supranational despite its intergovernmental origin (that nonetheless retains great significance)[33] cannot be understood without reference to the free movement of EU citizens and the fundamental effect that it (and the ensuing (perceived) lack of control of the EU Member States over their internal borders) has had in intensifying and legitimising the control of external migration as an exigent political priority and turning it into a crucial co-operation issue.[34] Moreover, and most importantly, in recent years external migration has become demonised and constructed as a threat to the security, stability and welfare of the (supposedly homogenous) EU Member States as anxieties about social cohesion and boundaries have come to the fore.[35] This anxiety over security has been transferred to the

[31] Council Regulation 343/2003/EC of 18 Feb 2003 establishing the criteria and mechanisms for determining the Member State responsible for examining an asylum application lodged in one of the Member States by a third-country national [2003] OJ L 50/1.

[32] The Council Directive on minimum standards for the qualification and status of third-country nationals and stateless persons as refugees or as persons who otherwise need international protection and the content of the protection granted was finally adopted in Apr 2004 (Directive 2004/83/EC [2004] OJ L 304/12); at the same time political agreement was also reached on the so-called Asylum Procedures Proposal (Proposal COM(2002)326 final/2 [2002] OJ C 291 E/143). The latter was adopted in 2005 as Directive 2005/85/EC [2005] OJ L 326/13.

[33] Most centrally, Member States retain the primary role in the admission of non-EU nationals for longer residence (see Art 63 TEC); see also eg Art 67 TEC.

[34] See Joppke, above n 7; Geddes, above n 13. See also S Lavenex and E Uçarer, 'The Emergent EU Migration Regime and Its External Impact' in S Lavenex and E Uçarer (eds), *Migration and the Externalities of European Integration* (Lanham, Mld, Lexington Books, 2002); E Uçarer, 'Guarding the Borders of the European Union: Paths, Portals and Prerogatives' in *ibid.*

[35] J Huysmans, 'Migrants as a Security Problem: Dangers of "Scrutinizing" Societal Issues' in Miles and Thränhardt (eds), above n 19. See also D Bigo, 'Migration and Security' in V Guiraudon and C Joppke (eds), *Controlling a New Migration World* (London, Routledge, 2001).

European arena where the linking of immigration to internal security issues, with roots in the TREVI Group and the tentative Schengen co-operation, has progressed rapidly as co-operation has deepened. In the setting of a Union without internal borders and with free movement of people this has highlighted 'compensatory' efforts to 'stem the flows' through deepening co-operation in the areas of policing and immigration, which are now fundamentally intertwined in the EU arena.[36] Considering the perceived danger posed by immigrant communities (and the intensified threat of terrorism after the Madrid and London bombings) this trend is unlikely to abate in the near future.

Bearing in mind how self-interested the Area of Justice and Home Affairs is, it is not unexpected that increased Union responsibility has gone hand in hand with strident rhetoric on immigration control and the development of various means to tackle 'problem' countries vis-à-vis irregular migration.[37] After the Amsterdam Title IV on 'visas, asylum, immigration and other policies related to the free movement of persons' was adopted with the aim of creating an Area of Freedom, Security and Justice, an impressive array of measures and instruments of control has been introduced. Restrictive Member State practices have increasingly become those of the EU, as the case of readmission clauses and agreements shows.[38] Many of the controls intended to stem the 'influx of immigrants' frequently take place outside the territory of the Union Member States, such as in consulates (visa regimes[39]), in the territories of other states (creation of concepts like 'safe third countries') and by transportation companies (carrier liability).[40] In short, the measures taken to combat 'bad' migration, be it irregular or simply unwanted (especially in the form of 'fake' asylum-seekers or family reunion) include measures not only to expel, and as efficiently and cheaply as possible, the undesirable aliens from Member States[41] but, importantly, to prevent them from ever

[36] P Turnbull, 'The Fusion of Immigration and Crime in the European Union: Problems of Cooperation and the Fight Against the Trafficking in Women' (1997) 3(4) *Transnational Organized Crime* 189; R Koslowski, 'Personal Security and State Sovereignty in a Uniting Europe' in V Guiraudon & C Joppke (eds), *Controlling a New Migration World* (London, Routledge, 2001).

[37] Note, eg, how the 'High-Level Working Group' on asylum and immigration (created in 1998) developed external immigration policy by drawing up action plans for (unilaterally) selected third countries to reduce migration flows (Afghanistan, Morocco, Somalia, Sri Lanka, Iraq and Albania).

[38] Readmission clauses have been included in association and co-operation agreements for several years; the EU no longer signs association or co-operation agreements lest the other side agrees to the standard obligation. As regards readmission agreements, since the entry into force of the Treaty of Amsterdam, the European Community has pursued agreements requiring third states to re-admit their own nationals, and those of third states. On these see M Schieffer, 'Community Readmission Agreements with Third Countries—Objectives, Substance and Current State of Negotiations' (2003) 5 *European Journal of Migration and Law* 343; D Bouteillet-Paquet, 'Passing the Buck: A Critical Analysis of the Readmission Policy Implemented by the European Union and Its Member States' (2003) 5 *European Journal of Migration and Law* 359.

[39] See Community Visa Regulation (Council Regulation 539/2001/EC [2001] OJ L 81/1), which lists illegal migration and public policy concerns about crime as relevant factors.

[40] A Cruz, *Shifting Responsibility. Carriers' Liability in the Member States of the European Union and North America* (Stoke-on-Trent, Trentham Books, 1995).

[41] Communication on a Community Return Policy on Illegal Residents, COM(2002)564 final, 14 Oct 2002.

reaching the territory of the Member States in the first place.[42] In the setting of the 2004 enlargement the old Member States used prospective EU membership (with the eventual right of free movement for nationals of the CEECs) as a carrot to make the accession states deal with the EU's (perceived or real) 'immigration problems'. Hence Central and Eastern European Countries, while being source countries for migrants, became the EU's 'buffer zones': in return for imposing stricter border controls at their Eastern borders and taking on part of the 'burden' created by asylum-seekers, the citizens of the CEECs have received benefits.[43] In practice, the export of EU immigration policy to the CEECs has involved moving 'the problem' eastwards and has, for instance, created negative side-effects for those of the CEECs that have strong economic, social or cultural links with non-acceding countries.[44] Yet, as was seen above, full free movement rights, the possibility of which was used as an incentive for the CEECs to co-operate, are at present inaccessible to the new EU citizens in many of the old EU-15.

Many of the anti-immigration measures alluded to above, such as limiting the definition of a refugee, have been (justly) criticised for threatening to undermine the EU Member States' other international obligations, most notably international human rights agreements and the 1951 Refugee Convention.[45] This collision of human rights and refugee protection with the trends in border management is in fact also one example of what Lahav and Guiraudon call a 'control dilemma'. This involves dealing with how to settle the national public security concerns (justified or not) about external migration with the constraints imposed by their liberal norms and the promotion of free trade, both of which rule out sealing borders as an option. Among others, Lahav and Guiraudon argue that it is this dilemma that has led to the movement of immigration control away from the core areas of the state to the transnational, especially the EU level (where it is less liable to of rights scrutiny) as well as to the local and private levels (airlines, employers' sanc-

[42] The most extreme and obvious example of the latter is the UK idea to build a centre for asylum-seekers in Croatia: that way asylum-seekers never reach EU territory in the first place, so costly repatriation (after the claims of the majority have been rejected) would be avoided: 'Secret Balkan camp built to hold UK asylum-seekers', *The Observer*, 15 June 2003. This plan, rejected at the Thessaloniki European Council in 2003, was revived again in 2004.

[43] And in case the carrot failed, there was the stick: eg, the threat of refusing visa-free movement if the CEECs fail to co-operate willingly has done wonders for inducing 'co-operation'—on this in Polish-German relations see R Freudenstein, 'Río Odra, Río Buh: Poland, Germany, and the Borders of Twenty-First-Century Europe' in P Andreas and T Snyder (eds), *The Wall around the West. State Borders and Immigration Controls in North America and Europe* (Lanham, Mld, Rowman & Littlefield Publishers, 2000). See also M Vachudová, 'Eastern Europe as Gatekeeper: The Immigration and Asylum Policies of an Enlarging European Union' in *ibid*; L Jesien, 'Border Controls and the Politics of EU Enlargement' in *ibid.*

[44] See E Jileva, 'Larger than the European Union: The Emerging EU Migration Regime and Enlargement' in Lavenex and Uçarer (eds), above n 34; H Grabbe, 'Stabilizing the East While Keeping Out the Easteners: Internal and External Security Logics in Conflict' in *ibid.*

[45] United Nations Convention Relating to the Status of Refugees, 189 UNTS 150 (hereafter 'the UN Refugee Convention'). On how EU action might further the criminalisation of asylum and racial discrimination see M Bell, 'Mainstreaming Equality Norms into European Union Asylum Law' (2001) 26 *European Law Review* 20.

tions).[46] Thus EU integration on (im)migration issues is not, as some have argued, a simple example of states 'losing control' in a globalising world, but a manifestation of evolving control policies, whereby states reassert their control over (unwanted) migration through EU co-operation, which is, moreover, less susceptible to domestic judicial constraints or political scrutiny.[47] Thus controls, which used to be located at the national border, have now been spread and are exercised in varied ways, in various places by a multitude of actors. Yet the dilemma of friction between human rights and xenophobic and nationalistic tendencies is not resolved when the issue is moved to the transnational level; it is merely transformed and has a more diffuse and fragmented character in the evolving regime.

It is evident that the fight against smuggling[48] and trafficking in human beings falls under this logic without difficulty, indeed far too easily, posing a number of crucial questions about the motivations behind the EU-driven 'fight against trafficking'. Human smugglers and traffickers have now joined the ranks of drug traffickers and terrorists as dangerous criminals to be targeted, not least because of the tremendous business opportunities and profits that (are seen to) await them for evading migration controls.[49] The response has been filled with tensions. On the one hand, European and Member State response to smuggling-cum-trafficking has been to put particular emphasis on co-operating, not only to expel irregular migrants but to combat the increase in the activities of middlemen and smugglers (especially when they take the form of transnational criminal networks), making use of the opportunities created by the migration regime, and to block the gaps of which these individuals and groups make use. On the other hand, the nature of a system that seeks to guarantee the privileges of the select few (nationals of Member States and other rich countries) at the cost of keeping everyone else out has been characterised at best as discriminatory and at worst as downright racist.[50]

[46] See G Lahav and V Guiraudon, 'Comparative Perspectives in Border Control: Away from the Border and Outside the State' in Andreas and Snyder (eds), above n 43. See also Joppke, above n 7, at 263, who makes a further distinction between external and internal controls, the latter of which is more visibly in collision with rights concerns—states therefore tend to opt for the former, which 'circumvents rights without openly violating them'.

[47] See V Guiraudon, 'De-Nationalizing Control: Analyzing State Responses to Constraints on Migration Control' in Guiraudon and Joppke (eds), above n 35; A Geddes, 'International Migration and State Sovereignty in an Integrating Europe' (2001) 39(6) *International Migration* 21.

[48] See Council Directive 2002/90/EC of 28 Nov 2002 defining the facilitation of unauthorised entry, transit and residence [2002] OJ L 328/17 and Council Framework Decision of 28 Nov 2002 on the strengthening of the penal framework to prevent the facilitation of unauthorised entry, transit and residence, 2002/946/JHA [2002] OJ L 328/1.

[49] Moreover, trafficking, smuggling and terrorism are increasingly linked together, although usually through unverifiable suspicions that the profits made from trafficking are used to fund terrorist activities or that potential terrorists are smuggled to the European Union. For an example of the latter see, eg, 'Blitz contro i mercanti di uomini', *La Repubblica*, 21 Jan 2005.

[50] See, eg, S Cohen, *No One Is Illegal. Asylum and Immigration Control Past and Present* (Stoke-on-Trent, Trentham Books, 2003). The racism claim can be linked with many things from the Race Directive, [2000] OJ L 180/22, to the so-called 'negative' and 'positive' visa lists drawn up in the framework of the EU—the negative list (of those countries whose nationals need a visa to enter an EU Member State) consists mainly of African and Asian states, while the positive list includes the CEECs and Latin America.

Moreover, a policy focused on control alone is doomed to fail as immigration control in itself does nothing about the reasons (root causes) why people want to migrate to the EU.[51] Nor can the 'fortress', transnationalised or not, ever be perfected to the necessary extent without gnawing away at the civil rights of individuals, including those of EU citizens. As a result, it seems reasonable to assume that policies seeking to prevent migration (to appease the public hostility to migrants) cannot stop it but are likely to keep driving the majority of would-be migrants to trying to beat the Member States at their own game by circumventing the rules. Since European borders cannot be sealed off completely, seeking to make the activities of traffickers more difficult may also increase their profits, as migrants have to pay more to ensure entry.

The issues relating to criminal law and policy on migration in general and trafficking in particular will be addressed in more detail below in Chapter 5.[52] Suffice it to say here that the fusion of immigration policy and criminal law measures, and the connecting of migrants with criminals, not only makes it difficult to recognise the pertinent differences between those victimised and those perpetrating crimes, but contributes to a generally hostile environment for 'third-country nationals', already seen by some as 'leeches' feeding on the welfare state, and now criminalised. It is ironic but not surprising that it is precisely this connection of trafficking with the fusion of policing and security concerns over what is seen as irregular (and essentially unwanted) external migration into the area of free movement, which explains why trafficking emerged as a European policy issue in the first place. It is likely that the link to migration and crime will keep trafficking on the agenda, despite the existence of other and better reasons to consider trafficking an important policy issue. It is emblematic that the phenomenon now referred to as 'trafficking' has not until very recently been called trafficking with any degree of consistency; nor should one be amazed if responses to it involved migration and crime control related measures like prosecution for irregular entry and/or removal. As will be argued below, under a migration control approach little else can be expected, as such approaches cannot easily, if at all, make a conceptual distinction between those victimised and irregular immigrants in general, when the latter are criminalised as a class.

However, from any perspective aiming effectively and coherently to address trafficking, it is plain that it is necessary to break the link between migration and crime/security oriented concerns and start talking about openness to labour migration. This is necessary, but easier said than done, considering the 'myths'

[51] This has been acknowledged to a degree but has resulted in rather short-sighted proposals that emphasise improving control in developing countries rather than long-term development that might alleviate the root causes of migration. See below ch 7.

[52] Albeit that the immigration and policing approaches to trafficking are fundamentally connected (and also connected to the ensuring of free movement), they are dealt with in different sections precisely because the interweaving of crime, migration and free movement issues obscures the mechanisms that operate to bind them together and the consequences this has for trafficking.

that dominate migration decision-making discourse.[53] The matter links with the views of those who see the transnationalisation of immigration policy as an inevitable (and desirable) development considering the mismatch between global economy and national (restrictive) immigration policy, and those who assume that the involvement of EU institutions in policy-making will lead to a more balanced policy.[54] In this relatively tumultuous period of transition (as far as the Europeanisation of (im)migration policy is concerned), the logic of 'escape to Europe' still predominates in European-level policy-making, prioritising (some) Member States' domestic security-oriented concerns and leaving little room for other agendas, for example consideration for global themes such as human rights or economic justice, in forging convergence in this area.[55] While it is vital to keep challenging the foundation of migration myths, in a more positive vein it can be noted that the theme of 'migration as a resource' has emerged with increasing frequency, especially after the controversial UN report in March 2000 about the demographic need for migrants in Europe.[56] This is connected with the recent talk on the need to move towards open and proactive, rather than reactive, immigration policies.[57] At the EU level, this idea has been particularly, if cautiously, advocated by the Commission which, noting the declining demographic trend in Europe and the (generally) positive impact of immigrants on EU economies, argues for a more open immigration policy, especially as far as labour migration is concerned.[58]

Moves towards openness, while modest, can only be welcomed, even if what is to a degree problematic about the idea of relaxing migration controls to 'solicit' desirable migrants (such as IT or health care professionals required by boom sectors) is that, while it serves the aim of getting 'good' (educated, etc) legal migrants

[53] G Sciortino and F Pastore, 'Immigration and European Immigration Policy: Myths and Realities' in J Apap (ed), *Justice and Home Affairs in the EU. Liberty and Security Issues after Enlargement* (Cheltenham, Edward Elgar, 2004).

[54] S Sassen, 'Beyond Sovereignty: De-Facto Transnationalism in Immigration Policy' (1999) 1 *European Journal of Migration and Law* 177.

[55] For the conflicting agendas regarding migration see J Niessen, 'Overlapping Interests and Conflicting Agendas: The Knocking into Shape of EU Immigration Policies' (2001) 3 *European Journal of Migration and Law* 419. Note also that the Constitutional Treaty ([2004] OJ C 310/1) evidenced a security orientation: the common immigration policy is 'aimed at ensuring, at all stages, the efficient management of migration flows, fair treatment of third-country nationals residing legally in Member States, and the prevention of, and enhanced measures to combat, illegal immigration and trafficking in human beings' (Art III–267).

[56] United Nations Population Division, *Replacement Migration: is It a Solution to Declining and Ageing Population?* (ESA/P/WP.160, 2000, New York, UN Population Division of the Department of Social Affairs, 2001). For a recent overview of Europe's demographic trends see IOM, *World Migration 2005. Costs and Benefits of International Migration* (Geneva, IOM, 2005), ch 7.

[57] J Apap, 'Shaping Europe's Migration Policy New Regimes for the Employment of Third Country Nationals: A Comparison of Strategies in Germany, Sweden, the Netherlands and the UK' (2002) 4 *European Journal of Migration and Law* 309.

[58] See Communication from the Commission to the Council, the European Parliament, the European Economic and Social Committee and the Committee of the Regions on immigration, integration and employment, COM(2003)336, 3 June 2003. See also the recent Commission Green Paper 'On an EU approach to managing economic migration', COM(2004)811 final, 11 Jan 2005.

who serve the needs of national economies, this is not likely to lead to reduced restrictions placed on those not fitting that description. A perhaps more fundamental concern about these plans relates to the tacit assumption behind seeing (some) migrants as an 'economic asset', that is if (im)migrants could instead be proven to be a 'liability' to the receiving countries, the European Union would be justified in sealing the borders completely (whether that is possible is of course another matter).[59] Thus the current moves still have rather little to say about more principled matters of global economic justice or human rights. Finally, the challenge is to convince not only institutions such as the Commission but Member States' governments that the current policy is unworkable (let alone unethical) as it is still they who hold the keys to the door.

4.2 FEMALE MIGRANTS, MIGRATION POLICIES AND EXPLOITATION

4.2.1 From Structural Causes to Exploitative Situations

If and when it is true that 'in immigration law issues of sexuality, gender and the family are intimately linked to those of racism',[60] it is necessary to situate female (mostly irregular) migrants in the recent developments on European (im)migration policy. As was seen above, this presents a complicated picture of domestic rights controls hindering the effective stemming of (perceived) flows of migrants,[61] and a trend from uncoordinated and national solutions on asylum and immigration towards co-ordinated and European responses. The structures of international migration (already mentioned in Chapter 2) are further clarified in this section with reference to how they lead migrant women into the informal sector and exploitation, while the next section focuses on the actual response to trafficking in a migration setting. The emerging body of literature that studies female migrants (and to a lesser degree the legal regulation around it) sheds light on the processes that are causing the increasing 'feminisation of migration', and on how restrictive legal migration options concentrate female migrants, often entering though 'dependent' channels, into the informal and illegal sectors in the EU.[62] It is important to stress these processes, because at times a focus on individuals'

[59] Note how the transition period imposed on the nationals of the CEECs embodies this tension between freer migration policy and the 'threat' posed by free movement. The same applies to the suggested (possibly permanent) restrictions on Turkish nationals vis-à-vis Turkey's future accession.

[60] Cohen, above n 50, at 8.

[61] It is good to keep in mind that despite the talk of a 'migration crisis', and even though the number of migrants has more than doubled since 1970 (meaning that in 2005 around 191 million persons currently reside in a country other than that in which they were born), this still means that only about 3% of the world's population are migrants: see UN Department of Economic and Social Affairs, Population Division, *International Migration Report 2006,* (New York, UN Population Division of the Department of Economic and Social Affairs, 2006). Nor are EU Member States major receivers of migrants in relative terms. Instead of talking about a 'migration problem', it might be useful to note that the vast majority of people do *not* migrate, and ask why this is so.

[62] H Lutz, 'The Limits of European-ness: Immigrant Women in Fortress Europe' (1997) 57 *Feminist Review* 93.

motivations obscures from view the broader systemic factors that underlie migration options—prescribing the forms migration takes and the kinds of employment it entails. This is particularly hidden in individualist migration discourses, which tend to focus on the (assumed) qualities of migrants as resourceful cheaters or seekers of easy money. This is not to say the motives for migrating are not economic—often they are—but that the focus on the individual hides the complex structural constraints that make migrating, even with the risks that go with downward mobility and irregularity, the most viable choice.

The increase in and diversification of female migration has to be linked with the global processes that affect economies and societies today.[63] Women have become increasingly responsible not only for 'traditional' (and unpaid) 'women's work', like child care and household tasks, but also for the material wellbeing of children due to family breakdown and dislocation. In this respect, Sassen paints a grim picture of what is happening in many of the so-called third world countries hit by economic liberalisation and discovers systemic links between its costs (unemployment, the move from traditional modes of production to cash crops, government debt) and what she calls the 'feminisation of survival', or the increasing reliance on women to create alternative means of survival for themselves and their families at a time when governments can or will not produce health care, education or subsistence for a large part of their population.[64] The increasing participation of women in paid work can also be linked to the mobilisation of a cheap and flexible female workforce to produce consumer goods in third world factories of multinational companies which have moved there because of lower production costs. In many cases this mobilisation is also the first step into international migration, as it often involves migration from rural areas to industrialised zones. This mobilisation caused by industrialisation, the high turnover in many of these industries (due to employment practices) and accompanying unemployment contribute to the creation of uprooted people drawn into paid labour, which, together with Westernisation, combine to make emigration seem like the only option for many.[65] Hence the increase in female migrants who seek to support their families through migrating and sending home money from better paid work in more affluent countries.

The better paid work is in the West, which (perceiving itself as more or less 'full') at the same time has increasingly closed its gates to labour migration and declared that it does not want more migrant workers. One of the paradoxes of current labour migration is that in fact in all of the EU Member States there exists a demand for migrant workers and, importantly, especially for female migrant workers. This is due to several factors, ranging from the oft-mentioned

[63] For overviews of European trends see, eg, E Kofman, 'Female "Birds of Passage" a Decade Later: Gender and Immigration in the European Union' (1999) 33 *International Migration Review* 269; E Kofman *et al*, *Gender and International Migration in Europe* (London, Routledge, 2000).

[64] S Sassen, 'Women's Burden: Counter-geographies of Globalization and the Feminization of Survival' (2000) 53 *Journal of International Affairs* 503.

[65] S Sassen, *Globalization and Its Discontents* (New York, The New Press, 1998), ch 6.

demographic change in the developed world (which means the population is ageing fast) and increased female participation in the paid workforce, which (especially in Southern European countries where state provision for child care and care of the elderly is scarce) has involved the creation of an ever-growing 'care deficit' to the general shift towards service economies in the developed countries. Migrating for labour such as care and domestic work is tightly related to the growth of the (in particular informal) service sector in the West. The trend towards moving manufacturing off-shore hinges on cheaper labour costs; in the service sector cheap labour has to be imported from the third world to do the necessary but unattractive work. What these two have in common, of course, is that they are 'ways of securing a low-wage labour force and of fighting the demand of organized workers in developed countries'.[66] While some see the unprecedented female mobility between the developing and developed nations as revolutionary as far as traditional gender roles are concerned,[67] the dark side of the coin from the perspective of the EU Member States lies in the largely unacknowledged nature of this demand and the structural factors behind it.[68] In most EU Member States, the low-wage work associated with care functions is typically still considered 'women's work', as men refuse to do it or do so only reluctantly. Non-EU women are in essence being recruited to do the 'second shift' which the women of the West, as market citizens, are no longer willing or able to do. Instead of this being considered as a public problem requiring more equitable burden-sharing in relation to care work in families, the official provision of care services or the official recruitment of foreign labour,[69] the care problem remains (or has become) privatised, explaining, for example, the massive increase in the numbers of Filippina maids and nannies in some EU Member States.[70]

Migrating for work is, however, a risky survival strategy for migrants, not least because of the legal regulation of migration, as most (old) EU Member States have

[66] Sassen, above n 65, at 111.

[67] It can be argued that the increase in female participation in paid work, and especially female migration for work, challenges many of the taken-for-granted stereotypes: this reality shows the inadequacy of the 'male breadwinner' model, and challenges women's 'cultural association with home', the notion that women, as the providers of child care and household maintenance, are place-bound in ways that men (traditionally characterised by independence and mobility outside the home) are not: J Fitzpatrick and K Kelly, 'Gendered Aspects of Migration: Law and the Female Migrant' (1998) 22 *Hastings International and Comparative Law Review* 47.

[68] What also tends to remain hidden is the cost to migrant women themselves, who often leave behind their own children to take care of the children of others, as this enables them to earn the money to support their children and provide them with an education: see, eg, B Ehrenreich and A Hochschild (eds), *Global Woman. Nannies, Maids, and Sex Workers in the New Economy* (New York, Metropolitan Books, 2002) (2002), above ch 2 n 40; R Parreñas, *Servants of Globalization: Women, Migration and Domestic Work* (Stanford, Cal, Stanford University Press, 2001)

[69] See, however, Italy's recent legalisation of domestic workers, which is, however, reactive rather than proactive.

[70] Note also the consequences that this separation of European ('liberated', working women) and 'other' women (their maids) has for feminist reform projects. This dichotomy is false in the sense that it implies that for European women equality is a goal achieved, but it nonetheless reveals how issues of class, nationality and race make achieving equality a very different project for migrant women in Europe.

restricted or practically eliminated the possibilities of third-country nationals migrating to their area for work purposes (with the exception of high-level professionals). The restrictions introduced increasingly at the EU level (such as the visa requirements that apply to most migrant-sending countries) target in particular nationals of states with (perceived) high emigration potential—short term visitors can have visas denied if there is a perceived risk of overstaying.[71] The restrictions, however, only make migration more difficult and dangerous; they do not eliminate the structural reasons for migrating, such as the need for migrant workers in developed countries or the large informal sectors already in place, migrant workers' need to migrate or the social networks that connect the two.[72] As a result, many of those who seek to migrate for low-paid work are channelled into irregular or dependant forms of migration and work.[73] Typically, irregular migrants either migrate legally, for example (especially women) through family reunion or with short-term work permits, and then overstay,[74] or enter irregularly to begin with, usually with the aid of smugglers and the support of networks of acquaintances. This entails the use of fraudulent documents, irregular border crossings, resorting to smugglers who offer their services to prospective migrants, and trafficking in those migrants whose vulnerability makes them apposite targets for exploitation. Irregular status in the country of destination brings with it increased vulnerability, for the security that having a job brings is reduced, and in some cases eliminated, by the enormous potential for exploitation and abuse that goes with being in an irregular situation.

The service industries, especially the feminised sectors of care and domestic work which absorb a large proportion of female migrants, are typically associated with informality and irregularity of working conditions. This state of affairs is tacitly accepted in some EU Member States which, despite official rhetoric, are aware of the enormous usefulness of migrants for their economies, and thus perceive little need dramatically to tackle the grey areas in which illegal and exploitative work is being performed by irregular migrants. This tendency is particularly strong in

[71] See Community Visa Regulation (Council Regulation 539/2001/EC), above n 39. (This, of course, profiles individuals as risks based on the group in which they (are seen to) belong: see R Cholewinski, *Borders and Discrimination in the European Union* (Report for ILPA & MPG, 2002, London and Brussels, ILPA and MPG, 2002.)

[72] Migration is in many ways a self-feeding social process: not only do established (im)migrants form a network that helps newcomers, but migrant workers visiting home tell of the possibilities abroad, thus attracting new migrants: see, eg, D Massey *et al*, 'Theories of International Migration: A Review and Appraisal' (1993) 19 *Population and Development Review* 431; S Castles, 'Why Migration Policies Fail' (2004) 27 *Ethnic and Racial Studies* 205. On how a reliance on informal networks to beat the system fits the trajectory of 'homo sovieticus' in the post-communist CEECs see E Morawska, *Transnational Migrations in the Enlarged European Union: A Perspective from East Central Europe* (EUI Working Papers, RSC No 2000/19, Florence. EUI, 2000).

[73] Similarly, supply side bans on temporary migration, eg for domestic work, can create demand for smuggling by networks that later expand their operations to trafficking for prostitution: see Fitzpatrick and Kelly, above n 67.

[74] It is difficult, if not impossible, accurately to estimate the numbers of migrants that enter informal work in EU Member States through existing legal channels (such as family reunion, short-term labour or study).

countries where the informal economy in general is large (the southern European EU Member States being a classic example). Indeed, Italy's boom in migrant domestic workers relates not only to the (supposed) laxity of its external controls, but the fact that the domestic informal sector is colossal and scarcely controlled (as well as to a lack of adequate state provision to compensate for Italian women's rapidly increased participation in the paid labour force outside the home).[75] It is, of course, something of a generalisation to say that there is a structural need for non-EU women, as a flexible workforce, to do the work Europeans (men or women) are no longer willing to do. For instance, countries like Sweden, which (as noted before) have traditionally offered limited possibilities for informal work and where the state more generously provides child care facilities for working mothers and care for the elderly, the need for migrant workers to take care of domestic and care work has been much more limited, and hence the domestic worker phenomenon is less visible. However, the situation may be changing in this respect in Sweden too as the informal economy is expanding and welfare is becoming increasingly privatised. However, on the whole the growth of phenomena such as migration for domestic and care work shows that the need for these women is deeply embedded in the organisation of European societies.

The downside of this phenomenon for female migrants lies not only in the little room for choice over migration options (for instance family reunion and irregular channels) and the type of work they can get in the countries of destination (as some are, in fact, well-trained but end up being socially mobile downwards in terms of the type of work they do), but also in that female migrants in the informal service sector are often at the mercy of their employers. This applies even to those who have arrived legally and have all the requisite documents in order, as they are by immigration rules often tied to a particular employer who thus has a strong bargaining chip. This is not to mention more extreme situations in which employers have reportedly confiscates migrants' passports, etc.[76] In many cases this means that due to their precarious migration status informal or irregular workers, such as many domestic workers, are extremely vulnerable to sexual abuse and economic exploitation by employers.[77] Importantly, redress for this kind of exploitation is not easily available, as the precarious status of the employee means that going to the police entails the risk of expulsion rather than any possibility that the charges will be taken seriously. Domestic and sexual violence, for instance, is generally hidden and legitimised through systematic non-intervention by the police and judicial authorities in EU Member States, even when it involves a husband abusing his wife. It is not hard to imagine why an irregular female migrant,

[75] See V Chell-Robinson, 'Female Migrants in Italy: Coping in a Country of New Immigration' in F Anthias and G Lazaridis (eds), *Gender and Migration in Southern Europe* (Oxford, Berg, 2000); M Orsini-Jones and F Gattullo, 'Migrant Women in Italy: National Trends and Local Perspectives' in *ibid.* On domestic workers' organisation, see J Andall, 'Organizing Domestic Workers in Italy' in *ibid.*

[76] Lutz, above n 62, Kofman *et al*, above n 63.

[77] On the abuse suffered by domestic workers see, eg, Fitzpatrick and Kelly, above n 67, G Lazaridis, 'Filippino and Albanian Women Migrant Workers in Greece: Multiple Layers of Oppression' in Anthias and Lazaridis (eds), above n 75.

who often does not possess sufficient language skills or knowledge of her rights, would believe her employer when he says reporting his behaviour will not benefit her—something that is usually true.

This situation is not the result of a conspiracy against these women, but rather of the coming together of several factors, ranging from female migrants' low social status (due to gender as well as race and class) to the official reluctance to admit their usefulness as a flexible workforce (as that would require empowerment—and, inevitably, loss of flexibility). The destination states' ambivalence about recognising the plight of migrant workers and the structural need for their labour is evident in their unwillingness to become parties to the UN International Convention on the Protection of the Rights of All Migrant Workers and Members of Their Families.[78] The Convention, which explicitly extends human rights to migrant workers (and a core set of rights to those with irregular status) was adopted in 1990 and finally entered into force in July 2003. The Convention has, however, not been signed or ratified by a single EU Member State—in fact, practically all current parties to the Convention are major source countries of migrants such as the Philippines, Mexico, Morocco and Colombia.[79] Migrant-receiving countries see many of the Convention's obligations towards migrants (especially regarding economic and social rights) as costly, and the extension of some of the rights to irregular migrants as an incentive to migrate 'illegally', rather than a way of protecting irregular migrants who are vulnerable.[80]

The general situation of female migrants engaged in domestic and care work differs from that of women in prostitution, in that domestic and care work is considered 'legitimate' work despite the gender-specificity and informality that go with it. Yet migration for domestic and care work has a number of important links with migration for prostitution. Not the least significant connection is that both domestic/care work and prostitution can and do involve trafficking, and often for the same reasons, as both share the vulnerability that comes with irregularity and low status. Both are often performed in arduous conditions, with unsocial hours and usually entail hard and ill-protected work. Both are 'female' labour and draw female migrants for lack of better possibilities, albeit with the major difference that prostitution is particularly gendered (after all, domestic work *can* be performed by a man[81]) and, as it exists today, is premised on the gender-specific notions that demand that *women* (or children) perform it *for men*. Yet basically the same structural factors go a long way to explaining why the majority of women in prostitution in Western and (increasingly) Eastern European cities are (im)migrants;

[78] Hereafter the ICMW. For the text of the Convention, see UN Doc A/RES/45/158.

[79] The ICMW has 34 parties (May 2006).

[80] For a discussion on the actual modifications that the IMWC might (or might not) necessitate in European countries see, eg, D Vanheule *et al*, 'The Significance of the UN Migrant Workers' Convention of 18 December 1990 in The Event of Ratification by Belgium' (2005) 6 *European Journal of Migration and Law* 285. For further discussion of the ICMW, see below ch 6.

[81] See Chell-Robinson, above n 75, at 119–20, who notes an interesting pattern among domestic workers in Rome: as trained female migrants (nurses, etc) from the Philippines move 'up' to better jobs, their positions in domestic work are taken over by Filipino men.

the trend of western European women moving out of prostitution, to be replaced by other women who have fewer or no options, is just the most evident case.[82]

In addition to the gender-specific nature of prostitution, but related to it, the main difference between domestic/care work and prostitution is that the latter tends to be more stigmatised, more dangerous and more illegal, especially in the migration context. Exact patterns are difficult to establish, as prostitution as 'non-proper' work tends to be even more hidden than informal domestic work, but some comments about the connection with migration policy can be made. With a few exceptions (the Dutch one being the most famous), prostitution is not classified as work in EU Member States' legislation. Most Member States more or less tolerate prostitution by their nationals, however, at least as long as it entails no involvement by a third party, like a pimp, or does not cause a public nuisance. As was seen in Chapter 3, with some help from the European Court of Justice this 'tolerance' was widened to 'EU citizens' practising prostitution in another Member State, if the Member State in question accepts prostitution[83] (which would exclude, for instance, Sweden) and, more recently, based on the Association Agreements, to nationals of (then) applicant countries when 'genuinely self-employed'.[84] While the latter are of relevance for those Polish, Czech (etc) women who wish to and can migrate independently to practise prostitution in an EU Member State, the majority of women who would migrate for prostitution in the EU derive no benefit, as for them the possibility of migrating legally for prostitution is explicitly or implicitly denied by Member States (including the Netherlands), which, considering prostitution not a legitimate form of work *for non-EU nationals*, do not give work permits or visas for that purpose. Yet some of them apparently consider prostitution to be work, for when third country nationals are discovered to be practising prostitution in Member State they are expelled as working irregularly.

With trafficking, however, the problem is not just that women who want to migrate to work in prostitution cannot, but that women who do not particularly want to or strive for it are more or less forced to because of socio-economic imperatives and the need for assistance in order to migrate for (any) work under the current migration regimes. In terms of occupational choice, prostitution tends to be the last option short of not migrating.[85] As was discussed above, the line between

[82] In fact, considering how relatively well-paid prostitution can be compared to, eg, domestic work, it is revealing that so many migrant women do choose less well-paid work over prostitution.

[83] Joined Cases 115 and 116/81 *Adoui & Cornuaille*, [1982] ECR 1665.

[84] Case C-268/99 *Jany and Others*, [2001] ECR I-8615.

[85] Note that with gradual socio-economic improvement in the CEECs their role as source countries of women in prostitution in general, and certainly as regards trafficking victims, has decreased; at the same time countries such as the Ukraine remain important source countries. See, eg, D Hughes, 'The "Natasha" Trade: The Transnational Shadow Market of Trafficking in Women' (2000) 53 *Journal of International Affairs* 625; T Denisova, 'Trafficking in Women and Children for Purposes of Sexual Exploitation: The Criminological Aspect' (2001) 6(3–4) *Trends in Organized Crime* 30; D Hughes and T Denisova, 'The Transnational Political Criminal Nexus of Trafficking in Women from Ukraine' (2001) 6(3–4) *Trends in Organized Crime* 43.

trafficking and smuggling is a fluctuating one, as the two are interlinked through the complex patterns that allocate (migrant) women to low-paid jobs, reward them for bodily objectification, and allow hidden forms of coercion by powerful actors in the informal/criminal sector.[86] Migration rules mean that in most cases even if a woman wants to migrate (be it for prostitution or other work), she has to have some help to reach a Member State and to work there, as even informal networks of co-nationals cannot provide her with the necessary assistance to cross the obstacles put in the way of legal migration. Providers of irregular entry and employment are increasingly organised and sophisticated, and there is no guarantee that the smugglers are not in fact traffickers, especially if the woman is offered a package deal in which the smugglers/traffickers agree to arrange both entry and subsequent employment. The end result can be abuse and exploitation in the country of destination, with extortion (especially linked to involvement in stigmatised activities or irregular status) and violence, substandard living conditions and confiscation of earnings. The same scenario can meet women who are approached with offers of typical barmaid/nanny/maid work and those who know about possible involvement in prostitution.[87] In both cases, come the police raid, expulsion as an undocumented migrant is a real possibility.

Seen from a migration perspective, trafficking in women for sexual exploitation is the area in which moral panic over uncontrolled flows of non-nationals meets moral panic over promiscuous female sexuality, with familiar consequences. On one hand, migrant women who enter, stay or work in EU Member States irregularly are precisely the kind of unwanted aliens who are seen as 'flooding in'. As the increase in controls has been intensifying, those who manage to get in are likely to have engaged in some sort of foul play, thus exposing themselves to the label of (migrant) criminal. Being engaged in prostitution, moreover, for female migrants tends to be like burgling or stealing for male migrants: the stereotypical 'criminal activity of migrants'—with the telling exception that prostitution in itself is not criminal in most EU Member States. Effectively criminalised are non-EU citizen women who have been tainted by commercial sex and involvement in violating the boundaries of the emerging European polity. While the ambiguity about prostitution as criminal/legal should raise questions about the reasons behind it, in practice it has merely meant that when foreign women are found during a brothel raid they are apprehended, typically found to have insufficient documentation or to be engaged in illegal activities, and expelled without anyone bothering to ask how they got there. On the other hand, and to a lesser degree (due to the varied

86 See above ch 2.

87 Existing studies show no agreement as to the proportion of women belonging to the two groups—some studies find that the majority of women have been duped and coerced into prostitution, while others have found cases where the majority of women wanted to migrate for prostitution. And then there are the cases in between, which may actually form the largest group: women who wanted to migrate, not ruling out involvement in prostitution but with unrealistic assumptions about what it entails in practice. Compare J Vocks and J Nijboer, 'The Promised Land: A Study of Trafficking in Women from Central and Eastern Europe to the Netherlands' (2000) 8 *European Journal on Criminal Policy and Research* 379.

conditions involved in trafficking-related exploitation), (some) migrant women exploited in prostitution also fit the frame of 'sex slaves'. As such they are typically considered innocent, gullible women who have been duped by traffickers and middlemen, who are the 'real' criminals, demonised as members of precisely the dangerous migrant criminal networks the moral panic sees as the epitome of migration.

Yet in a migration discourse most migrant women exploited and trafficked as 'sex slaves' are not 'real' victims either, because they are still irregular migrants; they are seen as having contributed to their own victimisation, not only by believing the traffickers' promises, but (perhaps more importantly) by wanting to make 'easy money' by coming to the West. This label of 'victims who are not really victims' particularly applies to those women who knew in advance that they would be working in prostitution, and are thus susceptible to being stigmatised as 'migrant prostitutes' who asked for what they got. Interestingly, the only actor in the trafficking equation who remains completely anonymous, if not invisible in the migration discourse, is the indispensable (usually) non-(im)migrant prostitution customer, for whose entertainment migrant women are trafficked in.[88] This is particularly remarkable considering how often they may have reason to suspect (from her behaviour) that the prostitute they visit is actually a trafficking victim. The not unusual stories of the customer taking pity on the trafficked prostitute (and letting her, for example, use his cellular phone to call for help) should nonetheless be contrasted with the vast majority of customers who do not seem to care whether or not the prostitute serving them is the victim of exploitation.

4.2.2 Helping Trafficking Victims through Short-term Residence Permits?

The setting in which a trafficked woman's story of trafficking and abuse will be considered is framed by her identification as an 'illegal alien' engaged in the semi-criminal activity of prostitution. Although, thanks to NGO and IGO documentation and increased media attention, the EU Member States are now faced with a situation where this kind of abuse can no longer go completely unrecognised, and the need to tackle at least the most atrocious forms of trafficking has found its way to policy documents, this has in essence caused no rethinking of the broader frame of current migration policy. At present stopping immigration remains the foundation of the 'European' anti-trafficking policy in the sense that Member States' anti-trafficking laws and the Council Framework Decision of 2002 (see Chapter 5) focus on the criminal aspects of arranging this exploitative migration, and prevention is most often synonymous with prevention from coming ('keeping the women home') and whatever protection is given is tied up with the interests of

[88] While demand for cheap labour often pops up in policy documents, until quite recently this has related to the demand for informal labour in sweatshops, agricultural work, etc, and not prostitution. In feminist literature the issue of demand has of course been discussed for much longer and almost exclusively vis-á-vis prostitution. See further chapter 7.

catching the 'big fish' who organise movement across borders. Trafficking, rarely recognised as violence against women, is considered primarily as an abusive form of irregular immigration (an aberration if you will). This is evident not only when comparing the estimates of the numbers of women trafficked in with the numbers of women who are identified as trafficked in (and/or given protection, conditional or otherwise), but the 'migration mentality' that affects anti-trafficking activities can also be illustrated by looking at the treatment of those victimised by traffickers in the countries of destination.

For instance in the Netherlands, which has had anti-trafficking legislation for decades, anti-trafficking measures like giving the police a 'list of indicators' to identify victims of trafficking when they come into contact with possibly trafficked women (the list includes factors like lack of travel documents and having to hand over a major part of earnings, restrictions on freedom of movement) have resulted in increasing numbers of women being identified as trafficked. Yet, the evident tension in this approach is that the lack of papers is also evidence of irregular status under immigration rules, and thus a large number of trafficking victims are likely to be simply expelled from the country as undocumented workers or irregular migrants.[89] In cases where victims *are* identified, the expulsion of such individuals (who are, of course, not even the majority) is simply suspended (the so-called 'B-9 regulation'[90]), while they decide on pressing charges; this so-called reflection period lasts up to three months.[91] If the victims decide to press charges, they can obtain a short-term permit to stay with some assistance for the duration of the criminal procedure, after which they must leave the Netherlands; if they decide not to report the crime, they must leave the country immediately.[92] From the start the police have not seemed very enthusiastic about informing (identified) victims of their options (apart from prosecution) and referring them to assisting NGOs (mainly STV). While initially this might have been considered a teething problem, it is still reported that 'in a not inconsiderable number of cases' victims are not informed of the possibility of the reflection period but forced to decide immediately, contributing to the low number of reported cases.[93]

[89] It is impossible to know how many, as most statistics are not disaggregated enough; but considering that only 160 applications for B-9 (see below n 90) were submitted in 2002 and that estimates of actual trafficking victims amount to some thousands, the number is not insignificant: see A Korvinus, *Trafficking in Human Beings. Third Report of the Dutch National Rapporteur* (The Hague, Bureau NRM, 2005), 61. See also below ch 5.

[90] S B-9 of the Aliens Act Implementation Guidelines, previously known as the 'B-17 regulation' (after the original s B-17 of the Vreemdelingencirculaire, added in 1988).

[91] The importance of the reflection period (in countries where the permit is tied to criminal proceedings) cannot be over-emphasised. Studies show consistently that victims of trafficking need time more than anything else to recover from the shock and trauma, to realise what they have experienced, and to consider what their options are.

[92] On the law see A Korvinus, *Trafficking in Human Beings. First Report of the Dutch National Rapporteur* (The Hague, Bureau NRM, 2002), and Korvinus, above n 89. If the victim has not yet worked in the Netherlands in prostitution, the decision on reporting the crime has to be taken immediately.

[93] Korvinus, above n 92, at 73. See also Korvinus, *Trafficking in Human Beings. Second Report of the Dutch National Rapporteur* (The Hague, Bureau NRM, 2003) especially ch 3 for figures on the application of s B-9.

The draconian 'talk or walk' rules make seemingly perfect sense from a migration control perspective, as they do not reward the 'illegal alien' for her irregular entry and residence, but merely take advantage of any eventual information she may have on her traffickers. However, the rules and their application suffer from insufficient attention to the broader combination of factors that make reporting the offence in exchange for obtaining the extremely limited exception (or rather delay) to the general migration policy less attractive than disappearing underground, even if that means continued exploitation, or immediate expulsion, with all the risks that go with it.[94] These include the trauma caused by trafficking and related abuse, fear of reprisals against the victim or family members back home, the irregular migration situation, distrust of the police as corrupt (often due to experiences in countries of origin), the lack of local knowledge, the existence of large debt to traffickers and few provisions specifically assisting trafficking victims. In addition to completely ignoring the enormous risks that reporting a crime against traffickers entails for the victim, who is typically in a very disadvantaged and vulnerable position, this casts a shadow on the international commitments that the state has under human rights obligations. The continued sexual victimisation of female migrants in the hands of traffickers and exploiters, as well as the very real risk of re-trafficking after expulsion, raises serious questions about the state's violation of its obligations to *ensure* and protect the basic human rights of all within its jurisdiction without discrimination, regardless of their irregular situation or status. Even from a limited migration control perspective the aim of expelling 'migrant sex workers' can hardly be called a satisfactory solution, as it may (or may not, if she goes underground) rid the country of a small number of 'illegal migrant sex workers', but does not tackle or dismantle the trafficking network that will remain operational.

The same problems (non-identification of victims, permission to stay being conditional on giving evidence) that plague the Dutch approach are evident, if in a less accentuated form, in the Italian case study. Italy's 1998 unified text on immigration provides for an approach for the protection of identified victims of trafficking ('victims of severe exploitation').[95] The victims are to be given a six-month residence permit on humanitarian grounds; the permit is not in principle tied to testifying but instead to participating in a programme of social assistance arranged by NGOs.[96]

[94] See also below ch 5.

[95] Testo unico delle leggi sull'immigrazione (legislative decree no 286 of 25 July 1998), [1998] GU 191, Art 18: '[w]hen, during police operations or inquiries or proceedings for a criminal offence . . . or during aid interventions of social services of local bodies, situations of violence or serious exploitations of a foreigner are found, and concrete dangers emerge for his or her life, as effects of trying to escape from the influence of an association dedicated to one of the above mentioned crimes, or because of the declarations made during preliminary inquiries or during the proceeding, the chief of the local Police headquarter, also on Public Prosecutor's proposal, or with the favourable opinion of the same authority, releases a special permit of staying to give the opportunities to the foreigners to escape from the violence and from the influence of the criminal organisation and to participate in an assistance and social integration programme.'

[96] Or, rather, the release of a permit does not necessarily imply direct judicial co-operation by the victim, as two 'paths' are envisaged; the judicial one (victim will co-operate with the police and prosecutor) and the 'social path', which does not oblige the victim to press charges.

The permit is renewable, and allows the holder to seek work (to regularise the situation more permanently). The provision of the 1998 law, which survived from an earlier decree that never became law,[97] 'de-links', at least in theory, recovery programmes and protection from the interests of prosecution. It is more humane and involves more NGO intervention than the Dutch one.[98] Regarding prostitution, the system can be perceived as relying, at least to some extent, on the perceived need to rescue 'innocent' women from prostitution and return them to a 'normal' life. However, it is reported that unless the victims of trafficking immediately declare themselves as such, it is likely that they will be considered irregular aliens and will, after a period of detention, be ordered to leave Italian territory (and if they are apprehended a second time they will be expelled).[99] It has also been reported that in practice there appears to be a degree of friction between not only immigration officials and the police but also the NGOs involved; for instance the police are not willing to provide possible victims with the right to stay if they refuse to testify, more or less coercing them to co-operate with the proceedings.[100]

In contrast to the longer evolution of the trafficking-related migration policy exception in the Dutch and Italian contexts, until 2004 Sweden did not have a system of victim protection as far as trafficking victims were concerned, albeit that exceptions to the implementation of immigration rules (on expulsion) could in principle be made on humanitarian grounds.[101] The problem of irregular migration and trafficking for prostitution has emerged in Sweden only lately and is not as widespread as in the other two Member States, where prostitution, migrant involvement in it and trafficking for it have been visible for longer. In the wake of European initiatives (see below), in 2003 the Swedish Government proposed to insert a new provision into the Aliens Act to allow for the issue of a time-limited residence permit to a victim or witness 'if this is deemed necessary in order to conclude a preliminary investigation or the main proceedings in a criminal case'.[102] The new provision took effect from October 2004.[103] It is clearly an instrument of

[97] Decree 477 of 13 Sept 1996, [1996] GU 477, passed by the Dini Government.

[98] On the 1998 law see Geddes, above n 13, 158. On the involvement of the women's movement see D Danna, 'Italy: The Never-ending Debate' in J Outshoorn (ed), *The Politics of Prostitution. Women's Movements, Democratic States and the Globalisation of Sex Commerce* (Cambridge, Cambridge University Press, 2004), at 169–75. On the intervention experiences of NGOs see F Carchedi *et al* (eds), *I Colori della Notte. Migrazioni, sfruttamento sessuale, esperienze di intervento sociale* (Milan, Franco Angeli, 2000), part 3.

[99] E Niesner and C Jones-Pauly, *Trafficking in Women in Europe: Prosecution and Victim Protection in a European Context* (Bielefeld, Kleine Verlag, 2001), at 79–80; I Orfano, *Country Report: Italy* (Research based on case studies of victims of trafficking in human beings in 3 EU Member States, Antwerp, Payoke et al, 2003).

[100] A van der Kleij, *Provisions for Victims of Trafficking in Bonded Sexual Labour, ie Prostitution—in 6 European Countries—Belgium, Germany, Italy, the Netherlands, Spain and the United Kingdom* (Amsterdam, BlinN, 2002); Orfano, above n 99. See also below ch 5.

[101] This, however, rarely took place in practice. See Stiftelsen Kvinnoforum, *Översyn av socialt stöd till kvinnor, flickor och pojkar offer för människohandel i Sverige* (Stockholm, SK, 2002).

[102] Proposal 2003/04:35, Människosmuggling och tidsbegränsat uppehållstillstånd för målsägande och vittnen m.m. (20 Nov 2003). See also SOU 2002:69, Människosmuggling och offer för människohandel.

[103] Lagen 2004:206 om ändring i utlänningslagen (1989:529).

police investigation and prosecution rather than victim assistance; an application for such a temporary permit can be made only by the authority responsible for the police investigation (Chapter 2, section 4a of the Act), who is also the only one allowed to appeal against a negative decision by the migration authority (Chapter 7, section 3a of the Act). There is no exact time limit on the permit; depending on the complexity of the investigation (or appeal against the judgment), the residence permit may be extended upon application by the prosecutor. On the positive side, during their stay in Sweden victims will be entitled to health care and medical attention as well as social welfare.

The spirit of restrictiveness is echoed, and indeed the Swedish law is in large part inspired, by the 2002 Commission Proposal for a Directive on a short-term residence permit for victims of trafficking—or, rather, those (and only those) who agree to 'co-operate' with the authorities against their traffickers.[104] The Commission Proposal, which had as its legal basis Article 63(3) TEC,[105] and which therefore lumped together trafficking and smuggling victims, was extensively criticised for (again) failing to recognise that trafficking (and smuggling) victims are not 'migrant criminals'.[106] Despite talk on recognising the rights of those trafficked, the proposal was clearly based on the potential usefulness of some victims as sources of information rather than the remotest consideration for the actual situation in which exploited migrant women find themselves.[107] Political compromise on the proposal was reached in November 2003 (with the UK and Ireland opting out), and it was formally adopted in April 2004, the Member States being given until August 2006 to comply with it.[108] The Directive, which covers smuggling only optionally, provides for a (domestically determined) period of reflection after which a temporary residence permit for at least six months can[109] be given (public policy and national security permitting[110]) if the victim is useful in terms of investigations or judicial proceedings, has shown a clear intention to co-operate and has severed all relations with exploiters. The permit is not renewed

[104] Commission Proposal for a Council Directive on the short-term residence permit issued to victims of action to facilitate illegal immigration or trafficking in human beings who cooperate with the competent authorities, COM(2002)71 final, [2002] OJ C 126 E/393.

[105] Competence to adopt measures on immigration policy (in areas of conditions of entry and residence, standards on procedures for the issue of long-term visas and residence permits and illegal immigration and illegal residence).

[106] See Human Rights Watch, *Commentary on the European Commission Proposal for a Council Directive 'on the short-term residence permit issued to victims of action to facilitate illegal immigration or trafficking in human beings who cooperate with the competent authorities'* (Briefing Paper, Brussels, HRW, 2002).

[107] On the corresponding US law, see W Chapkis, 'Trafficking, Migration, and the Law. Protecting Innocents, Punishing Immigrants' (2003) 17 *Gender & Society* 923.

[108] See Council Directive 2004/81/EC of 29 Apr 2004 on the residence permit issued to third-country nationals who are victims of trafficking in human beings or who have been the subject of an action to facilitate illegal immigration, who cooperate with the competent authorities [2004] OJ L 261/19.

[109] Unlike in the original proposal, there seems to be no obligation to give such a permit if the conditions are fulfilled.

[110] Art 8 of the Directive, above n 108.

if the conditions cease to be fulfilled,[111] and can be withdrawn on grounds of 'in particular' (the list is not exhaustive) renewed contact with the suspected exploiters, authorities' belief in fraudulent co-operation or a fraudulent complaint, public policy or national security, lacking co-operation on the part of the victim and discontinued proceedings.[112]

In the final Directive the treatment offered during and after the reflection period was further reduced and made even more discretionary than in the Commission proposal; as a result the fact that victims of trafficking have typically experienced repeated and often aggravated sexual violence is barely mentioned (see below). During the period that the short-term permit covers, victims are to be guaranteed a minimum standard of living; access to emergency medical treatment; translation and interpretation ('where appropriate'); (optional) free legal aid; and 'necessary medical or other assistance to the third-country nationals concerned, who do not have sufficient resources and have special needs, such as pregnant women, the disabled or victims of sexual violence or other forms of violence'.[113] Member States are also expected to define the rules for victims' access to the labour market, vocational training and education during the period of the residence permit.[114] Additional conditions on participation in schemes for third country nationals can be imposed on permit-holders.[115] While the Directive does not foreclose the adoption of more favourable national provisions, it does seem less than probable that there will be significant developments in the direction of increased openness to the victims' plight, as most Member States are adopting this kind of system for the first time and are thus unlikely to start by greatly exceeding the scope or benefits provided for by the Directive. Indeed, considering the perceived need to be seen as tough on irregular migration, the Directive might even encourage Member States which have in some respects more generous provisions (most notably Italy) to reduce the 'generosity' of their existing systems so as not to 'attract' unwanted immigrants.

Melis is right when she states bluntly that in a migration setting protecting the rights of trafficking victims through residence permits is, as regards the Member States, 'against their actual immigration policies' that seek to discourage migration.[116] Thus, the Directive, while foreseeing that a limited number of exploited victims (who are of use and thus deserving) can stay temporarily, also entails an inherent desire to minimise the number of people who could make use of the instrument and, deep down, the assumption (as with asylum-seeking earlier) that

[111] Ibid, Art 13. After the period the permit covers is over, normal immigration law applies (note, however, that the preamble states that Member States should consider the fact that the victim already has a residence permit issued on the basis of this Directive if the victim applies to stay on another ground).

[112] Ibid, Art 14.

[113] Ibid, Art 9.

[114] The formulation (maybe on purpose) does not specify whether this means freedom of choice over whether to allow such access or only over how this access is arranged. See ibid, Art 11.

[115] Ibid, Art 12.

[116] B Melis, *Negotiating Europe's Immigration Frontiers* (The Hague, Kluwer Law International, 2001), at 190.

the opportunity will be misused by clever migrants looking for loopholes.[117] This will probably mean that in the future 'bogus' trafficking victims will emerge, just as 'bogus' asylum-seekers have; if the consequences were to be analogous to the consequences for asylum-seeking (in other words further tightening of the regime due to unfounded claims), that would mean the (already strict) conditions for receiving such a permit would be increasingly tightened. So it remains likely that those 'true' trafficking victims who actually benefit from this kind of limited opportunity will be few and far between, and those who do benefit will be the most useful ones, that is 'useful' in the sense of agreeing and being able to help to capture the 'real' criminals, those having some kind of information on trafficking operations beyond their individual experience. Those with little relevant information (those drugged or isolated, or children) or those with little reason to co-operate, for instance due to having relatives who have been threatened by traffickers in the country of origin or having the economic imperative to work no matter what, are hardly ideal candidates for success.

To criticise the Directive for its meagre content is of course not to argue that temporary residence permits for a specific category of trafficking victims would be the best way of approaching the issue in the first place. Indeed, the whole idea of a specific avenue for (some) trafficking victims seems inherently the product of a logic that is so focused on restrictions that the only way to approach any problems is through carving out limited exceptions to generally ungenerous rules. Rather than further developing a specific regime for trafficking victims (even one that would envisage a permit for *all* victims, with family reunion rights for their children, which has sometimes been suggested), their treatment might have been integrated into the general asylum/humanitarian protection structures with the right to stay and work accordingly. Moreover, an almost completely unexplored issue is some trafficking victims' potential right to asylum based on the Geneva Convention or other humanitarian leave to stay based on the principle of non-refoulement, owing to, among others, a real risk of retribution, violence and/or re-trafficking if returned to country of transit or origin.[118] Extending the right to asylum or subsidiary protection, for instance based on the threat of torture or inhuman or degrading treatment, on trafficking grounds could be justified, and even required, in some cases where the country of origin cannot guarantee protection from further violence, for example re-trafficking.[119] Certainly, there is no

[117] This tension is also noted by S Peers, 'Key Legislative Developments on Migration in the European Union' (2004) 6 *European Journal of Migration and Law* 67, at 87.

[118] The European Parliament has mentioned (but not elaborated on) the possibility of seeking asylum for trafficking victims (see, eg, European Parliament Resolution on trafficking in women for the purpose of sexual exploitation, [1998] OJ C/14/39). On asylum and trafficking see also R Hopkins and J Nijboer, *Towards Policy and Practice Recommendations for Dealing with the Growing Problem of Women Trafficking: A Dutch Response* (Conference Paper from the University of Nottingham Trafficking in Persons Conference, 27–28 June 2003).

[119] Note that the new Council Directive 2004/83/EC, above n 32, explicitly covers gender-based persecution, and in some circumstances extends to persecution committed by non-state actors. For arguments on the trafficking–asylum nexus see J Demir, *Trafficking of Women for Sexual Exploitation: A Gender-Based Well-Founded Fear?* (New Issues in Refugee Research, Working Paper No 80, Geneva,

reason why the ban on refoulement, covered by Article 3 of the European Convention of Human Rights, should not apply with regard to trafficking situations, as in any case the fact that there might be a concrete danger of torture or inhuman or degrading treatment or punishment in case of repatriation should raise questions about the risks involved.[120] Yet while the necessity of examining repatriation risks and protection needs both before and after return to the country of origin features in some best practice documents, there is thus far little by way of official affirmation of this in the individual Member States or the Union.[121]

Given the existing political climate, the lack of a visible link between trafficking and asylum (or even humanitarian leave) is unsurprising, considering that in order to make sense any such move towards a more expansive interpretation would very likely have to go hand in hand with making the general migration/asylum regime less tilted towards control, rather than trying to block existing gaps in the restrictive regime. While this is desirable, not least because it would make trafficking less useful for migrants and thus profitable, it is improbable that this will occur in the short term, considering the general converging tendencies in the Members States to interpret the right to asylum and migration issues restrictively rather than expansively. Still, that is no excuse for failing to make the connection. In the meantime it is relatively clear that residence permit schemes, no matter how perfected, can never 'solve' the trafficking problem. This is not only because they lack the logical basis that would recognise the harm that trafficking victims have suffered and the dangers they often face, and thus fail to understand the motivations of trafficking victims in deciding whether or not to collaborate (owing to psychological distress, trauma and a reasonable fear of reprisals against themselves) and the very limited advantage they can derive from a permit that allows them to stay only a few months (and then sends them to exactly the same conditions they sought to escape—with the additional risk of retaliation and re-trafficking). It is also because even when these permit systems are refined to reach more trafficking victims, they do nothing about the systemic consequences of restrictive immigration policies or about the structural reasons that make people migrate, however illegal, exploitative and dangerous migration is.

UNHCR, 2003) and (vis-à-vis the US) M Raghu, 'Sex Trafficking of Thai Women and the United States Asylum Law Response' (1997) 12 *Georgetown Immigration Law Journal* 145.

[120] That Art 3 ECHR implies an obligation on the part of the state not to remove someone where there are grounds for believing that upon such expulsion the person will face a real risk of being subjected to treatment contrary to Art 3 was first decided by the ECtHR in *Soering v United Kingdom* (1989) 11 EHRR 439. Even though the burden of proof is high, the argument that trafficking victims could rely on Art 3 could be based on the one hand on cases such as *Cruz Varas v Sweden* (1992) 14 EHRR 1, *Vilvarajah v UK* (1992) 14 EHRR 248 and *Chahal v UK* (1997) 23 EHRR 413 (restating the applicability of Art 3 to expulsion) and on the other hand on *Ahmed v Austria* (1997) 24 EHRR 278 and *HLR v France* (1998) 26 EHRR 29 (on the sufficiency of non-state cause of danger when there is a a real risk and the state cannot provide protection).

[121] On this see also below ch 6, which discusses repatriation and human rights obligations as well as the new Council of Europe Convention on action against trafficking in human beings, which was expected to aim at a proper human rights balance on anti-trafficking co-operation.

4.3 CONCLUDING REMARKS

While the Europeanisation of migration and asylum policies has brought trafficking onto the migration agenda, and is producing much convergence on issues relevant to trafficking (most specifically vis-à-vis the residence permit), the results at present point to mixed success at best. Some Member States which have not been affected by or taken trafficking seriously are waking up to the subject, not least because of the trafficking–migration link. Yet, at present, in the response to trafficking migration-related security concerns meet the ambiguities of prostitution policies; the moral condemnation of prostitution as *female* deviance, together with the de facto criminalisation of irregular migration, means that only a marginal number of trafficked women are recognised as victims of sexual and physical violence. Even when there is a space for acknowledging their victimisation, their irregularity makes them 'lesser' (or less 'natural') victims, which is evident in the absence of any protection system that would secure assistance and protection to *all* exploited migrants and ensure that they are not subject to further violence. The effective criminalisation of migrants and the lack of legal and safe migration opportunities, especially for women, are major factors in exposing prospective migrants to vulnerability, marginalisation and criminality. At present, migration laws give traffickers the opportunity and the tools with which to control their victims. While trafficking is a complex phenomenon the prevention of which cannot be reduced to migration opportunities alone (on this in conjunction with 'root causes' approaches see Chapter 7), the effect of the migration regimes in Member States remains a crucial factor in exposing women to the risk of trafficking.

The bottom line is that ultimately the success of measures such as criminalisation of trafficking or granting a right of stay to victims crucially depends on the parameters of (im)migration policies in general: criminal provisions targeting trafficking can tackle trafficking to some degree (see Chapter 5), but the residence permit cannot become a sufficiently widespread practice in a setting where the trend is to criminalise migration itself. It is thus necessary to ask what kind of migration policy would be better suited to the aim of reducing the harm of trafficking, and how the process of Europeanisation of (im)migration policy interacts with this. The obvious, if very general, answer is that a more open policy for labour migration is needed; it should start with the recognition in the Member States that migration is not by nature a criminal or a security problem, but a global phenomenon providing opportunities as well as challenges for migrants, non-migrants and their societies. At the same time, trafficking also depends on a generally gendered labour market, as well as on prostitution not being attractive enough an option for women to guarantee a supply of willing, cheap prostitutes even when recognised as 'work'. This should not only stir up some debate on the place of sexuality in terms of European values, but also on how legitimate it would be to open the door to the free movement of *only* sex workers as opposed to other categories of workers. Finally, the economic justification for welcoming migrants of course (almost too) neatly fits in with EC/EU integration, as it is driven by economic imperatives. However, at this point, when the EU is striving so hard to become more than an economic actor, failing to connect (im)migration to more principled issues of freedom of movement, the fight against racism, xenophobia and nationalism and economic and social justice is not exactly impressive, in particular as these concerns are accentuated in the light of the current security/crime discourse. This dimension is the focus of the next chapter.

5

Criminal Justice Co-operation Against Trafficking

AN UNDERSTANDING OF trafficking in women for the purpose of sexual exploitation as a criminal justice issue is at the core of anti-trafficking efforts, in the sense that it is through the means of criminal law that the problem is mainly tackled in domestic systems and also as regards the direct competence of the European Union. A criminal justice approach is in a way commonsensical, due to the links trafficking has with the exploitation of prostitution, which is often dealt with as a law and order or a criminal problem, and with irregular migration, as it is the concern over trafficking as a form of 'illegal' (criminal) migration that has made it the target of crime prevention and crime control measures. The linking of trafficking with concerns over international (or, rather, transnational) crime and security in particular has ensured that there have been significant efforts towards addressing trafficking, both in the most affected Member States and at the level of the EU vis-à-vis the Area of Freedom, Security and Justice. The criminal justice approach to trafficking is a response that resonates with the current crime and security discourse, under which criminal law harmonisation and more effective enforcement seem the (apparently) easy and necessary solution to a tricky problem. Thus criminalisation and criminal harmonisation are the clear targets of the 1997 Joint Action on trafficking and the subsequent Council Framework Decision on trafficking in 2002, whereas Europol and Eurojust are hailed as the facilitators of co-operation on the ground.

Yet, just as prostitution and migration are much more than a law and order problem (and, as some would argue, not really that at all), trafficking also invokes far more complex issues than just those relating to law enforcement, transnational organised crime and criminal law harmonisation. Indeed, much like the so-called 'war on terrorism', the (organised) crime rhetoric often tends to cover up simplistic cause and effect analyses that are used to justify a repressive response. In the case of trafficking, the response is targeted at this 'modern form of slavery'; at the same time the moral panic over migration and sexuality is mobilised to defend subsequent demands for tighter entry controls, law enforcement measures and morality-based crime prevention. This raises several questions. As regards crime control measures in the Member States, one must ask whether these can inadvertently worsen the situation of those most vulnerable while doing little to thwart the trade.

Since the interests served by an intensified law enforcement response are not necessarily those of trafficking victims, the drawbacks to them can be significant. In the framework of an Area of Freedom, Security and Justice, the question is how the law and order fight against trafficking resonates not only with security but with freedom and justice. It is also not clear how much harmonisation is possible or even desirable, considering the variations in prostitution and trafficking operations and attitudes to them between Member States (regarding, for example, penalties), not to mention the more principled questions of the aim of criminalisation.

The following chapter will chart these issues with regard to current anti-trafficking policies in the European context. The general argument of this chapter is twofold. First, it is claimed that criminal law in itself is a problematic tool in addressing trafficking, and especially so if it is seen as a cure-all. Trafficking in women for sexual exploitation is, apart from being a criminal problem, a gendered phenomenon that raises particular difficulties from a criminal justice perspective. In particular, criminal justice systems have been criticised for being 'male' in the typical sense, that is preferring and adjudicating behaviour in terms of gendered stereotypes about both men and women—and these in a trafficking context crucially reflect on the way laws and law enforcement deal with female victims and male perpetrators of prostitution-related offences (or, for that matter, male victims and female perpetrators). Secondly, it is argued that the current EU responses to trafficking in women for sexual exploitation are crucially premised on an understanding of the phenomenon as a form of transnational organised crime that stems from and fits all too easily with the fears raised over free movement and the national security concerns over external migration. This serves to reinforce the prominence of repressive responses and to sideline arguments relating to the fact that trafficking is not (only) a security problem, but brings up global concerns of equality and justice not easily, if at all, remedied by individual policing and law enforcement operations. As criminal law approaches to trafficking still fall clearly within the Member States' realm of action, the issue of trafficking and the limits of a criminal law approach are tackled first, after which trafficking as a 'European-wide criminal offence' and the possibilities and limits of European law enforcement action are examined.

5.1 TRAFFICKING OFFENCES IN THE MEMBER STATES

5.1.1 On the Goals and Contents of the Criminal Provisions

There is nothing new about the use of criminal law to control prostitution, even if modern criminal provisions specifically on the exploitation of migrants in the Member States have until recently been the exception rather than the rule.[1] The

[1] Even those EU Member States, which have had no trafficking provisions, have now adopted (or are in the process of adopting) them and others have amended existing statutes. This is mostly due to the UN Trafficking Protocol and the Council Framework Decision, discussed below in section 5.2.1. For information on Member States' implementation of the latter, see Report from the Commission

Netherlands and Italy have over a reasonably long period taken some action against trafficking for prostitution, and influenced developments beyond the national level; Sweden, less affected by trafficking until recently, has followed behind and is one of those Member States where anti-trafficking legislation is very much driven by international and European developments. In all three countries the issue has been (re)defined by the recent (perceived or real) increase in irregular immigration and transnational criminal activity in connection with prostitution. Prostitution laws as such are of course embedded in the interaction between national and international levels—the most famous example being the already mentioned nineteenth century/early twentieth century wave of 'abolition' that swept over Europe by demanding the abolition of state regulation of prostitution (for instance compulsory medical controls) and brothels in the Netherlands and Sweden. In Italy history took a detour and the *case chiuse* were eventually closed down in 1956.

In the Netherlands, the issue of trafficking for prostitution has been resurfacing over a relatively long period, and until very recently has always been specifically bound up with the issue of prostitution.[2] Traffic in women for prostitution was first criminalised with the abolitionist wave in 1911, followed by the criminalisation of trafficking in children, and accordingly involved delivering women for prostitution (regardless of consent).[3] From the 1970s onwards, the expansion of the sex industry, which undermined the local 'tolerance' policy (that tolerated it as long as no serious disturbance was caused), coincided with the rise in the number of foreign women in prostitution and the emergence of organised recruitment that also involved abuse and violence.[4] The turn of the 1990s saw the innovative distinction between 'forced' and 'free' prostitution, according to which the latter—the manifestation of which was a substantial sex industry—was to be considered as a normal sector of the economy, and only the former, involving violence or abuse, was to be combated. The definition of trafficking was reformulated first by the Attorney-General and then the Criminal Code in 1993, the new version including as trafficking the bringing of a person (reformulated to cover all human beings) into prostitution with violence, deceit or abuse of authority. Even though the Netherlands follows the forced/free distinction, and thus allows prostitution as a freely chosen form of work, this approach is not followed with regard to non-EU nationals, who cannot be given permits for the purpose of working in

based on Art 10 of the Council Framework Decision of 19 July 2002 on combating trafficking in human beings, COM(2006)187 final (2 May 2006).

[2] The provision that brings other forms of exploitation (labour exploitation) and the removal of human organs within the scope of the trafficking provision entered into force in 2005. Its adoption was due to the UN Trafficking Protocol which has a wider definition. On the UN Trafficking Protocol see below section 5.2.1.

[3] J Outshoorn, 'Sexuality and International Commerce. The Traffic in Women and Prostitution Policy in the Netherlands' in T Carver and V Mottier (eds), *Politics of Sexuality. Identity, Gender, Citizenship* (London, Routledge, 1998).

[4] C Sterk-Elifson and C Campbell, 'The Netherlands' in N Davis (ed), *Prostitution: An International Handbook on Trends, Problems, and Policies* (Westport, Conn, Greenwood Press, 1993).

prostitution.[5] The justification for such a move was the assumption that non-EU women are more vulnerable to abuse; thus all involvement must be inherently exploitative and should be criminalised.[6] At the same time it was made impossible for non-EU women to migrate for prostitution independently, the motivation being that it is not 'in the interest of the Dutch State as such' to permit non-nationals to work in prostitution.[7]

The prostitution provisions were reconsidered in 2000. In line with the forced/free distinction adopted previously, the ban on brothels (Article 250*bis* of the Dutch Criminal Code) and the ban on the consensual 'exploitation' of prostitution were lifted, local regulations provided for and the penalties for forced exploitation of prostitution and trafficking increased. Profiting from voluntary prostitution is now completely outside the purview of criminal law and brothels are subject to local administrative controls. A municipal licence is needed, for which closing hours, supervision with regard to labour law, and medical aspects have to be addressed; it must also be confirmed that the brothel does not hire irregular immigrants.[8] Article 250a (since January 2005 replaced by a new Article 273a) of the Criminal Code was changed to provide for the punishable forms of exploitation of prostitution. It was made punishable by up to six years' imprisonment to force (through physical coercion or violence, threat thereof, or dominance ensuing from it) or to deceive someone to make them engage in 'sexual activities with a third party against remuneration' (forced prostitution); to *recruit, bring back or abduct* another person with the intention of *inducing* this person to make him- or herself available to engage in sexual activities with a third party for remuneration in another country (trafficking), and to induce a minor to engage in prostitution or to take advantage of forced or child prostitution. The penalties rose to eight years' imprisonment in cases involving joint (two or more) offenders, if the minor in question was under 16 or if grievous bodily harm was caused; the penalties rose to 10 years' imprisonment if the offence was committed by two or more parties against a minor or resulted in grievous bodily harm.[9]

[5] Implementation regulation on migrant workers, Uitvoeringsbesluit, Art 3. See also Outshoorn, above n 3, 197.

[6] J Outshoorn, 'Regulating Prostitution as Sex Work: the Pioneer Case of the Netherlands' (2001) 36 *Acta Politica*, 155, at 167. On the debates see also J Outshoorn, 'Voluntary and Forced Prostitution: the "Realistic Approach" of the Netherlands' in J Outshoorn (ed), *The Politics of Prostitution, Women's Movements, Democratic States and the Globalisation of Sex Commerce* (Cambridge, Cambridge University Press, 2004).

[7] R Hopkins and J Nijboer, *Country Report: The Netherlands* (Research based on case studies of victims of trafficking in human beings in 3 EU Member States, Antwerp, Payoke et al, 2003), at 340. Removing the ban on migrating for 'sex work' has been suggested by some but has not led to serious proposals for change.

[8] Administrative sanctions can be applied if a brothel is found to be violating the conditions of the licence; sanctions include warnings, temporary closure, or revocation of the licence. This, along with the new requirement that sex workers carry identity documents, is one of the aspects that indicate that the seemingly sexually libertarian reform entails a strong desire to control prostitution activities: see also J Outshoorn, 'Pragmatism in the Polder: Changing Prostitution Policy in The Netherlands' (2004) 12 *Journal of Contemporary European Studies* 165.

[9] On this legislation see A Korvinus, *Trafficking in Human Beings. First Report of the Dutch National Rapporteur* (The Hague, Bureau NRM, 2002).

The reasoning behind Article 250a interestingly undermined the 'sex work' logic (evidenced in the legalisation of brothels and the acceptance of consensual 'exploitation' of Dutch/EC women in prostitution), making the policy internally inconsistent. This was because it was not prostitution as such but *migrant* prostitution that was considered undesirable—this was evident as the trafficking law reform in 2000 was entangled in discussions on asylum-seekers and irregular workers. For instance Outshoorn reports on parliamentary discussions and comments regarding the fear over 'uncontrollable streams of foreign prostitutes'[10] and so on. The situation is now somewhat different. Whilst Article 250a was placed in the Criminal Code under 'Crimes against morality', since 2005 the new Article 273a has been located under 'Offences against personal freedom'.[11] Unlike Article 250a, which—having the aim of ridding the prostitution scene of irregular immigrants and criminal elements—categorised any assisted movement of non-EU nationals for the purpose of prostitution, even under circumstances that would typically consider voluntary 'migrant prostitution' as a crime, Article 273a now incorporates the UN Trafficking Protocol definition of trafficking.[12] As sentences remain largely the same (except for the introduction of harsher penalties when the crime results in serious injury, or endangers the life of a person, or results in death) the most substantial change is that the new provision brings to an end the anomaly in which the trafficking provision (Article 250a) was at odds with the general 'sex work' position.

The criminalisation of trafficking, as well as the Dutch arrangement for residence permits for victims of trafficking (B-9 regulation), can be characterised as aiming at more effective law enforcement with a limited exception to migration rules on expulsion. As was seen above, the B-9 regulation creates the possibility of granting a temporary residence permit to a (possible) victim of trafficking as well as to a witness of trafficking, in order for them to report the crime of trafficking, assist in the investigations and/or testify in court.[13] If there is the smallest suspicion that trafficking may be involved, the (possible) victims are to be granted a period of reflection in order to allow them to consider whether or not they want to report the crime of trafficking (witnesses are not granted this period of reflection, but have to decide at once).[14] A temporary residence permit is issued only to those who agree to co-operate in actions against those who illegally trafficked them. To victims this temporary residence permit can be granted for the duration of the criminal investigation and the court proceedings at first instance and on appeal; for a witness it is valid for as long as her presence in the country is

[10] Outshoorn (2001), above n 6, 167.

[11] Note also that according to the official distinction between human smuggling and human trafficking, the former has since 1993 been separately criminalised in Art 197a of the Penal Code. The person who is assisted (the smuggled person) is not liable to be punished on the basis of Art 197a (but it is possible that this person can be liable on the basis of another Art, for instance Art 231, ie forged documents).

[12] On the 2005 legislation, see A Korvinus, *Trafficking in Human Beings. Third Report of the Dutch National Rapporteur* (The Hague, Bureau NRM, 2005), ch 2. On the UN Trafficking Protocol, see below section 5.2.1.

[13] See above section 4.2.2.

[14] About the system see Korvinus, above n 9; Korvinus, above n 12, and below section 5.1.2.

deemed by the prosecutor to be necessary. The permit must be renewed annually as long as the victim's presence is useful. After the trial the victim is generally supposed to return to her country of origin. The system thus seeks to make use of victims in the investigation and prosecution of the case against traffickers; as it connects residence permits to the temporary need for the victim as witness, permanent residence is not envisaged.

As in the Netherlands, in Italy trafficking as a crime has gained increasing prominence. As regards prostitution, Italy is an abolitionist country in name, if not always in practice, adopting an implicit forced/free distinction. The debates around *legge* Merlin (the 'Merlin law' that in 1956—along abolitionist lines—banned the facilitation of prostitution, the exploitation of prostitution, organising prostitution in closed surroundings (clubs, apartments) and brothel-keeping (renting a house) and set out penalties of between 2 and 6 years for breach) have in truth never abated. As in the rest of Europe, the 1990s was the decade during which the issue of prostitution and what to do about the criminal regulation around it resurfaced with ever-increasing frequency due to the perceived and real influence of foreign (and local) criminals, its involvement in prostitution and the exploitation of irregular migrants.[15] For a non-national it is not possible to obtain a permit to work in prostitution as it is not considered work under the Merlin law; non-nationals (without a valid permit granted on other grounds) will be served with an order to leave the territory. Until recently, Italy has had no specific anti-trafficking law, but has dealt with trafficking through various Articles of the Criminal Code. The legal provisions used to cover trafficking in women range(d) from slavery, child prostitution and pornography (Articles 600–604 of the Penal Code) to facilitating the moving ('enticing') of migrants for the purpose of prostitution and the exploitation of prostitutes (*legge* Merlin, Article 3) and to facilitating irregular immigration (Immigration Law of 1998, Article 12[16]). In 2003, the slavery provisions in the Criminal Code were finally modernised to include reducing into slavery or servitude (also for prostitution), trade in persons, and acquiring slaves.[17] Penalties range from eight to 20 years' imprisonment. Besides providing for the specific offence of trafficking in human beings, the new provisions introduce the offence of criminal association with the intention of engaging in people trafficking, thus connecting it more firmly with the fight against organised crime.

Ambiguity in policy is evident in Italy, where official abolitionism is challenged by the actual practice of tolerance and political parties that at frequent intervals

[15] G Campani, 'Trafficking for Sexual Exploitation and the Sex Business in the New Context of International Migration: the Case of Italy' (1998) 3 *South European Society and Politics* 231.

[16] Art 12 of the 'testo unico' (decree no 286 of 25 July 1998 [1998] GU 191) on immigration criminalises aiding or abetting illegal immigration with up to three years imprisonment; the same Art contains harsher penalties if the aim is to exploit or persuade people into prostitution.

[17] Law of 11 Aug 2003 no 228 'Misure contro la tratta delle persone' ([2003] GU 195). About the new legal framework see E Savona *et al*, *Tratta di persone a scopo di sfruttamento e traffico di migranti. Rapporto finale di sintesi della ricerca* (Transcrime Report No 8, Rome, Ministry of Justice, 2004), ch 10.

introduce regulationism or the reopening of brothels into the debate (the reopening was supported by all parties of the second Berlusconi government (2001–6) as a possible way of cleaning the streets and controlling the spread of disease).[18] In 2003, a Bill was introduced which, in order to eradicate the nuisance caused by prostitutes and cruising customers, would provide for a fine for customers and stricter sanctions for (voluntary) prostitutes.[19] While in Italy the moral panic over migration, crime and prostitution also sparked demands for a repressive response, especially against foreign women in prostitution, the notable feature is the relatively strong emphasis on helping identified victims to free themselves from criminal association.[20] As was discussed in the previous chapter, in principle there are two paths available for victims of trafficking immediately to obtain residence permits for six months with access to services and schooling.[21] The social path requires that the victim is in a 'situation of violence or exploitation' (here the list of offences causing this is obviously wide and not limited to trafficking) and that there is a danger to personal safety. This can, of course, emerge in the course of a police investigation, but local authorities, associations and NGOs can also act as reference points. The judicial path requires that there is an inquiry into listed offences (under *legge* Merlin, serious offences listed in the Code of Criminal Procedure—bodily harm, rape and so on). In both cases the *Questura* (police headquarters) issues the permit; but the paths are separate, and thus in theory it is irrelevant if the victims who wish to report the offence against them agree to testify.[22] In both kinds of cases victims are to be issued with renewable residence permits provided that they participate in assistance and integration programmes. This permit may be converted for education or work reasons (normally in practice the latter), but also revoked in case of interruption of the social assistance programme or 'incompatible behaviour'.[23]

Sweden, after a long abolitionist period (when the typical forms of exploitation were criminalised but prostitution itself was not), criminalised the buying of

[18] Considering the current repressive spirit and the traditional problem of weak enforcement activity, re-opening brothels may lead to traffickers importing their *manodopera* (workforce) ostensibly legally, making the work of exploiters easier and more organised. Arguably it may also worsen the situation of the women and drive them further underground and indoors, away from people who might help (now that many women work in the streets, there is a chance that they can ask for help).

[19] See disegno di legge n. 3826 promulgated on 26 Mar 2003: Art 1 proposes fines of €200–1000 for customers (€2,000–4,000 for repeat offenders) and fines of €200–3,000 for prostitutes (and detention of 5–15 days for repeat offenders) while Art 2 proposes holding prostitutes criminally liable for 'STD damage' to customers based on the frequency of their medical check-ups. On the proposal see E Aghatise, 'Trafficking for Prostitution in Italy' (2004) 10 *Violence Against Women* 1126, who condemns it as the implicit reintroduction of a regulatory system.

[20] See G Zincone (ed), *Secondo rapporto sull'integrazione degli immigrati in Italia* (Bologna, Il Mulino, 2001), at 621–54.

[21] See legislative decree no 286 of 25 July 1998, [1998] GU 191, Art 18 and the implementation decree of the President no 394 of 31 Aug 1999, [1999] GU 258) and above section 4.2.2.

[22] On the Art 18 legislation and its predecessors see D Petrini and V Ferraris, 'Analysis of Art. 18 within the Framework of Legislation Concerning Immigration and Measures Aimed at Fighting Organised Crime. The History and Rewarding Nature of Present and Previous Legislations' in Regione Emilia-Romagna and Associazione On the Road (eds), *Article 18: Protection of Victims of Trafficking and Fight Against Crime* (Martinsicuro, On the Road Edizioni, 2002).

[23] On the implementation of the system see below section 5.1.2.

sexual services in 1999 and trafficking in human beings in 2002. Procuring and promoting prostitution remain offences with penalties of up to four years' imprisonment (and six years' for aggravated offences). In Sweden, too, the law reforms were linked to the entry of foreign (often Baltic) women and girls into the prostitution market, which had until recently been very small, unorganised and considered relatively harmless. The sudden influx of often quite young and, above all, non-EU women in prostitution and the increasing visibility of the issue led to demands that the government tackle the exploitation of the women and girls involved through harsher penalties which would act as a disincentive to trafficking. A strong penal discourse initially supported criminalisation of both the seller and the buyer in prostitution to prevent and suppress prostitution.[24] Eventually the side that supported the criminalisation of the client only won, and prostitution became represented as a choice but, unusually, not for the prostitute but for the customer, whose demand feeds the trade. Under the Act Prohibiting the Purchase of Sexual Services, 'a person who obtains casual sexual relations in exchange for payment' shall be sentenced to a fine or imprisonment of up to six months. The client criminalisation provision was more heavily debated only after it had already been passed. Its labelling of prostitution as a form of violence against women was criticised for extending criminal liability on symbolic grounds,[25] but also because it can be interpreted as a knee-jerk reaction to the fear that Sweden was being 'taken over' by foreign prostitutes, especially from the East.[26] A fusion of concern over exploited girls with the fear of migrants (and with the law and order concern) does come across; for example, one of the grounds used for justifying this law reform was the particular habits of the 'girls from the east' (suggesting they were more 'used to' unprotected sex than Swedish women).[27]

As regards trafficking, the existing legal avenues, such as using criminal definitions like (aggravated) pimping, or measures provided for by the Aliens Law, were held to be insufficient to cover the wide range of practices that trafficking involves. The existing provisions, some from the 'white slavery' period ('bring someone to a state of emergency', meaning to force someone into prostitution abroad), were also deemed too strict and outdated to be useful in the current environment.[28] The trafficking provision (that entered into force in July 2002) relates to prostitution and

[24] Y Svanström, 'Criminalising the John—a Swedish Gender Model?' in Outshoorn (ed), above n 6.

[25] See, eg, C Lernestedt and K Hamdorf, 'Sexköpskriminaliseringen—till skydd av vad?—del I', (2000) 11 *Juridisk Tidskrift* 846; C Lernestedt and K Hamdorf, 'Sexköpskriminaliseringen—till skydd av vad?—del II' (2001) 12 *Juridisk Tidskrift* 111.

[26] It has also been argued that the law reflects the Swedish anxieties about joining the EU, some Member States of which regulate prostitution. See D Kulick, 'Sex in the New Europe. The Criminalization of Clients and Swedish Fear of Penetration' (2003) 3 *Anthropological Theory* 199.

[27] See A Gould, 'Sweden's Law on Prostitution: Feminism, Drugs and the Foreign Threat' in S Thorbek and B Pattanaik (eds), *Transnational Prostitution. Changing Patterns in a Global Context* (London, Zed Books, 2002).

[28] See Straffansvaret för människohandel, Proposal 2001/02:124 (14 Mar 2002). See also Sexualbrottkommitténs Betänkande, SOU 2001:14 (Report by the Sexual Crimes Committee) and Justitieutskottets betänkande, Straffansvaret för gränsöverskridande människohandel, 2001/02:JuU27 (Report by the Parliamentary Committee on Justice).

other sexual exploitation and is strongly influenced by the UN Trafficking Protocol and European developments. Placed in the 'Crimes against freedom' chapter in the Criminal Code, it imposes criminal responsibility for the crime of trafficking in human beings on anyone who: (1) by the use of unlawful coercion, deception or of any other similar improper means induces another to go to or to be transported abroad for the purpose of sexual offences, prostitution or other forms of exploitation for sexual purposes; (2) for such a purpose and by the use of such improper means as mentioned transports, harbours or receives someone who has arrived in a country under such conditions; (3) commits any such act against a victim who has not attained 18 years of age, even if no improper means have been used.[29] Attempt, preparation and conspiracy to traffic in human beings for sexual purposes or failure to report such a crime were also made punishable. Trafficking was originally defined as a cross-border crime (unlike in the UN Trafficking Protocol), but the provision was amended in 2004, and the requirement was removed.[30] The sentences range from a minimum of two years' to 10 years' imprisonment or, in less serious cases, to a maximum of four years in prison. As was seen above in Chapter 4, an Aliens Law provision was introduced to reinforce the anti-trafficking measures with a system of temporary residence permits for victims who are useful for the investigation or prosecution of trafficking.

As was discussed above in Chapter 3, current prostitution policy in all three countries reflects an attempt to strike difficult balances between the view of women as sufficiently independent/rational to decide what to do with their bodies and the view of them, especially foreign (non-EC) ones, as insufficiently independent to do this without state control or protection from exploitation through the use of criminal law. Yet they also incorporate a strong desire to do (or to be seen as doing) something about an issue which raises strong negative sentiments in many segments of society and, therefore, the three countries aim to limit the visibility and scale of and/or criminal involvement in prostitution through the use of criminal law. Inspired by a strand of feminism, Sweden struck the balance at deciding that prostitution is a social evil that has to be eradicated; inspired by another branch of feminism, the Netherlands is at the other end, wanting to cleanse prostitution of non-sex work elements. Italy for the time being seems resigned to the continuing existence of the phenomenon while condemning those involved, yet admitting that the worst by-products must be tackled. In these processes migrants frequently feature, but as bad examples rather than as people to be taken into consideration in the content of the reform. If there is any consensus among these countries, it stems from the 'foreign takeover' in prostitution, involuntary as it may be. There is much more convergence as regards prostitution vis-à-vis migration and foreigners (non-EU women in prostitution, their

[29] Criminal Code, Ch 4 s la (as amended by Lagen 2002:436).

[30] Lagen 2004:406. Criminalisation now extends to all forms of trafficking in persons, including trafficking within national borders, and also to trafficking for other forms of exploitation, such as forced labour and slavery and the removal of organs.

exploitative pimps, the traffickers that keep on delivering women without papers and so on), that is, as a security and law and order concern.

Yet the laws pay little attention to those they mainly affect, namely the ranks of prostitutes that are now composed of non-EU (or new Member State) women. In Sweden the law's underlying stance is fairly clear; prostitution is bad for all women, foreign or not, and bad for society; but even though women in prostitution are considered victimised by the involvement in it, foreign women in prostitution can be simply expelled under the Aliens Law (if assumed not to have enough money or to be able to support themselves through 'honest means'). In the Netherlands, sex workers are up to a point considered as workers, but this logic has tended to break down regarding non-EU citizens; if a woman in prostitution is without valid papers this arouses suspicion of either trafficking or irregular migrant prostitution. In Italy the law treats prostitutes as an unavoidable nuisance that has to be removed from sight and controlled for public order reasons; this applies to migrant women as well, even though it is acknowledged that they are particularly vulnerable to abuse. In all three countries the main goal is to remove irregular migrants and to prevent more from coming; at the same time they form the greatest proportion of women in prostitution. The de facto criminalisation of migrant prostitution—that goes hand in hand with the migrant 'takeover'—shows the artificiality of considering 'domestic' and 'foreign' prostitution as separate issues; both involve complex issues of control, inequality and freedom which should be kept in mind when considering the European challenge in this area as regards harmonisation and co-operation.

5.1.2 Applying the Laws: Female Caricatures and Invisible Men

The law, as it appears on the statute books, is one matter; the law in practice is quite another. This is especially the case with regard to prostitution which, due to its typically semi-legal status, is often a partially hidden phenomenon and which, owing to the controversies surrounding the harm and its perpetrator, is not easily adaptable to coherent legal regulation, let alone enforcement. And trafficking in women for sexual exploitation for its part is one of the most hidden and controversial crimes, not least because the nexus with prostitution and migration means that its victims are even more silenced than victims of crime in general.

In the Netherlands the police and prosecution authorities have made serious efforts to tackle trafficking.[31] At present, however, the long-term effects of the legalisation reform on trafficking are still unclear. The amendments have not been a panacea, as reports still cite prostitutes in irregular situations, but now the phenomenon is more hidden as administrative controls focus on the legalised sector (at the same time there is still demand for 'irregular' women, as Dutch women,

[31] For a summary see Korvinus, above n 9, 81–104. See also EMZ, (2003b) *Prevention and Fight against Trafficking: Institutional Developments in Europe. Netherlands Report* (Berlin, Europäische Migrationszentrum, 2003).

wary of the regulatory obligations and increased control, have moved away from the official prostitution sector).[32] The enforcement of the laws that legalise consensual prostitution (by those who have their papers in order) and that seek to suppress irregular immigration for prostitution and exploitation seems to be less effective than was hoped, at least in the short term, not least because the administrative checks are resource-intensive.[33] In practice, the checks also emphasise administrative control more than prostitutes' rights. It is also reported that after *Jany and Others*—which in principle allows women from EU Candidate Countries (and the new Member States), such as Romania and Bulgaria, to set up shop as long as they act independently of exploiters[34]—exploitation around prostitution continues, because a need has been created for mediators to 'arrange' the independence required (as small entrepreneurs women in prostitution must submit a business plan and organise starting capital), creating space for new forms of dependence and exploitation.[35] The situation of dependence is of course worse for non-EU nationals, since their involvement in prostitution is banned by the regulations on foreign workers and they are thus forced into hiding. At the same time repressive law enforcement action against irregular migrants in prostitution (like the famous raids that took place in Amsterdam and the Hague in 2002, during which a number of Bulgarian and Romanian women were expelled) means that trafficking victims are also easily repatriated, despite the list of trafficking indicators.[36]

Trafficking investigations and prosecutions are typically highly dependant on victims (or witnesses) reporting the crime and providing information and eventual testimony. The most serious problems are the reluctance of victims to put themselves on the line through reporting and testifying, on the one hand, and, on the other, the lack of attention to the needs and indeed rights of victims, considered irregular immigrants. As to the first, the reputation of the police is often poor in the eyes of victims, who have been told by traffickers that the police are corrupt or that they will simply be expelled, only to be picked up by traffickers again; the fear of retaliation against victims and their family members in countries of origin makes many reluctant to stand up to exploiters; and sometimes the existing

[32] For the most recent translated report by the national rapporteur see Korvinus, above n 12; see also A Daalder, *The Lifting of the Ban on Brothels. Prostitution in 2000–2001* (House of Representatives Documents, Just 02-801, The Hague, Wetenschappelijk Onderzoek- en Documentatiecentrum, 2002). NGO sources report that while some legalised their situation (through marriage, Case C–268/99 *Jany v Staatssecretaris van Justitie* [2001] ECR I-8615, etc), most 'went underground' and kept moving from place to place to avoid detection (there are also signs of illegal brothels). See, eg, TAMPEP, *Transnational AIDS/STD Prevention among Migrant Prostitutes in Europe/Project. TAMPEP 5, Volumes 1–3* (Amsterdam, TAMPEP, 2002).

[33] Korvinus, above n 12.

[34] The Association Agreements 'do not in principle preclude a system of prior control which makes the issue by the competent immigration authorities of leave to enter and remain subject to the condition that the applicant must show that he genuinely intends to take up an activity as a self-employed person without at the same time entering into employment': Case C-268/99 *Jany and Others* [2001] ECR I-8615, at para 66.

[35] Hopkins and Nijboer, above n 7.

[36] A problem also noted by the national rapporteur: See Korvinus, above n 9.

debt-bonded relationship with the trafficker, together with the need to make some money 'no matter what', means that reporting is simply not an option.[37] As to the second, the fact that many victims stay in the Netherlands without a valid permit tends to lead to their quick expulsion. The implementation of the law, despite a relatively open definition, suffers from a lack of police capacity and priority.[38] Investigating trafficking offences is notoriously resource-intensive and time-consuming; prosecutions are not always very successful; and resources spent on trafficking are diverted away from perhaps more high-profile crimes.[39] It has also been reported that the lack of priority has reflected the prostitution-related nature of trafficking (akin to a public order problem); indeed, it has been suggested that to move trafficking from sexual offences to 'organised crime' would gain it greater priority as the latter is considered more serious than 'vice'.[40] There have also been problems of police organisation (as the decentralisation of the police creates unnecessary confusion and bureaucracy).[41]

These problems are highlighted with regard to the residence permit system. As was discussed above, the system applies to victims of (sex) trafficking who report the crime and agree to testify; it is thus an exception to migration rules that aims at guaranteeing the success of criminal trials. As such, it grants a 'reward' (temporary residence permit for the duration of the investigation and trial plus access to some services) to those, and only those, victims of trafficking who co-operate. Those who refuse or are refused B-9 have no access to services. While formally the system is meant both as a victim protection and as a prosecution instrument, in practice it is mostly the latter—and as such does not seem to work too well, as the level of reporting by victims is low.[42] In addition to the above-mentioned barriers it is reported that in practice victims may not be informed of the existence of a B-9 permit or it may be that no reflection period is granted and the decision on whether or not a woman wants to proceed with the case has to be made immediately; this not only denies victims the right granted by the letter of the law, which is generous on this point, but means they have no opportunity to recover from the experience and seriously consider their options. Often an actual prosecution/trial is required for the victim to obtain the permit to stay; those who merely report the offence and who perhaps are not deemed 'useful' (for instance it is plain there will be no prosecution, for whatever reason) may not be given the permit, in contra-

[37] Hopkins and Nijboer, above n 7; C Rijken, *Trafficking in Persons. Prosecution from a European Perspective* (The Hague, TMC Asser Press, 2003), especially ch 6.

[38] Note that the legalisation of the sex industry has directed the attention of police forces towards the regulated sectors, meaning that less capacity remains for monitoring 'irregular' prostitution: see Daalder, above n 32.

[39] Korvinus, above n 9, Korvinus, above n 12.

[40] Hopkins and Nijboer, above n 7. This, however, gives rise to the danger that the 'organised crime response' might be even more repressive than the response by 'vice', which (with all its faults) tends to be more sensitive to the difficult situation of victims. In line with, eg, the national rapporteur's suggestion the trafficking provision now comes under the heading of 'crimes against personal freedom'.

[41] Korvinus, above n 9.

[42] *Ibid*; A Korvinus, *Trafficking in Human Beings. Second Report of the Dutch National Rapporteur* (The Hague, Bureau NRM, 2003); Korvinus, above n 12.

vention of the law. According to the National Rapporteur's surveys 40 per cent of *identified* victims (those who have not been expelled or who have not disappeared underground) report the fact of their being trafficked in; of these, around 70 per cent have made use of the period of reflection; around a quarter of reporting victims are not granted permits.[43]

Moreover, as an option the B-9 has its obvious limits: it is clear that the right to stay in the Netherlands will terminate as soon as the trial does. Victims are, for instance, not allowed to work, as they might then integrate too much into the Netherlands. The end result for victims is to be sent home notwithstanding the fact that they may face revenge by traffickers or ostracism by communities, and certainly the conditions from which they sought to escape in the first place still exist. Thus, as an encouragement to co-operate the permit seems inadequate.[44] At the same time, it is possible to characterise even a small concession, such as the temporary right to stay for evidence purposes, as a 'bribe'; unsurprisingly, at trial defence attorneys attempt to use B-9 to discredit witnesses, arguing that their testimony has been 'bought' with permission to stay to testify.[45] It has been argued that the suggested possibility of allowing victims to work during B-9 would be 'too much' and only increase the 'bought' claims or act as an attraction to economic migrants.[46] At the same time, to grant the temporary right to work is 'too little', for what is the use of getting a job in the Netherlands if, after the trial, a victim is going to be repatriated in any case? A lack of attention to this issue maintains the trafficking circuit, as desperate repatriated trafficking victims make for easy prey, which means that this is not only a human rights problem but a law enforcement one.

As to trials, the procedure tends to be very upsetting for victims, with repeated interrogation and so on (reminiscent of rape trials). As trafficking cases are often complicated, there is a need for experienced prosecutors to formulate charges. In a way that resembles the attitudes of some police officers, it is reported that judges consider those victims who knew in advance of their likely involvement in prostitution to be 'less' victimised (compare the rape of women in prostitution).[47] It seems that relatively few trafficking cases are actually identified, and that of these many do not make it through the filtres of the police and prosecution. For instance, a total of 132 cases were registered by the police in 2001, of which 63 per cent were prosecuted—compared with an estimatethat 'at least 3,500' people a year become victims of trafficking.[48] Of the cases brought to trial 88 per cent

[43] Korvinus, above n 9; Korvinus, above n 42; Korvinus, above n 12.

[44] In 2004, as a response to the national rapporteur's call, a National Plan of Action to Combat Human Trafficking was adopted, highlighting the need to counsel victims upon their return to their countries of origin as well as to improve the implementation of the B-9 permit and to raise awareness of prostitution customers (with a hotline to report trafficking). But the 2005 report still cites significant gaps with regard to the repatriation of victims to countries of origin.

[45] Hopkins and Nijboer, above n 7.

[46] Not that B-9 seems not to be very attractive as it is; it accounted for only 3–5 per 1,000 residence permits granted in 1999–2000: Korvinus, above n 42, 12.

[47] Hopkins and Nijboer, above n 7.

[48] E Van Dijk, *Mensenhandel in Nederland 1997–2000* (Zoetermeer, KLPD/NRI, 2002).

resulted in conviction in 1995–2001, with 84 per cent resulting in imprisonment for offenders.[49] Regarding the offenders, it should be noted that not all are members of organised crime groups. A case study of Dutch police files demonstrates the existence of small loosely organised cliques of professionals as well as larger organised crime groups from Eastern and Central Europe or from the Netherlands.[50] Similarly, the Dutch national rapporteur notes that traffickers can be individuals, isolated criminal groups or criminal networks—while criminal networks cover about 60 per cent, they are not the only type of traffickers.[51] As to the transnational element, while this is frequently present, at the same time the largest national group among traffickers are the Dutch themselves.[52]

In Italy the fluid situation of prostitution laws, in which prostitution is not a crime but much to do with it is, and where women in prostitution are both condemned and need to be saved, is mirrored by ambiguous law enforcement practice. Traditionally, prostitutes have been harassed by the police who (mis)use the laws against the exploitation of prostitution to target prostitutes themselves, or who arrest them for obscene acts in public places or acts against public morality.[53] In some areas the customers of prostitution have also been targeted; a practice reminiscent of the Swedish criminalisation of clients (which is clearly not intended by the Merlin law itself), it reflects the desire to reach those perceived by some (especially under Catholic morality) to be to blame for prostitution.[54] This does not, however, mean that the prostitute (forced or not) would be considered innocent, but rather demonstrates the spread of punitive measures. The enforcement of the Merlin provisions against prostitutes themselves at some point resulted in most Italian women (apart from drug addicts) moving away from the streets to minimise hassle with the police, albeit that indoor prostitution can also lead to a charge of keeping a brothel.[55] Since the early 1990s, the prostitution business has not only grown and become very diversified but is also increasingly sophisticated and ethnically segregated. Most notoriously the streets are now filled with African and Eastern European women, and links have been established between organised crime from countries of origin and domestic Italian criminal groups.[56]

[49] Korvinus, above n 42, 47–56.

[50] G Bruinsma and G Meershoek, 'Organized Crime and Trafficking in Women from Eastern Europe in the Netherlands' (1997) 3(4) *Transnational Organized Crime* 105.

[51] Korvinus, above n 42; Korvinus, above n 12.

[52] Korvinus, above n 9; Korvinus, above n 42; Korvinus, above n 12.

[53] See, eg, M Gibson, 'Italy' in Davis (ed), above n 4.

[54] See, eg, M Virgilio, 'Article 18 Within the Framework of Criminal Legislation Aimed at Combating Crime Against Migrants' in Regione Emilia-Romagna and Associazione On the Road (eds), above n 22, at 76–9.

[55] Gibson, above n 53.

[56] Associazione LULE, *Vite di strada* (Abbiategrasso, LULE, 2001); P Monzini, *Il Mercato delle Donne. Prostituzione, Tratta e Sfruttamento* (Rome, Donzelli editore, 2002); F Carchedi *et al* (eds) *I Colori della Notte. Migrazioni, sfruttamento sessuale, esperienze di intervento sociale* (Milan, Franco Angeli, 2000), part 2; I Orfano, *Country Report: Italy* (Payoke et al, Research based on case studies of victims of trafficking in human beings in 3 EU Member States, 2003).

Acquiring accurate information of prostitution-related offences such as trafficking meets the usual barriers relating to underground industries; in Italy these are increased by multiple criminal definitions, variable judicial practices across regions, a lack of national data and monitoring systems, and the general problem of rather widespread organised criminal activity in the country.[57] As to prosecuting trafficking under existing criminal definitions, the judiciary were at least at first reluctant to use slavery offences (extremely grave and considered rare) for cases of trafficking in adults, preferring the prostitution-related Merlin offences, criminal association, or individual offences, such as kidnapping.[58] More recently there have also been a few cases of adult women (as opposed to children) as victims who have been tried under the slavery provision, and in future the new slavery definitions should be used.[59] The trafficking-related case load has increased considerably since 1997; but the field is still very heterogeneous, and there are variations on jurisdictional choices (especially regarding the offence used for prosecution) according to area; some districts are reportedly more aware and active than others. A limited but illustrative case study points to the prevalence of the use of Article 3 of the *legge* Merlin (recruitment for prostitution, inducing prostitution in public places, inducing transfer for prostitution, organisation of recruitment for prostitution) over other possible criminal offences, and notes the presence of Italians among defendants as a sign of local–international criminal co-operation.[60]

The so-called Article 18 instruments have helped to increase the number of victims who denounce traffickers.[61] More flexible than the Dutch, with two different paths, the system gives a high degree of discretion on the issue of victim permits to local police headquarters. As a downside the system is also more fragmented and slower than the Dutch one, even if in principle it ought to be faster.[62] Unsurprisingly, the majority of permits, over two thirds, are given to victims who follow the judicial path.[63] In practice the offences that allow for the judicial path have been widely interpreted (also to cover, for instance, immigration law's Article on smuggling). Still the humanitarian path does exist; and both in reality intertwine (the stories of social path victims are verified in the beginning; and such victims can be called to testify in pre-trial hearings and so on). Also this law is very heterogeneously applied throughout the country; for instance some areas are

[57] S DeCarli and A Di Nicola, *Italy, National Report* (Trento, Transcrime, University of Trento et al, 2002).

[58] See, eg, M Virgilio, 'Law and Rights' in A Signorelli and M Treppele (eds), *Services in the Window* (Trieste, Asterios Editore, 2001).

[59] Virgilio, above n 54, at 80–3.

[60] See M Virgilio 'Judicial Activity Aimed at Combating Crimes Against Migrants' in Regione Emilia-Romagna and Associazione On the Road (eds), above n 22.

[61] For statistics see Dipartimento per le Pari Opportunità, *Protezione e assistenza alle vittime della tratta, i dati del monitoraggio* (Rome, Equal Opportunities Department, 2005).

[62] Orfano, above n 56.

[63] V Ferraris *et al*, 'National Data Concerning Residence Permits, Projects and Procedures, and Connected Juridical Routines' in Regione Emilia-Romagna and Associazione On the Road (eds), above n 22.

known to apply only the judicial path to trafficking victims.[64] The problem of victims dropping out and disappearing is a large one; on the first year of application only 31.5 per cent of those initially enrolled in the social assistance programme made a request for a permit.[65] Apart from the structural problems of the Italian legal system, there have been teething problems, for instance delays in the *Questura* granting permits. There is also a need to develop attitudes to victims' rights in compensation procedures, to protect them from criminal retaliation, provide interpreters and so on. Trafficking cases are strongly and sometimes exclusively based on the victims' declarations, and their credibility is thus central—and, like in the Netherlands, the 'bought' argument is sometimes brought up in Italy because, owing to the dominance of the judicial path, in some cases the permit clearly must seem like a reward for testimony.[66]

As in the Netherlands, there is relatively predictable, in light of the conflicting interests at stake, friction in the co-operation between immigration and police (on the illegal immigrant–crime nexus), as well as between assisting NGOs and the police. On the one hand, one of the strengths of Article 18 is a horizontal and vertical approach with multi-party involvement. There is close collaboration between the police and those who offer assistance.[67] On the other hand, police involvement represents the desire to repress what is seen as moral degradation; those migrant women who do *not* collaborate (as 'innocent' victims should) may simply be picked up and sent back to their countries of origin (or transit).[68] The same attitude, however, also applies to some NGOs implementing the social assistance programme, even though the original idea of the law was not to 'rescue' prostitutes as such.[69] The police reportedly have a sense of removing the workforce of the organisation when they expel women, since when the women are removed they have to be replaced with others, which in turn costs the criminals money. The police also make a distinction between those who are 'really victims' and those who know of the 'permits route'; in other words, the police suspect instrumental use of the social path when women do not denounce exploiters.[70] Indeed, it is reported that sometimes victims

[64] Orfano, above n 56, 187.

[65] Ferraris *et al*, above n 63. Reasons are again obvious (fear, the need to earn money, even if in prostitution, etc).

[66] Note also the similarities between the Art 18 judicial path and the favourable treatment afforded to the so-called *pentiti* ('repented'), former members of a Mafia-type organisation that have abandoned their organisation and started helping the authorities in investigations, and who receive protection and benefits in exchange for the information they deliver.

[67] Orfano, above n 56.

[68] Efforts for the more effective expulsions of illegal immigrants have intensified in recent years. Note also that Italy has signed several readmission agreements with major countries of origin for trafficking victims, eg Albania and Nigeria.

[69] Many of the NGOs running the programmes of social assistance and integration are Catholic and consider any further involvement in prostitution as a violation of the conditions of participation in the compulsory programme. Thus the revocation grounds of the Art 18 permit, notably that of 'incompatible conduct', have been interpreted by some assisting NGOs as covering involvement in prostitution: the permit is revoked if a victim of trafficking is later found in street prostitution.

[70] Aghatise, above n 19. At the same time one of the problems for the police is that victims cannot always identify their exploiters. This highlights a general problem in relying on victims for evidence. Sometimes they simply do not know enough to be useful—and this can be perceived as not co-operating.

are not informed of the opportunity to avail themselves of the assistance and integration programme. Yet the report dealing in particular with this issue claims that Article 18 does *not* undermine immigration policy, precisely because the facts relating to even social path victims are verified and thus indirectly contribute to the investigation.[71] Perhaps more importantly, victims who are treated humanely, given time to recover and get their lives in order are more willing to seek justice and trust and co-operate with the police.[72] They are also less likely to be re-trafficked. Thus the system can offer a real chance to escape exploitation, and can be of use even to those victims who do not know enough to be useful in any investigation. Indeed, again it may be noted that the implementation of repressive strategies, especially ones focusing on violations of immigration law, prostitution raids and expulsions, does not favour the achievement of the aims of the law but is counterproductive even from a long-term law enforcement point of view.

In Sweden the application of the 1999 client criminalisation law (with the allocation of an initial budget of 7 million Swedish crowns) did, as anticipated, clean the streets of big cities of prostitution, although it may be that much of the business has just been driven underground, making it potentially more dangerous for women in prostitution.[73] The implementation of the law has suffered to a degree from low priority and evidence problems. The crime, the definition of which requires a 'temporary sexual relation for payment', is difficult to prove without intercourse taking place under the eyes of the police; this also tends to confine the application of the law to visible forms of prostitution, such as street prostitution, and this indeed has decreased. There are only estimates of the scale of prostitution in, for example, massage parlours or through escort services or of whether or not violence against women in prostitution has intensified or diminished as a result of the law.[74] There is a basic tension between the general obligation of the police to prevent crime and obtain relevant evidence, as the goal of the law is to protect women in prostitution from prostitution, but its enforcement depends on the supposedly harmful acts taking place. Prostitution is also perceived by some to be a crime against public order or 'a victimless crime', contradicting the logic of prostitution as exploitative, which underpins the letter of the law.[75] In many instances

[71] See articles in Regione Emilia-Romagna and Associazione On the Road (eds), above n 22.

[72] About this argument see M Giammarinaro, 'La rappresentazione simbolica della tratta come riduzione in schiavitù' in Carchedi *et al* (eds), E Niesner and C Jones-Pauly, *Trafficking in Women in Europe: Prosecution and Victim Protection in a European Context* (Bielefeld, Kleine Verlag, 2001). See also M Svevo, E Garavaglia and M D'Amico (eds), *Polizia e Traffico degli esseri umani. Sistema dei controlli e protezione delle vittime* (Proceedings of the Conference entitled 'Police and Trafficking in Human Beings') Associazione Irene. Milan, 10 June 2002).

[73] In order to avoid the customer being detected, the deal has to be struck quickly, which gives the prostitute no chance to assess whether he is, eg, potentially violent. The law has reduced demand, especially for customers afraid for their reputations. These were mostly (if not entirely) so-called 'good customers' (non-violent, etc) so, together with the need to avoid police controls, this has meant that the remaining customer population is more risky for prostitutes.

[74] C Holst and P Lindström, *Förbud mot köp av sexuella tjänster* (Stockholm, BRÅ-rapport, 2000:4); Socialstyrelsen, *Kännedom om prostitution 2003* (Stockholm, Socialstyrelsen, 2004).

[75] A Nord and T Rosenberg, *Rapport: Lag (1998:408) om förbud mot köp av sexuella tjänster* (Malmö, Polismyndigheten i Skåne, 2001).

the only successful cases are those in which the customer confesses. It has also been reported that the legal system tends to treat customers leniently, fines are low and public humiliation is avoided when possible, thus, for example, correspondence about the matter is sent to work and not home.[76]

There is at the time of writing a lack of information on the effects of the Swedish trafficking provisions, as they are fairly recent. The estimates of trafficked women show a slight increase (400–600 women in 2003 from an estimate of 200–500 in 2002) but this could simply be because previous estimates have been too low.[77] The first case of trafficking charges was the so-called *Solna* case[78] which failed on the trafficking count—the conviction for aggravated pimping and sentenced to four years' imprisonment was later upheld on appeal. The case interestingly illustrates the problems with a trafficking law that sets very high evidentiary requirements. For victims over 18 years of age it is necessary to prove unlawful coercion, deception or any other similar improper means (the latter is clarified in the *travaux préparatoires* for the law) *in inducing leaving or being transported* for prostitution. This is problematic in cases where the victim may know or suspect the type of work required in the destination country but is not aware of the exploitative *conditions*, especially in cases when there is nothing but the victim's word against the word of the accused when it comes to the initial deception or improper means.[79] This happened also in the *Solna* case, where it was held that 'any other similar improper means' does not include simply exploiting the fact that a neighbouring country (in this case Estonia) has a much lower standard of living and that there are people in desperate economic situations, willing to take up any offer without knowing much about what to expect. But this is often the case, as most trafficking arguably is mundane; it does not involve dramatic kidnappings, but abusing power and control over people in much weaker economic and social circumstances. As it is, there has to be substantial evidence of deception before a conviction can be secured; less spectacular cases do not satisfy this threshold and may result only in a conviction for pimping, which is considered less serious.[80]

Trafficking investigations are not only difficult but require expertise that is still lacking, and are very expensive (for example phonetapping and interpreters and

[76] Rikskriminalpolisen, Kriminalunderrättelsetjänsten, *Handel med kvinnor: Lägesrapport 5* (Rapport 2003:1, Stockholm, Rikskriminalpolisen, 2003).

[77] Rikskriminalpolisen, Kriminalunderrättelsetjänsten, *Människohandel för sexuella ändamål. Lägesrapport 6* (Rapport 2004:2, Stockholm, Rikskriminalpolisen, 2004). For the latest report, which offers no estimates, see Rikskriminalpolisen, Kriminalunderrättelsetjänsten, *Människohandel för sexuella ändamål. Lägesrapport 7* (Rapport 2005:4, Stockholm, Rikskriminalpolisen 2005).

[78] Case B 2636-02, *Solna Tingsrätt*, upheld on appeal to the Svea Hovrätt. See also Rikskriminalpolisen, Kriminalunderrättelsetjänsten, above n 77.

[79] The heavy burden of proof is noted also in the latest report by the National Rapporteur: Rikskriminalpolisen, Kriminalunderrättelsetjänsten, above n 77.

[80] The first conviction based on the new trafficking Art was handed down in Oct 2003 in Gothenburg, and involved one under age girl in the context of clear deception and force: Case B 7477-03, *Dagens Nyheter*, 16 Oct 2003. In 2004 there were 29 reports for trafficking offences; however, there were no convictions of trafficking but several related offences, such as procuring: Rikskriminalpolisen, Kriminalunderrättelsetjänsten, above n 77.

the housing of victims). There is still a lack of routine to deal with trafficking cases, and links between various authorities for exchanging information are weak. In Sweden, too, the lack of resources to back the political will to act has been visible; for example, the 15-person trafficking project unit of Stockholm's police force was closed down in 2003. This resonates with the negative police attitudes which have been reported ('it's only prostitutes anyway'). In the same year, however, 30 million crowns (about €3 million) were budgeted for police work against trafficking between 2004 and 2006.[81] In general Sweden, which has never had a trafficking or prostitution problem on the same scale as, for instance, the Netherlands or Italy, still seems to be more unattractive to traffickers (the 1999 law is seen as having a positive preventive effect on the scale of trafficking as there is less money to be made from scared customers[82]). The exploiters must work in a more organised manner (eg, arrange to have several flats for prostitution in different parts of a town or province) and this incurs costs, making exploiting prostitution less profitable.[83] The relative lack of trafficking cases, however, also means that there is insufficient know-how on dealing with cases which do arise. Above all, investigations have been hampered due to the fact that usually the victims, who would be needed as witnesses, have been expelled from the country soon after discovery, as it has not been clear who, if anyone, has responsibility for them; and thus they are not available for the trial without great cost. This is the reason behind the introduction in 2004 of the temporary residence permit for victims of trafficking. The interest of the state in securing criminal proceedings against traffickers and the need for victims' co-operation quite explicitly feature as the motivation behind the provision.[84]

What is apparent in all three countries is a collision between the purposes of immigration policy and the aims of law enforcement agencies; this collision tends to undermine the residence permit arrangements that seek to keep the victim of a crime available for evidentiary purposes. At the same time the interests of the victims are subordinate to the (short-term) interests of the investigation and prosecution. Objectively it is often *not* in the interests of the women to co-operate, but this in turn is perceived by the authorities as a sign of guilt. Indeed, a stereotypical image of the 'guilty victim' keeps occurring, hampering the identification of the trafficked as victims rather than perpetrators. This, however, is by no means a police problem alone. Moreover, the guilt and shame felt by trafficking victims themselves quite often makes some of them blind to the exploitation they have endured, resulting in feelings of unworthiness and so on. The elision from trafficking to migrant prostitution, be it prejudice or a defence mechanism, underlines how the persistent dualisms of guilty/innocent, victim/perpetrator,

81 *Ibid.*

82 Scared, that is, to approach prostitutes in Sweden—note reports of Swedish men contacting prostitutes in neighbouring countries: eg, Socialstyrelsen, above n 74.

83 Rikskriminalpolisen, Kriminalunderrättelsetjänsten, above n 76.

84 The latest reports state that 5 such permits were granted in the first year of application: see Rikskriminalpolisen, Kriminalunderrättelsetjänsten, above n 77.

passive/active[85] often do not match the reality of being trafficked. Often trafficked women have been severely victimised, but have in many cases knowingly broken immigration law. Sometimes they know or guess in advance that sexual services will be expected, but have no idea what that means in practice, and frequently they are controlled and manipulated in ways that allow some agency, but at the same time negate the possibility for real choice and exploit their situation. Real-life women, trafficked or not, are not 'either/or' but often 'both and'. Therefore they do not fit the fixed categories of female stereotypes (women as either protected or persecuted), and that is why enforcement action tends to hit back at victims—though the 'innocent' victim is to be protected, few real-life trafficking victims are innocent enough.

At the same time, traffickers, other exploiters and customers of prostitution are typically absent in discussions regarding both law reform and the enforcement of the law, apart from when the customer is blamed for prostitution (either because of religious morality or from a gender equality perspective); and in these cases it seems to be more a matter of public order or a slap on the wrist (for the Swedish law's fines are more or less on the same scale as those for shoplifting). As to traffickers, their wickedness seems to be taken for granted and needs no explanation. Often they are portrayed as rational (if criminal) businessmen seeking to maximise their profits, and thus the matter of motivation is shrugged off. Unlike male traffickers, it is the occasional female traffickers who usually draw the attention of commentators as their exploitative behaviour towards other women is seen as needing an explanation. Interesting as this need to explain female involvement is, what is troubling is that the lack of attention to the male perpetrator seems to be almost a sign of resignation to the fact that this is what (some) men are like, as if trafficking and exploiting women was caused by some innate male characteristic which makes some men treat women as objects to be sold and used. It is of course a staple feminist critique that male offending is considered more 'natural' than female (with the notable and relevant exception of prostitution); this, along with the claim that there is a relative lack of enforcement when the victims of crime are women (again, especially if they are prostitutes or non-nationals) speaks volumes about the priorities and prejudices behind law enforcement also when it comes to trafficking.[86]

Ignoring temporarily that law, especially criminal law, is a blunt instrument when it comes to addressing complex and gendered social phenomena, it is remarkable how much emphasis seems to be put on drafting definitions (important as they are), debating conceptual issues and so on as if, once everyone manages to agree on these, the problem will be solved. Yet even before the boom of crimi-

[85] Note that for instance in the above-mentioned *Solna* case, above n 78, an ideal of female passivity emerges; women who seek to change their desperate economic circumstances get no protection; women are either to stay and suffer (or rely on potential male financial aid) in the country of origin or risk migration at their peril (as in the *Solna* case).

[86] For an introduction to the issue of gender and criminal law see D Nicolson and L Bibbings (eds), *Feminist Perspectives on Criminal Law* (London, Cavendish Publishing, 2000).

nalising trafficking and then harmonising criminal provisions around it, all (old) EU Member States had laws that could and should have been used to prosecute those who brutalised women in prostitution. It would have been enough to apply the existing laws with equal protection to women, non-nationals and prostitutes, starting with rape, kidnapping and blackmail.[87] It would have been enough to admit that all victims of crime must have some rights due to their common humanity. In short, the problem has less to do with a lack of (harmonised) anti-trafficking laws than with a lack of priority, accorded to trafficking investigations when those whose rights are trampled upon are mere 'foreign prostitutes'. It may be that to have specific harmonised anti-trafficking laws will improve the situation (see below); it may be that they do not. Minimising the exploitation of female migrants depends on whether Member States start treating women in prostitution, irregular migrants and trafficking victims as human beings of equal value to the rest of us. It can be argued that adopting special laws for prostitution in general and also for trafficking for sexual exploitation merely entrenches the notion that the issue *is* a criminal one, and that it can be solved through introducing more and more specific and sophisticated criminal law strategies, arrangements for victims of trafficking who co-operate, and so on.

This brings to light the further problem, namely that of the ultimate reach of criminal sanctions *tout court.* As attractive as it is, on the one hand, to call for more enforcement to punish exploiters and to deter offending, on the other, the fact that a criminal justice approach targets individuals (be they prostitutes or traffickers), and essentially on a reactive basis, obscures the broader structural and ideological nature of the problem. Trafficking as a phenomenon is a collective one; it is the deep-rooted disadvantaging of certain groups of women, often from certain national and ethnic groups, that effectively selects them for abuse. Widespread ideologies of sexual objectification of the female sex channel the least powerful of women as the workforce in the global sex market, and there are wider social problems, such as maladministration, corruption and excessive Western consumerism, that provide the structural background for the exploitation of women through trafficking and sexual exploitation. In short, trafficking is a structural problem, and where it is entrenched no amount of criminal enforcement can ever do more than catch a few of the perpetrators, expel (or 'save') some of the victims and confiscate a minimal percentage of the profits. As long as the structural problems and the ideology behind trafficking remain unaddressed, there will be new traffickers, new victims and more money to be made. Increasing repressive law enforcement and improving the facilities for the victims will prevent some offending and help to increase the number of successful cases, but it will not stop the trade where it already flourishes, even if it may displace it in less established areas. In fact, law enforcement may inadvertently increase trafficking in places where it is well-established, as traffickers will need to make more money when their proceeds are

[87] The lack of legal and practical protection against male violence, especially male violence against prostitutes, is of course another frequently criticised aspect often found in feminist analyses: see above ch 2.

cut through confiscation and the liberation of their 'workers', and can do this through recruiting more women or through exploiting them more.[88]

One should thus be wary of demanding harsher penalties, especially when those can be passed on to the most vulnerable, and at worst serve to divert attention from more proactive measures.[89] This is not to say that prosecuting traffickers should stop or that nothing should be done. It is to say that in the larger picture of anti-trafficking action, criminal justice can never be more than a supplement in the efforts to reduce the exploitation of prostitution and trafficking. It cannot be a substitute for broader social exertions regarding the elimination of the conditions of wide-ranging social and economic problems and gender inequality that feed the trade (see below Chapter 7). Nor can it replace the treating of victims of trafficking as humans. The current emphasis on criminalising trafficking and related measures remains the minimum solution under conditions where there is little or no intention to pursue *broader* change, for instance the loosening of the emerging European migration regime, especially for the sake of poor or non-professional women who are at present victimised in the informal sector. One should be careful about using criminal law as the default response to complex social problems or as a tool for managing concern over globalisation or security. The debates on whether or not prostitution should be criminalised or regulated tend to trivialise the issue into 'concrete action' that cannot solve the difficult and multi-faceted prostitution problem; to reduce measures against trafficking to criminal law provisions, distinctions such as forced/free and criminals/victims are simply not enough in terms of effective and long-term solutions.

5.2 TRAFFICKING AND THE THIRD PILLAR

5.2.1 Harmonising or Not—Repressive Emphasis with Vague Results

As was examined in Chapter 4, reluctantly but irrefutably Member States have come to recognise the need for their co-operation in the area of migration control, with significant consequences as regards trafficking. At the same time, even after Amsterdam, EU competence to take explicit anti-trafficking action lies in the less harmonised and even more jealously guarded area of criminal co-operation, which was not moved from Title VI to Title IV but remains for now in the intergovernmental Third Pillar (renamed 'Provisions on Police and Judicial Co-operation in

[88] On how pursuing the proceeds of organised crime can worsen the situation of its victims see J Sheptycki, 'Global Law Enforcement as a Protection Racket' in A Edwards and P Gill (eds), *Transnational Organised Crime. Perspectives on Global Security* (London, Routledge, 2003), at 48–50.

[89] That traffickers' but also customers' risks (Sweden) tend to become those of the prostitutes provides a particularly pertinent lesson, as the laws in both the Netherlands and Sweden were 'feminist' law reforms. Yet in both countries the laws are often enforced against a marginalised and vulnerable group of women. The fact that there is no consensus on prostitution even among the authorities of a country (let alone between countries) means that the laws around prostitution are applied arbitrarily; this in itself points to the necessity to formulate provisions carefully so that enforcement does not target those not intended to come within their reach.

Criminal Matters'). The saga of Justice and Home Affairs is of course (in)famous and often repeated.[90] After Amsterdam the objective in this area is (in line with amended Article 2 TEU) to 'provide citizens with a high level of safety within an Area of Freedom, Security and Justice by developing common action among the Member States in the fields of police and judicial co-operation in criminal matters and by preventing and combating racism and xenophobia'.[91] Security, now a constitutional objective, is to be achieved 'by preventing and *combating crime, organised or otherwise*, in particular terrorism, *trafficking in persons and offences against children*, illicit drug trafficking and illicit arms trafficking, corruption and fraud' through closer police co-operation, judicial co-operation and the approximation of rules on criminal matters.[92]

That trafficking in women is by now relatively firmly entrenched in this particular setting of EU action is fairly clear. Just as Amsterdam ranked trafficking among the topics requiring increased co-operation, the Vienna Action Plan included trafficking in human beings as requiring effective measures to guarantee security and justice and as a target for criminal justice harmonisation.[93] The Tampere Conclusions (that place trafficking in human beings under the rubric of 'Management of Migration Flows') declared the determination to combat traffickers and urged 'the adoption of legislation foreseeing severe sanctions against this serious crime'. On a less repressive note it also acknowledged that the rights of victims of trafficking 'shall be secured with special emphasis on the problems of women and children'.[94] The Millennium Plan on Organised Crime again used a discourse of securitisation while emphasising the need to focus harmonisation efforts on a limited number of sectors, including 'trafficking in human beings, particularly exploitation of women' and the 'sexual exploitation of children'.[95] The 2002 Comprehensive Action Plan to combat illegal immigration and trafficking in human beings for its part links both issues to organised criminal networks.[96] And of course, last but certainly not least, there is the Framework Decision (replacing

[90] For overviews see S Peers, *EU Justice and Home Affairs Law* (Harlow, Pearson Education Limited, 2000); S Lavenex and W Wallace, 'Justice and Home Affairs' in H Wallace, W Wallace and M Pollack (eds), *Policy-making in the European Union* (Oxford, Oxford University Press, 2005). On Police and Judicial Co-operation in particular see L Ferola, 'The Fight Against Organized Crime in Europe. Building an Area of Freedom, Security and Justice in the E.U.' (2002) 30 *Journal of International Legal Information* 53; S Skinner, 'The Third Pillar Treaty Provisions on Police Cooperation: Has the EU Bitten Off More Than It Can Chew?' (2002) 8 *Columbia Journal of European Law* 203.

[91] Art 29 TEU. Note the emphasis on EU *citizens'* safety.

[92] Note that the Draft Constitution ([2004] OJ C 310/1) in Art III-271 included 'trafficking in human beings *and* sexual exploitation of women and children' as particularly serious offences meriting criminal harmonisation.

[93] Council and Commission Action Plan of 3 Dec 1998 on how best to implement the provisions of the Treaty of Amsterdam on an area of freedom, security and justice [1999] OJ C 19/1.

[94] Tampere European Council (15–16 Oct 1999), Presidency Conclusions (available at http://www.europarl.europa.eu/summits/tam_en.htm).

[95] The Prevention and Control of Organised Crime: a European Union Strategy for the Beginning of the New Millennium [2000] OJ C 124/1.

[96] Comprehensive Plan to combat illegal immigration and trafficking of human beings in the European Union, 28 Feb 2002 [2002] OJ C 142/23.

the 1997 Joint Action), which is an example of approximation or the 'creation of EU-wide criminal offences'.[97]

The previous chapter noted how the goal of stemming migrant flows has coincided with the demonisation of migration as a threat to the 'internal security' of the Area of Freedom, Security and Justice.[98] A similar process can be recognised as regards the amorphous bogeyman of 'organised crime',[99] and indeed it is the concurrence of the two which demonstrates the twice securitised, and by now entrenched, place of trafficking in women at the nexus of migration and crime concerns. The official argument goes that since organised crime has extended its scope and acts on a transnational scale, any serious policy against it must be structured along transnational lines with transnational structures and bodies.[100] The migration–crime–security link provides a powerful impetus for co-operation despite sovereignty concerns—which, however, vitally inform the way co-operation is perceived and the form it takes. Concern over organised crime, and especially the involvement of non-nationals in it, and the attendant aim of developing cross-border co-operation to combat it is of course a recurring rather than a novel theme.[101] The roots of the current period go back to the 1970s, most famously to TREVI, which was concerned with terrorism and extremism in the 1970s, and more recently to Schengen co-operation.[102] As is well known, much of the action in this area involves Home Offices and security experts (with something of a predisposition towards securitisation), and is justified through the fears that in an area of free(er) movement of (some) people, goods and services criminal elements will make use of the opportunities provided.[103] The notion that certain forms of (irregular) migration in fact involve serious crimes against migrating women fits, at least on a superficial level, quite well with law enforcement objectives, and thus trafficking has climbed up the agenda.[104]

Arguably, legal harmonisation and the creation of an EU-wide offence of trafficking in humans were considered necessary because, to be able to agree on

[97] V Mitsilegas, J Monar and W Rees, *The European Union and Internal Security. Guardian of the People?* (Houndmills, Palgrave Macmillan, 2003), at 95.

[98] See the discussion about this above in section 4.1.2.

[99] On the problems of agreeing on a definition of organised crime see V Mitsilegas, 'Defining Organised Crime in the European Union: the Limits of European Criminal Law in an Area of "Freedom, Security and Justice"' (2001) 26 *European Law Review* 565. On the threat of 'transnational organised crime' see M Massari, 'Transnational Organized Crime between Myth and Reality' in F Allum and R Siebert (eds), *Organized Crime and the Challenge to Democracy* (London, Routledge, 2003).

[100] W Rees, 'Transnational Organized Crime, Security and the European Union' in *ibid.*

[101] See M Anderson, 'European Police Co-operation—History and Theory' in F Longo (ed), *The European Union and the Challenge of Transnational Organised Crime* (Milan, Giuffrè, 2002).

[102] At present the perception of threat and the quest for security are of course fuelled by the overriding priority of international terrorism, possibly financed by organised crime.

[103] See, eg, M Elvins, 'Europe's Response to Transnational Organised crime' in Edwards and Gill (eds), above n 88; on the 'professional managers' of this unease see D Bigo, 'Security and Immigration: Toward a Critique of the Governmentality of Unease' (2002) 27(supp) *Alternatives* 63.

[104] For other reasons see also B Locher, *International Norms and European Policy-Making: Trafficking in Women in the EU* (CEuS Working paper 2002/6, Bremen, Centre for European Studies, 2002). Locher argues that the emergence of feminist-minded co-operation and effective norm-linking at the European level also facilitated the placing of trafficking on the political agenda.

co-operation to tackle it, it must first be agreed what exactly one is talking about. Above all, the quest for a harmonised definition was given a boost by the adoption of the most commonly mentioned reference point in the criminalisation discussion, the United Nations Convention against Transnational Organised Crime[105], its supplementing Protocol 'to Prevent, Suppress and Punish Trafficking in Persons, Especially Women and Children'[106] and another Protocol 'Against the Smuggling of Migrants'.[107] Indeed, European action should also be set against the global initiative to criminalise trafficking and smuggling, for the European concern over both is not specifically European, in the sense that it to a large degree stems from, among others, economically developed countries' anxieties over global changes, such as the breakdown of the Cold War order and globalisation. These have given the impetus to regional action, which, on the one hand, implements some of the global initiatives but, on the other, arguably also tries to go beyond them owing to regional homogeneity, which may be a myth but is still claimed to facilitate deeper regional developments. In a sense, then, EU action can be evaluated in the light of 'implementing' the UN Trafficking Protocol and also developing a more characteristically European approach to the crime of trafficking as well as smuggling.

The UN Trafficking Protocol is now famous for establishing the first internationally agreed definition of the crime of trafficking in humans, for advancing national and regional initiatives and for facilitating crime control co-operation. It is the first instrument since the 1949 United Nations Convention[108] (which at the time consolidated earlier international agreements aiming to suppress trafficking in women and children[109]) to address trafficking under international law. The 1949 Convention was notorious for containing no definition of what it actually meant by trafficking.[110] The interesting thing is that it, like the UN Trafficking

[105] United Nations Convention against Transnational Organized Crime, A/55/383, which entered into force on 29 Sept 2003; current parties 119 (May 2006).

[106] Protocol to Prevent, Suppress and Punish Trafficking in Persons, Especially Women and Children, supplementing United Nations Convention against Transnational Organized Crime, A/55/383, Annex II (hereinafter UN Trafficking Protocol). It entered into force on 25 Dec 2003 and has 97 parties (including Austria, Belgium, Denmark, France, the Netherlands, Portugal, Spain, Sweden and the UK among the EU-15).

[107] Protocol Against the Smuggling of Migrants by Land, Sea and Air, A/55/383, Annex III (hereinafter UN Smuggling Protocol). It entered into force on 28 Jan 2004 and currently has 89 parties (May 2006).

[108] Convention for the Suppression of the Traffic in Persons and of the Exploitation of the Prostitution of Others, 96 UNTS 271 (hereinafter 'the 1949 Convention').

[109] These international instruments include the 1904 International Agreement for the Suppression of the Slave Traffic (1 LNTS 83), the 1910 International Convention for the Suppression of White Slave Traffic (3 LNTS 278), the League of Nations Covenant, and League of Nations treaties: the 1921 Convention for the Suppression of Traffic in Women and Children (9 LNTS 415) and the 1933 International Convention for the Suppression of the Traffic in Women of Full Age (150 LNTS 431).

[110] The 1949 Convention, above n 108, simply obliges state parties to 'punish any person who, to gratify the passions of another: procures, entices or leads away, for purposes of prostitution, another person, even with the consent of that person; exploits the prostitution of another person, even with the consent of that person' (Art 1). On the Convention see, eg, L Reanda, 'Prostitution as a Human Rights Question: Problems and Prospects of United Nations Action' (1991) 13 *Human Rights Quarterly* 202, at 209–11; J Chuang, 'Redirecting the Debate over Trafficking in Women: Definitions, Paradigms, and Contexts' (1998) 11 *Harvard Human Rights Journal* 65, at 75–8.

Protocol, understood trafficking as a criminal issue—but while its focus was on abolishing state control over prostitution, the latter focuses exclusively on trafficking as a form of 'serious transnational organised crime'. States parties to the UN Trafficking Protocol are required to criminalise trafficking in human beings in accordance with the given definition[111] (along with attempted, participation in and organisation of trafficking), when (in accordance with the parent Convention) these are committed transnationally and involve an organised criminal group, which is flexibly defined in the parent Convention. Establishing trafficking as a criminal offence means incorporating the essence of the definition in the Protocol; national criminal legislation may use simpler and clearer language which, considering the openness of the definition, can pose problems of further divergence.[112] The UN Trafficking Protocol also includes provisions for the prevention of trafficking and largely discretionary but wide-ranging measures for the protection of victims. The latter are optional, as the Protocol is a compromise that aims to reassure receiving countries concerned about their ability to decide on migration/prostitution control.[113] Nonetheless, the provisions are there, evidencing the incorporation, although not with equal emphasis, of all the three Ps of anti-trafficking action in the Protocol (namely prosecution, prevention and protection, considered in Chapter 1).

In the EU, the Council Framework Decision on combating trafficking in human beings was adopted in July 2002.[114] The definition of the Framework Decision largely copies that in the UN Trafficking Protocol. Paragraph 1 of Article 1 states:

> Each Member States shall take the necessary measures to ensure that the following acts are punishable:

[111] Art 3 states:

> '(a) "Trafficking in persons" shall mean the recruitment, transportation, transfer, harbouring or receipt of persons, by means of the threat or use of force or other forms of coercion, of abduction, of fraud, of deception, of the abuse of power or of a position of vulnerability or of the giving or receiving of payments or benefits to achieve the consent of a person having control over another person, for the purpose of exploitation. Exploitation shall include, at a minimum, the exploitation of the prostitution of others or other forms of sexual exploitation, forced labour or services, slavery or practices similar to slavery, servitude or the removal of organs;
> (b) The consent of a victim of trafficking in persons to the intended exploitation set forth in subparagraph (a) of this article shall be irrelevant where any of the means set forth in subparagraph (a) have been used;
> (c) The recruitment, transportation, transfer, harbouring or receipt of a child for the purpose of exploitation shall be considered "trafficking in persons" even if this does not involve any of the means set forth in subparagraph (a) of this article;
> (d) "Child" shall mean any person under eighteen years of age.'

[112] About the ambiguities of the definition see, eg B Sullivan, 'Trafficking in Women. Feminism and New International Law' (2003) 5 *International Feminist Journal of Poltics* 67. Symptomatically, there is little agreement on what the definition actually covers. See, eg, J Raymond, 'The New UN Trafficking Protocol' (2002) 25 *Women's Studies International Forum* 491. Compare J Doezema, 'Who Gets to Choose? Coercion, Consent, and the UN Trafficking Protocol' (2002) 10(1) *Gender and Development* 20.

[113] A Gallagher, 'Human Rights and the New UN Protocols on Trafficking and Migrant Smuggling: A Preliminary Analysis' (2001) 23 *Human Rights Quarterly* 975.

[114] Framework Decision 2002/629/JHA, [2002] OJ L 203/1.

the recruitment, transportation, transfer, harbouring, subsequent reception of a person, including exchange or transfer of control over that person, where:

(a) use is made of coercion, force or threat, including abduction, or
(b) use is made of deceit or fraud, or
(c) there is an abuse of authority or of a position of vulnerability, which is such that the person has no real and acceptable alternative but to submit to the abuse involved, or
(d) payments or benefits are given or received to achieve the consent of a person having control over another person

for the purpose of exploitation of that person's labour or services, including at least forced or compulsory labour or services, slavery or practices similar to slavery or servitude, or for the purpose of the exploitation of the prostitution of others or other forms of sexual exploitation, including in pornography.[115]

Paragraph 2 repeats the UN Trafficking Protocol's compromise clause on the role of consent and states that 'the consent of a victim of trafficking in human beings to the exploitation, intended or actual, shall be irrelevant where any of the means set forth in paragraph 1 have been used.[116] The definition is essentially the same as in the UN Trafficking Protocol, yet equally amorphous, as contested terms such as 'exploitation' or 'an abuse a position of vulnerability' are not explained.

The Framework Decision introduces a number of specific provisions that are not found in the UN Trafficking Protocol, for example, the demand that sanctions against trafficking be 'effective, proportionate and dissuasive', a minimum of maximum penalty for aggravated offences,[117] the liability of legal persons, and provisions on jurisdiction.[118] Most importantly, though, it omits practically all of the UN Protocol's (optional) provisions on prevention of trafficking and the protection of victims of trafficking.[119] The Framework Decision is thus even more clearly than the UN Trafficking Protocol (which, too, is primarily a law enforcement tool aiming at improving international co-operation against organised crime with only 'soft' provisions on victim protection and prevention measures) designed to be a prosecution and punishment tool. This goes hand in hand with the criminalisation

[115] Note that the Framework Decision makes a distinction between 'exploitation of labour and services' and exploitation of prostitution; there is thus an interesting tension with free movement law, under which prostitution is a job like any other, and Third Pillar rules, which seem to regard it as a special case of exploitation.

[116] In cases of child trafficking (ie concerning victims who are under 18) none of the means set out in para 1 of Art 1 is necessary (paras 3–4): of Art 1 UN Trafficking Protocol, above n 111.

[117] Ie, when the offence has deliberately or by gross negligence endangered the life of the victim; has been committed against a victim who was particularly vulnerable (minors are considered so, or those subjected to sexual—as opposed to other—exploitation), has been committed by the use of serious violence or has caused particularly serious harm to the victim; or has been committed within the framework of a criminal organisation (Art 3 of the Framework Directive).

[118] For an overview see, eg, T Obokata, 'EU Council Framework Decision on Combating Trafficking in Human Beings: A Critical Appraisal' (2003) 40 *Common Market Law Review* 917.

[119] What remains in Art 7 is a reference to conducting an investigation independent of accusation by the victim, and vis-à-vis children a reference to the Framework Decision on the standing of victims (which lists types of information, protection, compensation and support which Member States should provide for victims of crime), which, however, has limited scope and does not take sufficient account of the specific character of trafficking in human beings: see Council Framework Decision of 15 March 2001 on the standing of victims in criminal proceedings, 2001/220/JHA [2001] OJ L 82/1.

of human smuggling.[120] The repressive emphasis was justified by a lack of EU competence to venture too deeply into victim protection and the plan later to introduce an instrument more specifically regarding victims—the Directive on temporary residence permits for victims of trafficking which was adopted in April 2004. As was discussed above in Chapter 4, the Directive does not really deal with victims but witnesses, or arguably even considers them akin to *pentiti*,[121] and the residence permits give access to the most minimal and rigid 'protection' imaginable to a limited category of 'useful victims'. Thus it is the punitive side of the UN approach that is amplified in the EU response which is even more concerned with prosecution. Moreover, as not that much use has been made of the existing EU competence that could be utilised to address trafficking beyond the criminal/immigration framework, for example as regards aid for trafficking prevention or the long-term funding for programmes that would facilitate long-term victim support and reintegration measures (see below Chapter 7), it seems difficult to avoid the conclusion that a specifically European, as opposed to global, anti-trafficking response is firmly laid on a repressive foundation.

It is of course an often-made claim, and also admitted above, that it is simpler to agree on repressive measures against migration or even crime than on broader policy aims. As regards trafficking, agreeing on its criminalisation was relatively easy, in that most Member States did not have a definition deeply entrenched in national legal traditions, as trafficking as an independent offence is fairly new—most international 'harmonisation' has thus far focused on the exploitation of prostitution, and even that has not been defined. Moreover, just as the UN Trafficking Protocol's definition is wide and vague as a result of arduous negotiations during which it was impossible to agree on anything more specific,[122] the 'harmonised' definition of the Framework Decision leaves the specifics open. Considering the diversity in the prostitution policies of Member States, at least as regards those Member States that already have a trafficking offence on the books, it in effect harmonises little but at the same time entrenches the notion that trafficking is, above all, a criminal matter. The same issue arises with the Directive on residence permits, which is subordinate to national laws—where Member States retain the right to define the length of the period of reflection, the availability of psychological assistance, victims' access to legal aid, rules on the ability to work and access to education. This may in itself not be a bad thing considering the diversity of trafficking situations in different Member States, the tenuous trust between the Member States and the open questions about the proper role of the Union in pursuing convergence in the divergent criminal justice sphere.[123] However, if it is

[120] See Council Framework Decision 2002/946/JHA, [2002] OJ L/328/1.

[121] See above n 66.

[122] On the negotiations on the definition see Gallagher, above n 113, 984–8.

[123] On the contested nature of criminal law harmonisation see A Klip and H van der Wilt (eds), *Harmonisation and Harmonising Measures in Criminal Law* (Amsterdam, Royal Netherlands Academy of Arts and Sciences, 2002); A Weyembergh, 'Approximation of Criminal Laws, the Constitutional Treaty and the Hague Programme' (2005) 42 *Common Market Law Review* 1567.

assumed that the Union's role was and is to be to pursue further *European* policy on trafficking based on any kind of 'regional consensus', it at present evidences a clear trend towards more repressive and at the same time an unclearly defined law enforcement consensus over migration matters than anything else.

5.2.2 Anti-trafficking Co-operation: Security, Justice or Freedom?

The EU approach has brought trafficking firmly under the umbrella of its 'security threats' which merit an intensified repressive response, and the development of and continuing emphasis on suppression is evident also in practical co-operation. The attention paid to the involvement of transnational organised crime and its allegedly huge profits made from trafficking in humans may even ring true especially where organised crime has been able 'rapidly [to] adjust to new market opportunities'.[124] Considering the money allegedly made from trafficking and the frequently transnational nature of trafficking, which means that more than one state is often somehow involved (territory, suspects, financing, etc), what has frequently been lamented by many Member States is the relative lack of international and European co-operation in practice. Difficulties in investigating and prosecuting trafficking tend to mean that only a part of the chain can be tackled in one country in cases where mutual legal assistance simply does not yield results for reasons such as delays, problems in identifying the relevant authorities, other organisational or procedural problems or even relatively banal issues such as language problems.[125] This is a problem not only of the Member States; indeed, the difficulties in co-operation have been highlighted with regard to non-EU countries of origin or transit. Unsurprisingly, the intensification of European co-operation has been called for, also as regards the new Member States and remaining Candidate Countries.

The EU, as is well known, has responded to this call for improved co-operation in the field of crime, focusing (unsurprisingly) on the transnational element and in particular on the involvement of organised crime. A number of practical instruments have recently been introduced, often building on and intensifying the Council of Europe's efforts. The project of building a European criminal justice space has taken many steps forward.[126] These developments include the

[124] A Aronowitz, 'Smuggling and Trafficking in Human Beings: The Phenomenon, the Markets that Drive It and the Organisations that Promote It' (2001) 9 *European Journal on Criminal Policy and Research* 163.

[125] For a detailed investigation into these issues, see Rijken, above n 37, especially chs 4–6.

[126] Note also the role of EU funding, eg through the STOP Programme(s) on trade in human beings and all forms of sexual exploitation which ran until 2003; STOP is now subsumed under the AGIS Programme which is to help legal practitioners, law enforcement officials and representatives of victim assistance services from the EU Member States to set up Europe-wide networks and exchange information and best practices. During its first years AGIS has co-financed several projects on trafficking (as well as two that also partially addressed trafficking), mainly on network-building training and conferences.

Convention on Mutual Assistance in Criminal Matters[127] (and later the European Evidence Warrant) and the controversial European Arrest Warrant, in which trafficking was included as one of the crimes that facilitates the return of suspects.[128] Regarding the institutional framework, the most important development is, of course, Europol.[129] Its mandate, which is likely to generate some harmonising effect, is to improve the effectiveness and co-operation between authorities of the Member States in preventing and combating serious international organised crime (that now includes all forms of serious crime, as mentioned in the annex to the Europol Convention) including trafficking in human beings/illegal immigration as one of its main priorities.[130] In addition to the exchange of information between liaison officers (based in The Hague), analysis of trends and methods of crime, hosting experts' meetings (for instance biannual ones on trafficking) and arranging training for law enforcement officers, Europol is, slowly and controversially, moving in a more operational direction.[131] With regard to trafficking in humans it places the phenomenon quite squarely under an 'illegal migration' inspired framework[132] which is, interestingly, lamented at least by both the Swedes and the Dutch, and is with increasing frequency mentioned as a background actor in law enforcement operations that target criminal networks, for instance, the co-ordination of operation Leda in 2003. The more recent judicial counterpart of Europol, Eurojust[133] is to coordinate the prosecution and investigation of cross-border crimes, including trafficking in humans.

The obvious criticism of the organised crime/illegal immigration lens, through which for instance Europol sees trafficking in women for sexual exploitation, is

[127] Council Act of 29 May 2000 establishing in accordance with Art 34 TEU the Convention on Mutual Assistance in Criminal Matters between the Member States of the European Union, [2000] OJ C 197/1.

[128] Council Framework Decision of 13 June 2002 on the European arrest warrant and the surrender procedures between Member States, 2002/584/JHA, [2002] OJ L 190/1. For criticism of the EAW see S Alegre and M Leaf, 'Mutual Recognition in European Judicial Co-operation: A Step Too Far Too Soon? Case Study—the European Arrest Warrant' (2004) 10 *European Law Journal* 200. Note that in 2005 the German Constitutional Court annulled a law of July 2004 which implemented the EAW in Germany (BVerfG, 2 BvR 2236/04, 18 July 2005), (2005) 58 NJW 2289.

[129] See Convention on the establishment of a European Police Office [1995] OJ C 316/2.

[130] For criticism of the de facto extension of Europol's competence to cover all serious crime see, eg, Elvins, above n 103.

[131] See Council Act of 28 Nov 2002 drawing up a Protocol amending the Convention on the establishment of a European Police Office (Europol Convention) and the Protocol on the privileges and immunities of Europol, the members of its organs, the deputy directors and the employees of Europol [2002] OJ C 312/1. On the trend towards increasing operational activities note, eg, the participation in joint investigation teams: Council Framework Decision of 13 June 2002 on joint investigation teams, 2002/465/JHA [2002] OJ L 162/1.

[132] W Bruggeman, *Illegal Immigration and Trafficking in Human Beings Seen as a Security Problem for Europe.* (Conference Paper from the EU/IOM STOP European Conference on Preventing and Combating Trafficking in Human Beings, Brussels, 18–20 Sept 2002).

[133] Council Decision of 28 Feb 2002 setting up Eurojust with a view to reinforcing the fight against serious crime, 2002/187/JHA [2002] OJ L 63/1. Eurojust is composed of national prosecutors, magistrates or police officers of equivalent competence, nominated by each Member State according to its legal system, in a network that is to facilitate co-ordination and support of criminal investigations in organised crime cases.

that while it does make trafficking a priority concern, it tends to focus on just the egregious and obvious forms of crime and those networks that make the most money or that are involved in committing other transnational crimes as well (drug trafficking, money laundering, and so on); money is thus invested in intelligence and law enforcement co-operation that may be visible but not necessarily most useful in the long term.[134] A similar remark can be made regarding initiatives such as the EU Forum for the Prevention of Organised Crime, which discuss trafficking but mostly through a transnational law enforcement paradigm.[135] Yet even if it is clear that organised criminal activity, transnational or otherwise, organised or not, can be and is involved in trafficking, whether trafficking can be even primarily connected with organised crime is anybody's guess. What comes through from the limited research into trafficking is a wide range as regards the many kinds of operations and individuals that are involved. Although trafficking groups can be classified in several ways, for instance be divided into small, medium and large-scale operations,[136] it is extremely difficult to give generalised descriptions that fit all aspects of trafficking operations. To say this is not to discourage the development of improved co-operation or better methods of protecting witnesses against organised crime but to point out that even more rigorous and effective law enforcement co-operation against organised crime is unlikely to stop trafficking. The lopsidedness of law enforcement strategies regarding the multiple realities of the mechanisms and driving forces of trafficking means that they remain a blunt tool to address a complex reality.

In terms of broader concerns, the technically oriented and secretive decision-making of the new European institution(s) has frequently been criticised from the point of view of accountability and transparency, not to mention suspects' rights, especially as recent developments seem to be taking these institutions towards more operative action in this field.[137] The consequences for anti-trafficking strategies are not only that the priorities and aims of the co-operation can be suspected of stemming from and reinforcing the migration–crime nexus but also that they are largely invisible to the outsider. At the same time it is questionable how much an exclusive *EU* approach to improving law enforcement can do about the global co-operation challenges caused by trafficking. The lack of attention to global challenges is to a degree ameliorated by the 2004 EU enlargement as far as

[134] See, eg, Sheptycki, above n 88; M den Boer, 'The European Union and Organized Crime: Fighting a New Enemy with Many Tentacles' in E Viano (ed), *Global Organized Crime and International Security* (Aldershot, Ashgate, 1999), at 17–18.

[135] See, eg, European Forum on Prevention of Organised Crime, Workshop, 'Prevention of Trafficking in Human Beings' on 30 June 2003, Minutes and summary conclusions of the Chairman (Brussels, DG Justice and Home Affairs, 2003).

[136] Eg, B Ghosh, *Huddled Masses and Uncertain Shores* (The Hague, Martinus, Nijhoff, 1998), at 28 lists 'small and occasional' traffickers (who recruit and traffick in a few women at the request of brothel-owners), 'large-scale' traffickers (who use their extensive networks to organise trafficking from several countries and who cater to the demands of third parties) and 'medium-scale' traffickers (a hybrid of the first two who often recruit the women for their own clubs).

[137] For recent criticism see S Douglas-Scott, 'The Rule of Law in the EU—Putting the Security into the "Area of Freedom and Security and Justice"' (2004) 29 *European Law Review* 219.

co-operation with the new Member States is concerned, but does not solve the issue as far as other sending and transit countries are concerned. For improved co-operation, for instance, to tackle trafficking operations that in part take place outside the EU, a firmly and explicitly international angle is needed. This is particularly so if and when a large part of trafficking takes place from outside the enlarged Union as well as within it. Thus any co-operation among the EU Member States should at all cost avoid the reduction or cessation of co-operation with non-EU countries. In other words, building trust among Member States, especially after enlargement, should not lead to growing mistrust of others.

Moreover, in the grand scheme of things, there seems to be a tendency to mobilise criminal law, now at the transnational level, to answer all sorts of anxieties brought on by globalisation at the national level. This discourse is (unsurprisingly) now dominated by terrorism which is used as a justification for all sorts of initiatives, but in a less direct way trafficking fits the picture equally well. Indeed, some have highlighted the incoherent (and, some might argue, even random) manner in which certain concerns make it into the European agenda as harmonisation or co-operation targets.[138] Trafficking is where increasing human mobility, contested sexuality and fear of crime meet, and thus a convenient excuse for legitimating enforcement action for the 'protection of EU citizens' from alien elements that are seen as causing instability and/or crime. The Area of Freedom, Security and Justice is of course famous for laying more emphasis on security than on freedom or justice. Indeed, in this regard one may note, for example, the reinterpretation in the Vienna Action Plan that freedom also consists of 'freedom to live in a law-abiding environment in the knowledge that public authorities are using everything in their collective power . . . to combat and contain those who seek to deny or abuse of that freedom'.[139] However, the security (or freedom) sought through this kind of action is essentially a 'negative' style of security; freedom in the context of 'lack of threats'[140] (irregular migrants or crime) rather than 'positive' and broader security. In this respect one may note, for instance, the discourse on 'human security' that is sometimes used as the reverse of 'negative' human rights to express the positive need for protection from violence.[141] In this sense the superficial and exclusive understanding of security resonates well with the negative and limited freedom embodied in EC free movement law (see above Chapter 3).

To conclude, there has been very little serious discussion on and research into how effective, useful or justified (or not) this kind of transnational law enforcement approach to trafficking has been (or can be).[142] Furthermore, precisely because the perceived need to reinforce the European law and order approach to

[138] See Weyembergh, above n 123.

[139] Vienna Action Plan, above n 93, para 6.

[140] Mitsilegas, Monar and Rees, above n 97, at 84.

[141] For discussion of the concept see, eg, R Paris, 'Human Security: Paradigm Shift or Hot Air?' (2001) 26 *International Security* 87.

[142] On the need for this kind of discussion on the legitimacy and priorities of transnational law enforcement in general see Sheptycki, above n 88, at 52–3.

internal security threats, such as trafficking, mandates increasing monitoring and control, it involves dangers beyond the obvious realm of anti-trafficking action. The security that is allegedly threatened by crimes such as trafficking is that of EU citizens, who may or may not feel safer knowing that massive intelligence and law enforcement operations are taking place. Therefore, as in the migration context, a particularly strong exclusion tendency emerges along with the desire to control those not deemed part of the community—most obviously non-EU nationals, especially those who are defined as 'illegal' or 'criminals'. Yet increasing surveillance and control can get out of hand, especially if they are not matched by adequate checks and balances. The increasing Europeanisation of law enforcement is not necessarily benevolent even for the EU citizen considering the (in)famous transparency and accountability problems of the current Third Pillar.[143] Thus attempts to use the fear of trafficking, or other security threats for that matter, to legitimise far-reaching security-oriented developments should be scrutinised, not only because they tend to fuse crime and migration even further (and to perceive developing massive monitoring systems and closing the gates on the unwanted as nearly inevitable) but also because the people whose security is ostensibly protected through the fight against transnational crime are likely also to be affected.

5.3 CONCLUSIONS

In many ways the criminal framework is still very much dominated by national concerns, which provide a powerful structure that informs the way in which the Area of Freedom, Security and Justice is framed. Responses to trafficking to a high degree stem from national frameworks for dealing with prostitution-related problems, even if the element of migration has acted as the catalyst in emphasising the importance of taking common action. At the same time it seems obvious that at present EU action gives preference to the use of criminal justice co-operation in order to stem migration flows, rather than to extending the protection of the individual and collective freedom and bodily integrity of migrants, indeed possibly undermining the efforts of some Member States to protect (some of) them. Therefore, the surprising apparent concern about trafficking in women (surprising, that is, considering the frequent lamenting of the 'indifference' on the part of European institutions, politicians and the public to the plight of migrants in general) proves to be, in the practical light of the Third Pillar anti-trafficking activity, in fact quite consistent with the criticism that its emphasis is at present firmly on

[143] See, eg, M den Boer, *Taming the Third Pillar. Improving the Management of Justice and Home Affairs* (Maastricht, European Institute of Public Administration, 1998); Peers, above n 90. See also P de Hert, 'Division of Competencies between National and European Levels with regard to Justice and Home Affairs' in J Apap (ed), *Justice and Home Affairs in the EU. Liberty and Security Issues after Enlargement* (Cheltenham, Edward Elgar, 2004). Note that the Draft Constitution ([2004] OJ C 310/1) proposed to remedy some of these through the extension of ECJ competence (law enforcement operations carried out to maintain law and order or to safeguard internal security would still have been excluded from ECJ jurisdiction according to Art III-377) and the incorporation of the Charter of Fundamental Rights.

repressing and prosecuting trafficking, an approach that is at best relatively indifferent to those trafficked. While the repressive emphasis is to some degree understandable in terms of a global compromise such as the UN Trafficking Protocol, the EU as a more homogenous regional actor should be able to go beyond this focus. The emphasis on criminalising trafficking and related law enforcement measures appears to be the minimum solution in the conditions where there is no will or capacity to pursue broader measures, such as relaxing the general migration regime.

On a more positive note, while in terms of the role of the Union vis-à-vis trafficking the present focus tends to be heavily reliant on improving international police co-operation and other measures aimed at prosecution, this is not necessarily a worthless pursuit as such. In addition, the European level criminal justice response to trafficking is part of a very specific and rapidly evolving setting. The fact that most Member States have taken quite some time to ratify the UN Trafficking Protocol points to the dynamic and evolving nature of this area of law, as the delay has much to do with Member States wishing to wait and see what happens in the European sphere of harmonisation before amending their domestic legislation. The European responses are still emergent rather than fully formed. Now that the Framework Decision and the Directive on short-term permits have been adopted, however imperfect they may be in some respects, it may be the time to highlight the extent to which the limitations of these instruments speak clearly to the need for a more holistic approach. The EU could have a valuable role in this precisely because of its untapped potential to assist in striving towards a wider framework and avoid over-focusing on narrowly understood criminal justice and migration control measures. Certainly, if the EU aims to have a more constructive and broader role in sustained and more comprehensive anti-trafficking efforts, it should not remain prisoner to the lowest common denominator logic that characterises so much of JHA activity at present.

6

Trafficking and Human Rights

> . . . the current mass involvement of migrant women in the global sex industry has implications which go beyond the issue of the individual rights of the women (and men) involved, who may be looking to better themselves and their families. The issue, to put it bluntly, is that the poverty of certain regions of the world makes their women available to the men of the industrialised world for sex in return for money. This is much more than a labour rights issue or an issue to do with unequal development. It is a basic human rights issue because it entails such a massive form of discrimination.[1]

AT THE MOST general level, an anti-trafficking approach based on the universal rights of women is about basic norms and values. It stems from the recognition that trafficking is one of the various kinds of unjustifiable treatment that women face because and as a consequence of their gender. The aim of such an approach is to seek effectively to challenge the existing reality in which women who are trafficked in are both essential as a group for the functioning of globalised sex industries and yet of little consequence as human beings. In many ways one of the greatest achievements of the contemporary anti-trafficking movement is that it has not only brought the trafficking issue to the fore but provided ways to frame the issue of trafficking in terms of human rights, as opposed to seeing it (solely) as a problem of state control over borders and territory or of individual criminals. The primary motivation behind (and effect of) the affirmation that trafficking is a violation of human rights is to make the victim of trafficking 'visible' as a subject, emphasising her dignity and integrity, despite her prima facie irregular status as an 'illegal' non-citizen. This formulation transforms the victim into a subject whose basic rights have been violated by exploiters and whose rights can also be violated in the process of implementing anti-trafficking measures. Such an emphasis on the victims' need for *and* entitlement to respect—often with the focus on the traffickers' culpability in violating the victims' human rights and on state policies' lack of action against or even (often inadvertent) contribution to trafficking—thus tries to shift attention from states' right to control to the victims' humanity and the states' obligation to protect.

[1] M Dottridge, *International Instruments Against Traffic in Persons—When the 'Excellent' is the Enemy of the 'Good'* (NGO Consultation with the UN/IGOs on 'Trafficking and the Global Sex Industry: Need for Human Rights Framework', Geneva, 21–22 June 1999), at 82–3, quoted in J Morrison and B Crosland, *The Trafficking and Smuggling of Refugees: The End Game in European Asylum Policy?* (New Issues in Refugee Research, Working Paper No 39, Geneva, UNHCR, 2001), at 59–60).

Considering the many ways in which trafficking offends human dignity and violates basic human rights, it is not surprising that the idea of a 'human rights approach' to trafficking and what choices moving towards such an approach would involve have been advocated by lobbyists and academics alike, as it is seen as posing a real alternative to the dominant framing of the debate—and, indeed, it is possible to identify the influence of human rights discourses in the practice of some states.[2] Human rights also have particular appeal for those sympathising with the women's movement for the obvious reason that these are seen as precisely what women have been deprived of. The rights discourse in particular is, traditionally, considered to be a powerful one (considering rights as trumps and so on) and it is for this reason that so many embrace the 'human rights approach'. However, not much attention has been given to the fundamental reasons for which formulating anti-trafficking approaches (only) through reference to human rights might be considered problematic, despite its seeming benefits in providing solutions for trafficking victims, both present and future. Most importantly, often the arguments on the human rights of trafficking victims seem to remain rather superficially at the level of rhetorical exhortations that are easily made (and as easily, it seems, ignored) but which do not challenge existing political priorities. To examine why this is so, this chapter discusses 'rights talk' around trafficking, both recognising its benefits and scrutinising the problems and limitations that this choice carries with it. The emergence of an international human rights discourse around trafficking is discussed first; attention then turns to the problems that the rights approach presents at the level of domestic exclusion of migrant women. These issues are then looked at in the setting of the European Union.

6.1 FEMALE MIGRANTS AND INTERNATIONAL HUMAN RIGHTS

6.1.1 Actual Victims of Trafficking: Included if Invisible?

There are many sides to the claims made about practices such as trafficking in women for sexual exploitation and international human rights. First, and most typically, it is increasingly commonplace to find the statement that trafficking is above all a 'violation of human rights'.[3] What this usually involves is a moral and ethical claim that trafficking is unjust, but also more specifically that the exploitation of migrants in such ways involves harms that have been recognised by international human rights treaties, which result in state obligations to protect women from them.[4] Secondly, and in some ways most urgently, it has now

[2] On the whole, the process is similar to identifying sexual violence committed in the setting of armed conflicts as a gender-specific human rights concern, long neglected but at present increasingly recognised as a legitimate concern (and even 'mainstreamed' in some ways).

[3] See, eg, European Parliament Resolution on trafficking in human beings [1996] OJ C 32/88.

[4] See S Farrior, 'The International Law on Trafficking in Women and Children for Prostitution: Making It Live Up to its Potential' (1997) 10 *Harvard Human Rights Journal* 213; A Kartusch, *Reference Guide for Anti-trafficking Legislative Review with Particular Emphasis on South Eastern Europe* (Warsaw, OSCE/ODIHR, 2001), at 13–16; L Kelly and L Regan, *Stopping Traffic: Exploring the Extent of, and*

become standard to demand, like the UN Special Rapporteur on violence against women, that 'any remedy or strategy proposed to combat trafficking and provide assistance to victims of trafficking must be assessed in terms of whether and how it promotes and provides protection for the human rights of women'.[5] Finally, it is possible to make a convincing argument for considering that trafficking as a phenomenon stems from existing and prevalent human rights violations against women, especially regarding their social and economic rights.[6] These three issues of course link with the so-called 'three P approach' of 'prosecution, protection and prevention' that was highlighted in Chapter 1 as necessary for a more comprehensive approach: anti-trafficking measures should take effective action against violations and provide those victimised with remedies while protecting them from re-victimisation, and seek to prevent trafficking in the first place. This section deals with the first two claims, while the next section focuses on the third.

Enormous strides have been made in recent years with regard to formulating trafficking as a human rights issue, to the extent that one commentator states that it seems 'almost trite' to repeat the human rights dimension.[7] In certain ways this is so, certainly amongst those actors most firmly advocating the development of a human rights dimension. To mobilise the force of human rights discourse behind anti-trafficking, the case has to be made for harms of trafficking in women for sexual exploitation to be 'read' into existing human rights instruments,[8] in order to argue that the substance of many international human rights conventions covers trafficking.[9] Most importantly, the International Covenant on Civil and Political Rights[10] and the European Convention for the Protection of Human Rights and Fundamental Freedoms[11] set out a number of relevant fundamental rights and freedoms such as the right to life,[12] the prohibition of torture and inhuman/degrading treatment,[13] the prohibition of slavery, servitude and forced labour,[14]

Responses to, Trafficking in Women for Sexual Exploitation in the UK (London, Home Office, Police Research Series Paper 125, 2000), at 13–14.

[5] R Coomaraswamy, *Trafficking in Women, Women's Migration and Violence against Women* (Report of the Special Rapporteur on Violence against Women, its Causes and Consequences, UN Doc E/CN.4/2000/68), at paragraph 80.

[6] Eg, Farrior, above n 4, 231–2.

[7] R Piotrowicz, 'Irregular Migration Networks: The Challenge Posed by People Traffickers to States and Human Rights' in B Bogusz *et al* (eds), *Irregular Migration and Human Rights: Theoretical, European and International Perspectives* (Leiden, Martinus Nijhoff Publishers, 2004), at 146.

[8] The use of this kind of 'trafficking falls under' argument could be called what Kingdom refers to as a 'conversion strategy', ie the idea that 'women's rights' can be reconceptualised by appropriating 'conventional rights' for women: E Kingdom, 'Body Politics and Rights' in J Bridgman and S Millns (eds), *Law and Body Politics* (Aldershot, Dartmouth, 1995).

[9] See in particular S Toepfer and B Wells, 'The Worldwide Market for Sex: a Review of International and Legal Prohibitions Regarding Trafficking in Women' (1994) 2 *Michigan Journal of Gender & Law* 83; Farrior, above n 4.

[10] International Covenant on Civil and Political Rights, 999 UNTS 171 (hereafter the ICCPR).

[11] European Convention for the Protection of Human Rights and Fundamental Freedoms, 218 UNTS 221, CETS No 5 (hereafter the ECHR).

[12] ICCPR, Art 6; ECHR, Art 2.

[13] ICCPR, Art 7 (also covers 'cruel' treatment); ECHR, Art 3.

[14] ICCPR, Art 8; ECHR, Art 4.

the right to liberty and security of person,[15] the right to an effective remedy,[16] the right to the equal protection of the law[17] and the prohibition of discrimination in the enjoyment of rights.[18] In light of the 'virtually slavery-like' conditions at times involved in trafficking and the victims' subsequent engagement in prostitution, the Slavery Conventions, which deal with slavery, compulsory and forced labour, are also pertinent to trafficking for prostitution and similar purposes—and linking trafficking to slavery, of course, not only harks back to the 'white slavery' past of trafficking as a concept but evokes strong universal condemnation.[19] Similarly, the ILO Conventions on forced labour have been evoked with regard to trafficking in women for involuntary servile work.[20] And, finally, the 1990 International Convention on the Protection of the Rights of All Migrant Workers and Members of Their Families (ICMW) is increasingly mentioned, as it explicitly extends the scope of fundamental human rights to be granted to *all* migrants, both documented and undocumented.[21]

As trafficking is most often committed by third parties (non-state actors as opposed to state actors[22]), this sort of argument necessarily goes hand in hand with the claim that this fact alone does not justify state inaction in the face of apparent violations. Reference is made to the general acceptance that the ICCPR obligation of states 'to respect and to *ensure*' (Article 2)[23] and the ECHR obligation 'to *secure*' (Article 1) the rights to persons in their jurisdiction are not simply matters of a negative obligation to refrain from violating these rights but also involve a positive state obligation (of the type usually created by 'positive', economic and social rights) to take action to secure/ensure the enjoyment of protected rights.[24] Indeed, for instance the practice of the European Court of Human Rights affirms that (Article 1 together with) certain of the Convention rights can entail a positive obligation, often involving the duty to create and implement

[15] ICCPR, Art 9; ECHR, Art 5.

[16] ICCPR, Art 2(3); ECHR, Art 13.

[17] ICCPR, Art 26; implicit in ECHR, Art 14.

[18] ICCPR, Art 2–3; ECHR, Art 14. Note also Protocol No 12 to the ECHR, which involves a general prohibition of discrimination (meaning that the prohibited discrimination does not have to link with one of the rights enumerated in the ECHR, as is currently the case with Art 14).

[19] See the 1926 Slavery Convention (60 LNTS 253) and the 1956 Supplementary Convention on the Abolition of Slavery, the Slave Trade, and Institutions and Practices Similar to Slavery (266 UNTS 40). See also S Drew, 'Human Trafficking: A Modern Form of Slavery' (2002) 4 *European Human Rights Law Review* 481.

[20] In particular the Forced Labour Convention (1930, ILO Convention No 29, 39 UNTS 55), the Abolition of Forced Labour Convention (1957, ILO Convention No 105, 320 UNTS 291) and the recent ILO Convention Concerning the Prohibition and Immediate Action for the Elimination of the Worst Forms of Child Labour (1999, ILO Convention No 182, adopted 17 June 1999).

[21] As was seen above (see ch 4), EU Member States have been reluctant to sign and ratify this convention.

[22] There are, of course, cases where state officials, namely corrupt police or immigration authorities, have been actively involved in trafficking, but these are more the exception than the general rule.

[23] See, eg, the Human Rights Committee's General Comment No 3: Implementation at the national level (Art 2) (29 July 1981).

[24] Coomaraswamy, above n 5; L Chiang 'Trafficking in Women' in K Askin and D Koenig (eds), *Women and International Human Rights Law. Vol. 1* (Ardsley, NY, Transnational, 1999).

legislation (the obligation to protect life by law, the obligation not to provide 'inhuman' conditions and the duty to guarantee a fair trial and effective remedies).[25] Pertinently, the prohibition of torture and inhuman and degrading treatment (Article 3) can involve a duty, through law, to protect people from such treatment.[26] Implicit positive obligations have also been read into the duty to secure other rights listed in the Convention, when the *effective* protection of a right so demands.[27] It can thus be argued vis-à-vis trafficking (as some have hypothesised with regard to kidnapping by terrorists[28]) that there exists a positive obligation with regard to, for instance, the right to liberty and security of the person to prevent violations and to investigate and take action against violators.[29]

While these arguments are convincing, there are significant problems in such a line of reasoning about trafficking harms being covered by existing international human rights law. Concerns relating to this are exemplified by the fact that such an argument indeed must be made. In other words, human rights (or, indeed the structures of international law in general) have not been immune to gender-blindness any more than other areas of law; and it has of course been argued time and again that the human figure protected by 'human rights' has been implicitly (and sometimes explicitly) male.[30] There is no need to go through that familiar terrain here—suffice it to say that human rights traditionally cover harm to 'humans' as they were understood when the relevant human rights instruments were drafted, and that as a result certain goods are preferred and protected over others. Thus, apart from the Convention on the Elimination of All Forms of Discrimination against Women, which requires states parties to 'take all appropriate measures, including legislation, to suppress all forms of traffic in women and exploitation of prostitution of women',[31] the harms of trafficking are not

[25] For a recent treatise on the matter see A Mowbray, *The Development of Positive Obligations under the European Convention on Human Rights by the European Court of Human Rights* (Oxford, Hart, 2004).

[26] Eg, *A v United Kingdom* (1999) 27 EHRR 61; *Z and Others v United Kingdom* (2002) 34 EHHR 97.

[27] See *Marckx v Belgium* (1979–80) 2 EHRR 330 on Art 8 (respect for private and family life). On Art 8 see also *Airey v Ireland* (1979–80) 2 EHRR 305; *X. & Y. v Netherlands* (1986) 8 EHRR 235.

[28] See D Harris, M O'Boyle and C Warbrick, *Law of the European Convention on Human Rights* (London, Butterworths, 1995), at 101–2.

[29] There are Art 3 cases on this aspect. See, eg, *Assenov and Others v Bulgaria* (1999) 28 EHRR 652.

[30] For general overviews see J Peters and A Wolper (eds), *Women's Rights, Human Rights* (New York, Routledge, 1995); R Cook (ed), *Human Rights of Women. National and International Perspectives* (Philadelphia, Penn, University of Pennsylvania Press, 1994). For an intrdoduction to both international law and human rights as gendered, see H Charlesworth and C Chinkin, (2000) *The Boundaries of International Law* (Manchester, Manchester University Press, 2000).

[31] See Convention on the Elimination of All Forms of Discrimination against Women (CEDAW), 1249 UNTS 13, Art 6. The Art includes no description of the 'appropriate measures' required; its interpretation draws, among others, from the more general obligations to eliminate the existing discrimination against women (set out in Art 2 of the Convention). The Committee on the Elimination of Discrimination against Women, in its General recommendation No 12 on Violence against women (6 Mar 1989), links trafficking to poverty and unemployment and the need for equal protection and maintains, at para 24(h), that States Parties should describe in their reports 'the measures, including penal provisions, preventive and rehabilitation measures, that have been taken to protect women engaged in prostitution or subject to trafficking and other forms of sexual exploitation'.

explicitly covered by existing international human rights instruments.[32] It is of course no coincidence that CEDAW is the one international human rights treaty to mention trafficking in women, as it is the instrument that seeks to remedy the original myopic vision of human rights regarding gender discrimination. Similarly, the fact that it is necessary to mount an argument about states' positive obligations relates to the traditional position of civil and political rights (such as most of those of the ICCPR and the ECHR) at the apex of the hierarchy of rights that primarily (albeit not exclusively) relate to the state–individual relationship, guaranteeing the freedom of individuals (who are members of the political community) from state interference. Even when it is agreed that more than simple non-interference on the part of the state is required (as discussed above), there is no clear and definitive answer to what falls within the required action to prevent private parties from violating these rights, and the threshold can be quite high.[33]

It is precisely because the specific harms that are commonly directed at migrant women have typically been marginalised and/or segregated in mainstream human rights discourse that arguments are needed to 'include' trafficking harms under the provisions of existing human rights instruments.[34] Despite vigorous campaigning by activists, abuse (such as sexual violence or reproduction-related restrictions on women's sexual freedom) that arguably violates so-called 'women's human rights', most often committed by private actors with relative impunity, still tends to remain relatively marginalised as a mainstream human rights harm.[35] Yet even though there is no consensus on prostitution as such as definitely (in)compatible with women's human rights in principle, it is certainly the case that, as prostitution typically takes place in EU Member States today, it is fraught with what could be characterised as serious human rights problems. Typically these relate to violence and abuse of women in prostitution by their customers (and occasionally by law enforcement officers), which are allowed to continue with impunity, as well as to widespread discrimination against women in prostitution on the part of the authorities. The situation of many migrant women in prostitution, let alone that of trafficking victims, has typically been even more precarious due to the fact that guaranteeing effective protection from violence fits ill with prevalent negative stereotypes about migrant (especially non-white) women, the victims' mostly irregular residence status and the generally dismissive atmosphere regarding 'illegal' immigrants in many EU Member States. Yet it has taken a long

[32] Of the regional instruments, the American Convention on Human Rights prohibits 'traffic in women' under slavery in Art 6(1). Child trafficking is mentioned in the Convention on the Rights of the Child in Art 35. On the Charter of Fundamental Rights of the European Union, see below section 6.3.

[33] See, eg, *Osman v United Kingdom* (2000) 29 EHRR 245 (on Art 2 ECHR).

[34] See A Byrnes, 'Women, Feminism and International Human Rights Law—Methodological Myopia, Fundamental Flaws or Meaningful Marginalisation?: Some Current Issues' (1989) 12 *Australian Year Book of International Law* 205.

[35] C Romany, 'Women as *Aliens*: A Feminist Critique of the Public/Private Distinction in International Human Rights Law' (1993) 6 *Harvard Human Rights Journal* 87; R Cook, 'State Responsibility for Violations of Women's Human Rights' (1994) 7 *Harvard Human Rights Journal* 125.

time for this situation to be perceived as a human rights issue in any sense of the word, and it is still far from being universally accepted as one. In that sense repeating the human rights dimension is far from trite.

In the absence of anti-trafficking human rights norms with explicit and detailed obligations on required action, what has now become in some ways the central human rights question regarding trafficking is what an anti-trafficking response that 'promotes and provides protection for the human rights of women' would look like. While many agree on the need to criminalise trafficking, the lack of a human rights instrument that would *specifically* address the human rights issues that relate to the treatment of victims of trafficking has made this a crucial campaigning issue. The lack of explicit standards in human rights law was notable when the UN Trafficking Protocol was negotiated in 2000. As was seen above in Chapter 5, largely as a result of lobbying by activists, the Trafficking Protocol was subsequently drafted to include some flexible provisions on the treatment of victims. For instance, States Parties are encouraged to 'consider' implementing measures for the physical, psychological and social recovery of victims, invited to 'endeavour' to provide for the physical safety of victims and to 'consider' adopting measures permitting victims to remain in the destination country 'in appropriate cases'; repatriation 'shall be with due regard for the safety of that person and for the status of any legal proceedings related to the fact that the person is a victim of trafficking and shall preferably be voluntary'.[36] These provisions, limited and relatively weak as they are, owing to non-binding language ('appropriate cases', 'endeavouring'), were still a notable step forward in the sense that, despite the human rights attention that eventually focused on the Protocol, the instrument was not intended to be a human rights convention in the first place but an anti-crime instrument.[37]

The UN Trafficking Protocol notwithstanding (and tellingly enough), in terms of international human rights law there are still few absolutes about turning the human rights discourse into concrete policy measures to deal with trafficking victims (apart from the basic challenge posed by the human rights approach that focuses on the victims rather than the crime committed or immigration policy breached). Based on interpretations of what is required by states' human rights obligations and what best corresponds to the need to provide for humane treatment of trafficking victims, several rights-based measures have been suggested as stemming from general state duties to investigate human rights violations, take appropriate action against violators, and provide for remedies for those whose rights have been violated. The most concrete proposals on a human rights approach are formulated as guidelines aiming to elaborate on trafficking victims' hitherto neglected claims to legal protection, non-discriminatory treatment, an

[36] See the UN Trafficking Protocol, A/53/383, Arts 6–8.

[37] On the UN Trafficking Protocol as a 'missed opportunity' vis-à-vis human rights see A Jordan, 'Human Rights or Wrongs? The Struggle for a Rights-Based Response to Trafficking in Human Beings' (2002) 10(1) *Gender and Development* 28.

effective legal remedy and access to restitution, compensation and rehabilitation.[38] Such guidelines, which are not binding, expand on matters ranging from the non-criminalisation of trafficking victims (based on immigration violations or involvement in prostitution) and ensuring an adequate legal framework and access to justice, to legal standing and to support for physical and psychological recovery (housing, health care, and so on).

In many ways the most central issue related to the human rights of victims is protection from further victimisation, which is also hugely controversial as it is often directly linked with questions about the victims' (temporary or permanent) right to stay in the country of destination.[39] As was discussed above (in Chapters 4 and 5), arrangements for permits enabling a victim to stay in a country of destination at present primarily stem from the logic that trafficking victims can be useful as witnesses, rather than from any recognised desire to construct and expand effective human rights protection for such victims. It is around this issue that the discourse on human rights most clearly shows its scope but also its limitations. On the one hand, it backs up the claim that not only may it make sense from the point of view of prosecution to treat trafficking victims humanely (rather than as criminals), but that states by not doing so may actually be trampling on the victims' most basic human rights. Most obviously this relates to the right to seek asylum and to Article 3 of the ECHR,[40] which prohibits expulsion to face prohibited ill-treatment, as not only may some trafficking victims be potential asylum-seekers in the first place (before being trafficked[41]) but as some of them may face relevant ill-treatment or persecution if returned to their country of origin or transit without proper assessment of their individual situations (for instance where the country of origin cannot guarantee protection from further violence or where retribution by traffickers could amount to persecution).[42]

[38] See in particular Global Alliance Against Traffic in Women, Foundation Against Trafficking in Women and International Human Rights Law Group, *Human Rights Standards for the Treatment of Trafficked Persons* (Utrecht, GAATW,1999); UNHCHR, *Principles and Guidelines on Human Rights and Trafficking* (document E/2002/68/Add.1, 2002); Stiftelsen Kvinnoforum, *European Good Practice on Recovery, Return and Integration of Trafficked Persons* (Stockholm, Stiftelsen Kvinnoforum, 2003). Note also the OSCE Anti-trafficking Guidelines and the NATO Guidelines on combating trafficking in human beings for military forces and civilian personnel deployed in NATO-led operations.

[39] On the tensions raised by this issue, see Piotrowicz, above n 7, at 146–50.

[40] A similar argument can of course be made vis-à-vis Art 7 of the ICCPR, and in some rare cases, Art 3 of CAT (which includes an explicit prohibition against expelling, returning or extraditing a person where he or she might be tortured).

[41] See Morrison and Crosland, above n 1, for criticisms that the current restrictive policies contribute to the trafficking in (and smuggling of) asylum-seekers, as it is increasingly impossible for potential asylum-seekers to reach an EU Member State to seek asylum without resorting to networks which arrange facilitated migration (which makes asylum-seekers vulnerable, eg, to trafficking for sexual exploitation). See also K Koser, 'Asylum Policies, Trafficking and Vulnerability' (2000) 38(3) *International Migration* 91.

[42] See above section 4.2.2 on the relevant case law of the ECtHR regarding Art 3. This is still highly exceptional as there have been few cases of asylum or humanitarian protection granted to trafficking victims. One of these was in the UK, where the Immigration Appeal Tribunal accepted that an Albanian woman was faced with a real risk of persecution (and violations of Arts 3 and 8 ECHR) and was not being given sufficient protection by the Albanian authorities: *Secretary of State for the Home Department v K* [2003] UKIAT00023, 7 Aug 2003.

On the other hand, however, this line of argument shows how fragile the human rights framework around female migrants in irregular situations is. In some ways, human rights discourse directly challenges the current acquiescence regarding destination states' 'right to expel' trafficking victims as irregular migrants should they not be 'useful' enough, particularly as concerns victims originating from countries that do not or cannot provide adequate protection to individuals who have been trafficked. However, the fact that activists are required to make such exhortations about asylum and Article 3 ECHR (and so far with little success) shows that this is not the most obvious way of interpreting either path. Much has been said elsewhere about the gendered structures of asylum law (in particular the 1951 Geneva Convention) and how well (or rather badly) it has incorporated harms suffered by women, typically 'private' (for instance because they are suffered at the hands of non-state actors).[43] A similar argument can be made about Article 3 ECHR, with added comments on how the entire ECHR framework actually goes a long way towards accommodating the migration control/policing imperatives of States Parties.[44] Even though it is meaningful and indeed welcome to suggest a reinvention and even though some progress has been made in recognising gender-specific harms,[45] the fact that this rests on a fairly fragile foundation speaks volumes about the structural weakness of such frameworks when it comes to challenging the actual immigration and asylum practices of Member States and the Union (such as safe third country lists) and their potential for realising rights for migrant women who have been exploited but who are in an irregular migration situation. The real problem is thus not so much whether or not trafficking can be read implicitly to fall within existing human rights provisions, but that there seems to be little consensus, capacity, political will and pressure behind doing so with any consistency (and little official guidance as to what that may mean in practice).

6.1.2 Potential Victims of Trafficking: Marginalisation of the Marginalised?

The section above focussed on trafficking itself as a human rights violation and the treatment of the victims of such practices. This section discusses the argument that trafficking as a phenomenon is, in whole or in part, *caused* by human rights violations against women, especially, but not only, regarding their social and economic rights. This issue obviously implicates the third 'P', prevention. The contention is that trafficking is not only about individuals who violate the human rights of

[43] For early commentaries see, eg, D Neal, 'Women as a Social Group: Recognizing Sex-Based Persecution as Grounds for Asylum' (1988) 20 *Columbia Human Rights Law Review* 203; J Greatbatch, 'Gender Difference: Feminist Critiques of Refugee Discourse' (1989) 1 *International Journal of Refugee Law* 518.

[44] Apart from the case law that has developed Art 3 and Art 8 with regard to expulsion, the ECHR itself contains very few limits on state policies on entry and removal of individuals.

[45] See, eg, D Anker, 'Refugee Law, Gender, and the Human Rights Paradigm' (2002) 15 *Harvard Human Rights Journal* 133; N Kelley, 'Convention Refugee Definition and Gender-Based Persecution: A Decade's Progress' (2001) 13 *International Journal of Refugee Law* 559.

migrant women, but that it has 'root causes' which comprise a complex set of economic and social factors. In terms of human rights, this shifts the focus of the argument away from positive obligations regarding civil and political rights towards so-called positive rights. Here a valid argument can be made for stating that much of trafficking in women for sexual exploitation is, indirectly at least, connected with violations of women's economic and social rights,[46] and indeed various forms of discrimination against women, which channel a disproportionate number of women into poverty, poor education and limited opportunities for employment. Most typically, it has been argued that the failure of states of origin but also of transit and destination to pursue economic, social and cultural rights (such as a sufficient standard of living, working conditions and education for women and girls) with non-discrimination is 'causing' trafficking as it allows discrimination to continue and renders women vulnerable to seeking any possible means of escaping such discrimination and making a living, including taking up 'risky offers', and hence to being subjected to exploitative practices such as trafficking.[47] Connecting trafficking with this background is considered useful in shifting attention from the individual to the collective and structural level, and highlighting, for example, the gendered effects of economic restructuring in migrant-sending countries.

Again, however, laudable as the aim of connecting the root causes of trafficking to the lack economic and social rights is, there is also a certain irony in the connection that aims at providing an empowering reconceptualisation of rights. As is well known, the traditional construction of human rights is as 'freedoms from', which gives less room for incorporating collective goods, or values embodied in alternative (positive) notions of freedom.[48] This of course ties in with the (by now standard) complaint that international human rights discourse systematically privileges civil and political rights over economic, social and cultural rights in terms of both priority and enforceability. Most obviously, many economic and social rights are often framed in more flexible terms and considered policy goals rather than justiciable rights.[49] In light of recent judicial activity in the area, it

[46] Eg, the rights included in the International Covenant on Economic, Social and Cultural Rights (the ICESCR, 1966, 993 UNTS 3). The ICESCR contains, eg, rights to work (Art 6), the right to 'just and favourable conditions of work' (Art 7), women's right to equal pay for equal work (Art 7(a)(i)), the right to social security (Art 9), the right to 'an adequate standard of living', including food, clothing and housing as well as the 'continuous improvement of living conditions' (Art 11), the right to 'the highest attainable standard of physical and mental health' (Art 12) and the right to education (Art 13). The Covenant also provides that the states shall ensure these rights without discrimination (Arts 2(2) and 3).

[47] See, eg, Coomaraswamy, above n 5, para 54 ff.

[48] Eg, N Lacey, 'Feminist Legal Theory and the Rights of Women' in K Knop (ed), *Gender and Human Rights* (Oxford, Oxford University Press, 2004), at 38. See also above ch 3.

[49] Most famously, the duty set out in Art 2(1) of the ICESCR requires (only) that a state party 'undertakes to take steps . . . to the maximum of its available resources, with a view to achieving progressively the full realization of the rights recognized' (although these rights can also contain justiciable elements). On its interpretation see, however, eg, the so-called Limburg Priciples (UN Doc E/CN.4/1987/17, Annex) and General Comment No 3, The Nature of States Parties' Obligations (Art 2(1)), 14 Dec 1990, by the Committee of Economic, Social and Cultural Rights, both of which refute claims that there would thus be no immediate obligation to realise these rights.

would be too simplistic to say that all these rights are considered merely aspirational and programmatic, as some are sufficiently precise as to be justiciable.[50] However, many economic and social rights remain weaker than civil and political rights. Thus, if one accepts the argument that (some) economic and social rights are in certain ways disproportionately relevant for women (who constitute the majority of the world's poor, malnourished, unschooled and so on), not only directly but also indirectly, 'female' rights receive disproportionately little attention as 'proper' rights across the field from human rights organisations and national authorities. Despite rhetorical statements about the artificiality of making a division between 'negative' and 'positive' rights and the indivisibility of rights (true and increasingly acknowledged as it may be in certain quarters[51]), economic, social and cultural rights remain in many significant ways the poor cousins of civil and political rights, just as 'women's rights' tend to be located at the periphery of human rights discourse, ghettoised as a special interest. This is certainly even more so as regards the economic and social rights of migrant women.

Yet at the same time this line of argument *does* highlight the artificiality of conceptual divisions between 'negative' and 'positive' rights, and the actual interconnectedness of all human rights with regard to vulnerability to trafficking. Economic, social and cultural rights tie in with instruments such as the CEDAW, the comprehensive framework of women's rights, and the ICMW, which proposes to address the rights of migrants.[52] The Women's Convention provides a framework for realising equality between women and men in political and public life, but also in areas such as education, health and employment, whilst the ICMW makes it clear that basic economic, social and cultural rights apply even to irregular migrants. Whilst both Conventions have some flaws and omissions—for instance in that CEDAW pays very little attention to violence against women[53] and the ICMW has little to say on the specific problems facing female migrants in situations of flexible unregulated labour (in some ways both in this sense reflecting the time at which they were drafted)—both instruments nonetheless emphasise how intertwined the factors are that make migrant women vulnerable to exploitation.

[50] For an overview of economic and social rights see the articles in, eg, A Eide, C Krause and A Rosas (eds), *Economic, Social and Cultural Rights* (Dordrecht, Martinus Nijhoff Pusblishers, 2001); on justiciability see, eg, M Addo, 'Justiciability Re-examined' in D Hill and R Beddard (eds), *Economic, Social and Cultural Rights* (Basingstoke, Palgrave Macmillan, 1991); Report of the Expert's [*sic*] Roundtable Concerning Issues Central to the Proposed Optional Protocol to the International Covenant on Economic, Social and Cultural Rights (Geneva, International Commission of Jurists, 2002), ch II.

[51] See, eg, Vienna Declaration and Programme of Action (UN Doc A/CONF.157/23, 12 July 1993), which also, for the first time, recognises violenece against women as a human rights issue.

[52] In some ways similarly, the collective need but also lack of protection for (labour) migrants in practice can been highlighted with reference to the two ILO Conventions, the Convention on Migration for Employment (1949, ILO Convention No 97, 120 UNTS 70) and the Convention on Migrations in Abusive Conditions and the Promotion of Equality of Opportunity and Treatment of Migrant Workers (1975, ILO Convention No 143, 1120 UNTS 323). The latter requires respect for the basic rights of *all* migrants (Art 1).

[53] But note General recommendation No 12 on Violence against women by the Committee on the Elimination of Discrimination against Women, above n 31, as well as the roles played by the UN Special Rapporteur on Violence Against Women and the Special Rapporteur on Trafficking in Persons.

The structural conditions of sexual inequality and economic discrimination that deny women basic human rights because of their gender are crucially linked with the exploitation they may face once they migrate. Indeed, the issue of trafficking can even be linked to the third generation of rights, such as the right to sustainable economic and social development or group and collective rights.[54]

The problem lies in linking these human rights instruments, as well as in the persistent reluctance of states to agree to legally binding obligations and their weakness in terms of substantive obligations. This is highly relevant when one considers that trafficking is located in the nexus of economic, social and cultural rights, the rights of women[55] and the rights of migrant workers. The case of the ICMW illustrates the problems that relate to not only the famous disinclination of receiving states to recognise the economic and social rights of (in particular irregular) migrants, but the fragility of a legal regime of transnational migrants' rights in general. Beyond the well-known problem with ratification,[56] this links with how the immediate guarantor of human rights is still the state (and how, for instance, migrant workers thus remain dependent upon the receiving state for the protection of their rights). Moreover, the ICMW, even if ratified by states concerned about the economic burden migrants may impose, poses no fundamental challenges to state authority as regards the entry and residence of aliens.[57] In other words, in some ways revolutionary as the development of human rights standards applicable to all persons may be, far from eliminating the line between citizen and non-citizen in the creation of more universal post-national belonging,[58] the global expansion of human rights still in crucial ways respects the existing boundaries of states. Thus, even if ratified, the ICMW offer no panacea for remedying the inequalities that sustain the exploitation of migrant women.

Finally, and in some ways more ambitiously, while most human rights attention to trafficking focuses rather more modestly on the economic and social 'root causes' of trafficking in women, it is possible to argue that from the perspective of effective long-term prevention it is necessary to combine arguments about women's civil and political rights, about economic social and cultural rights and about even more aspirational 'rights' that relate to global economic issues with explicit arguments about bodily integrity and sexual autonomy. This sort of approach is adopted by some of those who discuss an emerging discourse of 'sex-

[54] On development see further below section 7.2.1.

[55] The CEDAW, despite a strong ratification base, is of course (in)famous for states' reservations. On the issue see R Cook, 'Reservations to the Convention on the Elimination of All Forms of Discrimination against Women' (1990) 30 *Virginia Journal of International Law* 643; B Clark, 'The Vienna Convention Reservations Regime and the Convention on the Discrimination against Women' (1991) 85 *American Journal of International Law* 281.

[56] The Convention has not been signed or ratified by a single EU Member State as migrant-receiveing countries view the obligations it involves with some suspicion—see above ch 4 for a fuller discussion.

[57] See for instance Art 79 of the ICMW: 'Nothing in the present Convention shall affect the right of each State Party to establish the criteria governing admission of migrant workers and members of their families'.

[58] Y Soysal, *Limits of Citizenship* (Chicago, Ill, University of Chicago Press, 1994), ch 8.

ual rights', which tries to elaborate sexual (and reproductive) rights in ways that emphasise the indivisibility of different generations of rights. Attempts at converting these kinds of arguments into explicit and concrete positive commitments have been fraught with difficulties.[59] At a conceptual level it is useful, however, to note how from this kind of perspective, for instance, women's bodily integrity and sexual autonomy, gender equality and social rights as enabling conditions merge. That this is rather far removed from traditional human rights thinking around trafficking emphasises how deep the structures that need to be challenged go, ranging from stereotypical gender roles to gender discrimination in education and health to global economic structures that regulate the conditions in which choices about sexual matters are made.

6.2 EXCLUSION OF MIGRANT WOMEN FROM DEBATES ON WOMEN'S RIGHTS

The international level has its problems, but devising domestic legislation or administrative policies to implement human rights obligations with an eye to reform also presents a set of interdependent and overlapping problems. These broadly relate to the factors that make it difficult to put human rights agendas to practice when they have into be translated into domestically-oriented debates about rights and redistribution. The content and formulation of human rights agendas raise questions about whether or not a broader notion of transnational structural reform that is needed to tackle trafficking can be achieved through reference to human rights alone, seeing as in domestic discourse they tend to become one policy consideration among many. As to the assumptions underlying rights discourse in particular, it can be argued that despite its empowering potential (the reason feminists have usually been positive about rights as strategies), rights discourse involves hazards when it comes to using it to advance the position of women in general and trafficking victims in particular. In short, problems emerge because existing inequalities mean that a discourse of rights, be it on 'women's human rights' or 'migrants' rights', may mitigate but also entrench subordination, and thus the prospect that rights agendas will ultimately 'solve' trafficking can be to some degree deceiving.

Some of the concerns about translating the moral momentum of a human rights imperative into practical application can be illustrated by reference to the above-mentioned CEDAW obligation in Article 6 that states 'shall take all appropriate measures, including legislation, to suppress all forms of traffic in women and exploitation of prostitution of women'. In terms of content, this obligation is

[59] See R Copelon and R Petchesky, 'Toward an Interdependent Approach to Reproductive and Sexual Rights as Human Rights: Reflections on the ICPD and Beyond' in M Schuler (ed), *From Basic Needs to Basic Rights* (Washington, DC, Women, Law & Development International, 1995); Y Tambiah, 'Sexuality and Human Rights' in *ibid*; R Petchesky, 'Sexual Rights: Inventing a Concept, Mapping an International Practice' in R Parker, R Barbosa and P Aggleton (eds), *Framing the Sexual Subject. The Politics of Gender, Sexuality and Power* (Berkeley, Cal, University of California Press, 2000). See also M Scheinin, 'Sexual Rights as Human Rights—Protected under Existing Human Rights Treaties?' (1998) 67 *Nordic Journal of International Law* 17.

extremely vague and indeterminate. It gives no guidance on what states must do in practice to be deemed to be 'taking appropriate measures'.[60] It could be argued this merely involves an obligation to introduce criminal provisions against such exploitation and to investigate allegations of such abuse with due diligence. Or it could be connected to much broader issues, such as to Article 5 CEDAW which urges states to take all appropriate measures 'to modify the social and cultural patterns of conduct of men and women, with a view to achieving the elimination of prejudices, and customary and all other practices which are based on the idea of the inferiority or the superiority of either of the sexes or on stereotyped roles for men and women'. Even though again the formulation is very open to interpretation, at least one commentator on trafficking has connected it to the requirement to resist the exploitation of prostitution and trafficking as rooted in cultural and social notions of female inferiority.[61]

These concerns can again be highlighted with reference to the debates in the Netherlands and in Sweden over prostitution and trafficking (see above Chapter 3). Indeed, their domestic debates over law reform are particularly pertinent as they concern conflicts over the human (especially female) body, which 'involve immense social, political, economic, sexual and psychological complexity'.[62] In these debates rights talk was indeterminate enough to support (part of) both feminist arguments about women's human rights. At the same time it has been observed how feminist discussions on sexuality, which seek to challenge the dominant perceptions, easily become 'trivialised' when they meet and use the discourse of rights; the discussion then degenerates into a 'line-drawing debate' that reduces complex lines of reasoning about broader reform into competing arguments.[63] This in part also explains why feminist analyses of prostitution ended up not only reduced into simplification but competing with each other.[64] In the frame of the Dutch and Swedish debates, even though both sought to undermine 'the dominant definitions of sexuality', when the issue was formulated in terms of

[60] Although note that the Committee on the Elimination of Discrimination against Women that oversees the Women's Convention now increasingly gives States Parties some (if usually fairly general) feedback on measures required by Art 6 when examining their reports. Often these relate to legislative measures and protection of victims: see, eg, Comments on the latest Swedish (UN Doc A/56/38, 2001, paras 354–355) and Dutch (UN Doc A/56/38, 2001, paras 211–212) reports. See also General Recommendation No 19, above n 31, which mentions penal provisions as well as preventive and rehabilitation measures.

[61] See Farrior, above n 4, at 227–30. Compare this to the Convention against Racial Discrimination, which states, '[e]ach State Party shall take effective measures to review governmental, national and local policies, and to amend, rescind or nullify any laws and regulations which have the effect of creating or perpetuating racial discrimination wherever it exists' (Art 2(1)).

[62] F Beveridge and S Mullally, 'International Human Rights and Body Politics' in Bridgman and Millns (eds), above, n 8, 247.

[63] F Olsen, 'Statutory Rape: A Feminist Critique of Rights Analysis' (1984) 63 *Texas Law Review* 387, at 389–90.

[64] The exploitation view becomes one of a 'human right' to sexual security and freedom from prostitution, and the work view one of a 'human right' to choose prostitution. Yet it is a huge leap from recognising that prostitution is often abusive and certainly not the job for everyone to affirming the 'right to prostitute', on one hand, and, on the other, from arguing that many women have few alternatives but to make a living out of prostitution to arguing 'the freedom from prostitution'.

rights, it resulted in significant reduction in complexity behind the arguments and demands: feminist demands to address prostitution were reduced to demanding legalisation or criminalisation, even though it was clear that more was needed. Many Dutch feminists did recognise that legalisation alone is unlikely to stop the abuse of women in prostitution if wider societal issues (such as the devaluing of women) were not addressed, and that while the law may respect the will of (some) women in prostitution it also respects the presently sexist foundations of the sex industry. Indeed, some called for women entrepreneurs to replace men as brothel-keepers and the cleansing of prostitution of exploitative, criminally-minded businessmen.[65] Swedish feminists emphasised the need for resources to help women get out of prostitution, as it was recognised that it is hugely unrealistic to consider the criminalisation of prostitution, without offering women in prostitution other options to gain a living, improvement in women's social and economic situation or the elimination of gender-based ideologies sustaining prostitution.[66]

This in turn links with a staple feminist concern that 'rights talk' ignores complex power relations that underpin actual access to formulating what should be done about guaranteeing human rights. Gender is one the existing axes along which access to formulating rights agendas is organised. The fact that rights talk over prostitution was indeterminate enough to support (part of) both feminist arguments about rights (despite its incapability to provide a satisfactory solution), the centrality of the legal arena together with the fact that rights assume equal agency of the parties mean that rights discourse can be manipulated for decidedly non-feminist purposes as well. Indeed, arguably these structural issues make rights talk much more open to interventions of the non-feminist kind and can thus be easily hijacked by those with more power.[67] The issue is evident in the prostitution and trafficking context where brothel-keepers and pornography-producers as well as religious fundamentalists even use ostensibly 'feminist' arguments for manifestly anti-feminist purposes (of liberating the sex industry from any restrictions on its operation or of emphasising religious–patriarchal constraints on migrant women's freedom). In the Dutch debates on legalising brothel-keeping, the argument was presented that provisions of the 1911 law that banned keeping a brothel unduly interfered with the right freely to choose one's occupation, *not* with regard to the prostitute but by preventing individuals who might be interested in choosing to keep a brothel as their occupation from exercising this right, guaranteed in the Dutch Constitution.[68] The (in)famous debate on banning pornography in the

[65] Compare this with the Dutch pornography debates over a decade earlier: feminists were drawn into a rights debate (which they lost). The implications are explored in C Brants and E Kok, 'Penal Sanctions as a Feminist Strategy: a Contradiction in Terms? Pornography and Criminal Law in the Netherlands' (1986) 14 *International Journal of the Sociology of Law* 269.

[66] On the lack of resources to provide women in prostitution with other alternatives, see L Sohl, 'Politisk vilja är inte allt—fram med pengarna!' (2003) 1 *Bang* 56.

[67] The argument about how the feminist claim of women's 'rights' to reproductive control can be appropriated by men is only the most well-known example: see Kingdom, above n 8.

[68] Art 19.3 of the Dutch Constitution reads: '[t]he rights of every Dutch national to a free choice of work shall be recognised, without prejudice to the restrictions laid down by or pursuant to and Act of Parliament'.

US context is an excellent example of the religious right appropriating feminist arguments to ban 'moral degradation'; for an illustration in the trafficking context, one need only think how some states come up with measures to prevent female migration altogether and justify these with the need to protect women's rights.

Indeed, and in some ways most crucially, those marginalised altogether, namely those who for various reasons have no means of voicing (or even perceiving) their concerns (at least in terms of rights), are frequently excluded at domestic level. The voice of non-EU migrant women was drowned under the weight of the criminal justice/migration policy imperative in the law reform processes in the Netherlands and Sweden. In the Netherlands, the legal reforms of the 1990s were much supported by the Dutch feminist community; due to the influence of the sex worker lobby in the Netherlands, a broad consensus in the feminist community found it necessary to support the human rights based claims of Dutch sex workers.[69] Feminists were influential in driving through the law reforms, which were considered something of a victory. Yet, despite claims of listening to sex workers and respecting their human rights, feminist campaigners did not manage to include the voice of migrant sex workers, despite their growing number; in general public and political debates they were barely visible, apart from being used as a threat to the stability of the existing sex industry and to Dutch sex workers' rights. In Sweden, in line with a 'prostitution is a human rights violation' view, feminists persuasively argued that respect for women's human rights required that prostitution be addressed as part of male violence against women. The view promoting client criminalisation gained legitimacy when it was connected to the emerging 'right' to freedom from sex-related violence.[70] Here too the law reform was heralded as a success for women's rights; yet again resources really for tackling the issue were scarce, and women in prostitution (migrants or not) were almost completely invisible in the debates. Perhaps this was due to their unwillingness/unpreparedness to take on the majority view in circumstances where their voices were bound to be ignored as those of 'victims who participate in their own exploitation'.

As a result, while the discourse on women's human rights was used to justify law reform both in the Netherlands and in Sweden, it was unable to take on the powerful voices that argued that no-migration policies and repressive law enforcement are necessary to protect (EU) citizens' rights. It is thus not surprising that migrants' rights were a complete non-issue in both countries. The Dutch Law was adopted because it was thought that legalisation and stricter controls might 'clean

[69] See J Outshoorn, 'Regulating Prostitution as Sex Work: the Pioneer Case of the Netherlands' (2001) 36 *Acta Politica* 155. See also J Outshoorn, 'Sexuality and International Commerce. The Traffic in Women and Prostitution Policy in the Netherlands' in T Carver and V Mottier (eds), *Politics of Sexuality, Identity, Gender Citizenship* (London, Routledge, 1998); E Venicz, *A Discourse of Impotence, Dutch Politicians and their Efforts to Control Migrant Prostitutes* (Conference Paper from the Conference Beyond boundaries, sexualities across cultures, July 1997, unpublished).

[70] On this see the Committee on Violence against Women, *Kvinnofrid. Huvudbetänkande au Kvinnovåldskommissionen* (SOU 1995:60).

up' the sex industry; the fact that Dutch prostitutes vigorously demanded their right to sexual self-determination created extra support for law reform.[71] The correct interpretation of the Dutch policy is not so much as tolerance but as pragmatism or indifference. Most importantly, there is some xenophobia behind the 'right to prostitute': the person to claim it has to be sufficiently close to the liberal subject of rights (EU citizens) to be allowed to 'choose'; at the same time many of those who claim it often do so under heavy economic restraints. There is an irony in that women's movements would end up supporting the marginalisation of a large number of women on the same grounds (not being enough like the autonomous liberal subject of rights) that women in general have had difficulty exercising rights. This is not to deny that foreign women may not run a higher risk of exploitation; however, instead of being able to challenge the structures that make this so, feminists took what limited reform they could get at the cost of exclusion of others. Nor is it difficult to link Swedish law reform to the fear that Sweden might become a market for foreign prostitutes; in a paradoxical way in Sweden all women in prostitution were excluded. In some ways both of these stories meet in Italy, where both the penalisation of customers and the reopening of *case chiuse* (brothels) are promoted with little or no reference to migrant women's human rights at all.

The valuable gains that have nonetheless been achieved by resort to human rights language over the years make it difficult to consider giving up the language even though (or perhaps because) it is indeterminate and malleable—and as such vulnerable to manipulation. At the same time in these debates the underpinning idea that human rights may actually *direct* the policy formation of prostitution and trafficking tends to get lost. Rather then leading to a transformation in which the human dignity of all, migrants included, is recognised as a fundamental priority, human rights become a policy consideration among others. The obvious reference here can be made to the famous article by Koskenniemi, in which he argues that 'rights talk' tends to become institutionalised and reduced to a legalistic paradigm in which deeper values are marginalised and that a proliferation of rights rhetoric without any deeper respect for them (apart from as a policy consideration) leads to a 'political culture of bad faith'.[72] That this is particularly relevant vis-à-vis actual and potential trafficking victims who are powerless both as women and as migrants in irregular situations merely serves to highlight the broader fact that rights talk, without any deeper transformation of both local and global structures that underpin the exploitation of migrant women, is less adept at remedying certain kinds of entrenched harms. Changing these requires reallocation of resources and deep institutional commitment to positively contributing to a more profound societal transformation at the local, regional and international levels.

[71] See Outshoorn (2001), above n 69.

[72] M Koskenniemi, 'The Effect of Rights on Political Culture' in P Alston (ed), *The EU and Human Rights* (Oxford, Oxford University Press, 1999).

Beyond the problems of expressing national concerns over sexual exploitation in terms of human rights, there is a specific problem with assuming that rights discourse in particular will solve the plight of trafficking victims (in other words, with the assumption that their situation can be improved through the exercise of atomistic agency in the legal arena), or at least that this alone would serve as the 'human rights approach'. This problem relates back to the basic liberal notions of the subject of (especially civil and political) rights as a self-possessing, able-bodied, independent and rational individual.[73] While it used to be bodily difference which was historically used to exclude those with female bodies from the exercise of rights, in practice rights discourse still tends to appear like a masculine construction (in line with the feminist criticism of the legal subject and rights conferred on it as 'male').[74] It assumes a self-possessing individual in control of his or her self, who exercises (negative) rights freely and actively. This ignores the reality in which different kinds of people, such as men and women, have dissimilar capacities to, for instance, enjoy control over their bodies and to decide on and consent to their use.[75] In the real world rights are exercised under conditions of social, economic and psychological restraints, which in many cases disproportionately affect groups such as women, or ethnic minorities, or migrants in an irregular legal position.[76] Rights constructed in an abstract and universal manner as 'freedoms from', without reference to actual economic, social and cultural possibilities actually to enjoy them, are thus prone to operate to the detriment of those who are less privileged. Assumptions of equal access to justice and the equality of the parties systematically work to the detriment of those with less power who less easily fit the model subject of rights.[77] In addition, this fact is hidden from view by the notion of the legal subject as a universal individual without specific characteristics.

Relating this back to the phenomenon of prostitution and trafficking, it is not difficult to see that strong constraints (such as poverty, marginalisation and discrimination) prevent women involved in prostitution from exercising whatever rights they may have on paper; indeed, it is a staple of feminist critique that this is the case even when prostitution is decriminalised.[78] These obstacles are, obviously, even stronger in the case of trafficking victims considering, for instance, language barriers, irregular status and unfamiliarity with the legal system. To take a specific example from the ranks of relatively empowered trafficking victims—

[73] See C MacKinnon, *Towards a Feminist Theory of the State* (Cambridge, Mass, Harvard University Press, 1989), Kingdom, above n 8.

[74] N Naffine, 'The Body Bag' in N Naffine and R Owens (eds), *Sexing the Subject of Law* (Sydney, LBC Information Services, 1997); N Naffine 'The Legal Structure of Self-ownership: Or the Self-possesed Man and the Woman Possessed' (1998) 25 *Journal of Law and Society* 193; N Naffine, 'Can Women be Legal Persons?' in S James and S Palmer (eds), *Visible Women: Essays on Feminist Legal Theory and Political Philosophy* (Oxford, 2002).

[75] Above chs 2 and 3.

[76] The most famous example of a potentially 'empty' right is the right to reproductive freedom (which, without access to, eg, abortion facilities and health care, means nothing) but this applies to 'sexual and reproductive rights' more broadly as well as their enjoyment requires enabling conditions.

[77] See, for instance, C Smart, *Feminism and the Power of the Law* (London, Routledge, 1989).

[78] See above ch 2.

that is those who have been identified, and assisted and who have legal residence rights, for instance for acting as witnesses—the right to sue one's traffickers is often brought up as part of a human rights approach to trafficking.[79] Despite a lack of special provisions, in many Member States there is nothing to prevent (identified) trafficking victims from suing their (captured and convicted) traffickers for compensation in normal civil procedure. Yet in practice this does not often take place, for merely 'having' a right does not empower one to exercise it, or to do so successfully.[80] In the case of trafficked women this discrepancy between rights on paper and rights in practice is perhaps most obvious: the victims are non-nationals, not infrequently from discriminated against racial or ethnic minorities, typically poor and traumatised by the experience, unfamiliar with the language and legal culture of the destination country, usually still in a precarious legal situation and often threatened with retribution by traffickers. Moreover, victims do realise they have been 'treated badly', but do not necessarily recognise themselves as having legal rights they could claim. They are thus far removed from the ideal subjects of rights who actively exercise their rights.

Of course this fact is often acknowledged (implicitly or explicitly) by those who point out that trafficking victims must have access to many kinds of assistance, ranging from legal assistance to social security and so on to enable them to see themselves as rights-holders who have a right to reparation.[81] While such assistance would certainly be a worthwhile step forward, past experience as regards rape, domestic violence and sexual harassment indicates that this is not necessarily enough, as this does not transform the structural frame in which rights operate. Despite support given by state authorities to protect and assist those women who are identified as trafficking victims, it remains that those who use rights are those who have already begun to help themselves (for instance by seeking a way out of their irregular situation). Even if one is not talking about compensation claims, in order to make sure that victims receive the necessary residence permits or can take part in the recovery programmes they are entitled to, much activity on the part of victims is required. This is also true with regard to access by trafficking victims to the social support that is necessary for their recovery from abuse (but never even formulated as a right). There are, of course, ways to alleviate this situation, most notably by encouraging greater NGO involvement in order to support victims in the legal process.[82] NGO involvement is most obvious in Italy, where specialised NGOs are (ideally) involved with the victims from discovery through the legal

[79] See, eg, Jordan, above n 37, at 34.

[80] Certainly for those trafficking victims who have been expelled to their country of origin it is nearly impossible for jurisdictional reasons alone. It is never easy to bring actions in the courts of another nation, but this is emphasised in trafficking cases where the victim rarely has the financial and administrative resources to assert her rights.

[81] On the 'rights awareness' transformation needed for seeking the help of the legal system (in the context of domestic violence) see S Merry, 'Rights Talk and the Experience of Law: Implementing Women's Human Rights to Protection from Violence' (2003) 25 *Human Rights Quarterly* 343.

[82] But compare the EC Directive on the temporary residence permit, [2004] OJ L 261/19, which can hardly be said to provide the basis for extensive NGO co-operation (see Arts 5 and 12).

process to eventual recovery, while a less extensive NGO role exists in the Netherlands, where NGOs, however, have a great deal of responsibility for assistance.[83] In Sweden, where welfare mechanisms are in general most formalised, the task has fallen to the social and welfare authorities (which in turn underlines the need for specialised staff, training and language skills).

However, even though such measures may mitigate the extreme forms of inequality before the law, they do not touch upon the structural assumption behind rights discourse; that of individual rights-holders aggressively pursuing thier rights in the legal arena is a useful way of settling matters. The matter also links to the above-mentioned adversarialism and competitiveness that go with rights holders pursuing their rights and the legalistic environment in which rights claims operate. The fact that rights discourse assumes that litigation also links with the proliferation of rights discourse almost inevitably leads to increasing conflicts between rights, where 'new' rights have to compete with other rights, many of which are far better established (such as the better entrenched rights of the (typically male) defendant in a criminal trial, which have clashed with the less-established 'rights' of victims of sexual violence or sexual exploitation).[84] In the desire to obtain the occasional gains that the resort to rights can provide, not many commentators care to highlight the fact that resorting to rights may even inadvertently reproduce rather than challenge existing power structures under present enforcement mechanisms of rights frameworks in which the marginalised rarely win more long-lasting victories that would result in actual societal transformation.[85] Indeed, targeting all efforts to gain such litigation victories for some individual trafficking victims may become a façade that conceals the abandonment of the deeper transformative message of a human rights approach.

How can the marginalised win more permanent victories and how could the transformative potential of the human rights approach be maximised? With a view to redeeming the deeper idea behind a human rights approach one may note that beyond the issues of rights discourse, much of the agenda, which is at present expressed in the language of rights, really connects with long-term goals of global economic justice (such as eradicating poverty and inequalities of gender, race and wealth). These can be formulated in terms of rights (to highlight, for instance, the entitlement of everyone to have his or her basic needs met), even though it may be recognised that relying on rights language is not always the most successful (or even appropriate) way of calling for equality in the distribution of global economic and social well-being, as rights tend to be about minimum rather than maximum

[83] See above section 5.1.2.

[84] This phenomenon has been most typically present at rape trials, with the result that victims of sexual violence are frequently intimidated and traumatised further by the questioning by the defence. This is not to say that defendants should be denied the right to question the victim, but rather to have reservations about the way it is allowed to be done. About the problems with prosecuting rape see, eg, S Estrich, *Real Rape* (Cambridge, Mass, Harvard University Press, 1987); S Lees, *Carnal knowledge. Rape on Trial* (London, Hamish Hamilton, 1996). These can of course be mitigated, if not eliminated, by developing gender-sensitive practices to deal with rape complainants in the courtroom.

[85] W Brown, 'Suffering Rights as Paradoxes' (2000) 7 *Constellations* 208.

standards. The global structural issues are central for successful anti-trafficking agendas aiming at a long-term preventative effect; yet it may be that empowering women, the reduction of complex inequalities and ameliorating social and economic injustices require a less dichotomised, legalistic and individualistic view of the good involved than human rights arguments alone seem to offer, even in terms of positive and collective rights.[86] This is not to suggest that the discourse on (women's) economic and social rights or sexual rights is meaningless, or that it should be abandoned; rather that it has to be deepened and made more determinate, for instance through a focus on capabilities of actually benefiting them.[87]

6.3 THE EUROPEAN UNION'S HUMAN RIGHTS DIMENSION

In some ways several of the above issues are even more pertinent with reference to the EU, considering its economic origins; although the EU is not, and never has been, what could be characterised as a human rights organisation, and indeed in many ways because of this fact much has been written about the EU and human rights in the context of 'market rights', ECJ jurisprudence, the potential accession of the Union to the European Convention on Human Rights and in general about the growing demand for an EU human rights policy and its relation to recent constitutional developments.[88] Most recently, the focus has been on developments such as the Charter of Fundamental Rights of the European Union, which for the first time clearly articulated the fundamental values the Union holds dear beyond its traditional orientation towards market integration.[89] The constitutional development of human rights discourse in the Union culminated with the inclusion of the Charter in Part II of the Constitution for Europe in 2004, at that time anticipating its binding nature vis-à-vis EU institutions and Member States when they implement Union law.[90] Both the Charter and the Constitution were arguably substantial steps forward, placing human rights closer to the heart of the EU at a time when it touches upon many fields beyond the market, and thus has a vastly increased capacity to affect the human rights of individuals (for instance in the establishment of the AFSJ). The current situation of the Constitution is of course less clear, with the current 'period of reflection' after the French and Dutch referenda that rejected the Constitution. What was always open to debate was how this

[86] See, however, Pogge's (moral rather than legal) argument that some entrenched inequalities (his argument is about severe poverty in the devoping world) are, as violations of human rights, traceable to the global economic regime that disadvantages the poor: T Pogge, *World Poverty and Human Rights* (Cambridge, Polity Press, 2002).

[87] A Sen, *Development as Freedom* (Oxford, Oxford University Press, 1999); M Nussbaum, *Women and Human Development. The Capabilities Approach* (Cambridge, Cambridge University Press, 2000).

[88] Comité des Sages, *Leading by Example: A Human Rights Agenda for the European Union for the Year 2000* (1998); P Alston (ed), *The EU and Human Rights* (Oxford, Oxford University Press, 1999). Compare these with A von Bogdandy, 'The European Union as a Human Rights Organization? Human Rights and the Core of the European Union' (2000), 37 *Common Market Law Review* 1307.

[89] Charter of Fundamental Rights [2000] OJ C 364/1. On the Charter see S Peers and A Ward (eds), *The European Union Charter of Fundamental Rights* (Oxford, Hart, 2004).

[90] See Treaty Establishing a Constitution for Europe [2004] OJ C 310/1, Art II-111.

nascent and patchy dimension of human rights in the EU ties in with phenomena such as trafficking.

Even though the legal future (if any) of the Charter remains unclear, it is worth a look as it sheds some light on where trafficking fits in and what concerns it raises in the light of the EU human rights dimension. Many of the rights, freedoms and principles[91] of the Charter 'recognised' by the Union (as stated in the preamble) are, like human rights discussed above, relevant for trafficking in similar ways. Most strikingly, the Charter explicitly also includes trafficking in Article 5 (under Part Dignity), where it is added after the traditional prohibition on slavery, servitude, forced and compulsory labour, reading '[t]rafficking in human beings is prohibited'. This is a welcome recognition that trafficking is indeed a fundamental rights problem.[92] Its inclusion under slavery is quite interesting in that, although there has been some attention to trafficking as 'slavery-like' in the international arena,[93] this has also met (not entirely unjustified) resistance from those reluctant to see the context of 'proper' slavery expanded far beyond its historical origins.[94] The actual content of the right itself is weaker than in the context of slavery (which reads that 'no one shall be held in slavery'), bringing to mind the criminal law harmonisation goal of the Framework Decision. Other immediately relevant rights are human dignity,[95] respect for physical and mental integrity,[96] prohibition of torture and inhuman/degrading treatment,[97] right to liberty and security of person,[98] right to asylum[99] and the guarantee against removal or expulsion to a country where there is a serious risk of imposition of the death penalty, torture or other inhuman or degrading treatment or punishment[100] (these in particular touch upon the repatriation of victims of trafficking as discussed above), equality before law,[101] non-discrimination,[102] equality between men and women,[103] and the rights to an effective remedy and to a fair trial.[104] In the

[91] Art 51 of the Charter, above n 89, speaks of 'respecting' the rights and 'observing' the principles.

[92] Noted also in A Ward, 'Access to Justice' in Peers and Ward (eds), above n 89, at 130; she also notes the danger of codifying, which may ossify future developments in trafficking as (only) a slavery issue. On this see also B de Witte, 'The Legal Status of the Charter: Vital Question or Non-Issue?' (2001) 8 *Maastricht Journal of European and Comparative Law* 81.

[93] Note, eg, the activity of the UN Working Group on Contemporary Forms of Slavery, which is mandated to address trafficking and exploitation of prostitution of others as 'slavery-like practices'.

[94] Another reason the inclusion of trafficking is interesting is that the other two major women's human rights concerns, domestic and sexual violence, were not included anywhere (they could have been referred to in the equality provision or under health). This, and the lack of reference to the Women's Convention, ratified by all Member States, are noted by D McGoldrick, 'The Charter and UN Human Rights Treaties' in Peers and Ward (eds), above n 89, at 115.

[95] Art 1 of the Charter, above n 89.

[96] Ibid, Art 3.

[97] Ibid, Art 4.

[98] Ibid, Art 6.

[99] Ibid, Art 18.

[100] Ibid, Art 19.

[101] Ibid, Art 20.

[102] Ibid, Art 21.

[103] Ibid, Art 23.

[104] Ibid, Art 47.

European context the Charter was also relatively novel, in that it included economic and social rights together with typically civil and political rights.[105] Notably many of these too, as in the Charter in general, are formulated in inclusive terms, referring to 'everyone'—for instance, Article 15(1) of the Charter which affirms the right of 'everyone' to engage in work and pursue a freely chosen occupation (while 'every worker' is entitled to rights elaborated in Articles 30 and 31 of the Charter).

However, there were also important limits to the Charter, not least because it was primarily drafted to make the rights 'visible' to citizens of the EU rather than to 'everyone'. Moreover, it established (even as part of the Constitution) no new competences, which is particularly relevant as regards social rights in core social areas detached from market integration.[106] Most crucially, non-discrimination based on nationality (Article 21(2)) applies only within the scope of the EC and EU Treaties (or the Constitution), which in practice means that non-Union citizens are excluded.[107] Other notable limitations include the freedom to seek employment, to work, to exercise the right of establishment and to provide services, which is limited to citizens of the Union,[108] and the entitlement of nationals of third countries to equal working conditions with citizens of the Union, which applies only to those legally resident and working in the Union.[109] Moreover, the general limitation clause in Article 52(1) provides, '[a]ny limitation on the exercise of the rights and freedoms recognised by this Charter must be provided for by law and respect the essence of those rights and freedoms. Subject to the principle of proportionality, limitations may be made only if they are necessary and genuinely meet objectives of general interest recognised by the Union or the need to protect the rights and freedoms of others'.[110] In this respect it is useful to point out that one of the objectives of the Union (and similarly in the Constitution) now relates to developing the Union as an Area of Freedom, Security and Justice for the benefit of its citizens. Thus there can be no doubt about the role of the human rights component compared to other more central EU objectives (such as the AFSJ, or the Internal Market), or about the intended beneficiaries of such a dimension.

[105] On the inclusion of social rights see M Gijzen, 'The Charter: A Milestone for Social Protection in Europe?' (2001) 8 *Maastricht Journal of European and Comparative Law* 33; J Kenner, 'Economic and Social Rights in the EU Legal Order: The Mirage of Indivisibility' in T Hervey and J Kenner (eds), *Economic and Social Rights under the EU Charter of Fundamental Rights* (Oxford, Hart, 2003). Note that a distinction was made in the Constitution between 'rights' and 'principles' of the Charter (Art II-112). While 'rights' would be enforceable within the scope of EU competence, including the impact of legislation (or failure to legislate), 'principles' are judicially cognizable only in the interpretation of acts and in the ruling on their legality.

[106] See Art 51 of the Charter, above n 89.

[107] The provision banning any discrimination on grounds of nationality (Art 12 TEC), the relevant point of reference here, has never been interpreted by the ECJ to apply to third country nationals. See above section 3.2.2.

[108] Art 15(2) of the Charter, above n 89.

[109] Ibid, Art 15(3).

[110] On the limitation clauses see S Peers, 'Taking Rights Away? Limitations and Derogations' in Peers and Ward (eds), above n 89.

Not only is the Charter ambiguous, but its significance is yet to be seen.[111] For instance, as Peers argued in 2001, 'at first sight, Article 15(1) appears to recognise a right to work for everyone, which could potentially be interpreted as a right of access to employment for all persons, conceivably even persons not legally resident or even not yet resident at all in the European Union'.[112] Were the Charter to survive the tumultuous upheaval after the rejection of the Constitution, provisions like this could have an impact on the parameters of external migration policy. At the same time the possibility may now seem remote, also because at present at least there appears to be limited political will as regards extending rights to migrants, especially irregular ones. It is of course possible, considering the recent softening of attitudes to external migration at least in some EU institutions,[113] that eventually the ECJ will end up urging reluctant Member States to be progressive as regards migrants' rights. At the other extreme, even if the Charter were to gain legally binding status at some point, the limitation clauses could be interpreted by the ECJ in various ways to justify restricting the rights of non-EU citizens to ensure 'an internal market where competition is free and undistorted'. The latter alternative, which favours the traditional freedoms over areas where the Union's reach is weaker, of course links with the four 'traditional' fundamental freedoms of the Union, which remain far more central to the Union (and on which there is still more experience in the ECJ than human rights). While the Charter alleviates some of the problems caused by the overriding focus on markets that has driven European integration by bringing out 'common values', in the light of ECJ jurisprudence it seems not entirely far-fetched that the balancing act may pay more heed to EU citizens' market right 'to buy access to sexual services' than to the 'dignity' of those selling them (see above Chapter 3).

Furthermore, if one takes seriously the concerns expressed above (by, for instance, Koskenniemi), the EU human rights dimension is of course a prime example of legalistic paradigms, competence disputes and utilitarianism overriding any deeper meaning rights may hold.[114] Even if one is more positive about rights discourse and litigation strategies, in any case the present developments around human rights obviously provide no quick panacea, even if successful outcomes result (considering for instance the many costs involved).[115] Rights litigation depends on individual litigants and pioneering lawyers. It is expensive and lengthy in general, and even more so in the European context (be it ECtHR or

[111] See M Poiares Maduro, 'The Double Constitutional Life of the Charter of Fundamental Rights of the European Union' in Hervey and Kenner (eds), above n 105, who argues that the Charter has the potential both to further constitutionalisation of the Union and to restrain it.

[112] S Peers, 'Immigration, Asylum and the European Union Charter of Fundamental Rights' (2001) 3 *European Journal of Migration and Law* 141, at 159.

[113] Note for instance the above-mentioned Commission Communication on immigration, integration and employment, adopted in June 2003, which for the first time considered issues such as the possible regularisation of irregular migrants and the granting of social rights to them in the context of the fight against social exclusion, COM(2003)336.

[114] Koskenniemi, above n 72.

[115] On access to justice see Ward, above n 92.

ECJ). Yet at the same time in the light of the measures adopted in the field of trafficking, and indeed the Area of Freedom, Security and Justice in general, litigation still seems an easier way of actually implementing rights than much of the current legislation. Examples abound of superficial references to the Charter in instruments the actual quality and content of which leave much to be desired in terms of ensuring human rights. Reference can be made to the Directives discussed above in Chapter 3[116] and indeed to the above-discussed Directive on temporary residence permits for victims of trafficking.[117] As regards the Directive on temporary residence permits, it is sufficient to add here that while it does contain a reference to the Charter in its preamble and also states that it is without prejudice to refugee protection, subsidiary protection, asylum-seeking and other human rights instruments, this is hardly enough to make the content human rights sensitive as such, when the central human rights imperative, which involves recognising that *all* trafficking victims have suffered human rights violations (from which the Member States have failed to protect them) and may be abused in the future, is not reflected in its content. In a similar vein, the lack of a proper human rights dimension in the Comprehensive Action Plan to combat illegal immigration and trafficking in human beings has been criticised elsewhere.[118]

Moreover, while there has until recently been a principled distinction between the protection afforded to migrants by human rights treaties and EU instruments on asylum and immigration, recent developments around the Council of Europe Convention on trafficking give rise to fears over the migration control approach embraced by the EU being imported into organisations traditionally based on promoting human rights. In 2004, the Council of Europe set up a Committee on action against trafficking in human beings (CAHTEH) with the aim of drawing up a binding European Convention against trafficking in human beings. The stated aims were to protect the victim as a person whose human rights have been violated, to pursue a proper balance between the human rights of victims and the interests of prosecution, and to set up a comprehensive legal framework for the protection of and assistance to victims and witnesses with specific and binding measures. After earlier versions the draft text was approved by CAHTEH in December 2004[119] and the Convention opened for signature in May 2005.[120] However, rather than prioritising the situation of victims, it is remarkably reminiscent of the EU instruments adopted, and adds little in terms of hard obligations

[116] See above section 3.2.2.

[117] See above section 4.2.2.

[118] Comprehensive Plan to combat illegal immigration and trafficking of human beings in the European Union, 28 Feb 2002 [2002] OJ C 142/23; about human rights and the plan, see R Cholewinski, 'European Union Policy on Irregular Migration: Human Rights Lost?' in Bogusz *et al* (eds), above n 7. To take an even more recent example, the Hague Programme ([2005] OJ C 53/1) notes the EU commitment to not only respecting but also actively promoting fundamental rights, but its substance seems to place far less attention on the implications of some of the planned policies.

[119] See Draft Council of Europe Convention on Action Against Trafficking in Human Beings, CM(2004)222 Addendum, 14 Dec 2004.

[120] In May 2006 the Convention (CETS no 197) had 29 signatures and one ratification (by Moldova). It will enter into force after 10 ratifications.

to protect and assist victims.[121] Rather, for example, the provision on the non-penalisation of victims seems so narrow that it makes one seriously question whether any 'trite' human rights dimension has affected it at all.[122] This is even more interesting considering that on occasion the Convention goes beyond the minimum standards agreed upon in other international instruments.[123] The modest general standard may have something to do with fears over ratification by the broader Council of Europe audience (some of which criminalise prostitution altogether), but reportedly also stems from the inflexible stand of the European Commission during the negotiations.[124] This raises serious questions about how much the fact that the uneven instrument certainly does not strike a 'proper balance' has to do with spreading EU migration policy aims at the cost of human rights—with the somewhat unusual result of making the EU measures in this field seem progressive.

While the possible future accession of the EU to the European Convention on Human Rights (which would have been facilitated by the troublesome Constitution: Article I-9(2)), would no doubt be welcomed by many, in the shorter term, the EU human rights dimension cannot remedy the underlying problems relating to the broader conundrums of human rights in the EU that also affect trafficking-related matters. Most obviously, this relates to the personal scope of beneficiaries (that is, EU citizens). Somewhat more broadly, the fact that at present the EU lacks the famous 'fully-fledged' human rights policy means that it is unavoidably inept and at any rate incoherent when it comes to formulating a human rights approach to anything, let alone to issues touching upon several contentious areas of competence and concerns over subsidiarity. The lack of coherent internal human rights policy has been highlighted in particular with regard to the recent enlargement, where the 10 Candidate Countries were scrutinised in terms of their human rights record while no similar scrutiny could be targeted at the 'old' Member States.[125] The matter is relevant more broadly in terms of EU external

[121] It too provides for a residence permit, to be granted 'either in one of the two following situations or in both', (a) when it is deemed necessary owing to the victims' personal situation, (b) when it is 'necessary for the purpose of their co-operation with the competent authorities in investigation or criminal proceedings' (Art 14 of the CoE Convention, CETS No 197). Victims' access to assistance is nearly as limited as in the Directive on residence permits ([2004] OJ L 261/19), with only 'necessary' medical and other assistance to be made available to the 'lawfully resident'.

[122] Art 26 reads: '[e]ach Party shall, *in accordance with the basic principles of its national legal system*, provide for the *possibility* of not imposing penalties on victims for their involvement in unlawful activities, to the extent that they have been *compelled to* do so' (emphasis added).

[123] Eg, on educational programmes for boys and girls during their schooling in order to prevent trafficking.

[124] See Recommendation 1695 (2005) by the Council of Europe Parliamentary Assembly, which states that the European Commission, negotiating on behalf of 22 Member States, 'systematically refused' to adopt provisions which would have widened the scope of protection beyond what had been agreed in the Directive on residence permits. In its opinion (No 253 (2005)) on the draft Convention the Parliamentary Assembly 'regrets the fact that the current wording of the draft is far from guaranteeing effective and sufficient protection of victims, contrary to the objective pursued' (para 8).

[125] This is not to say that the enlargement scrutiny was faultless when it came to trafficking. Although the EU called on the Candidate Countries to tackle trafficking in women and gave aid for this purpose (note the STOP programme), the measures required (and implemented) most often related to

relations as well, for the Union is a powerful player in the world arena, most relevantly for the trafficking context in the field of development co-operation.[126] Yet its desire to promote development and human rights, including the rights of women (which would play a pivotal role in preventing trafficking) is hampered by a lack of legitimacy and charges of hypocrisy that relate to the complex evolution of its human rights dimension and the shortcomings therein.

To conclude, trafficking is not unique as a human rights issue that in the Community context, if pursued at all, is still not being pursued such. To the extent that this stems from the exclusive ways in which EU law develops its notion of transnational rights (rights reserved to a select few for economic reasons), this is not surprising. It is poignant though that the Union that takes EC migrant and labour rights seriously still has myopia about such rights in general. Even though recent developments arguably open up new possibilities in terms of a real European debate about values, rights and belonging of all those living in the European polity, it has not yet resulted in breaking the silence on matters that would relate to a broader human rights approach to trafficking. One of these is the demand side of trafficking for exploitation, concerns over which could be formulated in the language of dignity and equality and human rights. While European gender equality law has in many ways been grounded on the labour market, in light of gender equality as an objective for the EC (Article 2 TEC), the task of gender mainstreaming (Article 3(2) TEC) and Union competence to act against discrimination (Article 13 TEC), there is certainly room for debate on trafficking *as* a gender equality *and* a human rights issue, connected to the devaluing of and discrimination against women, requiring active empowering measures. In this vein it is useful to recall provisions such as Article 5 CEDAW and ask what the EU could and should do to modify the social and cultural patterns of conduct of men and women, notions of the inferiority or the superiority of either of the sexes and stereotyped roles for men and women. What sort of structural changes would this necessitate in the EU?

6.4 CONCLUSIONS

In light of the previous chapters, one can have no quarrel with the obvious benefits of an approach which finds (or at least claims to find) ways of expressing the suffering of trafficking victims and their need for the recognition of their human dignity. While not a universal remedy, rights talk has highlighted the exploitation

strengthening border controls rather than improving the social and economic status of women in these countries. Most notably, in the general Phare programmes none of the EU support was earmarked for advancing equality more generally or for projects run by/for women.

[126] The relevance of human rights for the external policies of the EC under the First Pillar is explicitly recognised in Art 177 TEC, which states that Community policy in development co-operation 'shall contribute to the general objective of developing and consolidating democracy and the rule of law, and to that of respecting human rights and fundamental freedoms': see B Simma, J Aschenbrenner and C Schulte, 'Human Rights Considerations in the Development Co-operation Activities of the EC' in Alston (ed), above n 72. On development aid see below ch 7.

of migrant women. Recourse to rights has emancipating potential, especially for those traditionally denied the right to voice their concerns in terms of rights, and it helps to envisiage what could be achieved vis-à-vis modifying existing approaches as well as to form coalitions to campaign around the issue. However, this chapter has also identified reasons that make adopting a perspective based on human rights discourse problematic as the only basis for anti-trafficking measures. As a philosophical starting point the idea that trafficking victims have rights is crucial to anti-trafficking approaches, but it needs to be backed up with broader debates about the good promoted and how to go about advancing it beyond individual rights claims. As legal rights arguments with regard to trafficking are weak, relating as they do to the rights of female irregular migrants, it may be that it is more productive to refer to states' own interests in supporting migrants/women rather than rights aspirations. While there is no reason whatsoever not to point out the grounds on which states would arguably benefit in the long term from receiving migrants and supporting their rights, calling for rights should not be abandoned entirely precisely because the legal position of migrant women in general, let alone trafficking victims in particular, is so disadvantaged and precarious that giving up on rights discourse would leave them significantly worse off.

Even though rights discourse has been helpful, and indeed essential, in bringing the issue of trafficking in women for sexual exploitation to the fore, it also involves tension as 'rights talk' can remain superficial, individualistic and conflictual, while the practicality of implementing the broader rights agendas remains difficult. More broadly, rights discourse at present at least focuses more on the consequences of trafficking, rather than its causes. Even if reference to social and economic rights can be used to highlight the range of concerns that relate to trafficking in broader ways, whether these would always be best expressed in terms of rights is another matter. To highlight these concerns is not to argue that such an approach should be abandoned (in some ways it is quite the contrary); despite the problems of rights talk, it is nonetheless necessary to engage in it, even if converting rights into strategies which would work is fraught with practical and theoretical difficulties. The fear is that calling for 'rights' in the context of trafficking victims becomes *all* that (alternative) anti-trafficking efforts are reduced to, which might result in trafficking victims' rights remaining a dead letter (if that), without the possibility of facilitating deeper debates and structural change necessary for the long term prevention of trafficking. Since it is not only trafficking itself but the current EU Member States' policies regarding it (indirectly or directly) that raise serious human rights concerns, the challenge is to engage critically with rights, without deserting other avenues that could influence the transformation of the present inability to address the areas relevant for broader change. Rights arguments can and should play a part in these broader efforts, but should not become the exclusive focus. Other possible avenues will be discussed in the next chapter.

7

Towards a More Comprehensive Approach to Trafficking?

> Emancipation is a luxury. It's something a person can only afford when one has sufficient food, an apartment and when the kids are able to go to school. . . . Of every ten illegal women working in prostitution, nine are being exploited. It doesn't matter if they have been trafficked or not, or if they came here voluntarily with the intention of working as prostitutes. They are simply being tremendously exploited.[1]

> The automatic channelling of migrant women into sex work is an index of their status under national rule but it also speaks of the place of sex in that national space where laws protect the flourishing sexual life of male citizens as a privilege and a source of power.[2]

INDIVIDUAL HORROR STORIES about trafficking and related problems are now frequently found in the press. These stories are, however, mere manifestations of the broader global injustices that create exploitation. Trafficking in women for sexual exploitation in the Union Member States is a product of a complex interaction between and accumulation of several factors, such as poverty, exclusionary laws and practices against non-EU nationals, sexist ideologies, discrimination against women, violence and corruption. This multi-faceted fabric forms the essential setting for the acts that are now defined as trafficking in women for sexual exploitation. The problem with calling the cluster of practices that have been the topic of this work 'trafficking', while in many ways necessary in that this makes the issue a specific concern, is that one often tends to lose sight of the broader picture of the causes behind it. This is not to deny the responsibility of the individual actors who exploit migrant women. But it is to say that, divorced from these essential background factors, legal responses to trafficking become reduced to a matter of devising specific anti-trafficking laws, witness protection measures (such as the short-term residence permit) and so on, which, while maybe removing some of the trafficking victims, make room for others, because such measures do not address the circumstances that led to the exploitation in the first place. At the same time these measures serve to entrench the notion of trafficking as a

[1] M Álvarez, 'The Emancipation of Prostitutes as a Luxury' in F Polanía Molina and M Janssen, *I Never Thought This Would Happen to Me. Prostitution and Traffic in Latin American Women in the Netherlands* (Amsterdam, Foundation ESPERANZA, 1998), at 93–4.

[2] U Biemann, 'Remotely Sensed: A Topography of the Global Sex Trade' (2002) 70 *Feminist Review* 75, at 85.

special case of utmost exploitation—which flies in the face of the nature of trafficking as just an example of global injustices based on gender, nationality, race, wealth allocation and so on.

In a less imperfect world the ideal 'response' to trafficking would be a comprehensive one, not necessarily specifically targeting (only) trafficking. An ideal response to trafficking stems from a broader commitment not only to enforcing human rights and the equal protection of women but to eradicating poverty, gender inequality, the wealth demarcation between the rich and the poor and global economic and social injustices (through, for example, international debt relief). These factors are 'comprehensive' in a substantive sense; in every way because only thus could trafficking be 'eradicated': there might still be sporadic violence against migrant women, but everything that makes trafficking such a 'special' concern now would be connected to the larger setting. It is thus not necessary for a more comprehensive approach to trafficking to be explicitly and exclusively 'about trafficking'. Indeed, the title of this book, in talking about 'legal responses to trafficking in women' is in a way fundamentally misleading because it too has a tendency to reinforce the notion that trafficking is a separate concern, something that can be 'solved' through more extensive legal regulation, creating exceptional categories for trafficked women, and so on. As 'special' exceptions or add-ons to current policies these will never work alone. Indeed, much of the legal regulation, and the harmonisation aimed at, is a part of the problem and not the solution. Nor is it absolutely necessary for a comprehensive approach that every Member State devise a specialised anti-trafficking law; in that respect it would be enough if the Member States gave migrants' physical and mental integrity the same respect and priority as they give to their nationals' wellbeing (for instance, through the application of their normal criminal provisions on rape, blackmail and the exploitation of prostitution equally).

The problem with this way of thinking is that it easily leads to passivity and waiting around for a better world. In the long term more thorough solutions are needed but something also has to be done about trafficking now, even if it provides only short-term relief. This does not mean that more far-reaching goals should be discarded, but that goals ought to be set and achieved in the meantime too. In other words, it is necessary to work towards a comprehensive approach with a touch of realism about what can and cannot be achieved in the short and long run. Any 'comprehensive' approach is, therefore, one that tries to advance ideals of global justice, including gender equality, narrowing the gap between the rich and the poor (utopian as these ideals may seem), while at the same time matching these goals with those elements of current, planned and hypothesised anti-trafficking efforts that can be judged helpful or which, at the very least, do not make things worse, as further criminalisation of migrants would do. There is obviously a tension here: if one is too ideological little or no practical progress may be made (eradication of prostitution as it is known today as a demonstration of male dominance); if one is too practical (going for those few reforms that are considered 'achievable') there is a risk of losing sight of the long-term goals, which in turn can lead into not making any real headway at all (for instance simply creating and reproducing existing categories of innocent victims, and so on). Yet this is the basic tension that realistic attempts towards a more comprehensive approach to trafficking have to negotiate.

In what follows, the issue is (for practical reasons, if somewhat artificially) divided into two sections. The first draws some conclusions based on the previous chapters. Its main focus is on more immediate and practical problems that should be addressed in order to facilitate serious and effective policy action against trafficking. Much of it relates to migration policy and criminal justice issues. Migration policy in particular is, however, also a long-term issue, and forms a bridge to the latter section on long-term action. That section, which tries to identify and sketch out some future directions for the rather more ambitious transformation required, focuses on two subjects (selected from many): development issues that affect the 'supply' of women and the sexual ideologies that indirectly underpin trafficking by upholding the 'demand'. It is worth stressing that the separation of these issue into short- and long-term dimensions should not be taken to mean that long-term measures should be considered as something to discard for now; both short-term and long-term measures are something on which reflection should start now and in fact they should be thought of together, so that they inform each other, even though (or maybe precisely because) there are points of tension between them. The two sections on long-term action should again be read as informing each other, for supply and demand are interdependent.

7.1 ANTI-TRAFFICKING IN THE SHORT TO MEDIUM TERM

As was seen above, the Area of Freedom, Security and Justice, into which the phenomenon of trafficking is mainly seen in the Union as falling, is an extremely self-interested area of EU (and Member States') policy, examples of which abound. As the prevailing formulation of problems and solutions tends to prefer short-term perspectives that obscure many facets of trafficking that require a long time-span, it is not easy to come up with feasible immediate strategies for change. It is perhaps useful to start by outlining the main problems with the current European approach. Where appropriate, the issues outlined above in previous chapters will be considered alongside the most recent evidence, the Commission Communication and, above all, the Council Action Plan that were adopted in 2005, which map some familiar issues but introduce some additional elements that might impact on future developments.[3]

[3] The EU Plan on Best Practices, Standards and Procedures for Combating and Preventing Trafficking in Human Beings [2005] OJ C 311/1, drawn from the Commission Communication, Fighting Trafficking in Human Beings—An Integrated Approach and Proposals for an Action Plan, COM(2005)514 final. The Communication was inspired by the report of the Commission's Experts' Group on Trafficking in Human Beings. The Experts' Group was set up in 2003 (see Commission Decision 2003/209/EC of 25 Mar 2003 setting up a consultative group, to be known as the 'Experts Group on Trafficking in Human Beings' [2003] OJ L 79/25), and its first report was finished in late 2004: see Experts' Group on Trafficking in Human Beings, *Report of the Experts Group on Trafficking in Human Beings* (Brussels, European Commission, 2004).

The problems with the current approach to trafficking relate to the ever harsher exclusion of the 'unwanted' and the increasingly punitive measures against the uncooperative, be they countries or individuals. Migrant-sending countries are targeted with readmission clauses in bilateral agreements and even stand-alone readmission agreements; 'illegal' migrants are detained and then expelled. The EU as well, thanks to its Member States' near-hysterical obsession with 'migration pressures' based on questionable 'migration myths', has become increasingly unilateralist towards third countries and fixated with migration control policies as opposed to immigration policies. Its internal migration law mirrors this imbalance as regards the rights of third country nationals living in the Union. Not only are these policies unjust and deny the EU precisely the good name it wants to have in global politics as a serious defender of human rights in general, and as the promoter of a 'human rights and victim-centred approach' to trafficking[4] in particular, but fundamentally counterproductive (in the long term), even according to their own logic. Punishing sending countries (for instance through reducing trade with, or aid to and investment in them) for failing to restrict migration or denying sending countries the remittances from potential migrants that can help sustain the sending country's economy, simply means that more sending country nationals are likely to see migrating, however illegal and exploitative, as their only alternative to the increasing poverty of their homelands.

As for criminal policy, the continuing reinforcement of the migration–crime nexus ensures that criminal justice targets without or with very little differentiation all those who are formally irregular migrants. Growing awareness of trafficking and the subsequent temporary residence permit arrangements in some of the Member States have improved the situation of (some) identified trafficking victims but cannot, even when perfected through proper identification of trafficking victims,[5] be presented as the solution to the problem of trafficking in women for sexual exploitation. What the permits do is to remove a certain number of victims from circulation, but at the same time keep up the exploiters' demand for fresh blood. Moreover, these kinds of arrangements are far from perfected at present, as the Directive on the short-term residence permits cannot be regarded as anything but a failure in terms of a realistic European approach. The Directive conveys that in EU terms those victims who fail to co-operate or are not 'real' victims, and merit none of the (limited) security provided by a regularised situation in the country of destination. Indeed, arguably the European approach on this point might even fall under a good faith interpretation[6] of the obligations of the UN Trafficking Protocol, itself criticised for failing the victims of trafficking. Admittedly, the Directive is a small step forward, in that *all* Member States are to adopt some kind of arrangement under the Directive and, if they are serious about the fear of organised crime, having an effective arrangement might actually suit their crime control

[4] EU Plan, above n 3, para 3.
[5] EU Plan, above n 3, para 3(ii).
[6] See Vienna Convention on the Law of Treaties, 1155 UNTS 331, Art 26.

needs, thus opening the way to taking the victim's interests, at least to a certain degree, into consideration.

However, one has to be careful about this sort of optimism precisely because the needs of crime victims do not necessarily match state interests in criminal prosecution, and because there is, under the Directive, no EU consensus on treating all trafficking victims, let alone all irregular migrants, humanely.[7] To say that the Directive is a missed opportunity does of course not mean that individual Member States cannot or should not have higher standards. Indeed, explicit victim protection measures that are within the competence of the Member States should be encouraged, even if this means that the divergences between the positions in the Member States will persist. Particularly interesting is the example of Italy: precisely because its protection regime is more extensive, it has managed to empower women so that they can actually *choose* to take action against their traffickers, rather than being cajoled or coerced into taking such action. However, the fact remains that the Directive fails to maximise the potential of the *Union* to protect the human rights of victims, and can at worst lead to a race to the bottom, as Member States have shown a tendency to view this kind of arrangement as potentially luring in irregular immigrants in the guise of 'fake trafficking victims'. This could lead to a general harmonisation of standards downwards, and have grave long-term consequences for devising a more comprehensive approach. Moreover, as far as a European approach is concerned, the Directive is only the latest piece of evidence that reaffirms that the EU's (especially the Council's) and Member States' commitment to fighting trafficking is far short of being comprehensive. This does not bode well for a long-term EU approach, which was to bridge the gaps between Member States, and in doing so improve, rather than worsen, the state of affairs.[8]

This issue is related to the fact that also in countries which already have anti-trafficking legislation such legislation has the tendency of remaining at least underused and poorly implemented, if not a dead letter.[9] Much of this has to do with the issue of (migrant) prostitution which, as was seen, is not easy to 'solve' through legal reforms in a non-migration climate. Paradoxically, in the light of their different internal logics, both legalisation and client criminalisation, also despite their intuitive feminist appeal, when combined with a strict migration policy tend to lead to the same results as far as trafficking victims are concerned, for they remain presumptively 'illegal'. Thus, if one looks at the Dutch situation,

[7] See EU Plan, above n 3, para 4(vii), which states: 'Member States should, as appropriate and in line with national conditions and practice, provide protection and assistance to (. . .) victims *as a part of a balanced, effective prosecution*' (emphasis added).

[8] Until recently it seemed that for the time being the EU had just relinquished the leading role it could have taken to the Council of Europe, planning to draft a human rights based convention. However, those who considered that the Council of Europe was a more 'natural' forum for the adoption of a human rights sensitive instrument on trafficking were sorely disappointed by the final result; see above section 6.3. See also EU Plan, above n 3, para 3(vii), which recommends that Member States 'take into consideration' the CE Convention when implementing the Residence Permit Directive ([2004] OJ L 261 19) and developing national strategies.

[9] EU Plan, above n 3, Annex, Section 5, lists measures to improve investigation and prosecution and to further co-operation between the Member States.

legalisation serves those Dutch and EC women who are willing to opt for it. This has turned out to be a smaller proportion than was assumed, as the new legal status also obliges prostitutes to pay taxes and involves quite a lot of initial and continuing regulations and costs (and the promised eligibility for social security weighs little when it is considered that many women work in the sex industry for only a few years—not long enough for sustainable pension contributions). In the light of EU enlargement, legalisation might in theory improve the protection and status of some new EU citizens migrating for prostitution; in practice the independence and opportunities are less pronounced. As for non-EU women, as they as a rule cannot migrate (for prostitution or for any other purpose), they will almost invariably be in an irregular situation and unable to claim the protection that legalisation offers. This not only represents the point where the work logic breaks down, leaving a large proportion of women in prostitution open to abuse, but means that trafficking, even when the phenomenon is addressed, remains difficult to identify, let alone prove.

The Swedish laws consider women to be the 'victims' of prostitution, but in practice the policy leads to the expulsion of non-nationals found in prostitution. Again it can be seen that the law penalises the weakest, the migrant prostitutes and the trafficked, and that again there is a consistency problem: prostitution is violence against women, but it is the women in prostitution who are blamed for making money from this violence. If the aim is to prevent the self-denigration of prostitutes while affirming that prostitution is not socially desirable for anyone, then migrant women in prostitution should not be expelled merely for being found in the trade. This logic is reinforced as far as those who are trafficked are concerned, as they should be considered, under an 'exploitation' view, to be victimised in multiple ways. Italy, with its traditional abolitionist if increasingly control-oriented policy, differs at the level of policy from the Netherlands, in that prostitutes are not considered workers under any circumstances, and from Sweden, in that it considers only some women victimised in prostitution. In practice this ambiguity translates into strong stigmatisation of women in prostitution with some mercy given to those women who are obviously victimised. While Sweden has chosen to be a prostitution-free area, and the Dutch prefer to try and improve the protection of prostitutes, the obvious point of tension in all three countries is that trying to improve the legal situation of women in prostitution, especially those who are particularly vulnerable, fits uneasily with the desire to prevent external migration, as this contributes to vulnerability to trafficking. This contradiction also appears in the emerging EU approach.

Suggestions for improvement in the Member States tend to lead to a dilemma between complete legalisation of involvement in prostitution for all nationals and a more or less prohibitionist/control-inspired regime. Both are politically sensitive, create public opposition and come with attendant problems. With regard to the legalisation of sex work and giving work permits for it, this would be more coherent (as it would give women the chance to become independent workers, and thus challenge the stigma of 'whores'), and might to a degree alleviate trafficking to the extent that migrant women in prostitution might become more independent. However, it alone hardly provides an appealing solution unless the parameters of immigration policy become wider in general (in other words for other kinds of labour as well); even then it raises strong ethical questions about importing women from economically disadvantaged countries to do the sexual servicing expected by European men (see the next section). At the practical level, it is no panacea for the regulation and cleaning up of the sex industry, for legalisation also tends to create the conditions for the expansion of the sex industry and a subsequent demand for more women, which in turn cannot be met without resort to abusive methods. The likely expansion of the prostitution scene[10] will, without a strong, continuing and (inevitably) hugely costly input on monitoring the implementation of the regulations and attendant economic and social measures, simply lead to an illegal sex market thriving next to the legal.[11] As the costs of legalised prostitution are passed on to the women in prostitution and as customers seek cheaper sex, women in prostitution seek to circumvent the legal system. The expanding demand for sexual servicing of different kinds (often by 'exotic' women) also entails a very real risk regarding trafficking in that it makes the work of traffickers easier, for instance regarding importing women for exploitation. Those exploited will still be hidden from view or prima facie (irregular) workers.

At the same time there is good reason to be wary of the rise of new prohibitionism and punitive tendencies as well, even where the enforcement action primarily targets customers rather than prostitutes themselves, when the practical effect is that the burden is passed on to the women in prostitution—as with, for instance, kerb-crawling offences. While Swedish client criminalisation has arguably decreased the volume of the prostitution business, it at the same time hampers attempts at undermining the dichotomy under which the whore stigma is attached to 'illegitimate' (promiscuous) female sexuality. Moreover, this decline in the scope of prostitution and trafficking is, to some degree at least, bought at the cost of displacing the business to neighbouring countries or just less strictly monitored areas. While again resources to monitor implementation make a difference, there are also bigger problems that raise questions about the workability of the Swedish approach in areas which, unlike Sweden with its fairly limited market, have a large and active existing sex industry already and which can muster much less general support for client criminalisation. The punitive side of client criminalisation that calls for more law enforcement is reminiscent of the recent Italian proposals for punishing both prostitutes and clients for creating a public nuisance that are quite unconcerned with the social and economic side of the issue. A system of the Italian

[10] For an example from outside Europe, see the discussion about the effects of legalisation in Victoria, Australia, M Sullivan and S Jeffreys, *Legalising Prostitution Is Not the Answer: The Example of Victoria, Australia* (North Fitzroy, Coalition Against Trafficking in Women, 2001); J Bindel and L Kelly, *A Critical Examination of Responses to Prostitution in Four Countries: Victoria-Australia, Ireland, The Netherlands and Sweden* (London, Routes Out, 2004).

[11] Note the EU Plan, above n 3, para 4(iii): 'Member States should provide for necessary organisational structures, specialised personnel and adequate financial resources to their law enforcement authorities to effectively combat human trafficking'.

kind also tends to leave unaddressed hidden prostitution, which sustains prostitution while at the same time maintaining the notion of its illicitness. The punitive discourse around prostitution is nothing new; but while in theory one can perhaps appreciate the different logic behind the Swedish and the Italian approaches, in practice it can be that the stigma of criminalisation undermines the effectiveness of the Swedish argument (see further the following sections).

In short, and relatively unsurprisingly, the reforms have provided no legal cure-alls for the issue of prostitution. Some choices are better than others, but the 'solutions' put into practice in one country are not always transferable. For example the Dutch approach is based on the policies of 'tolerance' and draws its meaning from the rather culturally specific Dutch notion of 'pragmatic tolerance', as well as domestic feminist debates; similar solutions adopted elsewhere might lead to far stricter regularisation that ignores the wellbeing of women in prostitution. The limits of law reform are highlighted by the fact that laws with different underlying (feminist) perspectives can result in remarkably converging outcomes, in particular as regards those excluded from their scope.[12] In particular it cannot be emphasised enough that a prostitution policy which takes into account only (EC) nationals involved in it is anachronistic, incoherent and counterproductive. Whatever the chosen path, the policies need to acknowledge and seek to address the fact that at present the majority of women in prostitution are migrants, and most often non-EU nationals (and as such in a different legal situation from those with EU nationals' rights), and contemplate policy reform not only from a criminal justice but from long-term migration policy, human rights, development and gender equality perspective. In particular these should be associated with wider approaches seeking to address the causes and processes of migrant prostitution, and to promote gender equality both in countries of origin and destination as well as to forge a more profound value discussion on the shared (or not) sexual values of the European Union citizens.[13]

The previous paragraphs have already hinted at the central concern: the urgent need to rethink European (im)migration policies with the layered differentiations they entail. While the Directive and the Action Plan (which once more focuses on migration *control* measures) seem to indicate that the time is simply not ripe for that, in a more hopeful tone it could be added that perhaps the first signs of a change are visible in the gradual recognition that the EU needs a larger workforce,

[12] A matter noted (vis-à-vis the Netherlands and Sweden) also by J Freedman, 'Selling Sex: Trafficking, Prostitution and Sex Work amongst Migrant Women in Europe' in J Freedman (ed), *Gender and Insecurity. Migrant Women in Europe* (Aldershot, Ashgate, 2003). See also J Kilvington, S Day and H Ward, 'Prostitution Policy in Europe: A Time of Change?' (2001) 67 *Feminist Review* 78.

[13] In this respect the EU Plan, above n 3, under 'Broad Principles' rather promisingly states: 'in order to address effectively human trafficking an integrated approach is needed, having as its basis the respect of human rights and taking into account its global nature. This approach calls for a coordinated policy response notably in the Area of Freedom, Security and Justice, external relations, development cooperation, social affairs and employment, gender equality and non-discrimination; it should also benefit from a broad public–private dialogue'. However, most of these elements are not elaborated on—but see below the next two sections.

skilled and unskilled, than it has even with 10 new Member States on board. Thus some Member States[14] and the Commission advocate recruiting at least certain categories of migrant workers—but in the Council the issue is firmly embedded in a security discourse. Protection for the rights of migrant workers in general is of course essential in the process of opening the Member States up to non-EC migrants, and significant measures should be directed towards ensuring that steps are taken for this purpose.[15] For instance, migration programmes developed jointly between countries of origin and destination have been suggested in order to encourage non-abusive short-term migration (as many migrants do not leave to start a completely new life elsewhere, but to improve the conditions of the life they have in their countries) that could fill labour shortages and send remittances to countries of origin.[16] The problem with even this sort of logic, based on the declining demographic trends or skill deficits in the Member States, is of course that it does not challenge the underpinnings of the two migration regimes. In some ways such plans are thus a limited indication of a more reasonable immigration policy (for instance the Directive on long-term residents already shows that it is easier said than done to improve migrants' position), but it could be a start for a more sensible immigration policy that addresses migration not as a threat but as a social reality or even a matter of rights.

Regarding criminal justice, notwithstanding the problems inherent in using criminal law to tackle issues as contentious and complex as trafficking (see Chapter 5), there is potential room for the EU to improve awareness and co-operation among law enforcement agencies.[17] At the bare minimum trafficking crimes should be actively identified, investigated and prosecuted, and not dismissed or belittled, and victims' needs and rights should be taken into account in all operations. This is not sufficient in itself but necessary, even though the risk that it may become exclusive of all other measures is acute. In line with the UN Trafficking Protocol and the Framework Decision all Member States are obliged to adopt anti-trafficking criminal provisions. Obviously, reviewing criminal codes and amending or inserting provisions should go hand in hand with guaranteeing not to penalise victims of trafficking (or other penalties on irregular immigrants) and ensuring their protection in line with international obligations. A general non-discrimination clause in anti-trafficking legislation should be considered. In addition, a host of measures ranging from improving victim identification and

14 See, eg, D Schmidt, 'The New German Immigration Law' in J Apap (ed), *Justice and Home Affairs in the EU. Liberty and Security Issues after Enlargement* (Cheltenham, Edward Elgar, 2004).

15 Ratifying the ICMW would be a start; see, eg, S Peers, 'Irregular Immigration and EU External Relations' in B Bogusz *et al* (eds), *Irregular Migration and Human Rights: Theoretical, European and International Perspectives* (Leiden, Martinus Nijhoff Publishers, 2004), at 216, who says, '[t]he EU, if it chose, could play a significant role in building the institutional multilateral framework for addressing issues related to international migration, incorporating a positive approach to the UN Migrant Workers Convention'. The EU Plan, above n 3, does not mention the ICMW at all (but the Experts' Group's report did: see above n 3, at 24).

16 See, eg, Anti-Slavery International, *The Migration-Trafficking Nexus* (London, ASI, 2003).

17 And indeed a large proportion of the recommendations in the EU Plan, above n 3, focus on this element.

referral mechanisms,[18] developing multidisciplinary co-ordination and co-operation with NGOs, national action plans to address local situations, extending witness protection and developing measures for data collection and data protection as well as anti-corruption need to be emphasised in this respect. In addition to these, there is a plethora of specific measures oft-recommended, such as special anti-trafficking units in much afflicted Member States and joint investigations as well as the provision of gender-sensitive methods of investigation and judicial proceedings, and so on.[19]

While the EU can have a meaningful role to play in raising awareness[20] and contributing to the co-ordination of anti-trafficking measures at both the institutional and operational levels, what remains a crucial concern, however, is that anti-trafficking laws may be more anti-immigration measures masquerading as 'protection' than a serious commitment to such protection. While this also links in with the problems of prostitution law reforms, it is in any case imperative to back up any action on (migrant) prostitution and trafficking with appropriate sensitising, training, exchange of good practice and awareness-raising of authorities coming into contact with trafficking victims, not to mention resources for the police and judicial authorities. In this respect it is also useful to refer to EU funding. Since 2003, the STOP Programme has been replaced by a wider programme on the AFSJ called AGIS that aims to bring together legal practitioners, law enforcement officials and representatives of victim assistance.[21] Linked partly with criminal justice co-operation, another area in which the EU can make and has made a contribution is (short- and middle-term) prevention measures. The most famous of these measures has been the Daphne programme, which is now to run until 2008 with a total budget of €50 million, funding mostly NGO projects, including trafficking-oriented ones to combat violence across the Union.[22] Daphne funding has in the past been used for a variety of anti-trafficking activities by NGOs, such as: setting up networks between NGOs and promoting co-operation between NGOs and

[18] Organisation for Security and Co-operation in Europe, *National Referral Mechanisms. A Practical Handbook.* (Warsaw, OSCE/ODIHR, 2004).

[19] About these see, eg, Experts' Group on Trafficking in Human Beings, above n 3; Brussels Declaration, [2003] OJ C 137/1; C Rijken, *Trafficking in Persons. Prosecution from a European Perspective* (The Hague, TMC Asser, 2003) ch 7; E Niesner and C Jones-Pauly, *Trafficking in Women in Europe. Prosecution and Victim Protection in a European Context* (Bieleveld, Kleine Verlag, 2001); A Kartusch, *Reference Guide for Anti-trafficking Legislative Review with Particular Emphasis on South Eastern Europe* (Warsaw, OSCE/ODHR, 2001). The EU Plan, above n 3, endorses some but not all of these recommendations.

[20] The EU Plan, above n 3, Annex, Section 3.2. elaborates on the possibilities of awareness-raising.

[21] AGIS has co-financed some projects on trafficking, mainly on network-building, training and conferences. Funding information is available at http://europa.eu.int/comm/justice_home/funding/agis/funding_agis_en.htm (accessed 15 May 2006).

[22] See Amended Proposal for a Decision of the European Parliament and of the Council establishing a second phase of a programme of Community action (2004–8) to prevent violence against children, young people and women and to protect victims and groups at-risk (the Daphne II programme), COM(2003) 616 final (original proposal COM(2003)54 final); European Parliament and Council of the European Union Decision 803/2004/EC of 21 Apr 2004 adopting a programme of Community action (2004 to 2008) to prevent and combat violence against children, young people and women and to protect victims and groups at risk (the Daphne II programme), [2004] OJ L 143/1.

authorities; measures to protect target groups and prevent violence against them; studies and research; the dissemination of information; and the organisation of awareness-raising campaigns (both for the general public and for victims as well as those working with them).[23]

While STOP and Daphne are both necessary and in some ways commendable, it has to be asked whether initiatives like these are not rather too short-term and narrow as effective prevention measures; despite claims being made to ensure the continuity of projects.[24] A span of (at most) a few years is very short for sustained and coherent anti-trafficking efforts, be they about helping victims or about measures for the prevention of trafficking, especially when there is no guarantee that funding will be available after each period.[25] Projects funded, such as information campaigns and awareness-raising, certainly help, but can become an excuse for more sustained action and coherent long-term policy.[26] Also, the increased channelling of responsibility to a chronically under-funded NGO sector is not only likely to be insufficient (as NGOs lack the resources to lead the battle against trafficking), but can inadvertently give the message that the problem of trafficking is somehow a private matter, that aiding victims should be a matter of importance (only) to committed volunteers and that the Member States have no responsibility for trafficking victims. This is not to disparage the valuable work NGOs do, but to point out that they should not remain the only voice speaking on behalf of trafficking victims.[27] What needs to be done is not to designate this as an NGO problem for them to solve, but to address the discriminating structures that need to be challenged across the board.

To conclude, the current state of affairs falls quite a way short of the 'comprehensive and multidisciplinary' approach called for by the Commission in 1996—and the role of the European Union has not always been beneficial. Even considering the merits of paper-driven harmonisation and co-ordination measures such as the Framework Decision, the list of the achievements as regards 'comprehensiveness' is not very impressive apart from the soft law that tends to

[23] For information on projects see Commission Final Report on the Daphne Programme (2000–2003), Mar 2004.

[24] A Point also noted by J Goodey, 'Migration, Crime and Victimhood' (2003) 5 *Journal of Punishment and Society* 415; J Goodey, 'Recognising Organised Crime's Victims. The Case of Sex Trafficking in the EU' in A Edwards and P Gill (eds), *Transnational Organised Crime. Perspectives on Global Security* (London, Routledge, 2003).

[25] For instance, in terms of awareness-raising it would be more sustainable to spread information through public education (linked with addressing other issues that are risk factors, such as domestic violence and discrimination at work) rather than through short-term awareness-raising campaigns to warn potential migrants of the dangers of trusting middlemen or television advertisements (these can help but have a very short-term effect).

[26] European Women's Lobby, *Violence Against Women* (23 May 2000), available at www.womenlobby.org/Document.asp?DocID=90&tod=0926 (accessed 8 Feb 2005). Note that, eg, the Experts' Group on Trafficking in Human Beings, above n 3, at 6, supports a more long-term approach to funding.

[27] For an overview of NGO responses see M Tzvetkova, 'NGO Responses to Trafficking in Women' (2002) 10(1) *Gender and Development* 60.

remain a dead letter, such as the Hague Declaration.[28] This past is explained but not mitigated by the rapidly evolving nature of EU co-operation in many of the relevant spheres, the security emphasis of the Council that stems from (Member States') concerns and the lack of transparency and judicial control. In the light of the very real constraints on devising a far-reaching policy (such as the current constitutional crisis and Member State dominance in crucial areas), the greatest short-term potential of a *European* approach remains more modestly in using the EU as a forum that could facilitate co-ordination and priority-setting, monitor progress (or lack thereof),[29] promote best practice and endorse the coherence of relevant policies, and values debate about them.[30] At the same time the role of the Union needs to be carefully scrutinised to ensure that European developments, for instance improving police and judicial co-operation between Member States to facilitate exchange of information or joint investigation, avoid impeding international developments due to European action to form an Area of Freedom, Security and Justice. The latter, in particular, is a challenge in light of the migration–crime nexus that easily dictates a certain kind of unilateralism and eschews creating overall coherence in anti-trafficking policies.

7.2 PREVENTING TRAFFICKING IN WOMEN IN THE LONG RUN

7.2.1 Development, Migration and Gender Empowerment

The section above mainly dealt with what could, in some ways at least, be characterised as short-term concerns. Debates on interim adjustments are necessary, but cannot deliver on the fundamental structural issues, for preventing trafficking (beyond the more limited sphere of crime prevention) is contingent on supporting wider change, which is, however, for this same reason much more difficult. In addition to questions about policies around migration, one of the most relevant issues can be summarised as 'female empowerment'. As far as countries of origin are concerned, this means (broadly speaking) transforming existing power relations stemming, for example, from gender bias so as to broaden the range of options available to women through measures such as access to more and better education and living conditions, decent work and working conditions, and effective non-discrimination policies; in countries of destination this links with the protection of migrant workers' rights and the promotion of gender equality. As trafficking has much to do with the relative and absolute lack of power of (would-be) migrant women over their choices, the empowerment aspect links trafficking in women for sexual exploitation to complex and larger issues of gender equality

[28] Illustrative, in this sense, is the case of national rapporteurs, advocated by both the 1997 Hague and 2003 Brussels Declarations, but adopted by only a few Member States.

[29] Note that the current annual Europol reports on trafficking focus only on the organised crime dimension.

[30] The lack of coherence of the EU's activities (see Art 3 TEU) is pertinent in many ways, most obviously as regards external relations (see below).

such as sustainable development, international trade, environmental degradation and disasters[31] and conflict prevention. These issues also involve an evident link with the so-called 'root causes' discourse (examined above), whereby a complex mix of push and pull factors, such as poverty, lack of employment opportunities, discrimination on the one hand, and economic and social possibilities on the other, were discussed as affecting women's choices around migration and the risks involved with it.

Whatever the sporadic references to the 'root causes' of trafficking in AFSJ documents[32] may suggest, this discourse is currently appropriated by crime and in particular migration concerns that, while (for example) making a link between migration and development issues, treat the root causes at best superficially, and at worst threaten to 'infect' the entire development agenda.[33] Thus policy suggestions tend to be more about using EU clout to 'persuade' or punish migrant-sending countries—establishing better arrangements for migrant readmission, tougher penalties for smugglers and traffickers and scaring potential migrants—rather than about supporting safe migration in the short or middle term, let alone long-term equality and development in countries of origin that would ensure that migration is a choice rather than a dire necessity.[34] These also ignore, among other things, both women's complex role as migrants and the ways in which temporary migration makes short-term economic sense from the point of view of developing sending countries (as money sent by migrant workers contribute to development in their countries of origin). Ways to improve people's alternatives so that they can build better lives (in countries of origin or through migrating) are essentially, if not straightforwardly, linked to any serious long-term anti-trafficking efforts. But there are no quick fixes, and in fact this section comes with a caveat. The relationships

[31] On the fears over trafficking in children, which surfaced almost immediately in the aftermath of the tsunami of 26 Dec 2004, see, eg, 'L'ultima paura, la tratta dei bambini', *La Repubblica*, 3 Jan 2005.

[32] For instance the 2005 Plan includes the following statement (but little elaboration): '[d]evelopment cooperation also (sic) to include gender specific prevention strategies and strategies aimed at strengthening the economic, legal and political position of both women and children': EU Plan, above n 3, at 11.

[33] Consider, eg, the Action Plans by the High Level Working Group on Migration and Asylum; the Seville Conclusions (2002) that contemplate various measures, such as sanctioning third countries that fail to co-operate in the joint management of migration flows; the Council Conclusions on 19 May 2003 on migration and development, which encouraged complementarity between development and migration related policies; the AENEAS Programme, intended to provide assistance to third countries on stemming irregular migration and implementing readmission agreements; and the 2005 Strategy for the External Dimension of JHA (adopted by the JHA Council on 1–2 Dec 2005) that links organised crime to migration and its root causes. On the Action Plans see J van Selm, 'Immigration or Asylum or Foreign Policy: The EU's Approach to Migrants and Their Countries of Origin' in S Lavenex and E Uçarer (eds), *Migration and the Externalities of European Integration* (Lanham, Mld, Lexington Books, 2002). See also Peers, above n 15, for a commentary on how current EU migration policy damages external policy objectives. Compare the discussion in Communication from the Commission, Integrating migration issues in the European Union's relations with third countries, COM(2002)703 final, 3 Dec 2002 where the issue of policy coherence is at least raised (with a plea to sensitivity regarding development aims).

[34] Such focus is not exlusive to law enforcement authorities, but is sometimes quite uncritically supported by academic commentators as well: see, eg, U Smartt, 'Human Trafficking: Simply a European Problem?' (2003) 11 *European Journal of Crime, Criminal Law and Criminal Justice* 164.

between development, migration and trafficking are indirect, complex, poorly explored and imperfectly understood.[35] While arguably long-term development, and gender-sensitive development in particular, alleviates the root causes behind trafficking, in the shorter term development ties can actually increase ('unwanted') migration from assisted countries as a result of increased ties between countries and increased resources to migrate.[36] This, when combined with a restrictive migration policy it is of course a recipe for trafficking and exploitation.

Yet, in the long run, the only sustainable way ahead is to reduce the global wealth disparities, and do it in a way that increases women's abilities and choices.[37] These topics are extremely wide; to take just one example of relevant yet little explored EU action, this section discusses the issue of development co-operation, in particular 'gendering' and 'gender mainstreaming' it to prevent trafficking.[38] In other words, it scrutinises how development co-operation is used in this 'gender-sensitive' way, what problems this involves and how appropriate it is as a way of empowering women, and thus making them less vulnerable to exploitation. A similar examination could be made, for instance, regarding conflict prevention and democratisation, which arguably have the potential to reduce forced movement and displacement that make women vulnerable to trafficking.

Much has, of course, been written on gender mainstreaming and the European Union in recent years (and indeed many of the concerns raised relate to general problems with the concept).[39] In general terms, mainstreaming is a strategy that seeks to go beyond specific 'women's programmes' and to ensure that a gender perspective is taken into account in all relevant activities, such as policy development, research, legislation or resource allocation.[40] The potential of mainstreaming lies in making it possible to recognise gender considerations in areas previously represented as genderless, and including gender as a relevant factor in policy considerations across the board. In the area of development and development co-operation, the trend towards mainstreaming is reflected in a shift from 'women in development' (WID) to 'gender in development' (GID) in recognition that gender affects all areas of life, be they poverty, education or employment

[35] For a recent overview see N Nyberg-Sørensen, N Van Hear and P Engberg-Pedersen, 'The Migration–Development Nexus Evidence and Policy Options. State-of-the-Art Overview' (2002) 40(5) *International Migration* 3.

[36] This has been called a 'migration hump', which has to be overcome before people are encouraged to stay in the country of origin: see, eg, P Martin and J Taylor, 'Managing Migration: the Role of Economic Policies' in A Zolberg and P Benda (eds), *Global Migrants, Global Refugees* (New York, Berghahn Books, 2001).

[37] Thus one of the UN Millennium Goals is to '[p]romote gender equality and empower women': see United Nations Millennium Declaration, UN Doc 55/2.

[38] For a broad take on the kind of wide-ranging policy changes suggested by cosmopolitan perspectives (vis-à-vis new slavery more generally) see C van den Anker (ed), *The Political Economy of New Slavery* (Houndmills, Palgrave Macmillan, 2004).

[39] See, eg, (2002) 10(3) *Feminist Legal Studies Special Issue.*

[40] See, eg, T Rees, *Mainstreaming Equality in the European Union* (London, Routledge, 1998), at 40–8.

prospects.[41] Thus it is not considered sufficient to focus solely on traditional women's issues, such as maternity care, but indispensable to examine how gender underpins the range of options available to both women and men. This kind of framework obviously has strong links with anti-trafficking efforts aiming at diminishing the gendered reasons behind (gendered) exploitative practices such as trafficking.

The EU and in particular its Member States are, of course, the leading donors of development aid in the world, and thus exercise a large influence on global development co-operation. In the past development co-operation has tended to be rather gender-blind.[42] The three Member States examined in this study, each in its own way, already pay some attention to gender in their development co-operation activities. As regards EC competence, according to Article 177 TEC, Community policy shall be complementary to Member States' action—so Member States are free to pursue their own policies.[43] The European goal is to foster sustainable economic and social development, integration in the world economy and the campaign against poverty. Democracy and the rule of law as well as human rights and fundamental freedoms are to be developed and consolidated.[44] Sweden particularly emphasises a gender equality perspective as one of its six policy objectives and is a strong advocate of mainstreaming, albeit with varied results.[45] It has developed a manual on Gender Equality between Women and Men in Development Cooperation, and has also taken the first tentative steps towards explicitly linking trafficking to development through building up a strategy on fighting trafficking in human beings in Sweden's international development co-operation.[46] The Netherlands, like Sweden, is one of the few model students of development cooperation vis-à-vis standards on the amount of aid and a large donor country; it has had a 'women's policy' since the 1980s and gender mainstreaming is gradually finding its way into Dutch policy.[47] Italy, while a moderate donor in relative terms,

[41] Note, eg, the last Lomé Convention (IV), which included a clause entitled 'women in development', and the 2000 Cotonou Agreement, which uses the language of 'gender'.

[42] For an overview of Community policy see J McMahon, *The Development Co-operation Policy of the EC* (London, Kluwer Law International, 1998). On the implicit gender assumptions see E Turner, 'The EU's Development Policy and Gender' in M Lister (ed), *New Perspectives on European Union Development Co-operation* (Boulder, Colo, Westview Press, 1999).

[43] Member States do have an obligation to co-ordinate their development policies and may take joint action: see Art 180 TEC. For the changes that would have been made by the Draft Constitution [2004] OJ C 310/1, see Arts III-316–III-318, and the provisions on general external action, Arts III-292 ff.

[44] Development issues have only recently been tied together with human rights (or gender). For instance Community agreements have included a standard human rights clause since 1995: see, eg, M Bulterman, *Human Rights in the Treaty Relations of the European Community* (Antwerp, Intersentia, 2001).

[45] On Swedish development aid see OECD, 'Sweden' (2000) 1(4) *DAC Journal* 5.

[46] See Utrikesdepartementet, enheten för global utveckling, *Fattigdom och människohandel—En strategi för bekämpning av människohandel in Sveriges internationella utvecklingssamarbete* (Stockholm, Utrikesdepartementet, 2003).

[47] OECD, 'The Netherlands' (2001) 2(3) *DAC Journal* 5 But see also M Verloo, 'Making Women Count in the Netherlands' in F Beveridge, S Nott and K Stephen (eds), *Making Women Count. Integrating Gender into Law and Policy-making* (Aldershot, Ashgate, 2000).

is still a large donor in absolute terms, and illustrates some recognition to gender issues with the 1998 guidelines for the promotion of the role of women, including mainstreaming in its development co-operation arrangements.[48]

Gender mainstreaming arrived in the European arena in the mid-1990s; the European Commission (like, for instance, Sweden) takes a two-pronged approach to mainstreaming: it seeks to give systematic attention to gender across all instruments and interventions and in all phases, and also has specific actions for women in recognition that a mainstreaming approach entails the danger that, when equality is everyone's responsibility, it easily becomes no one's duty. The thematic evaluation of the success of the 1998 Council Regulation on the integrating of gender issues in development co-operation[49] (no longer in force) revealed similar problems to those of the Member States, namely that lack of necessary resources and an actual reduction of the gender budget line hampered effective implementation.[50] The Commission's 2001 communication involved a Programme of Action for the mainstreaming of gender equality in Community development co-operation.[51] It recognised the priority areas for Community development policy (support for macro-economic policies, poverty reduction strategies, social development programmes in health and education, food security and sustainable rural development, transport, institutional capacity building, good governance and the rule of law, trade and development, and regional integration and co-operation) and acknowledged gender as a cross-cutting issue in all of these themes. Noting the problems with the previous regulation, the Commission proposed a replacement.[52] This 2004 Regulation on promoting gender equality in development co-operation[53] is to implement measures with the objectives of supporting 'gender mainstreaming in *all* areas of development co-operation, combined with specific measures in favour of women of all ages, with the goal of promoting gender equality as an important contribution to poverty reduction'.[54]

The role of the EU in gendering development in the case of the ACP Partnership Agreements can be used as an example of the current state of affairs, prospects and problems involved in linking development issues to measures against trafficking in

[48] OECD, 'Italy' (2000) 1(3) *DAC Journal* 2. See also Italian Government, *The Position of the Italian Government on Trafficking in Human Beings* (Conference Paper from the EU/IOM STOP European Conference on Preventing and Combating Trafficking in Human Beings, Brussels, 18–20 Sept 2002, unpublished).

[49] Council Regulation (EC) No 2836/98 of 22 Dec 1998 on integrating of gender issues in development cooperation [1998] OJ L 354/5.

[50] Commission of the European Communities, Thematic Evaluation of the Integration of Gender in EC Development Co-operation with Third Countries, vol 1–3 (Brussels, EC Commission, Mar 2003).

[51] Communication from the Commission—Programme of Action for the mainstreaming of gender equality in Community Development Co-operation, COM(2001)295 final, 'warmly welcomed' in the Council Conclusions, 8 Nov 2001.

[52] Proposal for a regulation of the European Parliament and of the Council on promoting gender equality in development co-operation, COM(2003)465 final.

[53] European Parliament and Council of the European Union regulation 806/2004/EC of 21 Apr 2004 on promoting gender equality in development cooperation [2004] OJ L 143/40.

[54] Ibid, Art 3.

women.[55] After a gender-blind string of agreements, the last of the Lomé Conventions (No IV, signed in 1989) addressed how the status of women in development co-operation was to be supported, but this policy line was not translated into practice.[56] The Cotonou Agreement of 2000[57] was considered an improvement over Lomé, in that gender appears in many of its provisions.[58] In line with the calls for mainstreaming, Article 1, which deals with objectives, states that 'systematic account shall be taken of the situation of women and gender issues in all areas—political, economic and social'. Gender, as well as migration, is included in the topics for political dialogue in Article 8, and Article 13 on migration, which contains the obvious readmission clause for ACP nationals (and provides for negotiating an agreement that also covers third-country nationals), also contains a commitment to eliminate all forms of discrimination based on, among others, origin, race and sex and a statement of migrants' rights in repatriation.[59] Article 20(2) contains the commitment to gender mainstreaming: 'systematic account shall be taken in mainstreaming into all areas of cooperation . . . gender issues'. Gender as a cross-cutting theme is elaborated in Article 31, which contains the aim to 'improve, ensure and broaden the equal participation of men and women in all spheres of political, economic, social and cultural life'.[60]

There are both theoretical and practical concerns that can be expressed about the framework of the Cotonou Agreement with regard to the role of gender vis-à-vis trafficking prevention. These are intertwined and can be summarised by saying that in some ways the mainstreaming project may go too far, whilst yet not going far enough. Where it goes too far is in some of the assumptions underpinning the gender mainstreaming of development co-operation. In other words, it is open to a charge of cultural imperialism, to the extent that it is suggestive of an understanding that it is the proper role of the EU to impose judgements about what

[55] Another example might be the lack of gender mainstreaming in the latest enlargement process, where gender equality was included only as regards the distinct equal opportunities *acquis*: see C Bretherton, 'Gender Mainstreaming and EU Enlargement: Swimming Against the Tide?' (2001) 8 *Journal of European Public Policy* 60; S Steinhilber, *Women's Rights and Gender Equality in the EU Enlargement. An Opportunity for Progress* (WIDE briefing paper, Brussels, Network Women in Development Europe, 2002).

[56] K Arts, *Gender Aspects of the Cotonou Agreement* (WIDE Position Paper, Brussels, Network Women in Development Europe, 2001).

[57] Partnership Agreement Between the Members of the African, Caribbean and Pacific Group of States (ACP) of the one part, and the European Community and its Member States, of the other part, signed in Cotonou on 23 June 2000 [2000] OJ L 317/3.

[58] Note that the list of relevant human rights instruments in the (preamble) also includes the Women's Convention.

[59] See also the human rights clause, which states that 'the Parties undertake to promote and protect all fundamental freedoms and human rights, be they civil and political, or economic, social and cultural. In this context, the Parties reaffirm the equality of men and women' (Art 9).

[60] Art 31 also states that co-operation is to 'integrate a gender-sensitive approach and concerns at every level of development cooperation including macroeconomic policies, strategies and operations' and to encourage specific measures in favour of women, eg, 'access to basic social services, especially to education and training, health care and family planning' and 'access to productive resources, especially to land and credit and to labour market'.

women in poorer countries should want and how their lives could be improved.[61] Linked with the undeniable migration control concerns that also find expression in the Convention, this *may arguably* approach interference in the internal affairs of ACP States and is, moreover, symptomatic of the kind of unilateral bullying and cultural imperialism by a rich bloc that the poorer nations of the world frequently complain about. This is not to say that human rights or gender should not have a place in agreements (although it remains in some ways controversial[62]), just that, to the extent that it is permissible, it should involve careful consideration of local factors and cultural landscapes. Helping women to have decent lives with freedoms, economic resources, work opportunities and non-abusive relationships should not involve initiatives that ignore the local realities or treat women as 'development targets', but recognise the inevitable diversity and complexity in the setting of priorities.

With that caution in mind, at the same time it can be argued that intentions to mainstream gender do not go far enough, in that they tend to remain just rhetorical pronouncements rather than to involve a serious commitment to integrate gender analysis into all forms of co-operation. For instance, many areas of the Partnership Agreement, most notably the 'hard ones' of economic and trade co-operation, structural adjustment, or even tourism (keeping in mind the links between sex tourism and trafficking), do not pay any attention to gender, let alone 'mainstream it as a cross-cutting issue'. Moreover, even though the gender commitments on paper are getting stronger, little guidance is given on how gender mainstreaming should be done in practice. Some commentators have concluded that, for instance, Cotonou adds little to promote more humane and 'kinder' forms of trade (or which are more people-centred), as the focus on trade in Cotonou is on 'big business' rather than on small-scale businesses (which are more likely to be female-owned and run by female entrepreneurs).[63] This could lead to squashing the small entrepreneurs, and pushing a disproportionate number of women into deeper poverty or marginalisation. Apart from this aspect, more emphasis is laid on involving and including women (numerically speaking) rather than on changing 'relations, institutions, attitudes and beliefs about men and women that provides the basis that underpin the perpetual discrimination against and exclusion of women and girls'.[64]

[61] The concerns about overruling the desires of people affected by development projects and imposing potentially harmful consequences on them are of course a familiar concern with regard to development aid projects in general: see, eg, J Paul, 'The Human Right to Development: Its Meaning and Importance' (1992) *Third World Legal Studies* 17.

[62] Development and human rights (and the role gender plays in both) are arguably intimately linked, but the primacy of each element (and what to do in cases of conflicting objectives) remains contested. On development as a human right see, eg, Declaration on the Right to Development (GA res 41/128, 4 Dec 1986). For discussion see, eg, J Donnelly, 'Human Rights, Democracy, and Development' (1999) 21 *Human Rights Quarterly* 608; P Alston and M Robinson, *Human Rights and Development* (Oxford, Oxford University Press. 2005).

[63] Arts, above n 56; R Mate, *A Gender Analysis of the Cotonou Agreement and Its Implementation* (London, One World Action, 2003).

[64] See Mate, above n 63, 4.

Regarding trafficking in women in particular, concerns about the success of mainstreaming development co-operation tie to how development in migrants' countries of origin should not only enhance their opportunities in labour exporter countries (laudable as that aim is), but also (perhaps more importantly) challenge the notion that women need just 'better' opportunities to acquire some spending money (or an encouraging pat on the head). It is precisely this kind of belittling and apparent but superficial attempts to help which offer no genuine long-term prospects that many women seek to escape through migrating for work. In some respects this mirrors the issues discussed in the previous section and the consequences of many well-meaning income-generating programmes run by international NGOs with Daphne support in countries of origin. Linked to the 'sticking plaster' approach to women and development is the problem of a lack of any serious commitment to discussing the role of men (despite their role in trafficking, or sex tourism, or the spread of HIV) and the gender dynamics that underpin the exploitation of women more widely in both developing and developed countries. Yet this is fundamental for any project trying to break the links between gender, sexuality, poverty and exploitation.

The lack of systematic integration at operational and institutional level is an example of the general problems of mainstreaming in the EU, notwithstanding its transformative promise and certain positive outcomes. In a nutshell, gender mainstreaming policies, while currently existing, are not fully thought-out, put into practice, funded or sufficiently monitored. Pollack and Hafner-Burton argue that the success of mainstreaming efforts depends on how well or not it resonates with the dominant frames of European institutions. Thus, it has been successful, for example, vis-à-vis the area of structural funds (a field that is relatively open to interventions and where the mainstreaming argument can be formulated in terms of both efficiency and social justice to ensure its acceptance by Member States), and it has been remarkably unsuccessful in the area of competition policy with its closed policy process and the lack of obvious gender-relevant implications.[65] As regards development aid in particular, the authors find that, despite the preliminary assumption that this area would be fertile ground for mainstreaming, the lack of gender expertise, resources, priority-setting and a high level of de-centralisation at the level of operations make practical advancement difficult.[66] Although, despite continuing obstacles, some (and not negligible) progress has been made, problems such as lack of awareness, finances and expertise, not to mention accountability for implementation, remain.

Moreover, a common problem with integrating a gender perspective into EU law is that, even when to a degree successful in an area (as in development), it

[65] M Pollack and E Hafner-Burton, 'Mainstreaming Gender in the European Union' (2000) 7 *Journal of European Public Policy* 432.

[66] *Ibid*, at 445–46. See also Turner, above n 42; G Painter and K Ulmer, *Everywhere and Nowhere: Assessing Gender Mainstreaming in European Community Development Cooperation* (London, APRODEV and One World Action, 2002).

actually rarely challenges the structures and frameworks of EU law itself.[67] By not challenging the established divisions and priorities among policy areas, such as trade and development, it fails to destabilise the status quo. Yet to be credible, gender mainstreaming should not only be sensitive to diversity, backed with sufficient resources and expertise (that much is obvious), but also link gender, development and trade in ways that would negate the effects of EU protectionism, most notably the impact of the Common Agricultural Policy (but also some aspects of the AFSJ) on poorer nations. The Union, as is well known, undermines local growers and manufacturers in the developing world through the dumping of subsidised goods on their local markets, and import tariffs imposed by the EU reduce the potential for developing countries to export their products, especially those in competition with EU products, to the EU.[68] In the lack of a development-friendly trading system it is hardly credible for the EU to talk about free trade in agricultural products with agriculturally dependent developing countries when the EU itself continues to distort production and trade through considerable levels of public aid. Similarly, a serious gender mainstreaming policy should also address the politics of neo-liberalism that have gained ground in EU development policy.[69] While neo-liberal politics have little to say, explicitly at least, about gender (after all, they speak in the gender-neutral language of the markets, individuals and choice), the world in which neo-liberalism rules operate is a gendered world and neo-liberalism has its gender politics, as the downgrading or dismantling of equal opportunity programmes and women's policies and social services restrict the freedom of choice of those most dependant on them. Thus without any explicit masculinity politics, the gender compromises embodied in state structures have been subverted by right-wing governments that justify state retreat in the name of individual liberty and global competition.[70]

Much can also be said about how this kind of lack of coherence and balance undermines the EU's credibility and reveals the patchiness of its commitment seriously to fight poverty and gender equality in ways that would be necessary to alleviate the root causes of trafficking. This is where the far greater challenge lies. This touches on the conceptions of freedom discussed in Chapter 3 and the fact that, despite its present and growing spillover to many spheres of life, the main European competence lies in the fields where the vested interests prefer the status quo of economic freedom (which prevails over the social dimension). But it also

[67] J Shaw, 'Importing Gender: The Challenge of Feminism and the Analysis of the EU Legal Order' (2000) 7 *Journal of European Public Policy* 406, at 408.

[68] For this kind of ethical argument see C van den Anker, 'Contemporary Slavery, Global Justice and Globalization' in van den Anker (ed), above n 38.

[69] On how the EU's development policy has gradually rejected its origins and moved towards the IMF/World Bank stance which ignores the tensions between social sector policies on poverty reduction and structural adjustment-oriented macroeconomic reforms see W Brown, 'From Uniqueness to Uniformity? An Assessment of EU Development Aid Policies' in K Arts and A Dickson (eds), *EU Development Co-operation. From Model to Symbol* (Manchester, Manchester University Press, 2004); A Dickson, 'The Unimportance of Trade Preferences' in *ibid.*

[70] R Connell, *The Men and the Boys* (Cambridge, Polity Press, 2000), at 50–6.

relates to the human rights argument in Chapter 6 and the even broader debate about the spread and proper management of economic globalisation and ethical accountability for its excesses. It necessitates undertaking the broad task of evaluating the sometimes unforeseen migration consequences of the interaction of globalisation phenomena such as foreign investment and disruption of traditional livelihoods in developing countries.[71] The EU could take the lead in regulation, protection of the environment, action to uphold labour standards globally and safeguarding those most likely to benefit the least.[72] This, if anything, is a long-term project, but any serious attempts towards a coherent approach to development that would also undermine trafficking should face these questions head on. While at present any attempt to go beyond the current situation, namely an EU approach that superficially addresses but substantially marginalises the relevant issues (the will to migrate due to poverty, or the desire to escape threats, such as armed conflicts or human rights abuses), is likely to meet heavy resistance at the very least, failing to connect them to core areas of European integration which affect these (such as EU policies' effects on women outside the EU) is equally damaging in the long run.

7.2.2 Sexual Ideologies and the Market for Sexual Services

Besides the supply, discussions on reducing and preventing trafficking need to address the issue of demand for sexual services that underpins the sex market in general and, arguably, trafficking to fill jobs in that market. Despite the logic of the connection, this is a very controversial area within feminism as well as in other fields. Familiar disagreements arise as to whether this demand is legitimate at all, or only when all parties involved genuinely agree, and on whether the demand stems from male biological needs or socio-cultural factors. When comparing this controversy to the consensus that generally backs (albeit only at a general and abstract level) reducing the economic and demographic disparities that encourage women's migration and facilitate exploitation, such as trafficking, one can immediately notice a point of agreement that links with the previous section. Prostitution has a low appeal as a form of work for most women, and even when 'chosen' it tends to be chosen by those in a disadvantaged socio-economic position. As was discussed in Chapter 2, an 'exploitation' argument would agree that the low appeal of prostitution is because of the aversion of women to prostitution as a central site where their sexuality is turned into a subordinate object of male desire (which means that only those with no other economic options would engage in it). A 'work' position would argue that the problem is the stigma on and

[71] For an analysis of how US foreign investments, the attendant uprooting of people to export zones in offshoring countries and the creation of low paid jobs in the US have fed the cycle of migration to the US see S Sassen, *Globalization and Its Discontents* (New York, The New Press, 1998), ch 3.

[72] N Dower, 'The Global Framework for Development: Instrumentality or Contested Ethical Space' in van den Anker (ed), above n 38.

very low social status of the women involved: thus it is not the degrading nature of prostitution itself, but the degrading label and the sexist assumptions often found behind it (that women are either 'Madonnas' or 'whores') that lead only those women with few other options choose it, that have to be challenged. Both lobbies recognise that any durable solution on the supply side, especially with regard to trafficking, has to relate to empowering women economically and socially.

As regards the demand side, any feminist perspective involves recognition that the current situation of global and local wealth disparities and the gendered ideologies that underpin buying sex as a commodity exchange mean that a large number of women are available to fill the demands of prostitution customers who can continue to have very little awareness or interest in the harm they may cause to the women who service them.[73] Therefore the expansion of European sex industries, which need an ever-increasing number of women, should be more carefully scrutinised as to the role of the invisible men behind them in particular and their societal foundations more broadly. Considering the disagreement on the source of the problem of prostitution itself, it is hardly surprising that there is little consensus on what to do about the *demand* for prostitutes. Is it an unconditional evil, in that the motivations for prostitute use are always gender-oppressive, or is it harmful only when it is done with sexist and denigrating motivations or through highly risky acts (such as lack of condom use)? Many do see a problem in the customers of prostitution and the sexist ideologies that now accompany the sex industries more generally; even many of those supporting a 'work' view willingly concede that prostitution customers are frequently hostile or violent against women in prostitution and thus call for an attitude change in customers as well as society in general. Put simply, the questions are: while in contemporary European societies prostitution is, to a greater or lesser degree, patriarchal, is it possible to take patriarchy out of prostitution and, if so, under what conditions, and what does that mean for anti-trafficking action?

Such questions are difficult to answer not only because they are contested, but also because there is a relative dearth of serious research into prostitution customers in Western countries. This in part reflects a double standard according to which women are held responsible for what is more properly male than female sexual behaviour, but it also (related to this) has to do with the overly biological understanding under which seeking prostitutes is naturalised as innate male behaviour that needs no analysis.[74] Beyond such structural invisibility, customers

[73] For a limited but interesting survey of customers' attitudes about prostitute use, migrants and trafficking victims see B Anderson and J O'Connell Davidson, *Is Trafficking in Human Beings Demand Driven? A Multi-country Pilot Study* (IOM Migration Research Series, No 15, Geneva, IOM, 2003). For how the construction of prostitution as a commodity exchange hides gendered power relations and relies on imagining prostitute women as 'outside the community' see J O'Connell Davidson, '"Does She Do Queening?": Prostitution, Sovereignty and Community' in L Brace and J Hoffman (eds), *Reclaiming Sovereignty* (London, Pinter, 1997).

[74] For a good (if US-centred) overview of existing research see M Monto, 'Female Prostitution, Customers and Violence' (2004) 10(2) *Violence Against Women* 160. See also D Hughes, *Best Practices to Address the Demand Side of Sex Trafficking* (Kingston, RI, University of Rhode Island, 2004).

are also silent because it is in their interests not to draw attention to themselves; it would be inaccurate to say that no stigma is attached to prostitution customers by society in general and (often more importantly) by their female partners, even if the stigma is not as total as the moral condemnation of prostitutes. As customers usually seek to keep their activities hidden (and the justice system routinely assists them by sparing them public humiliation), research on them is emerging and tentative. What is manifest in the existing research on prostitute-using men is the great variety of their motivations: there is no single reason or internally coherent set of motivations that explains why some men are prostitution customers and others not. In line with the 'exploitation' critique, for a relatively large part of them prostitution is patriarchal, in that it is connected with a desire to be in control; for multiple partners and limited emotional involvement; as well as the attraction stemming from the illicit nature of prostitution (through the mystery and excitement of a risky encounter).[75] A sexually libertarian, commodified perspective on sex is shown in an interest in variety, control and immediate satisfaction. However, other (perhaps less common) motivations point to loneliness, shyness, need for contact and intimacy and so on, which are less explicitly about male dominance but rather about problems related to dominant social and cultural expectations about being male.

These motivations, common enough as they are in the Western cultural setting, can partly at least be explained through the notion(s) of hegemonic masculinity (and alternative masculinities). Hegemonic masculinity is the current dominant form of masculinity in Western societies that, operating at the level of 'common sense', characterises 'what it means to be a man'. This is bound with the ascendancy to power of certain men—to becoming a ruling bloc that inhabits and maintains positions of control and wealth (be it through violence, as under colonialism, or through institutional means, such as corporate and political power)—and how this power and wealth are used to legitimate and reproduce social dominance-based relationships. Hegemonic masculinity stands in power relation to femininity and to other masculinities, such as homosexuality and effeminacy.[76] As a cultural ideal it secures the dominance of some men (and the subordination of women) within the gender system. It is unattainable for most men, but still powerful, something that is obvious with regard to hegemonic sexuality, defined as asymmetrical heterosexuality. Many men in contemporary Western cultures are trained to view sex as the acquisition of physical pleasure through the taking of women, conquest, control, performance and self-assertion.[77] Sex is a sphere in which many men (and not only men) believe that men are naturally dominant and women correspondingly passive. Under hegemonic masculinity sex is, at least in part, sexy because power relations are eroticised. Ideologies deeming that men should be fearless and despise weakness, abhor revealing dependency or seeking

[75] M Monto, 'Why Men Seek out Prostitutes' in R Weitzer (ed), *Sex for Sale: Prostitution, Pornography and the Sex Industry* (New York, Routledge, 2000).

[76] R Connell, *Gender and Power* (Cambridge, Polity Press, 1987).

[77] V Seidler, *Rediscovering Masculinity. Reason, Language and Sexuality* (London, Routledge, 1989).

intimacy (as they can expose one to emotional rejection) mean that for some men it is safer or easier to channel this towards commodified sexuality (for instance pornography, sex tourism), as this provides the sexual without emotional risks. Yet this entails a paradox evident in those men who visit prostitutes not for the sex but for the company, touch and so on.[78] Indeed, hegemonic masculinity is closely related to what it suppresses and what resists (for instance alternative male sexualities) and challenges it (feminism). As such hegemonic masculinity is also unstable, changing and contestable.

When looking at the demand for prostitution one can see that hegemonic masculinity resonates with the commodified sex-buying logic of prostitutes' customers, while the intimacy and contact-seeking motivations seem to point to more or less hegemonically inclined men who either aspire to hegemonic masculinity through prostitute use or suffer from the restrictions that hegemonic masculinity puts on stereotypical male behaviour (sex as conquest). This ideology, which in societies marred by unequal power relations easily becomes a recipe for abuse, is then something that turning prostitutes into sex therapists or labelling all men as sexual predators will not change; it is the larger problem of masculinity and the tensions within it that need to be addressed. Thus reducing or transforming demand supported by hegemonic masculinity entails having to seek alternative ways out of men's problems of social and sexual identities and relationships. While there are no patent solutions for this, educational activities seem the obvious way forward, especially as regards the education of boys. Policy measures may also be considered to support (also through law) alternative masculinities that question and undermine the hegemony of the prevalent notion, which sees sex-buying as a normalised expression of male virility, no matter what the consequences to others or the social setting in which the transaction takes place.[79] Obvious examples of alternative masculinities are homosexual and nurturing masculinities, the latter of which (for example, stay-at-home fathers) in particular destabilises hegemonic masculinity that associates the ideal form of masculinity with toughness, aggressiveness and opposition to 'femininity'. Broadly speaking then this project involves challenging sexual stereotypes and undermining unequal gender relations. In addition it must interrogate the dominant masculinity through more widespread discussion on the inaccurate (if prevalent) perceptions of female sexuality as a thing that has little value to women themselves (apart from perhaps the financial), but a lot of value for men. This should be linked to issues such as differences between countries on the numbers of men who buy (or do not buy) sex, the rise of sex tourism, the increasingly widespread consumption of pornography as normal entertainment and the often not only gender-specific but highly racialised encounters that prostitution and trafficking presently involve.

In this respect it is crucial to note that there has been a remarkable lack of discussion of sexual ethics in Europe, apart from homosexuality and abortion inspired

[78] See Seidler, above n 77, 163.

[79] See, eg, T Truong, 'Gender, Exploitative Migration, and the Sex Industry: A European Perspective' (2003) 7 *Gender, Technology and Development* 31, at 48.

debates, despite the fact that the area of sexual ethics as a site of struggle is no longer exclusively monopolised by the Church, and in spite of the attention to trafficking for prostitution as a gendered phenomenon. Most importantly, real ethical debate over the legitimate (or not) expressions of male heterosexuality is rarely found. That many customers of prostitution are either ignorant of or indifferent to whether the prostitutes they visit are trafficked or not means they deem their sexual satisfaction more important than entertaining doubts about the 'legitimacy' of the women they use. This should raise huge questions about sexuality at a time when trafficked women 'outnumber, under-price and "outperform" EU-nationals' in sex industry's terms.[80] In terms of practical solutions care must be taken not to cause harm to those intended to be helped. For instance, while emphasising customer responsibility may not be a bad idea, some campaigns on the prevention of trafficking (most notably the Nordic–Baltic one[81]), which have focused attention on the role of prostitute-users as giving rise to trafficking activities, face real difficulties in trying to criticise sex-buyers without at the same time (further) stigmatising the sellers. At the same time the official Dutch sex industry's recent initiative to develop a quality mark for the legal sex sector (to improve its image as opposed to the 'illegal' side)[82] risks furthering the demarcation between the domestic and migrant women in prostitution and reinforcing the racial and national hierarchies of the sex industry. What a feminist strategy might want to emphasise instead is the larger background of discrimination in its varying forms, from the devaluing and marginalisation of migrants and their lack of legal rights to the prevalence of sexual stereotypes, gendered labour roles and the sexual objectification of women and children, which undermine economic and social equality and contribute to the extreme exploitation of some of the most vulnerable. The role and responsibility of, for instance, the media and education systems is again relevant here.

In addition, while comparatively speaking much attention is now devoted to violations of women's sexual rights such as trafficking, there has been very little discussion on the positive side of the coin, on women's entitlement not only to freedom from abuse of their sexuality but to affirmative expressions of sexuality as *theirs* (as opposed to, for instance, prostitution, which is essentially about a variation of male rather than female sexuality).[83] Even though the past ties between

[80] Goodey, above n 24, at 161.

[81] The Nordic–Baltic campaign, conducted in 2002 in Sweden, Norway, Denmark, Finland and Iceland (as countries of destination) and in Estonia, Latvia and Lithuania (as countries of origin/transit). On Nordic–Baltic co-operation see, eg, C Johansson Wennerholm, 'Crossing Borders and Building Bridges: the Baltic Region Networking Project' (2002) 10(1) *Gender and Development* 10.

[82] Ministry of Justice Press Release, 2 July 2004 on the Government's action plan on the regulation and protection of the prostitution industry (Plan van Aanpak Ordening & Bescherming Prostitutiesector).

[83] To connect this to the quotation at the beginning of ch 2: why is it so much easier to focus on danger instead of pleasure? See, eg, R Petchesky, 'The Body as Property: A Feminist Re-vision' in F Ginsburg and R Rapp (eds), *Conceiving The New World Order: The Global Politics of Reproduction* (Berkeley, Cal, University of California Press, 1995); R Petchesky 'Sexual Rights: Inventing a Concept, Mapping an International Practice' in R Parker, R Barbosa and P Aggleton (eds), *Framing the Sexual Subject. The Politics of Gender, Sexuality and Power* (Berkeley, Cal, University of California Press, 2000).

religious morality and sexuality (in particular morality-based repression of sexual female expression) mean that calling for debate on sexuality may seem a dangerous trip back to the past, far from abandoning discussion of sexual ethics, it is time to engage in this, not least because by giving up any discussion of morality, the subject is monopolised by the fundamentalists. It is necessary to strengthen the 'weak' arguments of non-fundamentalists and to explore what a progressive sexual ethic might look like, whether or not it should be a separate ethical strand or not, and so on.[84] Sexual freedom and individualism in it have not meant equality and justice, and thus sexual freedom is only represented as such; in reality it is bound up with gender, class, ethnicity and wealth. Who can afford to choose and what they can choose is a political issue, not a neutral one. Thus a debate needs to redefine what we mean by sexual freedom, consent, and so on. What is, for example, the logic that underpins how freedom with regard to sexuality should be understood: thin and superficial but easy to agree on, as opposed to a thicker understanding that requires more careful balancing with the haves and the have-nots; who enjoys the capability and material conditions actually to enjoy sexual self-determination and expression? Thus it connects to broader questions of fairness, values and justice.

Although these issues may, at first glance, seem far removed from the EU's response to trafficking in the absence of a Union role in areas such as media or education,[85] this fact instead means that in European terms it is even more important to stop and think about the implications of this matter. In many ways, the previous section led to questions about the kind of notions of masculinity and femininity that underpin and find expression in the politics of economic globalisation and free trade. Unrestrained neo-liberal globalisation ideology naturalises unequal power relations as immutable, endorsing the exploitation of the 'weak', and can, moreover, be linked to the commercialisation of sexuality in general (for example, the increased use of sexuality in advertisements, or new technologies such as the internet that facilitate the spread of pornography). Connell explicitly brings together current hegemonic masculinity and market capitalism, and argues that the former is embodied above all with those who control its dominant institutions (business executives, politicians, and so on).[86] He separates this hegemonic masculinity from the previous one (which he calls traditional bourgeois masculinity), in that the current form is increasingly sexually libertarian, with a growing tendency to commodify relations with women; this kind of masculinity is also marked by increasing ego-centricism, very conditional loyalties, and a declin-

[84] For one discussion of the ethical principles behind sexual rights, see *ibid*, at 91–5.

[85] See, for instance, the 2004 Directive on equal treatment regarding goods and services ([2004] OJ L 373/37), the scope of which was eventually cut down to exclude, eg, equal treatment in media and education due to a lack of consensus between Member States (because of the potentially far-reaching economic and social implications).

[86] Connell, above n 70.

ing sense of responsibility for others.[87] In terms of the future of the European project, this links with the need seriously to engage with what kind of profile Europe is (or is not) to have as a developing polity—the kind of social face it is to have to complement the economic; the structures and mechanisms it is to have to tackle discrimination, social exclusion and gendered ideologies and hierarchies; the ways of meeting the expectations of *all* (as opposed to a privileged group of EU citizens) regarding belonging—and what kind of global role it should seek as an economic and political actor?

7.3 FINAL REMARKS

Even though the last part of this chapter on long-term efforts to tackle trafficking divides them into two parts for presentational purposes, it should be kept in mind that in terms of substance this division remains highly artificial. Trafficking and responses to it are located in an environment where the material conditions that produce the supply of women to be exploited are very much bound with the ideological underpinnings of the market where the demand for sexual services remains unchallenged. This again connects back to Chapter 3 in which the market-oriented underpinnings of the European Union, and its multilateral governance in which preference of the economic over the social (left to the Member States) leads to the social being constrained by the mechanics of the economic, were discussed. While claiming to be (gender-)neutral, this ideology in practice benefits certain kinds of actors and acts. Although the intricacies of European governance may seem remote from the everyday prostitution acts of individual men and women, it is the conflation of material conditions (men's economic clout and corresponding constraints on women) with the market ideology in which sex becomes a commodity like any other which frames the concrete circumstances in which trafficking takes place. Thus the lack of will to engage in any debate over whether or not the Union should play a role in addressing demand for sexual services is actually a manifestation of a broader problem. To say this is not to claim that the European Union *is* the problem rather than the solution as far as trafficking in women for sexual exploitation is concerned; rather we have to recognise the multiple ways in which the European Union is part of the problem in order to conceive of ways of making it a part of the solution as well.

[87] It is therefore not surprising to find that in many countries much stricken by female poverty and discrimination prostitution is proposed by neoliberal circles as an alternative way out of unemployment and poverty for women. While it may be that some women are better off choosing prostitution, as a general solution to increasing female poverty and lack of prospects it is likely only to entrench gender inequality and discrimination against women.

Bibliography

BOOKS AND ARTICLES

Ackers, L (1998) *Shifting Spaces. Women, Citizenship and Migration Within the European Union* (Bristol, The Policy Press)

Addo, M (1991) 'Justiciability Re-Examined', in D Hill and R Beddard (eds), *Economic, Social and Cultural Rights* (Basingstoke, Palgrave Macmillan)

Aghatise, E (2004) 'Trafficking for Prostitution in Italy' 10 *Violence against Women* 1126

Albrecht, P and Braum, S (1999) 'Deficiencies in the Development of European Criminal Law' 5 *European Law Journal* 293

Alegre, S and Leaf, M (2004) 'Mutual Recognition in European Judicial Co-operation: A Step Too Far Too Soon? Case Study—the European Arrest Warrant' 10 *European Law Journal* 200

Alexander, P (1998) 'Prostitution: *Still* a Difficult Issue for Feminists' in F Delacoste and P Alexander (eds), *Sex Work. Writings by Women in the Sex Industry* (2nd ed) (San Francisco, CA, Cleis Press)

Alston, P (ed) (1999) *The EU and Human Rights* (Oxford, Oxford University Press)

—— and Robinson, M (eds), (2005) *Human Rights and Development* (Oxford, Oxford University Press)

Ambrosini, M (2001) 'The Role of Immigrants in the Italian Labour Market' 39(3) *International Migration* 61

Andall, J (2000) 'Organizing Domestic Workers in Italy' in F Anthias and G Lazaridis (eds), *Gender and Migration in Southern Europe* (Oxford, Berg)

Anderson, M (2002) 'European Police Co-operation—History and Theory' in F Longo (ed), *The European Union and the Challenge of Transnational Organised Crime* (Milan, Giuffrè)

Anker, D (2002) 'Refugee Law, Gender, and the Human Rights Paradigm' 15 *Harvard Human Rights Journal* 133

Apap, J (2002) 'Shaping Europe's Migration Policy New Regimes for the Employment of Third Country Nationals: A Comparison of Strategies in Germany, Sweden, the Netherlands and the UK' 4 *European Journal of Migration and Law* 309

Appleyard, R (2001) 'International Migration Policies: 1950–2000' 39(6) *International Migration* 7

Arlacchi, P (1999) *Schiavi. Il nuovo traffico di esseri umani* (Milan, Rizzoli)

Aronowitz, A (2001) 'Smuggling and Trafficking in Human Beings: The Phenomenon, the Markets that Drive It and the Organisations that Promote It' 9 *European Journal on Criminal Policy and Research* 163

Arts, K (2000) *Integrating Human Rights into Development Cooperation: The Case of the Lomé Convention* (The Hague, Kluwer Law International)

Bales, K (2000) 'Expendable People: Slavery in the Age of Globalization' 53 *Journal of International Affairs* 461

Barnard, C (1999) 'EC 'Social' Policy' in P Craig and G de Burca (eds), *The Evolution of EU Law* (Oxford, Oxford University Press)

BARRY, K (1979) *Female Sexual Slavery* (New York, New York University Press)
—— (1995) *The Prostitution of Sexuality* (New York, New York University Press)
BARTLETT, K and KENNEDY, R (eds) (1991) *Feminist Legal Theory: Readings in Law and Gender* (Boulder, Westview Press)
BEARE, M (1997) 'Illegal Migration: Personal Tragedies, Social Problems, or National Security Threats' 3(4) *Transnational Organized Crime* 11
BELL, M (1999) 'Shifting Conceptions of Sexual discrimination at the Court of Justice: from *P v S* to *Grant v SWT*' 5 *European Law Journal* 61
—— (2001) 'Mainstreaming Equality Norms into European Union Asylum Law' 26 *European Law Review* 20
—— (2002) *Anti-Discrimination Law and the European Union* (Oxford, Oxford University Press)
BENJAMIN, H and MASTERS, R (1964) *Prostitution and Morality* (New York, The Julian Press)
BENTON, S (1991) 'Gender, Sexuality and Citizenship' in G Andrews (ed), *Citizenship* (London, Lawrence & Wishart)
BERLIN, I (1969) 'Two Concepts of Liberty' in I Berlin, *Four Essays on Liberty* (London, Oxford University Press)
BERMAN, J (2003) '(Un)Popular Strangers and Crises (Un)Bounded: Discourses of Sex-Trafficking, the European Political Community and the Panicked State of the Modern State' 9 *European Journal of International Relations* 37
BEVERIDGE, F (2000) 'Same Song—Different Tunes: A Lesson in Harmony Singing?' in F Beveridge, S Nott and K Stephen (eds), *Making Women Count. Integrating Gender into law and policy-making* (Aldershot, Ashgate)
—— and MULLALLY, S (1995) 'International Human Rights and Body Politics' in J Bridgeman and S Millns (eds), *Law and Body Politics* (Aldershot, Dartmouth)
BIEMANN, U (2002) 'Remotely Sensed: A Topography of the Global Sex Trade' 70 *Feminist Review* 75
BIGO, D (2001) 'Migration and Security' in V Guiraudon and C Joppke (eds), *Controlling a New Migration World* (London, Routledge)
—— (2002) 'Security and Immigration: Toward a Critique of the Governmentality of Unease' 27(supp) *Alternatives* 63
BINGHAM, M (1998) 'Nevada Sex Trade: A Gamble for the Workers' 10 *Yale Journal of Law and Feminism* 69
BOTTOMLEY, A and CONAGHAN, J (1993) 'Feminist Theory and Legal Strategy' in A Bottomley and J Conaghan (eds), *Feminist Theory and Legal Strategy* (Oxford, Blackwell Publishers)
BOUTEILLET-PAQUET, D (2003) 'Passing the Buck: A Critical Analysis of the Readmission Policy Implemented by the European Union and Its Member States' 5 *European Journal of Migration and Law* 359
BOUTELLIER, J (1991) 'Prostitution, Criminal Law and Morality in the Netherlands' 15 *Crime, Law and Social Change* 201
BRANTS, C (1998) 'The Fine Art of Regulated Tolerance: Prostitution in Amsterdam' 25 *Journal of Law and Society* 621
—— and KOK, E (1986) 'Penal Sanctions as a Feminist Strategy: a Contradiction in Terms? Pornography and Criminal Law in the Netherlands' 14 *International Journal of the Sociology of Law* 269
BRETHERTON, C (2001) 'Gender Mainstreaming and EU Enlargement: Swimming Against the Tide?' 8 *Journal of European Public Policy* 60

Bridgeman, J and Millns, S (1998) *Feminist Perspectives on Law. Law's Engagement with the Female Body* (London, Sweet and Maxwell)

Brinkmann, G (2004) 'The Immigration and Asylum Agenda' 10 *European Law Journal* 182

Brown, W (1995) *States of Injury. Power and Freedom in Late Modernity* (Princeton, NJ, Princeton University Press)

—— (2000) 'Suffering Rights as Paradoxes' 7 *Constellations* 208

—— (2004) 'From Uniqueness to Uniformity? An Assessment of EU Development Aid Policies' in K Arts and A Dickson (eds), *EU Development Co-operation. From Model to Symbol* (Manchester, Manchester University Press)

Bruinsma, G and Meershoek, G (1997) 'Organized Crime and Trafficking in Women from Easter Europe in the Netherlands' 3(4) *Transnational Organized Crime* 105

Bryson, V (1999) *Feminist Debates* (London, Macmillan)

Bullough, V (1964) *History of Prostitution* (New York, University Books)

Bulterman, M (2001) *Human Rights in the Treaty Relations of the European Community* (Antwerpen, Intersentia)

Byrnes, A (1989) 'Women, Feminism and International Human Rights Law—Methodological Myopia, Fundamental Flaws or Meaningful Marginalisation?: Some Current Issues' 12 *Australian Year Book of International Law* 205

Cameron, S (2004) 'Space, Risk and Opportunity: The Evolution of Paid Sex Markets' 41 *Urban Studies* 1643

Campani, G (1998) 'Trafficking for Sexual Exploitation and the Sex Business in the New Context of International Migration: the Case of Italy' 3(3) *South European Society and Politics* 231

—— (2002) 'Crime, Trafficking, Prostitution and Drugs' in P Heywood, E Jones and M Rhodes (eds), *Developments in West European Politics 2* (Houndmills, Palgrave)

Caracciolo di Torella, E and Masselot, A (2001) 'Pregnancy, Maternity and the Organisation of Family Life: An Attempt to Classify the Case Law of the Court of Justice' 26 *European Law Review* 239

—— and Reid, E (2002) 'The Changing Shape of the "European Family" and Fundamental Rights' 27 *European Law Review* 80

Carchedi, F et al (eds) (2000) *I Colori della Notte. Migrazioni, sfruttamento sessuale, esperienze di intervento sociale* (Milan, FrancoAngeli)

—— Mottura, G and Pugliese, E (eds) (2003) *Il lavoro servile e le nuove schiavitù* (Milan, FrancoAngeli)

Carpenter, B (1998) 'The Prostitute and the Client: Challenging the Dualisms' 21 *Women's Studies International Forum* 387

Carrera, S (2005) 'What Does Free Movement Mean in Theory and Practice in an Enlarged EU?' 11 *European Law Journal* 699

Castles, S (2004) 'Why Migration Policies Fail' 27 *Ethnic and Racial Studies* 205

—— and Miller, M (1998) *The Age of Migration* (2nd ed) (Houndmills, Macmillan)

Chapkis, W (2000) 'Power and Control in the Commercial Sex Trade' in R Weitzer (ed), *Sex for Sale: Prostitution, Pornography and the Sex Industry* (New York, Routledge)

—— (2003) 'Trafficking, Migration, and the Law. Protecting Innocents, Punishing Immigrants' 17 *Gender & Society* 923

Charlesworth, H and Chinkin, C (2000) *The Boundaries of International Law* (Manchester, Manchester University Press)

—— —— and Wright, S (1991) 'Feminist Approaches to International Law' 85 *American Journal of International Law* 613

Chell-Robinson, V (2000) 'Female Migrants in Italy: Coping in a Country of New Immigration' in F Anthias and G Lazaridis (eds), *Gender and Migration in Southern Europe* (Oxford, Berg)

Chiang, L (1999) 'Trafficking in Women' in K Askin and D Koenig (eds), *Women and International Human Rights Law. Vol. I* (Ardsley, NY, Transnational Publishers)

Cholewinski, R (2004) 'European Union Policy on Irregular Migration: Human Rights Lost?' in B Bogusz et al (eds), *Irregular Migration and Human Rights: Theoretical, European and International Perspectives* (Leiden, Martinus Nijhoff Publishers)

Chorus, J et al (eds) (1999) *Introduction to Dutch Law* (3rd ed) (The Hague, Kluwer Law International)

Christman, J (1991) 'Liberalism and Individual Positive Freedom' 101 *Ethics* 343

Chuang, J (1998) 'Redirecting the Debate over Trafficking in Women: Definitions, Paradigms, and Contexts' 11 *Harvard Human Rights Journal* 65

Clark, B (1991) 'The Vienna Convention Reservations Regime and the Convention on the Discrimination against Women' 85 *American Journal of International Law* 281

Cohen, S (2003) *No One Is Illegal. Asylum and Immigration Control Past and Present* (Stoke-on-Trent, Trentham Books)

Collinson, S (1994) *Europe and International Migration* (London, Pinter Publishers)

Conaghan, J (2000) 'Reassessing the Feminist Theoretical Project in Law' 27 *Journal of Law and Society* 351

Connell, R (1987) *Gender and Power* (Cambridge, Polity Press)

—— (2000) *The Men and the Boys* (Cambridge, Polity Press)

Cook, R (1990) 'Reservations to the Convention on the Elimination of All Forms of Discrimination against Women' 30 *Virginia Journal of International Law* 643

—— (1994) 'State Responsibility for Violations of Women's Human Rights' 7 *Harvard Human Rights Journal* 125

—— (ed) (1994) *Human Rights of Women. National and International Perspectives* (Philadelphia, PA, University of Pennsylvania Press)

Copelon, R and Petchesky, R (1995) 'Toward an Interdependent Approach to Reproductive and Sexual Rights as Human Rights: Reflections on the ICPD and Beyond' in M Schuler (ed), *From Basic Needs to Basic Rights* (Washington DC, Women, Law and Development International)

Corrigan, K (2001) 'Putting the Brakes on the Global Trafficking of Women for the Sex Trade: An Analysis of Existing Regulatory Schemes to Stop the Flow of Traffic' 25 *Fordham International Law Journal* 151

Corso, C and Trifirò, A (2003) *. . . e siamo partite! Migrazione, tratta e prostituzione straniera in Italia* (Florence, Giunti)

Cotterell, R (1997) 'The Concept of Legal Culture' in D Nelken (ed), *Comparing Legal Cultures* (Aldershot, Dartmouth)

Cruz, A (1995) *Shifting Responsibility. Carriers' Liability in the Member States of the European Union and North America* (Stoke-on-Trent, Trentham Books)

Curtin, D and Meijers, H (1995) 'The Principle of Open Government in Schengen and the European Union: Democratic Retrogression' 32 *Common Market Law Review* 391

Dahl, T (1987) *Women's Law: An Introduction to Feminist Jurisprudence* (Oslo, Norwegian University Press)

Danna, D (2004) 'Italy: The Never-Ending Debate' in J Outshoorn (ed), *The Politics of Prostitution. Women's Movements, Democratic States and the Globalisation of Sex Commerce* (Cambridge, Cambridge University Press) de Groot, G (1992) 'European Education in the 21st Century' in B De Witte and C Forder (eds), *The Common Law of Europe and the Future of Legal Education* (Deventer, Kluwer)

De Hert, P (2004) 'Division of Competencies between National and European Levels with regard to Justice and Home Affairs' in J Apap (ed), *Justice and Home Affairs in the EU. Liberty and Security Issues after Enlargement* (Cheltenham, CO, Edward Elgar)

Decker, J (1979) *Prostitution: Regulation and Control* (Littleton, Fred B Rothman & Co)

Delacoste, F and Alexander, P (eds) (1998) *Sex Work: Writings by Women in the Sex Industry* (2nd ed) (San Francisco, CA, Cleis Press)

Demleitner, N (1994) 'Forced Prostitution: Naming an International Offense' 18 *Fordham International Law Journal* 163

den Boer, M (1999) 'The European Union and Organized Crime: Fighting a New Enemy with Many Tentacles' in E Viano (ed), *Global Organized Crime and International Security* (Aldershot, Ashgate)

—— (2001) 'The Fight Against Organised Crime in Europe: A Comparative Perspective' 9 *European Journal on Criminal Policy and Research* 259

Denisova, T (2001) 'Trafficking in Women and Children for Purposes of Sexual Exploitation: The Criminological Aspect' 6(3–4) *Trends in Organized Crime* 30

Di Pascale, A (2002) 'The New Regulation on Immigrants and the Status of Foreigners in Italy' 4 *European Journal of Migration and Law* 71

Dickson, A (2004) 'The Unimportance of Trade Preferences' in K Arts and A Dickson (eds), *EU Development Cooperation. From Model to Symbol* (Manchester, Manchester University Press)

Doezema, J (1998) 'Forced to Choose: Beyond the Voluntary v. Forced Prostitution Dichotomy' in K Kempadoo and J Doezema (eds), *Global Sex Workers: Rights, Resistance and Redefinition* (New York, Routledge)

—— (2000) 'Loose Women or Lost Women? The Re-emergence of the Myth of White Slavery in Contemporary Discourses of Trafficking in Women' 18 *Gender Issues* 23

—— (2001) 'Ouch! Western Feminists' 'Wounded Attachment' to the 'Third World Prostitute' 67 *Feminist Review* 16

—— (2002) 'Who Gets to Choose? Coercion, Consent, and the UN Trafficking Protocol' 10(1) *Gender and Development* 20

Donnelly, J (1999) 'Human Rights, Democracy, and Development' 21 *Human Rights Quarterly* 608

Douglas-Scott, S (2004) 'The Rule of Law in the EU—Putting the Security into the "Area of Freedom and Security and Justice"' 29 *European Law Review* 219

Dower, N (2004) 'The Global Framework for Development: Instrumentality or Contested Ethical Space' in C van den Anker (ed), *The Political Economy of New Slavery* (Houndmills, Palgrave Macmillan)

Drew, S (2002) 'Human Trafficking: A Modern Form of Slavery' (2002)4 *European Human Rights Law Review* 481

Drexler, J (1996) 'Governments' Role in Turning Tricks: The World's Oldest Profession in the Netherlands and the United States' 15 *Dickinson Journal of International Law* 201

Duncan, S (1994) '"Disrupting the Surface of Order and Innocence": Towards a Theory of Sexuality and the Law' II *Feminist Legal Studies* 3

Dworkin, A (1993) 'Prostitution and Male Supremacy' 1 *Michigan Journal of Gender and Law* 1

Edwards, S (1981) *Female Sexuality and the Law* (Oxford, Martin Robertson)

Ehrenreich, B and Hochschild, A (eds) (2002) *Global Woman. Nannies, Maids, and Sex Workers in the New Economy* (New York, Metropolitan Books)

Eide, A, Krause, C and Rosas, A (eds) (2001) *Economic, Social and Cultural Rights* (2nd ed) (Dordrecht, Martinus Nijhoff Pusblishers)

Eisenstein, Z (1988) *The Female Body and the Law* (Berkeley, CA, University of California Press)

Ellis, E (2005) *EU Anti-Discrimination Law* (Oxford, Oxford University Press)

Elvins, M (2003) 'Europe's Response to Transnational Organised crime' in A Edwards and P Gill (eds), *Transnational Organised Crime. Perspectives on Global Security* (London, Routledge)

Engbersen, G and van der Leun, J (2001) 'The Social Construction of Illegality and Criminality' 9 *European Journal on Criminal Policy and Research* 51

Enloe, C (1990) *Bananas, Beaches and Bases. Making Feminist Sense of International Politics* (Berkeley, CA, University of California Press)

Entzinger, H (2003) 'The Rise and Fall of Multiculturalism: The Case of the Netherlands' in C Joppke and E Morawska (eds), *Towards Assimilation and Citizenship: Immigration in Liberal Nation-States* (London, Palgrave)

Estrich, S (1987) *Real Rape* (Cambridge, MA, Harvard University Press)

Ewald, W (1995) 'Comparative Jurisprudence (II): The Logic of Legal Transplants' 43 *American Journal of Comparative Law* 489

Farrior, S (1997) 'The International Law on Trafficking in Women and Children for Prostitution, Making it Live Up to its Potential' 10 *Harvard Human Rights Journal* 213

Ferola, L (2002) 'The Fight Against Organized Crime in Europe. Building an Area of Freedom, Security and Justice in the E.U.' 30 *Journal of International Legal Information* 53

Ferraris, V et al (2002) 'National Data Concerning Residence Permits, Projects and Procedures, and Connected Juridical Routines' in Regione Emilia-Romagna and Associazione On the Road (eds), *Article 18: Protection of Victims of Trafficking and Fight Against Crime* (Martinsicuro, On the Road Edizioni)

Feve, S and Finzel, C (2001) 'Trafficking of People' 38 *Harvard Journal on Legislation* 279

Fijnaut, C et al (1998) *Organized Crime in the Netherlands* (The Hague, Kluwer Law International)

Fijnaut, C (ed) (2002) *The Administrative Approach to (Organised) Crime in Amsterdam* (Amsterdam, Public Order and Safety Department, City of Amsterdam)

Fitzpatrick, J and Kelly, K (1998) 'Gendered Aspects of Migration: Law and the Female Migrant' 22 *Hastings International and Comparative Law Review* 47

Flynn, L (1996) 'The Body Politic(s) of EC Law' in T Hervey and D O'Keeffe (eds), *Sex equality Law in the European Union* (Chichester, John Wiley & Sons)

Freedman, J (2003) 'Selling Sex: Trafficking, Prostitution and Sex Work amongst Migrant Women in Europe' in J Freedman (ed), *Gender and Insecurity. Migrant Women in Europe* (Aldershot, Ashgate)

Freeman, G (1995) 'Modes of Immigration Politics in Liberal Democratic States' 29 *International Migration Review* 881

Freudenstein, R (2000) 'Río Odra, Río Buh: Poland, Germany, and the Borders of Twenty-First-Century Europe' in P Andreas and T Snyder (eds), *The Wall around the West. State Borders and Immigration Controls in North America and Europe* (Lanham, MD, Rowman & Littlefield Publishers)

Friedman, L (1994) 'Is There a Modern Legal Culture?' 7 *Ratio Juris* 117

—— (1997) 'The Concept of Legal Culture: A Reply' in D Nelken (ed), *Comparing Legal Cultures* (Aldershot, Dartmouth)

FRUG, M (1992) *Postmodern Legal Feminism* (New York, Routledge)

GALLAGHER, A (2001) 'Human Rights and the New UN Protocols on Trafficking and Migrant Smuggling: A Preliminary Analysis' 23 *Human Rights Quarterly* 975

GEDDES, A (2000) *Immigration and European Integration. Towards Fortress Europe?* (Manchester, Manchester University Press)

—— (2001) 'International Migration and State Sovereignty in an Integrating Europe' 39(6) *International Migration* 21

—— (2003) *The Politics of Migration and Immigration in Europe* (London, Sage Publications)

GHOSH, B (1998) *Huddled Masses and Uncertain Shores* (The Hague, Martinus Nijhoff Publishers)

GIAMMARINARO, M (2000) 'La rappresentazione simbolica della tratta come riduzione in schiavitù' in F Carchedi et al (eds), *I Colori della Notte. Migrazioni, sfruttamento sessuale, esperienze di intervento sociale* (Milan, FrancoAngeli)

GIBSON, M (1993) 'Italy' in N Davis (ed), *Prostitution: An International Handbook on Trends, Problems, and Policies* (Westport, CT, Greenwood Press)

GIJZEN, M (2001) 'The Charter: A Milestone for Social Protection in Europe?' 8 *Maastricht Journal of European and Comparative Law* 33

GILLIGAN, C (1982) *In a Different Voice* (Cambridge, MA, Harvard University Press)

GOLDMAN, M (1997) *Revolution and Change in Central and Eastern Europe* (Armonk, NY, ME Sharpe)

GOODEY, J (2003a) 'Migration, Crime and Victimhood' 5 *Journal of Punishment and Society* 415

—— (2003b) 'Recognising Organised Crime's Victims. The Case of Sex Trafficking in the EU' in A Edwards and P Gill (eds), *Transnational Organised Crime. Perspectives on Global Security* (London, Routledge)

—— (2004) 'Sex Trafficking in Women from Central and East European Countries: Promoting a 'Victim-Centred' and 'Woman-Centred' Approach to Criminal Justice Intervention' 76 *Feminist Review* 26

GOULD, A (2002) 'Sweden's Law on Prostitution: Feminism, Drugs and the Foreign Threat' in S Thorbek and B Pattanaik (eds), *Transnational Prostitution. Changing Patterns in a Global Context* (London, Zed Books)

GRABBE, H (2002) 'Stabilizing the East While Keeping Out the Easteners: Internal and External Security Logics in Conflict' in S Lavenex and E Uçarer (eds), *Migration and the Externalities of European Integration* (Lanham, MD, Lexington Books)

GREATBATCH, J (1989) 'Gender Difference: Feminist Critiques of Refugee Discourse' 1 *International Journal of Refugee Law* 518

GREEN, P and GREWCOCK, M (2002) 'The War against Illegal Immigration: State Crime and the Construction of European Identity' 14 *Current Issues in Criminal Justice* 87

GUILD, E (2000) 'European Community Law from a Migrant's Perspective' (Nijmegen, Katholieke Universiteit Nijmegen)

—— (2004) 'Mechanisms of Exclusion: Labour Migration in the European Union' in J Apap (ed), *Justice and Home Affairs in the EU. Liberty and Security Issues after Enlargement* (Cheltenham, Edward Elgar)

GUIRAUDON, V (2001) De-Nationalizing Control: Analyzing State Responses to Constraints on Migration Control' in V Guiraudon and Joppke (eds), *Controlling a New Migration World* (London, Routledge)

Gushulak, B and MacPherson, D (2000) 'Health Issues Associated with the Smuggling and Trafficking of Migrants' 2(2) *Journal of Immigrant Health* 67

Hailbronner, K (2000) *Immigration and Asylum Law and Policy of the European Union* (The Hague, Kluwer Law International)

Hammar, T (1999) 'Closing the Doors to the Swedish Welfare State' in G Brochmann and T Hammar (eds), *Mechanisms of Immigration Control: A Comparative Analysis of European Regulation Policies* (Oxford, Berg)

Hansen, R and Weil, P (eds) (2001) *Towards a European Nationality. Citizenship, Immigration and Nationality Law in the EU* (Houndmills, Palgrave)

Harding, C (2000) 'Exploring the Intersection of European Law and National Criminal Law' 25 *European Law Review* 374

Harlow, C (2002) 'Voices of Difference in a Plural Community' in P Beaumont, C Lyons and N Walker (eds), *Convergence and Divergence in European Public Law* (Oxford, Hart Publishing)

Harris, A (1990) 'Race and Essentialism in Feminist Theory' 42 *Stanford Law Review* 581

Harris, D, O'Boyle, M and Warbrick, C (1995) *Law of the European Convention on Human Rights* (London, Butterworths)

Hauber, L (1998) 'The Trafficking of Women for Prostitution: A Growing Problem Within the European Union' 22 *Boston College International and Comparative Law Review* 183

Haveman, R (1998) *Voorwaarden voor strafbaarstelling van vrouwenhandel* (Deventer, Gouda Quint)

Haynes, D (2004) 'Used, Abused, Arrested and Deported: Extending Immigration Benefits to Protect the Victims of Trafficking and to Secure the Prosecution of Traffickers' 26 *Human Rights Quarterly* 221

Heinen, J (2000) 'The Impact of Privatization on the Female Workforce in Poland' in D Iatridis (ed), *Social Justice and the Welfare State in Central and Eastern Europe* (Westport, CT, Praeger)

Hervey, T and O'Keeffe, D (eds) (1996) *Sex equality Law in the European Union* (Chichester, John Wiley & Sons)

Hirschmann, N (2003) *The Subject of Liberty. Towards a Feminist Theory of Freedom* (Princeton, Princeton University Press)

Høigard, C and Finstadt, L (1992/1986) *Backstreets: Prostitution, Money, and Love* (University Park, PA, Pennsylvania State University Press)

Hooks, B (1981) *Ain't I a Woman? Black Women and Feminism* (Boston, South End Press)

Hughes, D (2000) 'The "Natasha" Trade: The Transnational Shadow Market of Trafficking in Women' 53 *Journal of International Affairs* 625

—— and Denisova, T (2001) 'The Transnational Political Criminal Nexus of Trafficking in Women from Ukraine' 6(3–4) *Trends in Organized Crime* 43

Huysmans, J (1995) 'Migrants as a Security Problem: Dangers of 'Securitizing' Societal Issues' in R Miles and D Thränhardt (eds), *Migration and European Integration. The Dynamics of Inclusion and Exclusion* (London, Pinter Publishers)

—— (2000) 'The European Union and the Securitization of Migration' 38 *Journal of Common Market Studies* 751

Iatridis, D (2000) 'The Social Justice and Equality Contexts of Privatization' in D Iatridis (ed), *Social Justice and the Welfare State in Central and Eastern Europe* (Westport, CT, Praeger)

Jaget, C (ed) (1980) *Prostitutes: Our Life* (Bristol, Falling Wall Press)

Jahn, A and Straubhaar, T (1998) 'A Survey of the Economics of Illegal Migration' 3(3) *South European Society and Politics* 16

Jalušič, V (1999) 'Women in Post-Socialist Slovenia: Socially Adapted, Politically Marginalized' in S Ramet (ed), *Gender Politics in the Western Balkans* (University Park, PA, Pennsylvania State University)

Jeffreys, S (1997) *The Idea of Prostitution* (Melbourne, Spinifex Press)

Jesien, L (2000) 'Border Controls and the Politics of EU Enlargement' in P Andreas and T Snyder (eds), *The Wall around the West. State Borders and Immigration Controls in North America and Europe* (Lanham, MD, Rowman & Littlefield Publishers)

Jileva, E (2002) 'Larger than the European Union: The Emerging EU Migration Regime and Enlargement' in S Lavenex and E Uçarer (eds), *Migration and the Externalities of European Integration* (Lanham, MD, Lexington Books)

Johansson Wennerholm, C (2002) 'Crossing borders and building bridges: the Baltic Region Networking Project' 10(1) *Gender and Development* 10

Joppke, C (2002) 'European Immigration Policy at the Crossroads' in P Heywood, E Jones and M Rhodes (eds), *Developments in West European Politics 2* (Houndmills, Palgrave)

Jordan, A (2000) 'Commercial Sex Workers in Asia: A Blind Spot in International Human Rights Law' in K Askin and D Koenig (eds), *Women and International Human Rights Law. Vol. II* (Ardsley, NY, Transnational Publishers)

—— (2002) 'Human Rights or Wrongs? The Struggle for a Rights-Based Response to Trafficking in Human Beings' 10(1) *Gender and Development* 28

Kappeler, S (1990) 'The International Slave Trade in Women, or, Procurers, Pimps and Punters' I *Law and Critique* 219

Kelley, N (2001) 'Convention Refugee Definition and Gender-Based Persecution: A Decade's Progress' 13 *International Journal of Refugee Law* 559

Kelly, L (2003) 'The Wrong Debate: Reflections on Why Force Is Not the Key Issue with Respect to Trafficking in Women for Sexual Exploitation' 73 *Feminist Review* 139

—— (2005) '"You Can Find Anything You Want": A Critical Reflection on Research on Trafficking in Persons within and into Europe' 43 *International Migration* 235

Kempadoo, K and Doezema, J (eds) (1998) *Global Sex Workers: Rights, Resistance and Redefinition* (New York, Routledge)

Kenner, J (2003) 'Economic and Social Rights in the EU Legal Order: The Mirage of Indivisibility' in T Hervey and J Kenner (eds), *Economic and Social Rights under the EU Charter of Fundamental Rights* (Oxford, Hart Publishing)

Kilvington, J, Day, S and Ward, H (2001) 'Prostitution Policy in Europe: A Time of Change?' 67 *Feminist Review* 78

Kingdom, E (1991) *What's Wrong with Rights? Problems for Feminist Politics of Law* (Edinburgh, Edinburgh University Press)

—— (1995) 'Body Politics and Rights' in J Bridgeman and S Millns (eds), *Law and Body Politics* (Aldershot, Dartmouth)

Kline, M (1989) 'Race, Racism, and Feminist Legal Theory' 12 *Harvard Women's Law Journal* 115

Klip, A and van der Wilt, H (eds) (2002) *Harmonisation and Harmonising Measures in Criminal Law* (Amsterdam, Royal Netherlands Academy of Arts and Sciences)

Kofman, E (1999) 'Female 'Birds of Passage' a Decade Later: Gender and Immigration in the European Union' 33 *International Migration Review* 269

—— and Sales, R (1992) 'Towards Fortress Europe?' 15 *Women's Studies International Forum* 29

Kofman, E et al (2000) *Gender and International Migration in Europe* (London, Routledge)
Koser, K (2000) 'Asylum Policies, Trafficking and Vulnerability' 38(3) *International Migration* 91
Koskenniemi (1999) 'The Effect of Rights on Political Culture' in P Alston (ed), *The EU and Human Rights* (Oxford, Oxford University Press)
Koslowski, R (2001) 'Personal Security and State Sovereignty in a Uniting Europe' in V Guiraudon and C Joppke (eds), *Controlling a New Migration World* (London, Routledge)
Kostakopoulou, T (2001) *Citizenship, Identity and Immigration in the European Union: Between Past and Future* (Manchester, Manchester University Press)
Kulick, D (2003) 'Sex in the New Europe. The Criminalization of Clients and Swedish Fear of Penetration' 3 *Anthropological Theory* 199
Lacey, N (1998) *Unspeakable Subjects: Feminist Essays in Legal and Social Theory* (Oxford, Hart Publishing)
—— (2004) 'Feminist Legal Theory and the Rights of Women' in K Knop (ed), *Gender and Human Rights* (Oxford, Oxford University Press)
Lahav, G and Guiraudon, V (2000) 'Comparative Perspectives in Border Control: Away From the Border And Outside the State' in P Andreas and T Snyder (eds), *The Wall around the West. State Borders and Immigration Controls in North America and Europe* (Lanham, MD, Rowman & Littlefield Publishers)
Laskowski, S (2002) 'The New German Prostitution Act—An Important Step to a More Rational View of Prostitution as an Ordinary Profession in Accordance with European Community Law' 18 *International Journal of Comparative Labour Law and Industrial Relations* 479
Lavenex, S and Uçarer, E (2002) 'The Emergent EU Migration Regime and Its External Impact' in S Lavenex and E Uçarer (eds), *Migration and the Externalities of European Integration* (Lanham, MD, Lexington Books)
Lavenex, S and Wallace, W (2005) Justice and Home Affairs' in H Wallace, W Wallace and M Pollack (eds), *Policy-Making in the European Union* (Oxford, Oxford University Press)
Lazaridis, G (2000) 'Filippino and Albanian Women Migrant Workers in Greece: Multiple Layers of Oppression' in F Anthias and G Lazaridis (eds), *Gender and Migration in Southern Europe* (Oxford, Berg)
Lees, S (1996) *Carnal Knowledge. Rape on Trial* (London, Hamish Hamilton)
Legrand, P (1996) 'European Legal Systems Are Not Converging' 45 *International and Comparative Law Quarterly* 52
—— (1997) 'Against a European Civil Code' 60 *Modern Law Review* 44
—— (1999) *Fragments on Law-as-Culture* (Deventer, WEJ Tjeenk Willink)
—— (2002) 'Public Law, Europeanisation and Convergence' in P Beaumont, C Lyons and N Walker (eds), *Convergence and Divergence in European Public Law* (Oxford, Hart Publishing)
—— and Munday, R (eds) (2003) *Comparative Legal Studies: Traditions and Transitions* (Cambridge, Cambridge University Press)
Leidholdt, D (1996) 'Sexual Trafficking of Women in Europe' in A Elman (ed), *Sexual Politics and the European Union* (Providence, NJ, Berghahn Books)
Lernestedt, C and Hamdorf, K (2000) 'Sexköpskriminaliseringen—till skydd av vad?—del I' 11 *Juridisk Tidskrift* 846
—— —— (2001) 'Sexköpskriminaliseringen—till skydd av vad?—del II' 12 *Juridisk Tidskrift* 111

LERUM, K (1998) 'Twelve-Step Feminism Makes Sex Workers Sick: How the State and the Recovery Movement Turn Radical Women into "Useless Citizens"' 2 *Sexuality & Culture* 7

ŁOBODZIŃSKA, B (1995) 'The Family and Working Women during and after Socialist Industrialization and Ideology? in B Łobodzińska (ed), *Family, Women and Employment in Central-Eastern Europe* (Westport, CT, Greenwood Press)

LUCAS, A (1999) 'Women and Prostitution' in K Askin and D Koenig (eds), *Women and International Human Rights Law. Vol. I* (Ardsley, NY, Transnational Publishers)

LUTZ, H (1997) 'The Limits of European-ness: Immigrant Women in Fortress Europe' 57 *Feminist Review* 93

MACCALLUM, G (1967) 'Negative and Positive Freedom' 76 *Philosophical Review* 312

MCGLYNN, C (2000) 'Ideologies of Motherhood in European Community Sex Equality Law' 6 *European Law Journal* 29

—— (2001a) 'Families and the European Union Charter of Fundamental Rights: Progressive Change or Entrenching the Status Quo?' 26 *European Law Review* 582

—— (2001b) 'Reclaiming a Feminist Vision: the Reconciliation of Paid Work and Family Life in European Union Law and Policy' 7 *Columbia Journal of International Law* 241

MCGOLDRICK, D (2004) 'The Charter and UN Human Rights Treaties' in S Peers and A Ward (eds), *The European Union Charter of Fundamental Rights* (Oxford, Hart Publishing)

MACKINNON, C (1987) *Feminism Unmodified* (Cambridge, MA, Harvard University Press)

—— (1989) *Towards a Feminist Theory of the State* (Cambridge, MA, Harvard University Press)

—— (1993) 'Prostitution and Civil Rights' 1 *Michigan Journal of Gender & Law* 13

MCLEOD, E (1982) *Women Working: Prostitution Now* (London, Croom Helm)

MCMAHON, J (1998) *The Development Co-operation Policy of the EC* (London, Kluwer Law International)

MAMELI, P (2002) 'Stopping the Illegal Trafficking of Human Beings. How Transnational Police Work Can Stem the Flow of Forced Prostitution' 38 *Crime, Law & Social Change* 67

MARCHAND, M, REID, J and BERENTS, B (1998) 'Migration, (Im-)mobility and Modernity: Toward a Feminist Understanding of the "Global" Prostitution Scene in Amsterdam' 27 *Millennium* 955

MARKESINIS, B (1994) 'Learning from Europe and Learning in Europe' in B Markesinis (ed), *The Gradual Convergence* (Oxford, Clarendon Press)

—— (1997) *Foreign Law and Comparative Methodology: A Subject and a Thesis* (Oxford, Hart Publishing)

MAROTTA, E (2001) 'Responding to Transnational Crime—the Role of Europol' in P Williams and D Vlassis (eds), *Combating Transnational Crime: Concepts, Activities and Responses* (London, Frank Cass)

MARTIN, P and TAYLOR, J (2001) 'Managing Migration: the Role of Economic Policies' in A Zolberg and P Benda (eds), *Global Migrants, Global Refugees* (New York, Berghahn Books)

MASSARI, M (2003) 'Transnational Organized Crime between Myth and Reality' in F Allum and R Siebert (eds), *Organized Crime and the Challenge to Democracy* (London, Routledge)

MASSEY, D et al (1993) 'Theories of International Migration: A Review and Appraisal' 19 *Population and Development Review* 431

MATHIEU, L (2003) 'The Emergence and Uncertain Outcomes of Prostitutes' Social Movements' 10 *European Journal of Women's Studies* 29

MEDVED, F and CULLEN, P (2002) 'Counteracting Human Trafficking: An Analysis of European Union Policy' in M Anderson and J Apap (eds), *Police and Justice Co-operation and the New European Borders* (The Hague, Kluwer Law International)

MELIS, B (2001) *Negotiating Europe's Immigration Frontiers* (The Hague, Kluwer Law International)

MERRY, S (2003) 'Rights Talk and the Experience of Law: Implementing Women's Human Rights to Protection from Violence' 25 *Human Rights Quarterly* 343

MILL, JS (1998) *On Liberty and Other Essays* (Oxford, Oxford University Press)

MILLER, D (1983) 'Constraints on Freedom' 94 *Ethics* 66

MILLER, E, Romenesko, K and Wondolkowski, L (1993) 'The United States' in N Davis (ed), *Prostitution: An International Handbook on Trends, Problems, and Policies* (Westport, CT, Greenwood Press)

MILLETT, K (1975) *The Prostitution Papers* (St Albans, Paladin Books)

MINDERHOUD, P (2004) 'Coping With Irregular Migration: The Dutch Experience' in B Bogusz et al (eds), *Irregular Migration and Human Rights: Theoretical, European and International Perspectives* (Leiden, Martinus Nijhoff Publishers)

MITCHELL, J (1987) 'Women and Equality' in A Phillips (ed), *Feminism and Equality* (Oxford, Basil Blackwell)

MITSILEGAS, V (2001) 'Defining Organised Crime in the European Union: the Limits of European Criminal Law in an Area of "Freedom, Security and Justice"' 26 *European Law Review* 565

—— MONAR, J and REES, W (2003) *The European Union and Internal Security. Guardian of the People?* (Houndmills, Palgrave Macmillan)

MITTELMAN, J (2000) *The Globalization Syndrome* (Princeton, NJ, Princeton University Press)

MONAR, J (2005) 'Justice and Home Affairs in the EU Constitutional Treaty. What Added Value for the 'Area of Freedom, Security and Justice'?' 1 *European Constitutional Law Review* 226

MONTGOMERY, H (1998) 'Children, Prostitution, and Identity' in K Kempadoo and J Doezema (eds), *Global Sex Workers: Rights, Resistance and Redefinition* (New York, Routledge)

MONTO, M (2000) 'Why Men Seek out Prostitutes' in R Weitzer (ed), *Sex for Sale: Prostitution, Pornography and the Sex Industry* (New York, Routledge)

—— (2004) 'Female Prostitution, Customers and Violence' 10 *Violence Against Women* 160

MONZINI, P (2002) *Il Mercato delle Donne. Prostituzione, Tratta e Sfruttamento* (Rome, Donzelli editore)

MOWBRAY, A (2004) *The Development of Positive Obligations under the European Convention on Human Rights by the European Court of Human Rights* (Oxford, Hart Publishing)

MURPHY, T (1997) 'Feminism on Flesh', VIII *Law and Critique* 37

NAFFINE, N (1990) *Law and the Sexes: Explorations in Feminist Jurisprudence* (Sydney, Allen & Unwin)

—— (1997) 'The Body Bag' in N Naffine and R Owens (eds), *Sexing the Subject of Law* (Sydney, LBC Information Services)

—— (1998) 'The Legal Structure of Self-Ownership: Or the Self-Possessed Man and the Woman Possessed' 25(2) *Journal of Law and Society* 193

—— (2002) 'Can Women be Legal Persons?' In S James and S Palmer (eds), *Visible Women: Essays on Feminist Legal Theory and Political Philosophy* (Oxford, Hart Publishing)

NASCIMBENE, B (2000) 'The Regularisation of Clandestine Immigrants in Italy' 2 *European Journal of Migration and Law* 337

NEAL, D (1988) 'Women as a Social Group: Recognizing Sex-Based Persecution as Grounds for Asylum' 20 *Columbia Human Rights Law Review* 203

NELKEN, D (ed) (2000) *Contrasting Criminal Justice. Getting from here to there* (Aldershot, Dartmouth)

NELKEN, D and FEEST, J (eds) (2001) *Adapting Legal Cultures* (Oxford, Hart Publishing)

NEUWAHL, N and ROSAS, A (eds) (1995) *The European Union and Human Rights* (The Hague, Martinus Nijhoff Publishers)

NICOLSON D and BIBBINGS L (eds) (2000), *Feminist Perspectives on Criminal Law* (London, Cavendish Publishing)

NIESNER, E and JONES-PAULY, C (2001) *Trafficking in Women in Europe: Prosecution and Victim Protection in a European Context* (Bielefeld, Kleine Verlag)

NIESSEN, J (2001) 'Overlapping Interests and Conflicting Agendas: The Knocking into Shape of EU Immigration Policies' 3 *European Journal of Migration and Law* 419

NOLL, G (2003) 'Visions of the Exceptional: Legal and Theoretical Issues Raised by Transit Processing Centres and Protection Zones' 5 *European Journal of Migration and Law* 303

NUSSBAUM, M (2000) *Women and Human Development. The Capabilities Approach* (Cambridge, Cambridge University Press)

NYBERG-SØRENSEN, N, VAN HEAR, N and ENGBERG-PEDERSEN, P (2002) 'The Migration-Development Nexus Evidence and Policy Options. State-of-the-Art Overview' 40(5) *International Migration* 3

OBOKATA, T (2003) 'EU Council Framework Decision on Combating Trafficking in Human Beings: A Critical Appraisal' 40 *Common Market Law Review* 917

O'CONNELL DAVIDSON, J (1997) "Does She Do Queening?': Prostitution, Sovereignty and Community' in L Brace and J Hoffman (eds), *Reclaiming Sovereignty* (London, Pinter)

—— (1998) *Prostitution, Power and Freedom* (Cambridge, Polity Press)

OECD (2000a) 'Italy' 1(3) *DAC Journal* 2

OECD (2000b) 'Sweden' 1(4) *DAC Journal* 5

OECD (2001) 'The Netherlands' 2(3) *DAC Journal* 5

OLSEN, F (1984) 'Statutory Rape: A Feminist Critique of Rights Analysis' 63 *Texas Law Review* 387

ORSINI-JONES, M and GATTULLO, F (2000) 'Migrant Women in Italy: National Trends and Local Perspectives' in F Anthias and G Lazaridis (eds), *Gender and Migration in Southern Europe* (Oxford, Berg)

OUTSHOORN, J (1998) 'Sexuality and International Commerce. The Traffic in Women and Prostitution Policy in the Netherlands' in T Carver and V Mottier (eds), *Politics of Sexuality. Identity, Gender, Citizenship* (London, Routledge)

—— (2001) 'Regulating Prostitution as Sex Work: the Pioneer Case of the Netherlands' 36 *Acta Politica* 155

—— (2004a) 'Pragmatism in the Polder: Changing Prostitution Policy in The Netherlands' 12 *Journal of Contemporary European Studies* 165

—— (2004b) 'Voluntary and Forced Prostitution: the 'Realistic Approach' of the Netherlands' in J Outshoorn (ed), *The Politics of Prostitution. Women's Movements, Democratic States and the Globalisation of Sex Commerce* (Cambridge, Cambridge University Press)

OVERALL, C (1992) 'What's Wrong With Prostitution? Evaluating Sex Work' 17 *Signs* 705

PAKES, F (2003) 'Tolerance and Pragmatism in the Netherlands: Euthanasia, Coffeeshops and Prostitution in the 'Purple Years', 1994–2002' 5 *International Journal of Police Science and Management* 217

PARIS, R (2001) 'Human Security: Paradigm Shift or Hot Air?' 26 *International Security* 87
PARREÑAS, R (2001) *Servants of Globalization: Women, Migration and Domestic Work* (Stanford, CA, Stanford University Press)
PATEMAN, C (1988) *The Sexual Contract* (Oxford, Polity Press)
PAUL, J (1992) The Human Right to Development: Its Meaning and Importance' 1992 *Third World Legal Studies* 17
PEERS, S (1999) 'Human Rights and the Third Pillar' in P Alston (ed), *The EU and Human Rights* (Oxford, Oxford University Press)
—— (2000) *EU Justice and Home Affairs Law* (Harlow, Pearson Education Limited)
—— (2001) 'Immigration, Asylum and the European Union Charter of Fundamental Rights' 3 *European Journal of Migration and Law* 141
—— (2002) 'Key Legislative Developments on Migration in the European Union' 4 *European Journal of Migration and Law* 85
—— (2003) 'Key Legislative Developments on Migration in the European Union' 5 *European Journal of Migration and the Law* 387
—— (2004a) 'Irregular Immigration and EU External Relations' in B Bogusz et al (eds), *Irregular Migration and Human Rights: Theoretical, European and International Perspectives* (Leiden, Martinus Nijhoff Publishers)
—— (2004b) 'Key Legislative Developments on Migration in the European Union' 6 *European Journal of Migration and Law* 67
—— (2004c) 'Taking Rights Away? Limitations and Derogations' in S Peers and A Ward (eds), *The European Union Charter of Fundamental Rights* (Oxford, Hart Publishing)
—— and WARD, A (eds) (2004) *The European Union Charter of Fundamental Rights* (Oxford, Hart Publishing)
PETCHESKY, R (1995) 'The Body as Property: A Feminist Re-vision' in F Ginsburg and R Rapp (eds), *Conceiving The New World Order: The Global Politics of Reproduction* (Berkeley, CA, University of California Press)
—— (2000) 'Sexual Rights: Inventing a Concept, Mapping an International Practice' in R Parker, R Barbosa and P Aggleton (eds), *Framing the Sexual Subject. The Politics of Gender, Sexuality and Power* (Berkeley, CA, University of California Press)
PETERS, J and WOLPER, A (eds) (1995) *Women's Rights, Human Rights* (New York, Routledge)
PETRINI, D and FERRARIS, V (2002) 'Analysis of Art. 18 within the Framework of Legislation Concerning Immigration and Measures Aimed at Fighting Organised Crime. The History and Rewarding Nature of Present and Previous Legislations' in Regione Emilia-Romagna and Associazione On the Road (eds), *Article 18: Protection of Victims of Trafficking and Fight Against Crime* (Martinsicuro, On the Road Edizioni)
PETTMAN, J (1997) 'Body Politics: International Sex Tourism' 18 *Third World Quarterly* 93
PHETERSEN, G (ed) (1989) *A Vindication of the Rights of Whores* (Seattle, The Seal Press)
—— (1996) *The Prostitution Prism* (Amsterdam, Amsterdam University Press)
PHOENIX, J (1999) *Making Sense of Prostitution* (London, Macmillan)
PHUONG, C (2003) 'Enlarging 'Fortress Europe': EU Accession, Asylum and Immigration in Candidate Countries' 52 *International and Comparative Law Quarterly* 641
PIOTROWICZ, R (2004) 'Irregular Migration Networks: The Challenge Posed by People Traffickers to States and Human Rights' in B Bogusz et al (eds), *Irregular Migration and Human Rights: Theoretical, European and International Perspectives* (Leiden, Martinus Nijhoff Publishers)
POGGE, T (2002) *World Poverty and Human Rights* (Cambridge, Polity Press)

POIARES MADURO, M (1999) 'Striking the Elusive Balance Between Economic Freedom and Social Rights in the EU' in P Alston (ed), *The EU and Human Rights* (Oxford, Oxford University Press)

—— (2000) 'Europe's Social Self: "The Sickness Unto Death"' in J Shaw (ed), *Social Law and Policy in an Evolving European Union* (Oxford, Hart Publishing)

—— (2003) 'The Double Constitutional Life of the Charter of Fundamental Rights of the European Union' in T Hervey and J Kenner (eds), *Economic and Social Rights under the EU Charter of Fundamental Rights* (Oxford, Hart Publishing)

POLANÍA MOLINA, F and Janssen, M (1998) *I Never Thought This Would Happen to Me. Prostitution and Traffic in Latin American Women in the Netherlands* (Amsterdam, Foundation Esperanza)

POLLACK, M and HAFNER-BURTON, E (2000) 'Mainstreaming Gender in the European Union' 7 *Journal of European Public Policy* 432

RADIN, M (1996) *Contested Commodities* (Cambridge, MA, Harvard University Press)

RAGHU, M (1997) 'Sex Trafficking of Thai Women and the United States Asylum Law Response' 12 *Georgetown Immigration Law Journal* 145

RAYMOND, J (2002) 'The New UN Trafficking Protocol' 25 *Women's Studies International Forum* 491

REANDA, L (1991) 'Prostitution as a Human Rights Question: Problems and Prospects of United Nations Action' 13 *Human Rights Quarterly* 202

RÉAUME, D (1996) 'What's Distinctive About Feminist Analysis of Law?: A Conceptual Analysis Of Women's Exclusion From Law' 2 *Legal Theory* 265

REES, T (1998) *Mainstreaming Equality in the European Union* (London, Routledge)

REES, W (2003) 'Transnational Organized Crime, Security and the European Union' in F Allum and R Siebert (eds), *Organized Crime and the Challenge to Democracy* (London, Routledge)

REGAN, E (ed) (2000) *The New Third Pillar: Cooperation Against Crime in the European Union* (Dublin, Institute of European Affairs)

RIJKEN, C (2003) *Trafficking in Persons. Prosecution from a European Perspective* (The Hague, TMC Asser Press)

RING, H (1995) 'Refugees in Sweden: Inclusion and Exclusion in the Welfare State' in R Miles and D Thränhardt (eds), *Migration and European Integration. The Dynamics of Inclusion and Exclusion* (London, Pinter Publishers)

ROBERTS, N (1992) *Whores in History: Prostitution in Western Society* (London, Harper Collins Publishers)

ROMANY, C (1993) 'Women as *Aliens*: A Feminist Critique of the Public/Private Distinction in International Human Rights Law' 6 *Harvard Human Rights Journal* 87

RUGGIERO, V (1997) 'Trafficking in Human Beings: Slaves in Contemporary Europe' 25 *International Journal of the Sociology of Law* 231

RUPNIK, J (2000) 'Eastern Europe: The International Context' in M Plattner and A Smolar (eds), *Globalization, Power, and Democracy* (Baltimore, MD, Johns Hopkins University Press)

RYDER, A (2004) 'The changing nature of adult entertainment districts: between a rock and a hard place or going from strength to strength?' 41 *Urban Studies* 1659

SALAZAR, L (1996) 'The European Community and Criminal Law: An Obstacle Course' in M Delmas-Marty (ed), *What Kind of Criminal Policy for Europe?* (The Hague, Kluwer Law International)

SALT, J (2000) 'Trafficking and Human Smuggling: A European Perspective' 38(3) *International Migration* 31

Sassen, S (1998) *Globalization and Its Discontents* (New York, The New Press)

—— (1999) 'Beyond Sovereignty: De-Facto Transnationalism in Immigration Policy' 1 *European Journal of Migration and Law* 177

—— (2000) 'Women's Burden: Counter-geographies of Globalization and the Feminization of Survival' 53 *Journal of International Affairs* 503

Scharpf, F (2002) 'The European Social Model: Coping with the Challenges of Diversity' 40 *Journal of Common Market Studies* 645

Scheinin, M (1998) 'Sexual Rights as Human Rights—Protected under Existing Human Rights Treaties?' 67 *Nordic Journal of International Law* 17

Scheiwe, K (1994) 'EC Law's Unequal Treatment of the Family: The Case Law of the European Court of Justice on Rules Prohibiting Discrimination on Grounds of Sex and Nationality' 1 *Social and Legal Studies* 243

Schieffer, M (2003) 'Community Readmission Agreements with Third Countries—Objectives, Substance and Current State of Negotiations' 5 *European Journal of Migration and Law* 343

Schloenhardt, A (1999) 'Organized Crime and the Business of Migrant Trafficking' 32(3) *Crime, Law & Social Change* 203

Schmidt, D (2004) 'The New German Immigration Law' in J Apap (ed), *Justice and Home Affairs in the EU. Liberty and Security Issues after Enlargement* (Cheltenham, Edward Elgar)

Sciortino, G (1999) 'Planning in the Dark: the Evolution of Italian Immigration Control' in G Brochmann and T Hammar (eds), *Mechanisms of Immigration Control: A Comparative Analysis of European Regulation Policies* (Oxford, Berg)

—— and Pastore, F (2004) 'Immigration and European Immigration Policy: Myths and Realities' in J Apap (ed), *Justice and Home Affairs in the EU. Liberty and Security Issues after Enlargement* (Cheltenham, Edward Elgar)

Seidler, V (1989) *Rediscovering Masculinity. Reason, Language and Sexuality* (London, Routledge)

Sen, A (1999) *Development as Freedom* (Oxford, Oxford University Press)

Shannon, S (1997) 'Prostitution and the Mafia: The Involvement of Organized Crime in the Global Sex Trade' 3(4) *Transnational Organized Crime* 119

Shaw, J (1996) 'Law, Gender and the Internal Market' in T Hervey and D O'Keeffe (eds), *Sex equality Law in the European Union* (Chichester, John Wiley & Sons)

—— (2000) 'Importing Gender: The Challenge of Feminism and the Analysis of the EU Legal Order' 7 *Journal of European Public Policy* 406

—— (2002) 'The European Union and Gender Mainstreaming: Constitutionally Embedded or Comprehensively Marginalised?' 10 *Feminist Legal Studies* 231

Sheptycki, J (2003) 'Global Law Enforcement as a Protection Racket' in A Edwards and P Gill (eds), *Transnational Organised Crime. Perspectives on Global Security* (London, Routledge)

Shrage, L (1989) 'Should Feminists Oppose Prostitution?' 99 *Ethics* 347

Simma, B, Aschenbrenner, J and Schulte, C (1999) 'Human Rights Considerations in the Development Co-operation Activities of the EC' in P Alston (ed), *The EU and Human Rights* (Oxford, Oxford University Press)

Simmons, M (1999) 'Theorizing Prostitution: The Question of Agency' 2 *Sexuality & Culture* 125

Skinner, S (2002) 'The Third Pillar Treaty Provisions on Police Cooperation: Has the EU Bitten Off More Than It Can Chew?' 8 *Columbia Journal of European Law* 203

SMART, C (1989) *Feminism and the Power of Law* (London, Routledge)

—— (1995) *Law, Crime and Sexuality: Essays in Feminism* (London, Sage Publications)

SMARTT, U (2003) 'Human Trafficking: Simply a European Problem?' 11 *European Journal of Crime, Criminal Law and Criminal Justice* 164

SMITH, K (2003) *European Union Foreign Policy in a Changing World* (Cambridge, Polity Press)

SMITH, P (ed) (1993) *Feminist Jurisprudence* (New York, Oxford University Press)

SOYSAL, Y (1994) *Limits of Citizenship* (Chicago, IL, University of Chicago Press)

SPENCER, M (1995) *States of Injustice. A Guide to Human Rights and Civil Liberties in the European Union* (London, Pluto Press)

STALKER, P (2000) *Workers Without Frontiers* (Boulder, CO, Lynne Rienner Publishers)

—— (2002) 'Migration Trends and Migration Policy in Europe 40(5) *International Migration* 151

STEINER, H (1994) *An Essay on Rights* (Oxford, Blackwell)

STERK-ELIFSON, C and CAMPBELL, C (1993) 'The Netherlands' in N Davis (ed), *Prostitution: An International Handbook on Trends, Problems, and Policies* (Westport, CT, Greenwood Press)

STOLTENBERG, J (1993) 'Male Sexuality: Why Ownership is Sexy' 1 *Michigan Journal of Gender and Law* 59

STYCHIN, C (2003) *Governing Sexuality. The Changing Politics of Citizenship and Law Reform* (Oxford, Hart Publishing)

SULLIVAN, B (2003) 'Trafficking in Women. Feminism and New International Law' 5 *International Feminist Journal of Politics* 67

SVANSTRÖM, Y (2004) 'Criminalising the John—a Swedish Gender Model?' in J Outshoorn (ed), *The Politics of Prostitution. Women's Movements, Democratic States and the Globalisation of Sex Commerce* (Cambridge, Cambridge University Press)

SZYSZCZAK, E (2001) 'Protecting Social Rights in the European Union' in A Eide, C Krause and A Rosas (eds), *Economic, Social and Cultural Rights* (2nd ed) (Dordrecht, Martinus Nijhoff Pusblishers)

TAMBIAH, Y (1995) 'Sexuality and Human Rights' in M Schuler (ed), *From Basic Needs to Basic Rights* (Washington, DC, Women, Law and Development International)

TAYLOR, C (1979) 'What's Wrong with Negative Liberty?' in A Ryan (ed), *The Idea of Freedom* (Oxford, Oxford University Press)

TAYLOR, I and JAMIESON, R (1999) 'Sex Trafficking and the Mainstream of Market Culture' 32 *Crime, Law and Social Change* 257

TEUBNER, G (1998) 'Legal Irritants: Good Faith in British Law or How Unifying Law Ends Up in New Divergences' 61 *Modern Law Review* 11

TIEFENBRUN, S (2001) 'Sex Sells but Drugs Don't Talk: Trafficking of Women Sex Workers' 23 *Thomas Jefferson Law Review* 199

TOEPFER, S and WELLS, B (1994) 'The Worldwide Market for Sex: a Review of International and Regional Legal Prohibitions Regarding Trafficking in Women' 2 *Michigan Journal of Gender & Law* 83

TRUONG, T (2003) 'Gender, Exploitative Migration, and the Sex Industry: A European Perspective' 7 *Gender, Technology and Development* 31

TURNBULL, P (1997) 'The Fusion of Immigration and Crime in the European Union: Problems of Cooperation and the Fight Against the Trafficking in Women' 3(4) *Transnational Organized Crime* 189

TURNER, E (1999) 'The EU's Development Policy and Gender' in M Lister (ed), *New Perspectives on European Union Development Cooperation* (Boulder, CO, Westview Press)

Twomey, P (2000) 'Europe's Other Market: Trafficking in People' 2 *European Journal of Migration and Law* 1

Tzvetkova, M (2002) 'NGO Responses to Trafficking in Women' 10(1) *Gender and Development* 60

Uçarer, E (1999) 'Trafficking in Women: Alternate Migration or Modern Slave Trade?' in M Meyer and E Prügl (eds), *Gender Politics in Global Governance* (Lanham, MD, Rowman & Littlefield Publishers)

—— (2002) 'Guarding the Borders of the European Union: Paths, Portals and Prerogatives' in S Lavenex and E Uçarer (eds), *Migration and the Externalities of European Integration* (Lanham, MD, Lexington Books)

Vachudová, M (2000) 'Eastern Europe as Gatekeeper: The Immigration and Asylum Policies of an Enlarging European Union' in P Andreas and T Snyder (eds), *The Wall around the West. State Borders and Immigration Controls in North America and Europe* (Lanham, MD, Rowman & Littlefield Publishers)

van Amersfoort, H (1999a) 'International Migration and Civil Rights: The Dilemmas of Migration Control in an Age of Globalisation' in E Guild (ed), *The Legal Framework and Social Consequences of Free Movement of Persons in the European Union* (The Hague, Kluwer Law International)

—— (1999b) 'Migration Control and Minority Policy: The Case of the Netherlands' in G Brochmann and T Hammar (eds), *Mechanisms of Immigration Control: A Comparative Analysis of European Regulation Policies* (Oxford, Berg)

van den Anker, C (2004) 'Contemporary Slavery, Global Justice and Globalization' in C van den Anker (ed), *The Political Economy of New Slavery* (Houndmills, Palgrave Macmillan)

—— (ed) (2004) *The Political Economy of New Slavery* (Houndmills, Palgrave Macmillan)

van der Leun, J (2003) *Looking for Loopholes. Processes of Incorporation of Illegal Immigrants in the Netherlands* (Amsterdam, Amsterdam University Press)

van Dijk, E (2002) *Mensenhandel in Nederland 1997–2000* (Zoetermeer, KLPD/NRI)

van Doorninck, M (2002) 'A Business Like Any Other? Managing the Sex Industry in the Netherlands' in S Thorbek and B Pattanaik (eds), *Transnational Prostitution. Changing Patterns in a Global Context* (London, Zed Books)

van Impe, K (2000) 'People for Sale: The need for a Multidisciplinary Approach towards Human Trafficking' 38(3) *International Migration* 113

van Ooik, R (2002) 'Freedom of Movement of Self-Employed Persons and the Europe Agreements' 4 *European Journal of Migration and Law* 377

van Selm, J (2002) 'Immigration or Asylum or Foreign Policy: The EU's Approach to Migrants and Their Countries of Origin' in S Lavenex and E Uçarer (eds), *Migration and the Externalities of European Integration* (Lanham, MD, Lexington Books)

Vance, C (1992) 'More Danger, More Pleasure: A Decade after the Barnard Sexuality Conference' in C Vance (ed), *Pleasure and Danger. Exploring Female Sexuality* (London, Pandora Press)

Vanheule, D et al (2005) 'The Significance of the UN Migrant Workers' Convention of 18 December 1990 in The Event of Ratification by Belgium' 6 *European Journal of Migration and Law* 285

Vanwesenbeeck, I and de Graaf, R (1998) 'Sex Work and HIV in the Netherlands: Policy, Research and Prevention' in T Sandfort (ed), *The Dutch Response to HIV. Pragmatism and Consensus* (London, UCL Press)

VERLOO, M (2000) 'Making Women Count in the Netherlands' in F Beveridge, S Nott and K Stephen (eds), *Making Women Count. Integrating Gender into Law and Policy-making* (Aldershot, Ashgate)

VERMEULEN, G (2000) 'The European Union Convention on Mutual Assistance in Criminal Matters' in De Kerchove and Weyembergh (eds), *Vers un espace judiciaire pénal européen* (Brussels, Institut d'Etudes europèennes)

VIRGILIO, M (2001) 'Law and Rights' in A Signorelli and M Treppele (eds), *Services in the Window* (Trieste, Asterios Editore)

—— (2002a) 'Article 18 Within the Framework of Criminal Legislation Aimed at Combating Crime Against Migrants' in Regione Emilia-Romagna and Associazione On the Road (eds), *Article 18: Protection of Victims of Trafficking and Fight Against Crime* (Martinsicuro, On the Road Edizioni)

—— (2002b) 'Judicial Activity Aimed at Combating Crimes Against Migrants' in Regione Emilia-Romagna and Associazione On the Road (eds), *Article 18: Protection of Victims of Trafficking and Fight Against Crime* (Martinsicuro, On the Road Edizioni)

VOCKS, J and NIJBOER, J (2000) 'The Promised Land: A Study of Trafficking in Women from Central and Eastern Europe to the Netherlands' 8 *European Journal on Criminal Policy and Research* 379

VON BOGDANDY, A (2000) 'The European Union as a Human Rights Organization? Human Rights and the Core of the European Union' 37 *Common Market Law Review* 1307

VON SRUENSEE, V (2000) 'Sex Trafficking: A Plea for Action' 6 *European Law Journal* 379

WALKER, N (2002) 'Culture, Democracy and the Convergence of Public Law: Some Scepticisms about Scepticism' in P Beaumont, C Lyons and N Walker (eds), *Convergence and Divergence in European Public Law* (Oxford, Hart Publishing)

WALKOWITZ, J (1982) *Prostitution and Victorian Society* (Cambridge, Cambridge University Press)

WARD, A (2004) 'Access to Justice' in S Peers and A Ward (eds), *The European Union Charter of Fundamental Rights* (Oxford, Hart Publishing)

WARD, I (2003) *A Critical Introduction to European Law* (2nd ed) (London, LexisNexis UK)

WEISS, F and WOOLDRIDGE, F (2002) *Free Movement of Persons within the European Community* (The Hague, Kluwer Law International)

WEITZER, R (2000) 'The Politics of Prostitution in America' in R Weitzer (ed), *Sex for Sale: Prostitution, Pornography and the Sex Industry* (New York, Routledge)

WEST, R (1988) 'Jurisprudence and Gender' 55 *University of Chicago Law Review* 1

WEYEMBERGH, A (2005) 'Approximation of Criminal Laws, the Constitutional Treaty and the Hague Programme' 42 *Common Market Law Review* 1567

WICHTERICH, C (2000) *The Globalized Woman* (London, Zed Books)

WIJERS, M and LAP-CHEW, L (1997) *Trafficking in Women, Forced Labour and Slavery-like Practices in Marriage, Domestic Labour and Prostitution* (Utrecht, STV)

WILLIAMS, P (1997) 'Trafficking in Women and Children: A Market Perspective' 3(4) *Transnational Organized Crime* 145

YOUNG, B (1998) 'Trafficking of Humans Across United States Borders: How United States Laws Can be Used to Punish Traffickers and Protect Victims' 13 *Georgetown Immigration Law Journal* 73

ZAJICEK, A and CALASANTI, T (1995) 'The Impact of Socioeconomic Restructuring on Polish Women' in B Łobodzińska (ed), *Family, Women and Employment in Central-Eastern Europe* (Westport, CT, Greenwood Press)

REPORTS AND WORKING PAPERS

Amnesty International (2004) *"So does that mean I have rights?" Protecting the human rights of women and girls trafficked for forced prostitution in Kosovo* (London, AI)

ANDERSON, B and O'Connell Davidson, J (2003) *Is Trafficking in Human Beings Demand Driven? A Multi-Country Pilot Study* (IOM Migration Research Series, No 15, Geneva, IOM)

Anti-Slavery International (2002) *Human Traffic, Human Rights: Redefining Victim Protection* (London, ASI)

Anti-Slavery International (2003) *The Migration-Trafficking Nexus* (London, ASI)

APAP, J and CARRERA, S (2003) *Towards a Proactive Immigration Policy for the EU?* (CEPS Working Document No 198, Brussels, CEPS)

—— and MEDVED, F (2003) *Protection Schemes for Victims of Trafficking in Selected EU Member Countries, Candidate and Third Countries* (Geneva, IOM)

ARTS, K (2001) *Gender Aspects of the Cotonou Agreement* (WIDE Position Paper on ACP-EU development co-operation, Brussels, WIDE)

ASSOCIAZIONE LULE (2001) *Vite di strada* (Abbiategrasso, LULE)

BINDEL, J and KELLY, L (2004) *A Critical Examination of Responses to Prostitution in Four Countries: Victoria-Australia, Ireland, The Netherlands and Sweden* (Glasgow, Routes Out)

BOS, N and KOOTSTRA, T (1997) *Starting a New life. For Better or Worse? Background Study of Victims of Traffic in Women in The Netherlands* (Utrecht, STV)

BRUSSA, L (1991) *Survey on Prostitution, Migration and Traffic in Women: History and Current Situation* (Strasbourg, Council of Europe)

CALDWELL, G, GALSTER, S and STEINZOR, N (1997) *Crime & Servitude: An Exposé of the Traffic in Women for Prostitution from the Newly Independent States* (Report of the Global Survival Network, Washington, DC, GSN)

CHOLEWINSKI, R (2002) *Borders and Discrimination in the European Union* (Report prepared for Immigration Law Practitioners' Association, London and Brussels, ILPA and Migration Policy Group)

COMITÉ DES SAGES (1998) *Leading by Example: A Human Rights Agenda for the European Union for the Year 2000. Agenda of the Comité des Sages and Final Project Report* (Florence, EUI)

COOMARASWAMY, R (2000) *Trafficking in Women, Women's Migration and Violence against Women* (Report of the Special Rapporteur on Violence Against Women, its Causes and Consequences, UN Doc. E/CN.4/2000/68)

DAALDER, A (2002) *The Lifting of the Ban on Brothels. Prostitution in 2000–2001* (The Hague, WODC)

DECARLI, S and DI NICOLA, A (2002) *Italy, National Report* (Trento, Transcrime, University of Trento et al).

DEMIR, J (2003) *Trafficking of Women for Sexual Exploitation: A Gender-Based Well-Founded Fear?* (New Issues in Refugee Research, Working Paper No 80, Geneva, UNHCR)

DEN BOER, M (1998) *Taming the Third Pillar. Improving the Management of Justice and Home Affairs* (Maastricht, European Institute of Public Administration)

Department for Migration and Asylum Policy (MAP) (2001) *Sweden in 2000. A Country of Migration* (Stockholm, Ministry of Foreign Affairs)

Department for Migration and Asylum Policy (MAP) (2002) *Migration 2002* (Stockholm, Ministry of Foreign Affairs)

Di Nicola, A et al (2005) *National Legislation on Prostitution and the Trafficking in Women and Children* (Trento, Transcrime for the European Parliament)

Dipartimento per le Pari Opportunità (2005) *Protezione e assistenza alle vittime della tratta, i dati del monitoraggio* (Rome, Dipartimento per le Pari Opportunita)

EMZ (Europäische Migrationszentrum) (2003a) *Overview reports on Finland, Ireland and Sweden* (RefTra Project—Prevention and fight against trafficking: Institutional developments in Europe, Berlin, EMZ)

EMZ (Europäische Migrationszentrum) (2003b) *Netherlands Report* (RefTra Project—Prevention and fight against trafficking: Institutional developments in Europe, Berlin, EMZ)

European Council on Refugees and Exiles (2001) *An overview of proposals addressing migrant smuggling and trafficking in persons* (ECRE Background paper, Brussels, ECRE)

Europol (2003) *European Union Organised Crime Situation Report* (The Hague, Europol)

Europol (2004a) *European Union Organised Crime Situation Report* (The Hague, Europol)

Europol (2004b) *Trafficking in Human Beings for Sexual Exploitation in the EU: A Europol Perspective* (The Hague, Europol)

Experts Group on Trafficking in Human Beings (2004) *Report of the Experts Group on Trafficking in Human Beings* (Brussels, European Commission)

Favell, A and Geddes, A (1999) *European Integration, Immigration and the Nation State: Institutionalising Transnational Political Action?* (EUI Working Papers, RSC No 99/32, Florence, EUI)

Global Alliance Against Traffic in Women, Foundation Against Trafficking in Women and International Human Rights Law Group (1999) *Human Rights Standards for the Treatment of Trafficked Persons* (Utrecht, Global Alliance Against Trafficking in Women)

Galiana, C (2000) *Trafficking in Women* (Brussels, European Parliament)

Guild, E (2002) *The Legal Framework of EU Migration* (The Political Economy of Migration in an Integrating Europe (PEMINT) Background Paper 2/2002, Coimlera, PEMINT)

Higgins, I (ed) *Migration and Asylum Law and Practice in the European Union* (FIDE 2004 National Reports, Cambridge, FIDE)

Hirsch, M (1996) *Plan of Action Against Traffic in Women and Forced Prostitution* (Strasbourg, Council of Europe)

Holst, C and Lindström, P (2000) *Förbud mot köp av sexuella tjänster. Tillämpningen av lagen under första året* (Stockholm, BRÅ-rapport 2000:4)

Hopkins, R and Nijboer, J (2003) *Country Report: The Netherlands* in Payoke, On the Road, de Roode Draad: Research based on case studies of victims of trafficking in human beings in 3 EU Member States, i.e. Belgium, Italy and The Netherlands (Antwerp, Payoke et al)

Hughes, D (2002) *Trafficking for Sexual Exploitation: The Case of the Russian Federation* (IOM Migration Research Series, No 7, Geneva, IOM)

—— (2004) *Best Practices to Address the Demand Side of Sex Trafficking* (Kingston, RI, University of Rhode Island)

Human Rights Watch (2002) *Commentary on the European Commission Proposal for a Council Directive "on the short-term residence permit issued to victims of action to facilitate illegal immigration or trafficking in human beings who cooperate with the competent authorities"* (Brussels, HRW)

IOM (1995) Trafficking and Pr*ostitution: the Growing Exploitation of Migrant Women from Central and Eastern Europe* (Geneva, IOM, Migration Information Programme)

IOM (1996a) *Trafficking in Women to Austria for Sexual Exploitation* (Geneva, IOM, Migration Information Programme)

IOM (1996b) *Trafficking in Women to Italy for Sexual Exploitation* (Geneva, IOM, Migration Information Programme)

IOM (1996c) *Trafficking in Women from the Dominican Republic for Sexual Exploitation* (Geneva, IOM, Migration Information Programme)

IOM (2000) There are ways to curb the worldwide traffic in migrants (2000) *Trafficking in Migrants*, No 21.

IOM (2001) *Victims of Trafficking in the Balkans* (Geneva, IOM)

IOM (2002a) Temporary residence permits: a new way to protect trafficking victims? (2002) *Trafficking in Migrants* No 25.

IOM (2002b) *International Comparative Study of Migration Legislation and Practice* (Dublin, IOM)

IOM (2005) *World Migration 2005. Costs and Benefits of International Migration* (Geneva, IOM)

Kartusch, A (2001) *Reference Guide for Anti-Trafficking Legislative Review with Particular Emphasis on South Eastern Europe* (Warsaw, OSCE/ODIHR)

Kelly, E (2002) *Journeys of Jeopardy: A Review of Research on Trafficking in Women and Children in Europe* (IOM Migration Research Series, No 11, Geneva, IOM)

Kelly, L and Regan, L (2000) *Stopping Traffic: Exploring the extent of, and responses to, trafficking in women for sexual exploitation in the UK* (London, Home Office, Police Research Series Paper 125)

Kootstra, T (1996) *Background Study on Basic Principles for a Code of Conduct Within the Member States of the European Union to Prevent and Combat Trafficking in Women* (Utrecht, Dutch Foundation against Trafficking in Women (STV))

—— (ed) (1996) *One year La Strada: Results of the First Central and Eastern Program on Prevention of Traffic in Women* (Utrecht, Dutch Foundation against Trafficking in Women (STV))

Korvinus, A (2002) *Trafficking in Human Beings. First Report of the Dutch National Rapporteur* (The Hague, Bureau NRM)

—— (2003) *Trafficking in Human Beings. Supplementary Figures. Second Report of the Dutch National Rapporteur* (The Hague, Bureau NRM)

—— (2005a) *Trafficking in Human Beings. Third Report of the Dutch National Rapporteur* (The Hague, Bureau NRM)

—— (2005b) *Trafficking in Human Beings. Supplementary Figures. Fourth Report of the Dutch National Rapporteur* (The Hague, Bureau NRM)

Lăzăroiu, S and Alexandru, M (2003) *Who is the Next Victim? Vulnerability of Young Romanian Women to Trafficking in Human Beings* (Geneva, IOM)

Limanowska, B (2002) *Trafficking in Human Beings in Southeastern Europe* (Belgrade, UNICEF, UNOHCHR and OSCE/ODIHR)

Locher, B (2002) *International Norms and European Policy Making: Trafficking in Women in the EU* (Bremen, Centre for European Studies, CEuS Working Paper No 2002/6)

London School of Hygiene and Tropical Medicine et al (2003) *The Health Risks and Consequences of Trafficking in Women and Adolescents. Findings from a European Study* (London, LSHTM, La Strada, STV, University of Padua, GAATW and LMU)

Mate, R (2003) *A Gender Analysis of the Cotonou Agreement and Its Implementation* (London, One World Action)

Monar, J (2000) *Justice and Home Affairs in a Wider Europe: The Dynamics of Inclusion and Exclusion* (ESRC 'One Europe or Several?' Programme Working Paper 7/00, Brighton, ESRC)

—— (2001) *EU Justice and Home Affairs in the Eastward Enlargement: The Challenge of Diversity and EU Instruments and Strategies* (Zentrum für Europäische Integrationsforschung (ZEI) Discussion Paper C 91, Bonn, ZEI)

Moore, A (ed) (2004) *Police and Judicial Co-operation in the European Union* (FIDE 2004 National Reports, Cambridge, FIDE)

Morawska, E (2000) *Transnational Migrations in the Enlarged European Union: A Perspective from East Central Europe* (EUI Working Papers, RSC No 2000/19, Florence, EUI)

Morrison, J and Crosland, B (2001) *The trafficking and smuggling of refugees: the end game in European asylum policy?* (New Issues in Refugee Research, Working Paper No 39, Geneva, UNHCR)

Muus, P (1996) *The Trafficking and Smuggling of Refugees: The End Game in European Asylum Policy?* (Amsterdam, European Research Centre on Migration and Ethnic Relations, SOPEMI)

Nord, A and Rosenberg, T (2001) *Rapport: Lag (1998:408) om förbud mot köp av sexuella tjänster* (Malmö, Polismyndigheten i Skåne)

Nottage, L (2001) *Convergence, Divergence, and the Middle Way in Unifying or Harmonising Private Law* (EUI Working Paper Law No 2001/01, Florence, EUI)

OECD (2005) *Trends in International Migration* (Paris, OECD, Annual Report 2004 Edition)

O'Neill Richard, A (2000) *International Trafficking in Women to the United States: A Contemporary Manifestation of Slavery and Organized Crime* (Washington, DC, DCI Exceptional Intelligence Analyst Program: An Intelligence Monograph)

Orfano, I (2003) *Country Report: Italy* in Payoke, On the Road, de Roode Draad. Research based on case studies of victims of trafficking in human beings in 3 EU Member States, i.e. Belgium, Italy and The Netherlands (Antwerp, Payoke et al)

Organization for Security and Co-operation in Europe (1999) *Trafficking in Human Beings: Implications for the OSCE* (Warsaw, ODIHR Background Paper 1999/3)

Organization for Security and Co-operation in Europe (2004) *National Referral Mechanisms. A Practical Handbook* (Warsaw, OSCE/ODIHR)

Painter, G and Ulmer, K (2002) *Everywhere and Nowhere. Assessing Gender Mainstreaming in European Community Development Cooperation* (London, APRODEV and One World Action)

Papademetriou, D and Hamilton, K (1996) *Converging Paths to Restriction: French, Italian and British Responses to Immigration* (Washington, DC, International Migration Policy Program, Carnegie Endowment for International Peace)

Polismyndigheten i Stockholms län, Länskriminalpolisens Underrättelserotel (2001) *Handel med människor för sexuella ändamål* (Stockholm, Länskriminalpolisen)

Raymond, J (2001) *Guide to the New UN Trafficking Protocol* (North Amherst, MA, Coalition Against Trafficking in Women)

Rikskriminalpolisen, Kriminalunderrättelsetjänsten (1999) *Handel med kvinnor: Lägesrapport* (1 januari–30 juni 1999), Rapport 1999:16 (Stockholm, RKP)

Rikskriminalpolisen, Kriminalunderrättelsetjänsten (2000) *Handel med kvinnor: Lägesrapport 2* (1 juli–31 december 1999), Rapport 2000:1 (Stockholm, RKP)

Rikskriminalpolisen, Kriminalunderrättelsetjänsten (2001) *Handel med kvinnor: Lägesrapport 3* (1 januari–31 december 2000), Rapport 2001:3 (Stockholm, RKP)

Rikskriminalpolisen, Kriminalunderrättelsetjänsten (2002) *Handel med kvinnor: Lägesrapport 4* (1 januari–31 december 2001), Rapport 2002:1 (Stockholm, RKP)

Rikskriminalpolisen, Kriminalunderrättelsetjänsten (2003) *Handel med kvinnor: Lägesrapport 5* (1 januari–31 december 2002), Rapport 2003:1 (Stockholm, RKP)

Rikskriminalpolisen, Kriminalunderrättelsetjänsten (2004) *Människohandel för sexuella ändamål. Lägesrapport 6* (1 januari–31 december 2003), Rapport 2004:2 (Stockholm, RKP)

Rikskriminalpolisen, Kriminalunderrättelsetjänsten (2005) *Människohandel för sexuella ändamål. Lägesrapport 7* (1 januari–31 december 2004), Rapport 2005:4 (Stockholm, RKP)

Riksrevisionsverket (2001) *Samverkan i gränskontrollen* ((Stockholm, RRV) Rapport 2001:1)

Savona, E et al (2004) *Tratta di persone a scopo di sfruttamento e traffico di migranti. Rapporto finale di sintesi della ricerca* (Transcrime Report No 8, Rome, Ministero della Giustizia)

Socialstyrelsen (2000) *Kännedom om prostitution 1998–1999* (Stockholm, Socialstyrelsen, SoS-rapport 2000:5)

Socialstyrelsen (2004) *Kännedom om prostitution 2003* (Stockholm, Socialstyrelsen)

Steinhilber, S (2002) *Women's Rights and Gender Equality in the EU Enlargement. An Opportunity for Progress* (briefing paper, Brussels, WIDE)

Stiftelsen Kvinnoforum (1998) *Trafficking in Women for the Purpose of Sexual Exploitation: Mapping the Situation and Existing Organisations Working in Belarus, Russia, the Baltic and Nordic States* (Stockholm, SK)

—— (2002) *Översyn av socialt stöd till kvinnor, flickor och pojkar offer för människohandel i Sverige* (Stockholm, SK)

—— (2003) *European Good Practice on Recovery, Return and Integration of Trafficked Persons* (Stockholm, SK)

Sullivan, M and Jeffreys, S (2001) *Legalising Prostitution Is Not the Answer: The Example of Victoria, Australia* (North Fitzroy, Coalition Against Trafficking in Women)

TAMPEP (1994) *Transnational AIDS/STD Prevention among Migrant Prostitutes in Europe/Project. Final Report* (Amsterdam, TAMPEP)

TAMPEP (1996) *Transnational AIDS/STD Prevention among Migrant Prostitutes in Europe/Project Final Report* (Amsterdam, TAMPEP)

TAMPEP (2002) *Transnational AIDS/STD Prevention among Migrant Prostitutes in Europe/Project. TAMPEP 5.* Volumes 1–3 (Amsterdam, TAMPEP)

UNICEF (2004) *Trafficking in Human Beings, Especially Women and Children, in Africa.* (Florence, UNICEF Innocenti Research Centre, Innocenti Insight)

United Nations Department of Economic and Social Affairs, Population Division (2006) *International Migration 2006* (New York, UN)

United Nations Fund for Population Activities (UNFPA) (2000) *State of the World's Population* (New York, UN)

United Nations High Commissioner for Human Rights (UNHCHR) (2002) *Recommended Principles and Guidelines on Human Rights and Human Trafficking* (Doc. E/2002/68/Add. 1)

United Nations Office on Drug and Crime (UNODC) (2006) *Trafficking in Persons. Global Patterns* (Vienna, UNDOC)

United Nations Population Division (2000) *Replacement migration: is it a solution to declining and ageing population?* (Doc. ESA/P/WP.160)

United States of America Department of State (2001) *Victims of Trafficking and Violence Protection Act 2000: Trafficking in Persons Report* (Washington, DC, Dept of State)

United States of America Department of State (2002) *Victims of Trafficking and Violence Protection Act 2000: Trafficking in Persons Report* (Washington, DC, Dept of State)

United States of America Department of State (2003) *Victims of Trafficking and Violence Protection Act 2000: Trafficking in Persons Report* (Washington, DC, Dept of State)

United States of America Department of State (2004) *Victims of Trafficking and Violence Protection Act 2000: Trafficking in Persons Report* (Washington, DC, Dept of State)

United States of America Department of State (2005) *Victims of Trafficking and Violence Protection Act 2000: Trafficking in Persons Report* (Washington, DC, Dept of State)

Utrikesdepartementet, enheten för global utveckling (2003) *Fattigdom och människohandel—En strategi för bekämpning av människohandel in Sveriges internationella utvecklingssamarbete* (Stockholm, Utrikesdepartementet)

VAN DER HELMS, T (1999) *The Amsterdam Intermediary Project: Ten Years Health and Social Care in Prostitution* (Amsterdam, Intermediary project)

VAN DER KLEIJ, A (2002) *Provisions for Victims of Trafficking in Bonded Sexual Labour, i.e. Prostitution - in 6 European Countries - Belgium, Germany, Italy, the Netherlands, Spain and the United Kingdom* (Amsterdam, Bonded Labour in Netherlands, BlinN)

VAN DER VLEUTEN, N (1991) *Survey on 'Traffic in Women'. Policies and Policy-Research in an International Context* (Leiden, Research and Documentation Centre Women and Autonomy (VENA))

VAN MENS, L and VAN DER HELM, T (1999) *Mobiliteit in de Nederlandse Prostitutie. Een Inventarisatie* (Utrecht, Europap)

VENICZ, E, NENCEL, L and VISSER, J (2000) *Trends in prostitutie en beleid* (Amsterdam, De tweede rapportage van de Profeitstudie)

VINK, M (2002) *Negative and Positive Integration in European Immigration Policies* (European Integration online Papers (EIoP), 6(13))

—— (2003) *Limits of European Citizenship: European Integration and Domestic Immigration Policies* (Belfast, QUB, Constitutionalism Web-Papers, ConWEB No 4/2003)

VISSER, J, Oomens, H and Boerman, F (1999) *Prostitutie en Nederland in 1999* (Amsterdam, De Profeit Studie)

ZINCONE, G (ed) (2000) *Primo rapporto sull'integrazione degli immigrati in Italia* (Bologna, Il Mulino)

—— (ed) (2001) *Secondo rapporto sull'integrazione degli immigrati in Italia* (Bologna, Il Mulino)

ZORLU, A and HARTOG, J (2001) *Migration and Immigrants: The Case of the Netherlands* (Amsterdam, Tinbergen Institute Discussion Paper TI 2001-042/3)

CONFERENCE PAPERS (on file with author)

BRUGGEMAN, W (2002) *Illegal Immigration and Trafficking in Human Beings Seen as a Security Problem for Europe.* Conference Paper from the EU/IOM STOP European Conference on Preventing and Combating Trafficking In Human Beings, Brussels, 18–20 September 2002

DIAMANTOPOULOU, A (2002) *Fighting Modern Slavery: The EU's Role in Supporting Victims of Trafficking.* Conference Paper from the EU/IOM STOP European Conference on Preventing and Combating Trafficking In Human Beings, Brussels, 18–20 September 2002

HOPKINS, R and NIJBOER, J (2003) *Towards Policy and Practice Recommendations for Dealing with the Growing Problem of Women Trafficking: A Dutch Response.* Conference Paper from the University of Nottingham Trafficking in Persons Conference, 27–28 June 2003

Italian Government (2002) *The Position of the Italian Government on Trafficking in Human Beings.* Conference Paper from the EU/IOM STOP European Conference on Preventing and Combating Trafficking In Human Beings, Brussels, 18–20 September 2002

ODIHR/OSCE (2001) *Europe Against Trafficking in Persons.* Conference Report from Berlin Conference, 15–16 October 2001

Regione Emilia-Romagna and Associazione On the Road (eds) (2002) *Stop Tratta. Atti del convengno internazionale*, Bologna, 23–24 May 2002

SANGHERA, Y (1997) *In the Belly of the Beast: Sex Trade, Prostitution and Globalization.* Appendix A in Moving the Whore Stigma. Report on the Asia and Pacific Regional Consultation on Prostitution, Bangkok, 17–18 February 1997

SVEVO, M, GARAVAGLIA, E and D'AMICO, M (eds) (2002) *Polizia e Traffico degli esseri umani. Sistema dei controlli e protezione delle vittime.* Pubblicazione degli atti della Conferenza Internazionale Polizia e traffico degli esseri umani. Sistema dei controlli e protezione delle vittime, Milan, 10 June 2002

TAVCER, C (2003) *From Poverty to the Trafficking of Women for Sexual Exploitation: A Study of Causal Factors of Trafficked Women from Moldova.* Conference Paper from the University of Nottingham Trafficking in Persons Conference, 27–28 June 2003

VENICZ, E (1997) *A Discourse of Impotence, Dutch Politicians and their Efforts to Control Migrant Prostitutes.* Conference Paper from the Conference Beyond Boundaries: Sexualities Across Cultures, Amsterdam, July 1997

Index

abolitionism 13–4, 38–40, 47–9, 101, 104–5, 124, 166
accountability 129, 131, 179
Adoui and Cornuaille Case 53–4, 86
AGIS Programme 127, 170
Area of Freedom, Security and Justice (AFSJ) 2, 6, 8–9, 43, 75, 99–100, 121–2, 130–1, 153, 155, 157, 163, 172
Association Agreements 54, 63, 86, 109
asylum 19, 61, 65, 69–76, 80, 94–6, 140–1, 154, 157
  see also persecution; refugee
asylum-seekers 30, 60, 69–70, 72, 75–6, 94, 103, 140
Austria 14
awareness of trafficking 43, 111, 164, 169–71, 179, 182

B–9 permit
  see Netherlands, residence permits
Belgium 3, 53, 123, 137
Berlin, I 44–5, 53
  see also freedom
biological urges 23, 29
body 2, 22, 26, 29, 146
Brussels Declaration 7, 170, 172

Candidate Countries 54, 109, 127, 158
care work 38, 57–8, 81–6
  see also domestic work
carrier liability 75
CATW 33–6, 46
Central and Eastern European Countries (CEECs) 55–6, 63, 76–7, 80, 86
Charter of Fundamental Rights 10, 59, 131, 153–7
choice (in prostitution) 15, 18, 24–5, 27–8, 30, 34–5, 40–1, 45–7, 50–2, 55–6, 65, 86, 106, 118
citizenship, European 52, 57, 60, 64–5
  see also EU citizens
client criminalisation 14, 49–51, 106, 112, 115–6, 148, 165–8
coercion (in prostitution) 18, 27–8, 34–5, 40, 45, 102, 107, 116
Cold War 28, 69, 123
commodification 2, 59, 183–4
Common Agricultural Policy 180
compensation for victims of trafficking 114, 140, 151
competence (EU) 6, 12, 43–4, 53, 59, 92, 99, 120, 126, 128, 131, 155–6, 158–9, 165, 175, 180
'comprehensive approach' to trafficking 1, 4–9, 13, 21–2, 36, 40–1, 132, 135, 162–3, 165, 171
consent 20, 23–4, 33–4, 101, 123–5, 150, 186
Contagious Diseases Acts 23
convergence 1, 8–13, 38, 63, 68, 70, 73, 79, 96, 107, 126, 168
  see also divergence
co-operation
  by victims of trafficking 90–3, 103, 110–1, 114–5, 117, 119
  EU 2, 5, 9–10, 13, 43, 72–7, 99, 108, 120–3, 127–32
  international 6, 123, 125, 129–30
Council Action Plan on trafficking 163–5, 167–70, 173
Council of Europe Convention against trafficking 95, 157–8, 165
country of destination 1, 3–5, 14–5, 17–20, 32, 35, 83–5, 87, 89, 116, 139–42, 151, 164, 168–9, 172
country of origin 3–5, 20, 90, 94–5, 104, 109, 112, 114, 127, 140, 142, 168–9, 170, 173, 179
criminal networks 30–1, 77, 88, 90, 112, 121, 128–9
criminalisation of migration 78, 87, 96, 108, 162
customers (of prostitution) 13, 16, 19, 22, 26, 28, 36, 38–40, 46, 48–52, 88, 105–6, 111–2, 115–8, 138, 149, 167, 182–5

Daphne Programme 43, 170–1, 179
data on trafficking 7, 16, 49, 89, 111, 113, 116, 170
debt bondage 18–9, 31, 35, 46, 90, 110
definition of trafficking 17, 32–4, 101–7, 113, 118, 123–5, 161
demand
  for migrant workers 73, 81–2, 85, 167
  for sexual services 24, 29, 35, 105, 108, 159, 167, 181–4
development co-operation 172–81
  gender mainstreaming in 173–80
dichotomies 27, 36, 45, 82, 167
Directive on the residence permit issued to victims of trafficking 92–4, 126, 132, 157, 164–5, 168

discrimination 23–6, 28, 31, 37–8, 55, 58–9, 62, 133, 136–8, 142, 144–5, 150, 154–5, 159, 161, 169, 172–3, 177, 185, 187
divergence 1, 3, 8–13, 27, 68, 70, 73–4, 124, 126, 165
  see also convergence
domestic work 15, 17, 82–6
  see also care work
domination 24

economic restructuring 29, 142
education 40, 45–6, 51, 59, 64, 81, 93, 105, 126, 142–3, 172, 174, 184–5
empowerment, women's 26, 34, 85, 153, 165, 172–174, 182
enlargement 43, 63, 74, 76, 129–30, 158, 166
equal treatment directives 59, 62, 186
essentialism 12
  in feminism 25–6, 34, 37
EU citizens 5, 43–4, 53, 55, 59–63, 76, 78, 86, 130–1, 148–9, 155–6, 168
Eurojust 99, 128
European Court of Justice 53–7, 131, 156–7
Europol 99, 128, 172
evidence 111, 115–6
exclusion of (non-EU) migrants 60, 63–5, 131, 149, 161
expertise 116, 179–80
expulsion 19–20, 32, 46, 49–50, 73, 75, 77, 86–7, 89–91, 108–11, 114, 117, 119, 140–1, 154, 164, 166

family 31, 58
family members 46, 57–8, 69, 90, 109
family reunion 58, 61–2, 70, 75, 83–4, 94
feminism 12, ch 2
  liberal 22, 39–40, 51
  radical 22, 24, 33, 39–40
feminist legal theory 21–2, 36–8
Finland 71
'foreignerisation' of prostitution 28–9, 52, 64, 85–6
former Soviet Union 4, 30, 55
Fortress Europe 15, 30, 67–70, 73, 78
Forum for the Prevention of Organised Crime 129
Framework Decision on combating trafficking in human beings 5–6, 88, 99, 121, 124–7, 154, 169, 171
France 14
free movement of persons (EC) 5, 8, 43–4, 52–55, 67, 74–6, 100, 130
  limitations to 53
freedom 15, 43
  barriers to 44–48, 50, 56, 65, 67
  in prostitution 27, 45–47
  negative and positive 44–52, 54–59
    negative 130
    positive 142
  of movement 30, 44, 89, 97
funding 126, 170–1

GAATW 34, 36
gender equality 5–6, 21, 27, 37, 51, 118, 145, 168, 172–6, 180
  EC policy on 53, 57–9, 159
gender mainstreaming
  see development co-operation
Germany 70
globalisation 2, 5, 28, 30, 35, 52, 55, 67, 120, 123, 130, 181, 186

Hague Declaration 20, 172
Hague Programme 62, 157
harmonisation 4, 10, 13, 73–4, 99–100, 121–3, 126, 130, 154, 162, 165, 171
health risks 19
hegemonic masculinity 183–4, 186–7
heterosexuality, expressions of 184
Hirschmann, N 45–6
homosexuality 47, 58, 183–4
human rights 5, 8–9, 35, 62, 74, 76–7, 85, 90, 130, 164–5, 168, 175, 178, 181
  civil and political 135–7, 142, 150
  economic, social and cultural 141–145
  fragility of framework 139, 141, 144, 155–6
  group/collective rights 144
  migrants' 85, 134, 136, 138, 141–4, 148–50
  of trafficking victims 135–40, 150–52
  positive obligations 136
  women's 134–149
  see also Charter of Fundamental Rights
human security 130

'illegal migration'
  see irregular migration
indirect discrimination 58
Internal Market 43–4, 52, 57, 60, 64, 74, 155
International Organization for Migration (IOM) 4, 32
immigration 44, 67, 69–73
immigration policy
  Europeanisation of 73–80
  openness to labour migration 78–80
  see Italy; Netherlands, Sweden – immigration policy
  see also migration control
irregular migration 2, 16–20, 31–2, 35–6, 68–9, 75, 77, 84–5, 89–90, 93, 101–4, 108–9, 144, 164
  irregular employment 17, 63, 83, 86–7, 167
  irregular entry 17, 30, 70, 78, 83, 87, 90
  irregular residence 17, 19, 72, 90, 138
Italy
  criminalisation of trafficking 104–5, 112–5

debates over women's rights and law reform 149
immigration policy 72–3
legal regulation of prostitution 49–50
residence permits for victims of trafficking 90–91, 105, 113–5

Jany and Others Case 54–5, 57, 59, 86, 109

kidnapping 18, 113, 116, 119, 137
Koskenniemi, M 149, 156

law
neutrality of 24, 26, 36
power of 38, 40
role of 21, 38, 41
women's experience and 26, 37
legal transplants 11, 37
legalisation (of prostitution) 14, 39, 47–8, 51, 103, 108–10, 147, 165–8
liberty
see freedom
litigation strategies 151–2, 156–7
long-term residents 62, 169

MacKinnon, C 24
media 18, 30, 88, 185–186
migration-crime nexus 78, 122, 129, 164, 172
migration control 9, 60–1, 69–79, 87, 90, 95, 120, 141, 157, 164, 168, 178
migration hump 174
migration patterns/trends 69
migration policy
see immigration policy
moral panic 23, 72, 87–8, 99, 105
morality
see prostitution – morality

national rapporteur(s) on trafficking 20
nationality 31, 37, 44, 62, 65, 155, 162
see also EU citizens; third country nationals
negative integration 53–4, 58
Netherlands
criminalisation of trafficking 101–4, 108–12
debates over women's rights and law reform 146–9
immigration policy 70–1
legal regulation of prostitution 47–8
residence permits for victims of trafficking 89–90, 103–4, 110–2
see also legalisation
NGOs 5, 19–20, 33, 88–91, 105, 114, 151–2, 170–1, 179
non-refoulement
see asylum; persecution

oil crisis 70
organised crime 2, 30–1, 35, 104, 110, 112–3, 121–5, 127–9, 164
ostracism 46, 111

Peers, S 61, 156
penalties 73, 100, 102–4, 106, 120, 158, 169, 173
persecution 69, 94, 118, 140–1
see also asylum; refugee
phases of feminism
'first phase' feminism 23
'second phase' feminism 24–25
'third phase' feminism 25–27
pleasure, sexual 21, 185–6
pornography 29, 54, 56, 104, 125, 147, 184, 186
poverty 24, 28, 31, 45–6, 55, 142, 150, 152, 164, 173–6, 178–81
see also root causes of trafficking
prevention (of trafficking) 4, 88, 124–6, 141–5, 170–187
prohibitionism 13–14, 38, 57, 166
prosecution (of trafficking)
see Italy; Netherlands; Sweden – criminalisation of trafficking
prostitution
as exploitation 24–5, 33, 39–40, 48–9, 50–1, 105–8, 148, 166
as work 14, 25–7, 33–4, 36, 39–40, 46–8, 51, 53–4, 56–7, 59, 103, 107–8, 148, 166
commonalities between 'work' and 'exploitation' 27–28, 34–35, 168
feminist law reform on 39–41, 47–48, 146–149, 168
heterogeneity of 28
morality and 5, 13–4, 22, 26–7, 49, 51, 54–5, 96, 183, 186
policy considerations 50–2, 56–7, 107–8
protection of victims
see Italy; Netherlands; Sweden – residence permits for victims of trafficking
public order 5, 13, 47, 108, 110, 115, 118

race 39, 62–3, 85, 152, 162, 177
racism/xenophobia 28, 71, 77, 80, 97, 121, 149
rape 12, 19, 105, 111, 119, 151, 162,
re-trafficking 20, 90, 94, 115
re-victimisation 20, 135, 140
readmission clauses/agreements 71–3, 75, 164, 173, 177
recovery 89, 110, 115, 139–40, 150–2
reflection period 89, 93, 110
see also Italy; Netherlands, Sweden – residence permits for victims of trafficking
refugee 69, 71–2, 74, 76, 157
see also asylum; persecution
regulationism 14, 23, 38, 50–1, 101, 105, 167
remittances 5, 81, 164, 169, 173
retribution 90, 94–5, 111, 140, 151

return/repatriation 19, 94–5, 104, 109, 111, 139–40, 154
rhetoric 2, 75, 83, 99, 134, 143, 149, 178
rights 25, 37–8, 57–63, 92, 109, 119, 164
  conflicts between 152
  discourse 134, 145, 147, 150, 152, 156, 160
  see also human rights
root causes of trafficking 9, 28, 31, 41, 78, 96, 142, 144, 173–4, 180
  see also structural causes (of trafficking)

safe third countries 75, 141
Sassen, S 81
Schengen 43, 60–1, 70, 72–5, 122
securitisation 60, 121–2
self-employment, 54, 61, 63
sex industries 14, 22, 28–30, 35, 39, 41, 50, 53–4, 101, 133, 147–9, 166–7, 182, 185
sex tourism 29–30, 33, 178–9, 184
sex work
  see prostitution as work
sexual ideologies 29, 41, 119, 147, 181–7
sexual slavery 18, 22
  see also prostitution as exploitation
sexual rights 144–5, 185
sexuality 13, 15, 21–4, 27, 40, 56, 59, 80, 87, 96, 99, 130, 146, 167, 179, 181, 183–186
short-term residence permits
  see Directive on the residence permit issued to victims of trafficking
  see also Italy; Netherlands; Sweden – residence permits for victims of trafficking
slavery 18, 43, 49, 99, 104, 106, 113, 124–5, 135–6, 154
Smart, C 25, 40
smuggling in human beings 17, 30, 32, 35, 49–50, 73, 77, 87, 92, 103, 113, 123–4, 126, 140
  commonalities with trafficking 35–6, 77
social cohesion 59, 74
socio-economic factors
  see root causes
soliciting 38, 48–50, 53
stereotypes 68, 87, 100, 117–8, 138, 145–6, 159, 184–5
STOP Programme 127, 158, 170–1
stigmatisation 20, 25–6, 37–8, 40, 46, 51, 86–8, 166–8, 181–3, 185
structural causes (of trafficking) 28, 33, 35–6, 80–5, 95, 119, 144–5, 149, 153, 160, 171–2
  see also root causes of trafficking
Sweden
  criminalisation of trafficking 105–7, 115–7
  debates over rights and law reform 146–9
  immigration policy 71–2
  legal regulation of prostitution 48–9
  residence permits for victims of trafficking 91–2, 107, 117
  see also client criminalisation

Tampere Conclusions 7, 61–2, 121
terminology, use of 18, 33–34
  see also definition of trafficking
terrorism 75, 77, 99, 121–2, 130, 137
third country nationals 5, 19, 44, 48–9, 52, 55, 60–5, 74, 78, 83, 86–7, 93, 101–3, 107–8, 131, 156, 164, 166–168, 177
Third Pillar 2, 61,120–1, 131
'three P approach' 4, 124, 135
Title IV 61, 63, 75, 120
torture or inhuman or degrading treatment 94–5, 135, 137, 154
trafficking in children 17, 32
trafficking in girls 15
trafficking in men 15–7, 32
Trafficking Protocol (UN) 103, 107, 123–6, 132, 139, 164, 169
transition period 63, 80
transnational organised crime
  see organised crime
transparency 129, 131
TREVI Group 75, 122
tsunami 173

unemployment 31, 69, 71–2, 81
United Kingdom 54, 74, 140
United Nations 79, 126
  see also Trafficking Protocol (UN)

values 24, 96, 133, 142, 149, 153, 156, 159, 168
victim
  label of 17
  as not really a victim 20, 88, 114, 117
violence against women 20, 28, 31, 48–51, 89, 106, 115, 135, 143, 148, 166

witnesses 91, 103–4, 109, 111, 117, 129, 140, 151, 170
'white slavery' 23, 32, 106, 136

www.ingramcontent.com/pod-product-compliance
Ingram Content Group UK Ltd.
Pitfield, Milton Keynes, MK11 3LW, UK
UKHW020832290926
15470UKWH00009B/1862/J

9 781841 136509